The Catholic Priest in the United States:

Sociological Investigations

The National Opinion Research Center Study,
The University of Chicago
directed by
Rev. Andrew M. Greeley, Ph.D.

1972
Publications Office
United States Catholic Conference
1312 Massachusetts Avenue, N.W.
Washington, D.C. 20005

A study conducted by:

National Opinion Research Center
The University of Chicago
6030 South Ellis Avenue
Chicago, Illinois 60637

FOREWORD

The radical and rapid social and moral changes in contemporary life affect the lives of many human beings, and particularly the lives of those dedicated to the service of God through the service of His people.

The Catholic priest experiences the normal difficulties of average human beings and reflects in his life the problems of the general population. Additionally, he experiences the normal problems of measuring up to the transcendental demands of his priestly vocation. He strives to be a man of God among men; to be in the world but not of it; to conform the world to Christ without being conformed to the world; to exercise a changeless ministry rooted in Christ and preach the timeless truths of the Gospel, amid the changing conditions and circumstances of earthly life and to be a witness and dispenser of a life other than this earthly life.

Since Vatican Council II the Catholic priest in a special way must preserve continuity amid continued change. He must personally accept, adjust to and promote among the people he serves the authentic changes of renewal introduced by the Ecumenical Council. Concurrently, he must resist the arbitrary and whimsical changes presented under the banner in the alleged spirit of the Council. Finally, the Catholic priest is exercising his ministry at a time when some people are trying to bury God and to construct a Godless Christian religion, committed to serve men in this earthly life only. Their concept of liberation does not encompass deliverance from sin to a life of grace — to a life in time and in eternity.

It is for these reasons that the Holy Spirit is impelling "the Church to open new avenues of approach to the contemporary world and is also suggesting and fostering fitting adaptations in the ministry of priests" (Decree on Priests, 22).

The current problems in the life and ministry of priests in the United States can best be appreciated in a historical context. God has blessed the Church in the United States with priests of outstanding apostolic zeal and piety, and through their efforts, has blessed the Church with unparalleled growth. Since 1920, through natural rather than immigrational accretion, the Catholic population increased from 17.7 to 47.8 million and the number of priests increased from 21 to 59 thousand for an increase of 266 per cent in population and 295 per cent in the number of priests.

Such gratifying growth could induce a sense of well-being and security. However, the National Conference of Catholic Bishops (NCCB), profoundly sensitive to the problems and needs of their priest collaborators, in April, 1967, directed its Committee on Pastoral Research and Practices to undertake an extensive study of the life and ministry of priests. When the members of this Committee completed their three-year term of office in 1969, they were named as an ad hoc committee to complete the study.

To ensure objectivity, the Committee — responding to the directives of the Conference — aggregated priests who would reflect the wide spectrum of views and practices current in the life and ministry of priests. The Committee of bishops and priests designed a plan for a comprehensive study along eight tracks — historical, doctrinal (both spiritual and theological), spiritual, pastoral, ecumenical, liturgical, sociological and psychological. Eight subcommittees — each chaired by a priest of recognized competence in his respective field — were established. Each priest chairman, after consultation with the bishop moderator, selected four members and as many consultants as were necessary.

The Committee carried out its task under the norm given by Pope Leo XIII when he opened the Vatican Archives: "not to dare utter a falsehood — not to fear to speak the truth." The Church has nothing to fear from truth. The sublime dignity of the priesthood was entrusted to human beings — to earthen vessels. The human frailties of the ministers of the mysteries of God clearly evince the presence of the Holy Spirit, who guides and directs the Church, preserves it and gives it growth, and to those members of the Church who respond to His promptings, He grants graces to attain heroic virtue and sanctity.

The Committee has scrupulously respected the professional integrity of all involved in the study. In obtaining extensive data through the sociological and psychological surveys, no expense was spared in retaining research agencies whose scholarly competence was generally acknowledged as being beyond question. In fact, never in its history has the Conference made so generous a study grant as that made for the study on the life and ministry of priests — the treasured collaborators of the bishops.

Each of the subcommittees, according to its own discipline, can contribute to a better understanding of the life and ministry of priests in the contemporary world. Sociological and psychological data may tell us how priests think and feel, live and work in carrying out their ministry. But to know what the priesthood is, and what its essential mission entails regardless of circumstances, we must look to the teachings of Christ as understood by the Church. Sociological and psychological data cannot be used, as Pope Paul noted in his Apostolic Exhortation of December 8, 1970, to reconstruct a Christianity cut off from the unbroken tradition which links it to the faith of the apostles. Such surveys, he said, are useful to discover thought patterns and serve as an invitation to proclaim more effectively a message which raises the mind to the level of divine realities.

The total study undertaken by the U.S. Bishops is now approaching completion. The historical study has been published. In this volume we present the complete report of the sociological survey conducted by the National Opinion Research Center. This publication and the publication of the complete psychological report reflect continued adherence to the norm "not to fear to speak the truth." This publication recognizes the great interest of many in the sociological survey, and most especially the 6000 priests who cooperated in the study and the nearly 60,000 priests for whom the former were stand-ins as a research sample. The publication should also allay the doubts and suspicions of those who believed that the research would be a closed project. This publication is a vote of confidence of the bishops in the priests of the United States — a confidence manifested in the terms of the contract with NORC, which was entered into before the survey was begun. By the terms of the contract, the bishops agreed that all the data collected — even that which could not possibly be included in a single report — will after two years be accessible to scholars recognized as such by the NORC.

The questionnaires used in the sociological survey were prepared by the professional staff of NORC after accepting suggestions about topics of interest from the full membership of the ad hoc committee, its subcommittees and from representatives of religious communities. The questions were designed for men of faith, committed to the supernatural, who believe in the cross and resurrection, who dispense the sacred mysteries and who radiate and resound Christ. The complete report is based on replies from nearly 6000 priests. It provides a wealth of data which are invaluable in understanding many of the problems encountered by priests today.

Even before the sociological survey and report were completed, it was decided to invite a team of eminently qualified sociologists who were in no way associated with the survey, to give an independent and objective evaluation of the report and the processes of gathering and analyzing the information that makes up the report. It is a commonly accepted procedure to commission such an evaluation of a research project of such magnitude. The evaluation, which will be published separately, affirms the great value of the "massive fund of information about priestly life and ministry." It also points out that the data can be of greater use through further study and analysis. The full potential of the study has yet to be achieved, and the evaluation points out the directions in which the maximum value of the data can be realized.

The NCCB has appointed a new committee to promote the pastoral implementation of the study. The Conference is addressing itself, in the light of faith and of the facts revealed by the surveys, to the task of easing and, as far as humanly possible, of eliminating the tensions current in priestly life and ministry. The NORC study will be extremely helpful in achieving this goal.

It is anticipated that the reaction to the publication of the results of this independent study and research will be uneven. The study has probed into sensitive and controversial areas. The data can provide ammunition for both sides of important issues. Some may charge the researchers of bias in selecting and analyzing controversial and delicate matters. The study is an irrefutable evidence of the deep concern of bishops for their priest co-workers. The National Conference of Catholic Bishops used the instrumentality of a massive sociological and psychological survey to enable the priests to speak frankly and directly about themselves and their problems to their bishops and religious superiors. Without discounting or minimizing the problems facing the priests, it is particularly comforting that, notwithstanding such problems, the report tells us that "A large majority of the clergy say that if they had the choice to make again, they would enter the priesthood." This perhaps is another way of saying that the priests would respond to the invitation of Our Lord to take up the cross and follow Him.

JOHN CARDINAL KROL
Chairman of the Ad Hoc Committee
For the Study on Priestly Life and Ministry

October 26, 1971

ACKNOWLEDGMENTS

The design and execution of the American Catholic Priesthood Study and the analysis of the data presented in this report were the responsibility of four staff members at the National Opinion Research Center. Theirs was in every way a concerted team effort, but the division of labor was roughly as follows.

Andrew M. Greeley, principal investigator, was responsible for drafting most of the final report. Richard A. Schoenherr, co-principal investigator, directed the overall project. Neal W. McDermott, O.P., research associate, assisted particularly in designing the items covering religious life, in supervising the preparation of the resignee sample, and in analyzing the personality orientation data. And John Mulhearn, research associate, helped in the general administration of the project, and in analyzing the data on professionalism and work satisfaction.

Their project staff included Robert M. Brooks, O. Praem., who analyzed the open-ended responses in the resignee questionnaire and spent long hours in preparing sampling lists; and James N. Watzke, C.S.C., who helped to design the questionnaire for resignees and to prepare that subsample. The team was completed by Bobbe P. Eaton and Florence M. McKinney, field supervisors; William C. McCready, Gloria R. Rauens, and Barbara Tzur, research assistants; Virginia Quinn and Donna J. Wainwright, secretaries; and Robert L. Walters, data-processing coordinator. The investigators and their associates wish to thank them for the enormous amount of excellent work that they performed.

Important contributions were made during different phases of the study by several colleagues, notably Thomas M. Gannon, S.J., who worked especially on the subject of religious communities, and Maurice J. Moore, S.J., who was especially helpful on the subject of changing attitudes on birth control; they are likewise acknowledged with gratitude.

The successful completion of this research would have been virtually impossible without the able assistance and generous cooperation of many people at NORC. Special thanks are due to William H. Bland, supervisor of the print shop, and Elroy C. Parker, xerox operator; to Rosie L. McClendone, sampling supervisor; to Jarvis U. Rich, director of data preparation, and Winona J. Adkins, Suzanne C. Morrison, Frank H. Schilling, Altha M. Scott, Edward I. Weston, Carmen Z. Wilson, and the army of coders, all members of the data-processing staff; and to Maxine A. Hart, keypunch supervisor.

The preparation of the final report would not have been possible without the help of Mary A. Spaeth, editorial director, and her assistant Elaine D. Richardson, who both contributed their editing skills; of Judith A. Schoenherr, who did the artwork; and last, but definitely not least, of Toshiko Takahashi and the steno pool, especially Nancy A. Nagel, Mary H. Okazaki, and Nella V. Siefert, who all typed above and beyond the call of duty to produce the report.

Several colleagues at NORC provided valuable help and suggestions during the project. Sincere gratitude is extended to Benjamin F. King for designing the sample and to Norman M. Bradburn, Ann H. Browning, Jae-On Kim, Norman H. Nie, Kenneth Prewitt, Paul B. Sheatsley, Joe L. Spaeth, James J. Vanecko, Sidney Verba, and Eve H. Weinberg for sharing their insights into the science and folklore of survey research.

TABLE OF CONTENTS

Page

Foreword iii

Acknowledgements vii

List of Tables x

List of Figures xviii

Chapter

1   Introduction 3
2   Backgrounds of the Clergy 23
3   Education and Vocation Decision Among the Clergy........... 37
4   The Personality of the Priest 53
5   The Spiritual Life of Priests 71
6   Attitudes and Values Among the Catholic Clergy 81
7   Structure and Power in the Life of a Priest 133
8   The Clerical Culture 155
9   The Work of Priests 171
10 Satisfactions and Frustrations in the Priesthood 199
11 The Morale of the Clergy 215
12 The Celibacy Issue 233
13 Future Plans 253
14 Recruiting for the Priesthood 267
15 A Look at the Resignees 275
16 Summary and Conclusion 311

Appendix

A   Sampling Methodology 317
B   Field Work and Response Rates 323
C   Description of Indices 333
D   Nonresponse 349
E   The Religious Clergy 359
F   Main Questionnaire 371
G   Resignee Questionnaire 431

References 447

Index 449

LIST OF TABLES

Table		Page
1.1	Distribution of Respondents by Age and Clerical Status	15
1.2	Correlations of Graduate Record Examination Score with Age and Education	18
2.1	Status of American Catholic Clergy by Age	24
2.2	Nativity by Clerical Status and for American Catholic Males	25
2.3	Nativity by Age	26
2.4	Socioeconomic Background by Clerical Status and for American Catholic Males	27
2.5	Socioeconomic Background by Age	28
2.6	Father's Ethnicity by Clerical Status and for American Catholic Males	29
2.7	Father's Ethnicity by Age	30
2.8	Family Experiences by Clerical Status	31
2.9	Family Experiences by Age	32
2.10	Religious Background by Clerical Status and for American Catholic Males	33
2.11	Religious Background by Age	34
2.12	Family Problems by Clerical Status	34
2.13	Family Problems by Age	35
3.1	Education of the Clergy	39
3.2	Education of the Clergy, by Age	40
3.3	Age at Entry to Seminary, by Clerical Status	40
3.4	Age at Entry to Seminary, by Age	41
3.5	Education since Ordination, by Clerical Status	42
3.6	Education since Ordination, by Age	43
3.7	Current Studies by Clerical Status	44
3.8	Current Studies by Age	44
3.9	Opinion of Seminary Education, by Clerical Status	46
3.10	Opinion of Seminary Education, by Age	47
3.11	Dating in Youth, by Clerical Status	48

Table   Page

3.12   Dating in Youth, by Age 49

3.13   Encouragement for Vocation, by Clerical Status 49

3.14   Encouragement for Vocation, by Age 50

4.1   Personality Scales 57

4.2   Personality Scales by Age of Active Diocesan and Religious Priests 62

4.3   "Hyper" and "Hypo" Self-Actualization for Active Priests and Resignees on Inner-Directed Scale 64

4.4   Active Priests and Others on Self-actualizing Scales 65

5.1   Spiritual Activities by Clerical Status 72

5.2   Spiritual Activities by Age 73

5.3   Recitation of Breviary, by Clerical Status 74

5.4   Recitation of Breviary, by Age 74

5.5   Religious Experiences by Clerical Status 76

5.6   Religious Experiences by Age 77

6.1   Attitudes on the Priesthood, by Clerical Status 85

6.2   Attitudes on the Priesthood, by Age 88

6.3   "Anomic" Attitudes by Clerical Status 90

6.4   "Anomic" Attitudes by Age 91

6.5   "Traditional" Religious Attitudes by Clerical Status 93

6.6   "Traditional" Religious Attitudes by Age 95

6.7   "Modern" Religious Attitudes by Clerical Status 97

6.8   "Modern" Religious Attitudes by Age 98

6.9   Attitudes on Masturbation, by Clerical Status 99

6.10   Attitudes on Masturbation, by Age 100

6.11   Attitudes on Premarital Sex, by Clerical Status 102

6.12   Attitudes on Premarital Sex, by Age 103

6.13   Birth Control Attitudes before *Humanae Vitae*, by Clerical Status 104

6.14   Birth Control Attitudes before *Humanae Vitae*, by Age 105

6.15   Birth Control Attitudes after *Humanae Vitae*, by Clerical Status 106

6.16   Birth Control Attitudes after *Humanae Vitae*, by Age........ 107

6.17   Birth Control Attitudes before and after *Humanae Vitae* .. 108

6.18   Birth Control Procedure in Confession before *Humanae Vitae*, by Clerical Status 109

6.19   Birth Control Procedure in Confession before *Humanae Vitae*, by Age 110

Table   Page

6.20 Birth Control Procedure in Confession after *Humanae
      Vitae,* by Clerical Status 111

6.21 Birth Control Procedure in Confession after *Humanae
      Vitae,* by Age 112

6.22 Birth Control Procedure in Confession before and after
      Humanae Vitae 113

6.23 Attitude toward *Humanae Vitae,* by Clerical Status 114

6.24 Attitude toward *Humanae Vitae,* by Age 115

6.25 Attitudes on Divorce, by Clerical Status 116

6.26 Attitudes on Divorce, by Age 117

6.27 Attitudes on Abortion, by Clerical Status 119

6.28 Attitudes on Abortion, by Age 120

6.29 Ecumenism by Clerical Status 120

6.30 Ecumenism by Age 121

6.31 Social Attitudes by Clerical Status 122

6.32 Social Attitudes by Age 125

6.33 Correlates of Religious Attitude Indices 127

6.34 Intercorrelations of Religious Attitude Indices 130

6.35 Explanation of Variance on "Modern"-Values Index 131

7.1   Actual Distribution of Power in Diocese, by Clerical Status 134

7.2   Actual Distribution of Power in Diocese, by Age 135

7.3   Ideal Distribution of Power in Diocese, by Clerical Status .. 136

7.4   Ideal Distribution of Power in Diocese, by Age 137

7.5   Actual Centralization of Authority, by Clerical Status 138

7.6   Actual Centralization of Authority, by Age 139

7.7   Ideal Centralization of Authority, by Clerical Status 140

7.8   Ideal Centralization of Authority, by Age 142

7.9   Actual Exercise of Personal Initiative, by Clerical Status .. 143

7.10 Actual Exercise of Initiative, by Age 143

7.11 Ideal Exercise of Initiative, by Clerical Status 144

7.12 Ideal Exercise of Initiative, by Age 145

7.13 Reforms in the Church, by Clerical Status 146

7.14 Reforms in the Church, by Age 148

7.15 Correlates of Power and Structure Indices 150

7.16 Intercorrelations of Power and Structure Indices 150

7.17 Explanation of Variance on Power-Conflict Index 152

7.18 Simple Correlations and Total Independent Effects of
      Selected Variables on Power-Conflict Index 153

Table		Page
8.1	Friendships by Clerical Status	156
8.2	Friendships by Age	156
8.3	Classification of Close Friends, by Clerical Status	157
8.4	Classification of Close Friends, by Age	158
8.5	Frequent Associates by Clerical Status	159
8.6	Frequent Associates by Age	160
8.7	Friendships with Priests, by Clerical Status	160
8.8	Friendships with Priests, by Age	161
8.9	Living Situation by Clerical Status	162
8.10	Living Situation by Age	162
8.11	Relations with Colleagues in Parish Setting, by Clerical Status	163
8.12	Relations with Colleagues in Parish Setting, by Age	164
8.13	Relations with Colleagues in "Nonparish" Setting, by Clerical Status	164
8.14	Relations with Colleagues in "Nonparish" Setting, by Age	165
8.15	Correlates of Colleague-Relationship Index	167
8.16	Explanation of Variance on Colleague-Relationship Index	167
9.1	Current Position for Priests by Age	172
9.2	Current Main Jobs by Clerical Status	173
9.3	Current Main Jobs by Age	175
9.4	Working Hours by Clerical Status	175
9.5	Working Hours by Age	176
9.6	Job Satisfaction by Clerical Status	176
9.7	Job Satisfaction by Age	177
9.8	Job Satisfaction by Current Position for Priests and Male Industrial Employees	178
9.9	Work Satisfaction by Current Main Job	180
9.10	Job Reactions by Clerical Status	181
9.11	Job Reactions by Age	182
9.12	Further Training Needed, by Clerical Status	183
9.13	Further Training Needed, by Age	184
9.14	Publications Read, by Clerical Status	185
9.15	Publications Read, by Age	186
9.16	Influential Authors Read, by Clerical Status	187
9.17	Influential Authors Read, by Age	190
9.18	Correlates of Work-Satisfaction and Professional-Comparison Indices	192

Table		Page
9.19	Explanation of Variance on Professional-Comparison Index	193
9.20	Explanation of Variance on Work-Satisfaction Index	193
10.1	Spiritual and Personal Fulfillment by Clerical Status	200
10.2	Spiritual and Personal Fulfillment by Age	201
10.3	Sources of Satisfaction, by Clerical Status	203
10.4	Sources of Satisfaction, by Age	205
10.5	Problems in the Priesthood for Self, by Clerical Status	206
10.6	Problems in the Priesthood for Self, by Age	208
10.7	Problems in the Priesthood for Others, by Clerical Status	210
10.8	Problems in the Priesthood for Others, by Age	211
10.9	Correlates of Reporting That "Loneliness of Priestly Life" Is a Problem	212
10.10	Explanation of Variance on Loneliness	214
11.1	Affect Scale Scores by Clerical Status	217
11.2	Affect Scale Scores by Age	217
11.3	Affect Scale Scores of Priests and College-Educated Males, by Age	219
11.4	Affect Scale Scores of Active Priests and Resignees	220
11.5	Recreation by Clerical Status	222
11.6	Recreation by Age	223
11.7	Correlates of Positive Affect, Negative Affect, and Affect Balance Scales	224
11.8	Explanation of Variance on Positive Affect Scale	225
11.9	Explanation of Variance on Negative Affect Scale	225
11.10	Simple Correlations and Total Independent Effects of Selected Variables on Positive Affect	227
11.11	Simple Correlations and Total Independent Effects of Selected Variables on Negative Affect	228
12.1	Attitude on Optional Celibacy, by Clerical Status	234
12.2	Attitude on Optional Celibacy, by Age	235
12.3	Future of Celibacy, by Clerical Status	236
12.4	Future of Celibacy, by Age	237
12.5	Attitudes toward Value of Celibacy, by Clerical Status	238
12.6	Attitudes toward Value of Celibacy, by Age	238
12.7	Attitudes toward Sexuality, by Clerical Status	240
12.8	Attitudes toward Sexuality, by Age	242
12.9	Going Out with Women Socially, by Clerical Status	244
12.10	Going Out with Women Socially, by Age	245

LIST OF TABLES—Continued

Table   Page

12.11 Patterns of Social Interaction with Women 245

12.12 Opinions on Social Relations with Women, by Clerical Status 246

12.13 Opinions on Social Relations with Women, by Age 247

12.14 Correlates of Social Interaction with Women and Desire To Marry 248

12.15 Explanation of Variance on Desire To Marry 250

12.16 Simple Correlations and Total Independent Effects of Selected Variables on Desire to Marry 251

13.1 Future Plans in the Priesthood, by Clerical Status 254

13.2 Future Plans in the Priesthood, by Age 254

13.3 Friends Leaving the Priesthood, by Clerical Status 255

13.4 Friends Leaving the Priesthood, by Age 256

13.5 Reasons for Staying in the Priesthood, by Clerical Status .. 256

13.6 Reasons for Staying in the Priesthood, by Age 257

13.7 Reasons for Leaving the Priesthood, by Clerical Status 258

13.8 Correlates of Future Plans To Stay in the Priesthood 260

13.9 Explanation of Variance on Future Plans To Stay in the Priesthood 262

13.10 Simple Correlations and Total Independent Effects of Selected Variables on Future Plans To Stay in the Priesthood 263

13.11 Future Plans in the Priesthood by Desire To Marry 265

14.1 Vocational Recruiting Attitude Four or Five Years Ago, by Clerical Status 268

14.2 Vocational Recruiting Attitude Today, by Clerical Status .. 269

14.3 Vocational Recruiting Attitude Four or Five Years Ago, by Age 270

14.4 Vocational Recruiting Attitude Today, by Age 271

14.5 Vocational Recruiting Attitudes Four or Five Years Ago and Today 272

14.6 Correlates of Vocational Encouragement 272

14.7 Explanation of Variance on Vocational Encouragement 273

15.1 Average Resignation Rates in American Dioceses and Religious Institutes, by Year 277

15.2 Quartile Distribution of Cumulative Per Cent Resignees from American Dioceses and Religious Institutes, 1966-69 278

xv

LIST OF TABLES—Continued

Table | Page
15.3 | Number of Resigned Priests from American Dioceses and Religious Institutes 279
15.4 | Characteristics of Parishioners with Whom Resigned Priests Worked 280
15.5 | Support and Opposition from Other Individuals in Last Assignment 280
15.6 | Evaluation of Experiences in the Ministry 281
15.7 | Crucial Events Influencing Decision To Leave 282
15.8 | Reasons for Leaving the Ministry 283
15.9 | Discussion and Support for Resignation from Other Individuals 283
15.10 | Counseling before Leaving the Ministry 284
15.11 | Displeasure with Aspects of the Laicization Procedures 285
15.12 | Personal Turmoil 285
15.13 | Marital Status of Resigned Priests 286
15.14 | Kind of Marriage Ceremony 286
15.15 | Marital Status of Wife (or Fiancee) before Present Marriage (Engagement) 287
15.16 | Religious Status of Wife (or Fiancee) 287
15.17 | Annual Income of Resigned Priests 288
15.18 | Professional Standards in Ministry and in Present Work 288
15.19 | Use of Talents in Ministry and in Present Work 289
15.20 | Present "Canonical" Status of Resigned Priests 289
15.21 | Reasons for Not Seeking Laicization 290
15.22 | Present Position of Resigned Priests in Relation to Church | 290
15.23 | Present Relationship to the Priesthood 291
15.24 | Future Plans in Priesthood 292
15.25 | Exercise of the Priesthood 293
15.26 | Marital Adjustment of Resigned Priests and College-Educated Males 295
15.27 | Marital Adjustment Balance Scale Scores of Resigned Priests and College-Educated Males 297
15.28 | Preferred Kind of Work for Exercise of the Priesthood 298
15.29 | Forms of Priestly Ministry 299
15.30 | Possible New Forms of Ministry for Priests 300
15.31 | Recommended Changes in the Roman Catholic Church 301
15.32 | Advice of Resignees to Laymen 301
15.33 | Advice of Resignees to Priests and Religious 304

LIST OF TABLES—Continued

Table		Page
15.34	Advice of Resignees to Bishops	305
A.1	Standard Errors of Estimate for Average Diocesan Resignation Rates and Total Number of Resignees, by Year	320
A.2	Standard Errors of Estimate for Proportion of Active Diocesan Priests Taking Certain Positions on Three Issues	321
B.1	Response Rate by Wave and Mailing for Sample of Active Priests	329
D.1	Alternative Models for Viewing Certain Findings in the Light of Nonresponse	350
E.1	Attitudes of Religious Priests toward the Religious Life	362
E.2	Attitudes of Religious Priests toward the Vows	364
E.3	Attitudes of Religious Priests toward Community Life	366
E.4	Explanation of Variance on Future Plans of Diocesan and Religious Priests to Stay in the Priesthood	368

LIST OF FIGURES

Figure   Page

1.1 Model for Causal Analysis of Priests' Characteristics 12

1.2 Path Diagram Relating GRE Score to Age and Education .. 17

4.1 POI Profiles for Sample Groups and for Priests 58

4.2 POI Profiles for Priests 60

4.3 POI Profiles for Selected Reference Groups 66

5.1 Path Diagram Relating Religious Experience to Prior Vari-
     ables. Active Priests Only 78

6.1 Path Diagram Relating "Modern" Values to Prior Vari-
     ables. Active Priests Only 129

7.1 Path Diagram Relating Power Conflict to Prior Variables.
     Active Priests Only 151

8.1 Path Diagram Relating Colleague Support to Prior Vari-
     ables. Active Priests Only 168

9.1 Path Diagram Relating Professional Comparison to Prior
     Variables. Active Priests Only 194

9.2 Path Diagram Relating Work Satisfaction to Prior Vari-
     ables. Active Priests Only 195

10.1 Path Diagram Relating Loneliness to Prior Variables.
     Active Priests Only 213

11.1 Path Diagram Relating Positive Affect to Prior Variables.
     Active Priests Only 230

11.2 Path Diagram Relating Negative Affect to Prior Variables.
     Active Priests Only 231

12.1 Path Diagram Relating Desire To Marry to Prior Variables.
     Active Priests Only 249

13.1 Path Diagram Relating Future Plans in Priesthood to Prior
     Variables. Active Priests Only 261

The Catholic Priest in the United States:

Sociological Investigations

CHAPTER 1

INTRODUCTION

In this introductory chapter we intend to treat three subjects:
1. The purpose of the research.
2. The phases of the present project.
3. The plan of this report.

The Purpose of the Research

This report is a description and analysis of the life and ministry of Roman Catholic priests in the United States of America. While it is intended to provide material for policy-making decisions, it is not oriented toward policy recommendations. In order to emphasize this point, we distinguish the following steps between the completion of data collection and policy decisions:

1. Description

In the first phase, the sheer raw facts that have been collected in the research project are presented. It will be reported, for example, that three per cent of the diocesan priests in the country are either certainly or probably going to leave the priesthood in the near future. No attempt is made to explain this phenomenon; the phenomenon itself is merely described. The first part of all the subsequent chapters in this report will be devoted to description.

2. Analysis of Explanation

In the second phase, an attempt is made to discover the underlying reasons behind the phenomenon. For example, an effort will be made to find out why three per cent of the diocesan priests in the country were preparing in 1970 to leave the priesthood and why another 10 per cent were uncertain about their future, as will be evident later in this report.

3

This issue — along with many others to be treated in the present volume — is extremely complicated. No simple, one-factor explanation can be found. However, among the causes that will be discovered for the inclination to leave the priesthood is having "modern" religious values. But the analysis simply does not stop with the description of such a relationship. Whenever possible, an attempt will be made to "explain the explanation." It might be asked, for example, whether "modern" values relate to a feeling of loneliness and whether this, in turn, relates to a propensity to leave the priesthood. As long as such "explanation of explanations" can be substantiated by the data in hand, we remain in the second phase. However, when it becomes impossible to substantiate a secondary explanation by the data, we pass to the third phase.

3. *Speculation*

In this phase, certain suggestions are made that might provide explanations of puzzles uncovered in the data, but such suggestions have no substantiation in the existing data. Thus, one member of the NORC research team has suggested on several occasions that the principal change in the priesthood in the last decade is that now it is possible to leave the priesthood but that discontent was strong a decade ago and may have been even stronger than it is at the present time. Speculation is interesting; it adds spice and variety to a report; and it is part of the craft of the social researcher. However, since there was no survey taken ten years ago, it cannot be said whether clerical morale is better or worse now than it was a decade ago. Hence, the speculation cannot be substantiated. We shall periodically engage in speculation in the course of the present report, but the reader may be assured that such speculation will be labeled as such.

4. *Recommendations*

In this phase, someone, after carefully inspecting the data, may suggest to policy-makers what appropriate decisions might be based on the explanations, analyses, and speculations in the report. When this phase is entered, research as such is finished. While research findings may strongly indicate that certain courses of actions would be appropriate, they cannot command such courses of action. All the researcher can say, for example, is that the absence of a specific change is likely to heighten a problem within the group studied. Beyond that, his competency as a researcher cannot go. He may make recommendations under pressure from a client, and there is nothing wrong with such recommendations so long as it is clear that when the researcher begins to make recommendations, he ceases to be a researcher and instead becomes a consultant. He is expressing his own personal opinion, however well informed and expert that opinion might be. In the present report, given the nature of the subject matter being studied, there will be no recommendations.[1]

5. *Policy Decisions*

Even if a researcher has been cajoled into making recommendations, it does not follow that simply because his recommendations have arisen from his research, they must automatically be accepted. In the final analysis, the role of policy-maker and researcher are distinct, except in the rare instance where one man occupies both positions. Since none of the NORC staff are members of the American ecclesiastical hierarchy, that combination of roles is excluded in the present instance. However skillful his research, and however wise his recommendations, the researcher realizes that policy-makers must consider factors other than those on which his competency bears. He may think the policy-maker has erred, but unless he misunderstands his own function, he has no right to assume that research automatically dictates either a policy decision or the methods of implementing that decision. The best the researcher can hope for is that his efforts become an important input both in the making and execution of policy. If he claims any more, then trouble and confusion are likely.[2]

Such a view of the research enterprise is implicit in any NORC report. It is made explicit in the introduction to this report because the NORC research team is well aware of the controversial and sensitive areas into which it has probed. We realize that our data could be used to provide ammunition for both sides of an important policy debate in the American Church. It is legitimate, of course, to use data in a policy debate as long as it is not torn from its context. But data in their proper context generally reveal that reality is gray. NORC specifically rejects the use of its empirical data in such a way as to argue that specific policies have been "scientifically proven." We are aware that in certain other countries, Catholic sociologists have on occasion argued that the wisdom of policies has been "scientifically" validated by social research. We reject both this notion and any use of the data in this report to support such a notion. This is a research monograph, not a series of policy recommendations, and much less a political treatise.

The Phases of the Research Project

We distinguish six phases in the research project: (1) preliminary, (2) data collection, (3) data processing, (4) construction of indices, (5) analysis and preparation of the report, and (6) review of the report.

1. Preliminary Phase

Work on NORC Study 5029 began on March 1, 1969. During the preliminary stage, the first step was the design of the study. In this step, the general subject, "Life of the Ministry," was developed into somewhat more specific categories, such as morale, relationships, spirituality, attitudes and values, and future plans. Some determination was also made on what general groups of respondents were to be surveyed. It was decided that in addition to a sample of diocesan and religious clergy in the United States, questionnaires would be sent to all the bishops and major superiors in the American Church, and a somewhat modified questionnaire would be sent to a sample of "resigned" priests.[3]

The next step was the specification and the operationalization of variables. In this step, the research staff asked itself what specific and concrete aspects in the life and ministry of the priest it was to observe through the means of its questionnaire. What are, for example, the various dimensions of "morale" and how might they be measured? Two of the dimensions that we decided upon were "occupational satisfaction" and "psychological well-being." The first of these variables was operationalized through the work-satisfaction index of Patricia C. Smith and her colleagues (Smith, Kendall, and Hulin, 1969); the second through the "happiness" index developed by Norman M. Bradburn (1969).

This early phase of the project was substantially complete by the summer of 1969, and the research team turned to the construction of the questionnaire — seven drafts in all. It was reviewed and revised both by the survey team and by senior colleagues at NORC. A penultimate draft of the questionnaire was pretested with a sample of 150 respondents, and after further consultation with NORC colleagues, the final version was prepared. (A separate modified questionnaire for resigned priests was also pretested with a sample of 100 resignees.) The final form of the main questionnaire was ready in November of 1969. (See Appendix F for a copy of the main questionnaire and Appendix G for excerpts from the resignee questionnaire.)

Through the entire preliminary effort of project design and questionnaire construction, constant consultation was in progress with NORC colleagues, with officers of various priests' organizations, with members of the bishops' Ad Hoc Committee for the Study of the Life and Ministry of the Priest (a whole day's consultation was devoted to the penultimate draft of the questionnaire), and with a special panel of consultants appointed by the sociology subcommittee of the Ad Hoc Committee for the Study of the Life and Ministry of the Priest. Members of this committee are Reverend Robert McNamara, S.J., Dean of the College of Arts and Sciences, Loyola University of Chicago; Professor James J. Vanecko, Department of Sociology, Brown University; Professor Donald Warwick, Harvard University; Monsignor George Higgins, United States Catholic Conference, Washington, D.C.; and Reverend Joseph Fichter, Divinity School, Harvard University. Other sociologists who were consulted were Sister Marie Augusta Neal, S.N.D., Emmanuel College, Boston; Dr. Edgar Mills, Ministry Studies Board, National Council of Churches; and Professor Jeffrey Hadden, Tulane University. The NORC team is grateful for the help of these distinguished scholars, but it goes without saying that these scholars should in no way be considered responsible for the design, the questionnaire, or the final report.

While the questionnaire was being designed, constructed, and pre-tested, the NORC sampling department was preparing and drawing a sample of the American clergy. Although it would have been relatively easy to draw a simple random sample of the American clergy, such a sample would have seriously impaired the staff's capacity to analyze not only individuals but also institutions such as dioceses and religious communities. Therefore, the sample that was actually drawn is a multistage probability sample that not only represents accurately the American priesthood but also makes possible the analysis of certain subinstitutions within the American Church. The sample design and execution is described in detail in Appendix A of the present report.

A further activity during the preliminary phase of the project was the preparation of a lengthy bibliography on the subject of the life and ministry of the priesthood. (This bibliography has not been included in the present report because of space limitations.)

2. Data Collection

One of the major problems encountered in the survey was experienced in the data-collection phase. We had assumed that the mailing service of *The Official Catholic Directory* could provide accurate lists of the names and addresses of the diocesan clergy in the United States. However, careful examination of the lists obtained for a number of large dioceses revealed inaccuracies, in many instances as high as 20 per cent. We therefore determined that *The Directory* lists could not be relied upon without undergoing the risk of substantial problems in attempting to obtain a high response rate, to say nothing of an accurate representation of American clergy. It therefore became necessary to seek lists of names and addresses of clergy from the individual dioceses and religious communities that had fallen into the sample. Generally speaking, the cooperation of dioceses and religious orders was excellent, although in some instances this cooperation required that the institution revise its own somewhat outdated lists.[4] Compiling an accurate list of the potential respondents and drawing the sample from that list caused a three-month delay in mailing the main questionnaires to active priests; the first wave went out in December, 1969, and the second wave in early 1970. The resignee questionnaire did not have its first mailing until July, 1970. The response was excellent for a mail survey of the present kind but the inevitable delays in the data-collection process prolonged the field work into the end of the summer of 1970. Full details of the field work and the response rates are provided in Appendix B of this report. In Appendix D we shall present illustrations of the implications of various assumptions that might be made about the attitudes of those who did not respond to the main questionnaire.

3. *Data Processing*

Preparation of the data for analysis began almost as soon as questionnaires arrived in NORC's mailroom. We presume that the reader of the present report is not interested in the mysteries of "editing," "coding," and "card punching." It is sufficient to say that the transfer of answers from the questionnaires of over 6,000 respondents to IBM cards (fourteen for each respondent) and thence to magnetic tapes and to discs is an immense, complicated, and time-consuming task in which many things can go wrong and almost always do.

4. *Construction of the Indices*

The fourteen decks of IBM cards contained over six hundred items to which the members of the sample had responded. Many of these items were designed in such a manner that they could be combined into indices which would represent not so much single answers as response patterns which, in their turn, would correspond to attitudinal or behavioral constellations. While many items were written with an *a priori* assumption that they would highly correlate with one another and thus become part of the indices, it was still necessary to establish empirically that such correlations existed. September, October, and November of 1970 were devoted to this task. More than six hundred items in the questionnaire were reduced through the construction of indices to approximately two hundred variables. A detailed description of the indices is presented in Appendix C.

5. *Analysis and Preparation of the Report*

The fall and winter of 1970–71 were devoted to the actual analysis of the data in preparation for the writing of this report. The method of analysis and presentation will be described in the next main section of this chapter.

6. *Review of the Report*

As the first draft of the chapters emerged from NORC's steno pool, they were reviewed first by members of the study staff and then by senior colleagues at NORC, in particular Paul B. Sheatsley and Joe L. Spaeth. This review process was extremely important in the preparation of this report because it provided members of the study staff with the perspective on their work that can frequently be lost during long immersion in the project. It also guaranteed them that whatever biases of their own may have crept into their analysis could be taken into account and eliminated.

A word must be said on the subject of "bias." In the language of controversy, an "objective" researcher is one whose findings agree with what the controvertialists hope research will discover, and a "biased" researcher is one whose findings disagree with what the controvertialists hope will be reported. In fact, there is no such thing as an unbiased researcher, particularly in the controversial and delicate matters under study in the present project. The wise social researcher does not pretend that he does not have feelings, hopes, inclinations, and expectations of his own, frequently rooted in the very depths of his personality. However, his training as a researcher teaches him how to take these biases into account in order to make sure that they do not interfere with the competency of his analysis. He also realizes that his reputation as a social scientist depends to a considerable extent on his ability to neutralize his own biases. In addition, if he is part of a major social science research center, he and his colleagues at the center realize that their collective reputation depends on the objectivity of his analysis.

The various members of the staff for this study of the life and the ministry of the priesthood have their own biases, ambivalencies, ambiguities, and uncertainties. In some instances, these cancel out one another.

In other instances, however, the advice and counsel of their non-Catholic colleagues has been vigorously sought with the precise purpose of making the present report as professionally competent as possible. We are therefore confident that the present volume is as unbiased as the collective efforts of a major social science center with thirty years of history behind it could possibly guarantee.

The Plan of the Report

The goal of any social research endeavor is explanation. The researcher is not merely interested in what is happening but in why it is happening. Hence, in the final analysis he is interested in "causal" explanation. It is not merely enough to know that variable A is related to variable B; one does all in one's power to establish that A causes B. A causal connection is rather easy to establish under some circumstances. If one knows, for example, that while in college a young man had planned to enter medical school and one discovers a statistical relationship between these plans and his present attendance at medical school, one can say that his plans while in college were in part a cause of his present attendance, although obviously not the only nor a completely effective cause.

The complexity of social reality is such that it is extremely difficult to determine the direction of a causal flow between two variables when a relationship has been demonstrated between these variables. For example, we shall point out in this report that there is a negative relationship between holding certain "modern" values about the nature of the Church and future plans to stay in the priesthood. We assume that the values are logically prior to the plans, though we cannot exclude the possibility that someone's values are in part the result of his future plans rather than the cause; nor can we rule out the chance that there is some "feedback" effect, that values and plans mutually affect each other.

What the researcher does is to establish certain "models" as tools for analyzing reality. These models are statements of causal relationships based on a number of specified assumptions about the flow of causality among the various variables he is considering. The assumptions are not arbitrary but are based on what the researcher thinks are the most solid theoretical or chronological reasons (one's values, for example, cannot be assumed to have caused one's parents' education). The model is an "as-if" device. The researcher analyzes his variables "as-if" the causal flow in reality is the way he has specified it in his model. The model can then be used as a tool for examining reality, but it does not claim to be an exact duplicate of reality. Another researcher might make a different set of assumptions and examine reality in a different fashion. What is important is that a researcher specify his assumptions before the data become available and that he make these specifications and the reasons for them explicit. A refusal to specify a causal model leaves both the researcher and his audience in a morass of correlations that cannot be arranged in any meaningful fashion. Once a model has been stated, the relationships are arranged in one meaningful fashion, though not necessarily in the only possible meaningful fashion.

In Figure 1.1 we present graphically the model on which the analysis in this report is based. The causal flow is from left to right. Each variable is assumed to have a possible direct and indirect causal relationship with each variable to its right. For example, age is assumed to have a possible causal influence on personality, religious experience, values, work problems, morale, the desire to marry, and future plans with regard to the priesthood. This influence may be direct or it may flow through any variable that intervenes between age and a later variable. Thus, age may have a direct influence on work problems as well as indirect influences through personality, religious experience, and values. Our work of analysis will be to put lines between these boxes and to put numbers on the lines to determine the actual existence of and the strength of causal relationships among the nine variables in the model.

Let us then make clear our assumptions:

1. We do not postulate a causal connection between age and family tension because there is no logical or chronological reason for doing so. They thus appear at the same level of the model.

2. We assume on the basis of general social science theory that personality is the result of background demographic and social psychological variables such as age and family tension.

3. We assume that religious experience — sense of contact with the Deity — is influenced by family background and in its turn is part of the psycho-religious equipment that one brings to the ministry.

4. We assume that religious values are shaped by background, personality, and experience of the Divine and that they in turn shape the reaction to one's work in the ministry.

5. We assume that the problems, frustrations, and difficulties (or the satisfactions, joys, and fulfillments) in one's work are shaped by an interaction of background, personality, religious experience, and values.

6. We view morale, or psychological well-being, as being the result of the reaction to one's work experience as interpreted in the light of back-

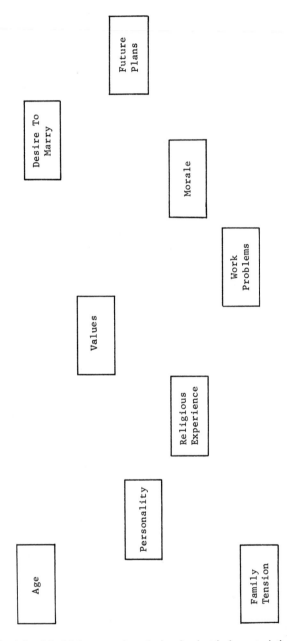

Fig. 1.1.—Model for causal analysis of priests' characteristics.

ground, personality, religious experience, and values and as a possible cause of the desire to marry and of the decision to resign from the priest-hood (or to stay in the priesthood).

7. We have placed the desire to marry in a rather late position in our model for three reasons. First of all, social science theory would lead us to predict that low satisfaction in priestly work would lead to a desire to marry as a compensation for the lack of "pay-off" in the work, while a high level of "pay-off" in terms of the satisfaction and fulfillments of the work might lead to a decline in the difficulties with celibacy. Secondly, an inspection of the percentages of those wishing to marry leads us to believe on empirical grounds that only a relatively small proportion of the clergy would in fact marry if they could. Finally, in terms of analytic strategy our model enables us to measure the increment to the amount of dissatisfaction priests experience that can be attributed only to the desire to marry. Or to put the matter somewhat differently, our strategy makes it possible to estimate the contribution of celibacy to resignation among the clergy, *net of all other sources of dissatisfaction.*

Model-building is not a completely rational business. Insight, instinct, and intuition go into it; and the statement of assumptions is usually an exercise in making explicit intuitive "feelings" about the shape of reality.[5] The ultimate test of a model is how useful it is for examining and under-standing reality. We think that the model used in this report will prove to have some utility. Other researchers may devise other models, and NORC has traditionally stood ready to make its data available for the use of other model-builders.

The model presented in Figure 1.1 is a version of one that was stated before inspection of the data began. The logic of our assumptions was explicit from the early stages of the project. However, this figure is much simpler than earlier versions of the model because, as in all model con-struction, many variables were dropped from the model when we found that they did not play an important role. Thus, we had assumed that variables such as parental education, age at entry to the seminary, amount of post-seminary education, being a member of a religious order, and size of one's diocese or religious order would correlate with the variables presently in the model. However, no important correlations (in excess of .2) emerged between these variables and those presently in the model. Occasionally a variable would correlate with one element of the model but with no other element and hence it was dropped. Thus, we found a relationship between family religious devotion and recollection of family tension. But religious devotion did not correlate with any of the other variables in the model and hence we dropped it from further analysis.

Furthermore, a number of different variables could be put in the specific boxes in Figure 1.1. There are several different indicators of values, of work problems, and of morale. The final decision of which ones to use depended on which displayed the strongest correlations with the variables to the right of the box about which the decision had to be made. Such decisions will be discussed in their proper places in subsequent chapters.

Only one variable was added to the model in the course of the analysis — the reports of respondents on whether loneliness was a serious problem for them in the priesthood. This variable was added because the desire to marry turned out to play such an important part in the model and we hypothesized (correctly as it turned out) that loneliness would strongly correlate with the desire to marry. That loneliness was not put into the model before inspection of the data was simply a mistake. It was something that should have been thought of but was not — a phenomenon that, by the way, is as common in social research as in any other human enterprise.

The decisions about which variables to drop from the original, far more elaborate model and which indicators to use in the specific boxes were based on inspection of several large correlation matrices. The inspection of these matrices and the determination of which variables went into them took place in light of the expectations and assumptions we have already stated. We shall not burden the reader of this report with the many pages of numbers that would be necessary to duplicate these matrices. However, copies of them are on file at NORC should any reader with social science training wish to examine them.

Each chapter will be divided into two sections — a descriptive section and an analytic section. In the descriptive section a set of two tables for each group of items under consideration will be presented and discussed. The first table in each set will present the responses of each subgroup within the larger survey — bishops, active diocesan priests, religious major superiors, active religious priests, and resigned priests (where applicable). In some tables there will also be information available from NORC's data file on the American Catholic population.[6] In the second table in each set the responses of different age groups of active diocesan and religious priests will be presented because our preliminary investigations showed that age is an extraordinarily important variable in explaining differences among the clergy. Pursuing the first of these tables will reveal to the reader the differences between priests and their leadership, between diocesan priests and religious priests, and between active priests and resigned priests. Pursuing the second table will enable the reader to know how the age groups within the clergy differ. Since resignees tend to be from the younger age group and bishops from the older group, a comparison between the two tables shows how both resignees and bishops differ from their respective age groups in the general population of the clergy.

For many readers, inspecting these tables and reading the accompanying text will sufficiently satisfy their curiosity about the study. However, for those interested in more detailed analysis, the second section of each chapter will explain and analyze the phenomena reported in the first section of the chapter. For those who do not wish to follow such complex and technical analysis in great detail, a summary of the analysis will be presented at the end of each chapter — in language we hope will not be too distant from English.

Table 1.1 presents the distribution of the numbers of respondents in the sample both by age and by status. These numbers, with small variations, are the case bases for the descriptive sections in all of the subsequent chapters.

TABLE 1.1

DISTRIBUTION OF RESPONDENTS BY AGE AND CLERICAL STATUS

Age of active priests:	*Distribution*
26-35[a]	1,121
36-45	1,544
46-55	1,165
Over 55	1,280
Clerical status:	
Bishops	165
Active diocesan priests	3,045
Resigned diocesan priests[b]	464
Major superiors	155
Active religious priests	2,110
Resigned religious priests[b]	286

[a] One respondent was 25 years old.

[b] All percentages for resignees in this report are based on these N's. Although, when the field work was finally completed, the total number of usable responses reached 873, it was too late to rerun the data using the larger case base. The additional 123 cases would not have significantly altered the percentages that we present.

In many chapters, immediately after the descriptive tables we present a correlation table showing how prior variables correlate with the factor under consideration. We shall then attempt to examine the complex interplay of direct and indirect cause among these variables.

Figure 1.2 illustrates the kind of analysis that will be attempted. Let us assume a population of students that is ordered on three different scales — their age, the number of years of education they have had, and their score on the Graduate Record Examination. Let us assume further that on their ages they may score anywhere from 1 to 25; on their education, anywhere from 1 to 16 years; and on their GRE score, anywhere from 0 to 100. The correlation coefficient is the measure of the extent to which there is a relationship between one's position on one of these scales and one's position on another scale. Thus, the relationship (r) of .32 between age and GRE score in Table 1.2 is a description of the extent of the relationship of where one is on the age scale and where one is on the GRE score scale. Since age is obviously something that is prior to taking the exam, it can be assumed that the position on the age scale is causally connected to one's exam score. In other words, the older you are, the more likely you are to get a good score. Moving to the next column, r^2, which is simply r multiplied by itself, is the amount of variance on one scale that can be explained by variance on another scale. The r^2 between age and GRE score is .10, which means that about 10 per cent of the variance on the GRE score scale can be explained by age. Age "causes" 10 per cent of the differences among the young people in their GRE score. But we also note from Table 1.2 that education relates to GRE score with a correlation of .30, so one's position on the education scale bears some relationship to one's performance in the exam. If age and education were completely independent of one another, their combined influence would give an R of .43 and an explanation of about 19 per cent of the variance on the exam score, but a moment's consideration makes it clear that there is a strong relationship between age and education and therefore a substantial part of their causal influence on exam scores would overlap.

The statistic R is a measure of their joint influence on GRE score, and the statistic R^2 is the measure of the explanatory power of the two variables combined. We see from Table 1.2 that the R of age and education together (presented in the education row of the table) is .35, and that the R^2 is .12. The overlap between age and education is therefore quite considerable because when one adds education to the model, the R goes up by only three points and the R^2 by only two points. The

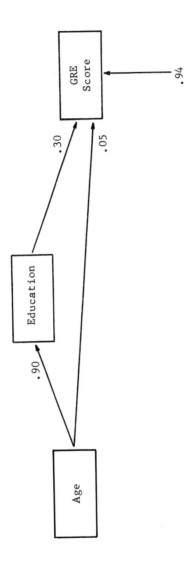

Fig. 1.2.—Path diagram relating GRE score to age and education.

TABLE 1.2

CORRELATIONS OF GRADUATE RECORD EXAMINATION
SCORE WITH AGE AND EDUCATION

Variable	r	r^2	R	R^2	R^2 Change
Age	.32	.10	.32	.10	.10
Education	.30	.09	.35	.12	.02

final column of the table, R^2 change, shows the increase in the explanatory power of the model by adding education to the causal system containing age and GRE score.

One might assume from looking at the table, then, that age was the principal "cause" of a high score on the GRE since our addition of education to the model only improves its explanatory power by two percentage points. However, another moment's consideration will reveal that this would be a false conclusion. In all likelihood, we would assume, what happens is that age is correlated with education and education, in its turn, with one's position on the GRE score scale. Age, then, "causes" the number of years that the young person has attended school, and this, in its turn, "causes" his position on the GRE measure.

The flow chart in Figure 1.2 illustrates this relationship.[7] There is a .90 correlation between age and education, a .30 correlation between education and GRE score, and a .05 relationship between age and GRE score with education taken into account. In other words, most of the influence of age flows through education to GRE score while a rather small proportion of the influence of age is direct. Older students get better scores mostly because they have had more schooling. The line linking age and GRE score is called the "direct path" between age and exam score, and the lines between age and education and between education and GRE score can be multiplied to produce the "indirect path" of age's influence on exam score. The measure of the indirect path is the product of the two path coefficients, or $.9 \times .3 = .27$. Thus, of the r of .32 between age and GRE score, .27 is indirect and .05 is direct.[8]

The advantage of the diagram in Figure 1.2 is that it enables us to consider simultaneously the direct and indirect paths by which a prior variable influences a subsequent variable. In this particular instance, for example, we note that even though the addition of education to our model only improves our explanatory power by two percentage points, education is, nevertheless, the principal channel by which age exercises its influence on GRE score. A small R^2 change, therefore, does not indicate that the variable which causes this rather small addition to the explanatory power of the model is unimportant.

It will be noted that there is a third arrow pointing into GRE score with a .94 at its base. This third arrow is called the "residual path." The square of the residual path coefficient indicates the amount of variance in GRE score not explained by the model. Thus, .94 squared is .88. Twelve per cent of the variance in GRE score is explained by age and education, and 88 per cent of the variance remains unexplained by the model. It can be said, therefore, that age and education do in fact play some causal role in a young person's performance on the GRE. But even when their full causal impact is taken into account, 88 per cent of the variance in the position of students on the score scale remains to be explained.

Social science does not expect to be able to explain 100 per cent of the variance. Such determinism of human attitudes and behavior can scarcely be expected to exist in reality, however much it may have been honored in philosophical textbooks in the past. The amount of explained variance that satisfies the researcher depends upon the nature of the analysis in which he is engaged. However, the fact that, as subsequent chapters will demonstrate, we are able to explain as much as one-half of the variance in future plans in the priesthood with a very complex causal model would be, we suspect, considered quite creditable by most of our sociological colleagues.

The use of correlation coefficients and path diagrams in causal models represents a major breakthrough in the methodology of social research because it enables the relationships between many variables to be specified much more clearly than mere percentage distribution tables would permit. However, something is lost when one proceeds from percentage tables to correlation models — particularly for the reader who is used to dealing with percentages. Therefore, periodically in the course of the analysis of this report, we shall turn away from the model and present some of the more familiar percentage distribution, or "contingency," tables.

While our path analysis method described in this section and used throughout the report may be unfamiliar to most readers, it is not especially difficult to understand or to follow when one becomes adjusted to it. For the reader who is interested in following in detail the complex set of relationships involved in the life and ministry of the priest, the little time and patience that will be required to become familiar with path analysis will be richly rewarded in a sophisticated understanding of the complexities of priestly attitudes and behavior.

Conclusion

The sample model presented in Figure 1.2 is a simple one involving only three variables and three paths, plus a residual path. As we proceed through the building blocks of our causal model in subsequent chapters, many more variables and paths will be used. Although such charts are somewhat complicated to read, they have the merit of persuading the reader that the reality represented by the chart is an extremely complicated one. There are no simple, easy explanations for any of the questions to which the Committee for the Study of the Life and Ministry of the Priest must address itself. It will only be by drastically tearing the findings of this report from their context that the reader will be able to present reality as uncomplicated.

For example, on the question of the morale of the clergy, it could be argued that since psychological well-being of the clergy is as high as that of the typical college-educated married man (and higher than that of single men),[9] there is no serious morale problem among the Catholic clergy in the United States. One can see the newspaper headlines, "Study finds no morale problem among priests." On the other hand, about five per cent of the diocesan priests resigned in the four-year period from 1966 to 1969, and when the questionnaires were adminstered, another three per cent said that they were either probably or definitely going to leave the priesthood and 10 per cent were uncertain about their future plans. Therefore, it must be argued that there is a very severe morale crisis. Furthermore, it could be pointed out that the job satisfaction of the typical American curate is not very different from that of an unskilled worker. Hence, the headline could be written, "Study finds morale crisis among priests."

Which of the two stories would be true? The only answer is that both of them would be true and neither of them would be true. Both of them would be true if they were seen as part of a much more complicated picture in which both stories had to be integrated. Neither of them would be true if they were seen as descriptions of the whole reality.

Again, one could make a plausible case from many of the tables in this report that bishops are more "conservative" than their priests — even in some instances than clergy in their own age brackets. On many moral and religious issues bishops are more likely to endorse a "traditional" position than are the rest of the respondents. On the other hand, on questions of social action and ecumenism the episcopal respondents are more inclined to endorse a "liberal" position than are other respondents, in some instances more "liberal" even than younger priests.

One could therefore justify a headline that would say, "Bishops more conservative than priests," and a headline that would say, "Bishops more liberal than priests." Both headlines could be true, but neither would be the whole truth without the other — and without the realization that however much "liberal" positions on one issue may correlate with "liberal" positions on other issues in the mind of the ideology, these correlations are much less likely to be found in reality. Most human beings are "conservative" on some issues and "liberal" on others. The clergy are no exception.

An earlier NORC report on Catholic education (Greeley and Rossi, 1966) was characterized by a national news magazine as "being mired in qualification." Unfortunately, there is no other way to describe social reality, for the human condition is mired in qualification. The reality of the life and ministry of the priest is more rather than less complicated than the path diagrams to be presented in this report.

To say that the reality is complicated is not to confess failure in the present research project. On the contrary, to be able to document the scope and nature of the complexity and hopefully to put to rest one-factor explanations is a legitimate goal of any research enterprise.

While this is the "final" report of the present project, it should still be emphasized that, like every "final" report, the present volume only skims the surface of the data. The basic outlines of the situation of the life and ministry of the Catholic priest in the United States are now clear. But further analysis can fill in details for many years to come.

1. In other NORC reports an occasional chapter of recommendations is added, but this is generally at the insistence of the client. See Spaeth and Greeley (1970).

2. On this subject, see Moynihan (1969).

3. The term "resigned" (or "resignee") is used in this report to describe those who have withdrawn from the active ministry. While this is a word that seems least objectionable to such priests, it must be emphasized that its use in the present report is entirely neutral and implies no theological or moral judgment either for or against those who have resigned.

4. All human organizations have a difficult time keeping accurate lists of the names and addresses of their members. One university that we know of does not even at the present time have a complete list of all its faculty members.

5. We share the feelings of such philosophers of science as Michael Polanyi and Thomas Kuhn that the quasi-artistic insight is at the core of scientific activity.

6. These data were collected for a study reported in Greeley and Rossi (1966).

7. It should be observed, incidentally, that the model illustrated in Figure 1.2 is completely mythical and does not represent any actual data on the relationship between age, education, and GRE scores.

8. In subsequent chapters the statistics on the path will not be an *r* but rather a *beta,* which is a "net standardized coefficient." Social science readers will know the difference between a *beta* and an *r;* non-social science readers can see the difference if they wish in some of the longer treatments of path analysis. See in particular Duncan (1966) or Spaeth and Greeley (1970), pp. 134-37.

9. This finding led Professor Bradburn to comment that if you're not married, it helps to be a priest.

CHAPTER 2

BACKGROUNDS OF THE CLERGY

The purpose of this chapter is to summarize background information on the American Catholic clergy: How old are they? Where were they born? What were their early family experiences? What kind of socio-economic class did they come from? What was the religious environment of their families? Were there tensions and problems in the family environment?

This information is of considerable interest in itself because never before has there been a systematic attempt to collect demographic, geographic, socio-economic, and social psychological data on the backgrounds of the American clergy. But in addition to the information being interesting in itself, it is also indispensable as a base from which to begin our exploration of the causality of the problems experienced in the life and ministry of the priest. Sociology and psychology leave us in no doubt that much of the behavior in the life of an adult is shaped by factors that were at work in his early childhood experiences.

Age

We observe in Table 2.1 that major superiors are more similar in their age to their subjects than bishops are to diocesan priests. Thus, 26 per cent of the major superiors are over fifty-five as are 29 per cent of the active religious priests, while, on the other hand, 68 per cent of the bishops are over fifty-five as opposed to 23 per cent of the active diocesan priests. Some idea of the age difference between bishops and the resignees from the diocesan priesthood can be gathered from the fact that only 3 per cent of the bishops of the country are forty-five and under, whereas 90 per cent of the diocesan resignees are under that age.[1]

The heaviest concentration of resigned priests is in the age bracket between thirty-six and forty-five, with 53 per cent of the diocesan resignees and 58 per cent of the religious order resignees in this age group. It is worth noting that the proportion of resignees thirty-five and under among religious (23 per cent) is not much greater than the percentage of

23

The Catholic Priest in the United States

TABLE 2.1

STATUS OF AMERICAN CLERGY BY AGE
(Per Cent)

Status	Age			
	26-35	36-45	46-55	Over 55
Diocesan:				
Bishops	0	3	29	68
Active priests	25	30	22	23
Resigned priests	37	53	9	1
Religious:				
Major superiors	2	27	45	26
Active priests	17	30	24	29
Resigned priests	23	58	18	1

actives in the same age category (17 per cent). On the other hand, the young diocesan resignees constitute 37 per cent of the resignee group while the young actives constitute 25 per cent of their group. Among those thirty-five and under, the resignation rate among diocesan priests is higher than that among religious priests, although as we shall see in Chapter 15, the overall role is higher for religious.

Nativity

Table 2.2 shows that of all the priest groups, only major superiors are notably more likely to have been born abroad than are American Catholic males. The resigned priests, presumably because of their lower age, are least likely to report foreign birth.

About two-fifths of the priests in the country were born in the northeastern region, which is approximately the same as the proportion of American Catholic males born in that region, but only about one-third of the bishops and major superiors come from this section of the country. It may well be that the concentration of large communities and dioceses in the Northeast explains why there are fewer leaders from that region: there may simply be fewer leadership positions. The only difference among all seven groups in Table 2.2 in the proportion born in the North Central states is that resigned diocesan priests seem to be overrepresented in this region of the country. Thirty-eight per cent of the active diocesan priests in the country come from this area but 45 per cent of the resigned diocesan priests were born in these states.

TABLE 2.2
NATIVITY BY CLERICAL STATUS AND FOR AMERICAN CATHOLIC MALES
(Per Cent)

Nativity	Diocesan			Religious			American Catholic Males[a]
	Bishops	Active Priests	Resigned Priests	Major Superiors	Active Priests	Resigned Priests	
Place of birth:							
Outside U.S.	6	11	2[b]	17	9	2[b]	10
In the Northeast[c]	32	35	34[b]	34	39	44[b]	43
In North Central states[d]	34	38	45[b]	38	41	37[b]	33
In metropolitan area with population over half-million[b]	42	34	48	36	32	46	33
Firstborn	32	34	44	29	33	37	—

[a] Data from Greeley and Rossi (1966).
[b] Based on where respondent grew up.
[c] Consists of the following states: Maine, New Hampshire, Vermont, Massachusetts, Rhode Island, Connecticut, New York, New Jersey, and Pennsylvania.
[d] Consists of the following states: Ohio, Indiana, Illinois, Michigan, Wisconsin, Minnesota, Iowa, Missouri, North Dakota, South Dakota, Nebraska, and Kansas.

Interestingly enough, 44 per cent of the resigned diocesan priests and 37 per cent of the resigned religious priests were the first children to be born in their families, both substantially higher than the proportion among active priests. Why the firstborn would be the most likely to leave the active ministry is not clear at this point, nor is it clear why resignees are more likely than other priests to have grown up in metropolitan areas with population of over a half-million.

We can see in Table 2.3 that even though the younger clergy are somewhat more likely than the older clergy to be firstborn, there are no important variations in either the size of the city where they grew up or in the region of the country where they were born, nor is there any appreciably less likelihood of the younger clergy being foreign born.

Socioeconomic Background

Using an NORC measure of occupational prestige, we can see from Table 2.4 that the fathers of clergy in all six categories score at least one full point higher on the occupational prestige index than do the fathers of typical American Catholic males. Thus, the clergy come from higher social-class backgrounds than do typical American Catholics. This phenomenon may result from the fact that clergy are disproportionately Irish, and the Irish, since they came before many of the other Catholic immigrant groups and already knew the language, have had greater occupational success than later immigrant groups.[2] Bishops and major superiors, however, are not much more likely than typical American

TABLE 2.3

NATIVITY BY AGE

(Per Cent of Active Diocesan and Religious Priests)

Nativity	Age			
	26-35	36-45	46-55	Over 55
Place of birth:				
Outside U.S.	9	10	10	11
In Northeast	35	35	37	39
In North Central states	41	40	39	37
In metropolitan area with population of over half-million [a]	32	34	34	32
Firstborn	38	33	34	30

[a] Based on where respondent grew up.

TABLE 2.4

SOCIOECONOMIC BACKGROUND BY CLERICAL STATUS AND FOR AMERICAN CATHOLIC MALES

Socioeconomic Background	Diocesan			Religious			American Catholic Males [a]
	Bishops	Active Priests	Resigned Priests	Major Supe- riors	Active Priests	Resigned Priests	
Mean occupational score of father (0-10)	3.3	3.3	3.3	3.4	3.3	3.2	2.2
Father high school graduate or more (per cent)	21	31	40	27	31	43	23
Mother high school graduate or more (per cent)	28	35	42	25	34	50	22

[a] Data from Greeley and Rossi (1966).

Catholic males to report that their fathers and mothers had at least graduated from high school. The resigned priests, on the other hand, whether they were diocesan or religious, are more likely to have come from higher educational backgrounds than the active priests.

The youth factor may be at work in the apparent relationship between parental education and resignation. As we can see in Table 2.5, the younger a priest is, the more likely his parents are to have at least graduated from high school. It is interesting to note, in comparing Tables 2.4 and 2.5, that in terms of occupational background, bishops come from a higher socioeconomic status than do active priests of the age group over fifty-five. This phenomenon may be explained by the Irish background of much of the episcopacy.

Ethnicity

This strong Irish influence is emphasized in Table 2.6. The Irish comprise 17 per cent of the American Catholic males, 34 per cent of the active religious priests, 38 per cent of the major superiors, 39 per cent of the active diocesan priests, and 49 per cent of the bishops. In other words, while only about one-sixth of the American Catholic population is Irish, better than one-third of the clergy is Irish, as is almost one-half of the hierarchy. The proportions of Germans and Scandinavians among the priests and hierarchy are about the same (about one-quarter), but the Italians, the French, the Poles, other Slavs, and the Latins are all underrepresented in the hierarchy. Italians are somewhat overrepresented among the major superiors while Poles are slightly underrepresented — in comparison with the proportions of these two ethnic groups to be found among the active religious priests. Only the Anglo-Saxons seemed notably overrepresented among the resigned priests in comparison

TABLE 2.5

SOCIOECONOMIC BACKGROUND BY AGE
(Active Diocesan and Religious Priests)

Item	Age			
	26-35	36-45	46-55	Over 55
Mean occupational score of father (0-10)	3.1	3.4	2.6	2.6
Father high school graduate or more (per cent)	42	32	26	25
Mother high school graduate or more (per cent)	46	35	30	27

TABLE 2.6

FATHER'S ETHNICITY BY CLERICAL STATUS AND FOR AMERICAN CATHOLIC MALES

(Per Cent)

Father's Ethnicity	Diocesan			Religious			American Catholic Males[a]
	Bishops	Active Priests	Resigned Priests	Major Superiors	Active Priests	Resigned Priests	
Anglo-Saxon	9	7	11	5	7	13	8
Irish	49	39	34	38	34	35	17
German or Scandinavian	25	24	29	21	25	25	20
Italian	3	5	5	8	5	3	19
French	3	7	7	6	9	11	9
Polish	1	6	5	5	7	3	9
Other Slav	2	3	2	4	4	1	9
Latin	1	2	2	2	2	1	7
Other	7	7	5	10	7	8	3
Total	100	100	100	99[b]	100	100	101[b]
Non-white	1	1	—[c]	1	1	—[c]	—[d]

[a] Data from Greeley and Rossi (1966).
[b] Not 100 per cent because of rounding.
[c] Not asked of resigned priests.
[d] Data not available.

with their proportions among the active clergy. Thus, 7 per cent of the active priests are Anglo-Saxon but 11 per cent of the resigned diocesan and 13 per cent of the resigned religious have Anglo-Saxon backgrounds. The explanation for this phenomenon may be that those with Anglo-Saxon backgrounds might well be the product of a marriage in which the father was a convert and hence somewhat less devout. We shall note later in this chapter that there is apparently some relationship between parents' being less than "very devout" and resignation from the priesthood.

One can find in Table 2.7 only two apparent relationships between the age and ethnic background of American Catholic priests. There are fewer Irish among those thirty-five and under than in the other three age categories and more Italians in the group forty-five and under than in the group over fifty-five. It may be possible, therefore, to tentatively suggest that the Irish have reached the stage of the acculturation process where they are somewhat less likely to send their sons to the priesthood than they were in the past (although even among those thirty-five and under, the Irish are still disproportionately overrepresented compared to their percentage in the total Catholic population). On the other hand, Italians seem to have reached that stage of the acculturation process where they are increasingly more likely to send their sons to the priesthood (although Italians are still underrepresented even among those thirty-five and under).

TABLE 2.7

FATHER'S ETHNICITY BY AGE
(Per Cent of Active Diocesan and Religious Priests)

Father's Ethnicity	Age			
	26-35	36-45	46-55	Over 55
Anglo-Saxon	8	7	9	6
Irish	34	37	35	39
German or Scandinavian	26	24	26	23
Italian	7	6	4	4
French	8	8	8	8
Polish	6	5	8	8
Other Slav	3	3	3	3
Latin	2	2	1	2
Other	6	8	6	7
Total	100	100	100	100
Non-white	1	1	0	1

Family Experiences

There is a substantial and growing literature on religious change indicating that leaving behind one's childhood church is related to certain family experiences. A family broken by divorce or death or a family where there were religious differences, emotional strain, or alcoholism, seems to be more likely to lead to apostasy in adult life. It was therefore hypothesized that there might be a connection between experiences as a child and resignation from the priesthood in adult life. Table 2.8 notes that there is virtually no difference among the six categories of clergy in proportions raised by both their parents. However, those who have resigned are more likely to report both that there was divorce or separation in their family background and that their mother was employed during their childhood years. It is also worth observing that active priests are very little more likely to report the occurrence of these two phenomena than are either bishops or major superiors. The apparent relationship between maternal employment and resignation may be a function of the younger age of resignees since we can observe in Table 2.9 that the mothers of priests forty-five and under were more likely to have worked when the priests were children than were the mothers of priests forty-six and over.

Religious Backgrounds

Table 2.10 shows that there are no important differences among the clergy in the percentages who were born Catholic of parents who were

TABLE 2.8

FAMILY EXPERIENCES BY CLERICAL STATUS

(Per Cent)

Item	Diocesan			Religious		
	Bishops	Active Priests	Resigned Priests	Major Superiors	Active Priests	Resigned Priests
Raised by both parents	90	91	92	91	92	92
Parents divorced or separated	1	3	7	4	3	9
Mother employed during childhood	13	20	25	15	21	25

TABLE 2.9

FAMILY EXPERIENCES BY AGE
(Per Cent of Active Diocesan and Religious Priests)

Item	Age			
	26-35	36-45	46-55	Over 55
Raised by both parents	93	91	91	90
Parents divorced or separated	2	3	4	4
Mother employed during childhood	22	23	20	17

Catholic. However, the clergy are more likely to come from Catholic families than are American Catholic males. Bishops are more likely to remember their fathers and mothers as very devout than are active diocesan priests, and the active diocesan priests, in their turn, are more likely to remember their fathers and mothers as very devout than are the resignees. Interestingly enough, no such pattern seems to exist among major superiors, active religious priests, and resigned religious priests. No immediate reason can be advanced to explain why such a pattern would exist among diocesan clergy and not among religious clergy. However, the theoretical hypothesis that there might be a relationship between resignation and family religious background does seem to have some support among diocesan priests.

But in Table 2.11, recollection of parents' religious devotion correlates somewhat with age. Therefore, the fact that bishops are more likely than active diocesan priests to describe their parents as very devout and resignees less likely to so describe them may result from the influence of the age factor.

Family Problems

The hypothesis that a strain in family background will relate to resignation from the priesthood is supported by the figures in Table 2.12. In every one of the ten comparisons that can be made between resignees and actives, the resignees are more likely to report problems in the family background, and in some instances, the differences are quite substantial. Thus, among the diocesan clergy 29 per cent of the resigned priests, as opposed to 17 per cent of the actives, report strain between mother and father; 12 per cent of the resigned, as opposed to 5 per cent of the actives, report strain with their mother; and 19 per cent of the resigned, as

TABLE 2.10

RELIGIOUS BACKGROUND BY CLERICAL STATUS AND FOR AMERICAN CATHOLIC MALES

(Per Cent)

Religious Background	Diocesan			Religious			American Catholic Males [a]
	Bishops	Active Priests	Resigned Priests	Major Superiors	Active Priests	Resigned Priests	
Born Catholic	98	98	—[b]	99	99	—[b]	89
Father Catholic	96	95	94	96	96	93	85
Mother Catholic	99	98	98	99	98	98	—
Father very devout	54	45	36	36	44	40	—
Mother very devout	83	73	64	68	73	63	—

[a] Data from Greeley and Rossi (1966).
[b] Not asked of resigned priests.

TABLE 2.11

RELIGIOUS BACKGROUND BY AGE

(Per Cent of Active Diocesan and Religious Priests)

Religious Background	Age			
	26-35	36-45	46-55	Over 55
Born Catholic	98	98	99	98
Father Catholic	95	96	95	95
Mother Catholic	98	98	99	98
Father very devout	42	43	45	47
Mother very devout	70	70	76	76

opposed to 11 per cent of the actives, report strain with their father. In all instances, however, bishops are less likely than the actives to report strain. Table 2.13 indicates that the tendency to report problems in the family background is only very slightly more pronounced among the younger priests than among the older, so it could well be that the differences among bishops, active priests, and resigned priests are an age phenomenon.

TABLE 2.12

FAMILY PROBLEMS BY CLERICAL STATUS

(Per Cent)

Family Problem	Diocesan			Religious		
	Bishops	Active Priests	Resigned Priests	Major Superiors	Active Priests	Resigned Priests
Strain between mother and father	6	17	29	14	18	31
Strain with mother	0	5	12	1	5	13
Strain with father	3	11	19	7	12	16
Father heavy drinker or alcoholic	6	13	17	17	12	16
Mother heavy drinker or alcoholic	0	1	2	1	1	4

A "family-tension" index was created from these three items dealing with strain in the family, and correlations were calculated between the index and various demographic and socioeconomic variables. None of the correlations are higher than .2, and only one correlation — that with age — comes close. In other words, with the exception of a −.17 correlation between age and remembrance of family tension, there is no evidence that family tension relates in an important way with family social status, family size, ethnic background, or parental education.[3]

On the other hand, when the relationship between the family-tension index and parental religious devoutness is considered, we find that remembrance of family tension has a correlation of −.32 with recollection of a devout father and a correlation of −.21 with recollection of a devout mother. Thus, those who remembered their parents as devout are somewhat less likely to remember tension in the family.

The reader may wonder why particular attention was paid to the family-tension variable. As we shall see in Chapter 13, a recollection of family tension explains 2 per cent of the variance in future plans for staying in the priesthood when age is held constant. This impact is apparently the result of the fact that those from families which are recollected as tense are somewhat less likely to have "religious experiences," somewhat more likely to have "modern" religious values, and somewhat more likely to have "morale" problems.

Conclusion

To summarize the findings of the tables in this chapter, bishops are older than typical American clergy; resignees are younger. Both bishops and resignees are more likely to come from large cities. The Irish are

TABLE 2.13

FAMILY PROBLEMS BY AGE
(Per Cent of Active Diocesan and Religious Priests)

Family Problem	Age			
	26-35	36-45	46-55	Over 55
Strain between mother and father	18	18	20	15
Strain with mother	6	4	5	5
Strain with father	12	12	12	10
Father heavy drinker or alcoholic	14	13	13	11
Mother heavy drinker or alcoholic	1	1	1	0

highly overrepresented in the clergy and dominate the hierarchy. Resignees are more likely to report divorce, working mother, and family tension, while bishops are less likely than typical American clergy to report these phenomena. Bishops are more likely than active diocesan priests, and the active priests more likely than resignees, to report very devout religious backgrounds in their families. However, virtually all the variables that differentiate among the three groups also correlate with age, and thus the tentative differences reported in these tables may all be attributable to age. Finally, major superiors seem to be much less different in most respects from their subjects than bishops are from diocesan priests.

We also note that a recollection of family tension — as measured by an index that will play a role in our further analysis — correlates with age (younger priests are more likely to describe family tension than are older ones) and with a remembrance of parents who were not so devout (the more devout the parents, the less likely the clergy are to describe family tension).

Of all the battery of background variables presented in this chapter, only age and family tension relate with a correlation above .2 with any of the variables to the right in our model as shown in Figure 1.1 Hence, these two variables will be used in our analysis of subsequent variables.

1. The mean age of the active priests in the sample is 46.6.
2. See Greeley and Spaeth (forthcoming).
3. The −.17 correlation between age and the family-tension index may seem somewhat at odds with the data reported in Table 2.13. The difference, however, is explained by the fact that while younger priests are no more likely to report strain in these relationships, they are more likely to describe these relationships as neutral, while the older clergy are more likely to describe their family relationships as warm and intimate. There may, of course, be a nostalgia factor at work here.

CHAPTER 3

EDUCATION AND VOCATION DECISION AMONG THE CLERGY

Since the time of the Council of Trent the Roman Catholic Church has maintained, in most countries, a separate educational system for its future clergy, including in almost all cases seminary colleges and professional training programs and frequently also seminary high schools. At the present time, this system of separate education is vigorously questioned and in many places it is being replaced by a "mixed" educational experience for seminarians in which future priests receive some of their training with lay students and some only with fellow seminarians. The principal argument used against the seminary system is that it isolates young men from the world and impedes their emotional maturation. In this chapter we shall discuss the educational background of priests both before and after they enter the seminary, their opinion of seminary education, their dating experiences before and during their seminary attendance, and the sources of encouragement for their decisions to become priests.

Description

In the descriptive section of this chapter we report the following principal findings:

1. It is not correct to assume that most priests enter the seminary as early adolescents or that they had no experience of dating young women before entering.

2. Resigned priests seem to have had somewhat more education after ordination than active priests.

3. While most priests think that the seminary equipped them moderately well for their priestly work, the majority also had highly critical, specific comments about the seminary, and only a minority approved of high school seminaries.

4. The most frequently mentioned sources of encouragement for a decision to become a priest are one's mother and a priest.

Turning to specific findings, Table 3.1 shows that about three-fifths of the priests in the country had at least graduated from high school before entering the seminary and that about two-thirds of all respondents had all their pre-seminary education in Catholic schools. Furthermore, 71 per cent of the bishops, 58 per cent of the major superiors, and 67 per cent of the active priests (diocesan and religious) had some sort of degree at the time of ordination, but more than 80 per cent of the resigned priests had a degree at that time. This difference between the resigned priests and the active priests cannot really be explained by the fact that the resigned priests are somewhat younger because we observe in Table 3.2 that there is only a slight correlation between youthfulness and having a degree at the time of ordination. As a matter of fact, resigned priests are even more likely to have had a degree at the time of ordination than are priests thirty-five and under.

Many, but by no means all, American priests entered the seminary in their early or middle teens (Table 3.3). Forty-five per cent of the bishops, 52 per cent of the major superiors, and 45 per cent of the active priests (both diocesan and religious) entered the seminary when they were seventeen years old or under, but interestingly enough, 57 per cent of the resigned diocesan priests had entered at this early age (as opposed to 45 per cent of the religious order resignees). Or, to look at the other end of the scale, 15 per cent of the active diocesan priests entered the seminary when they were over twenty-one compared to only 6 per cent of the resigned diocesan priests.

There is some correlation between time of entry to the seminary and age (Table 3.4). Thus, 8 per cent of the priests thirty-five and under were over twenty-one when they entered the seminary and 18 per cent of those over fifty-five were over twenty-one when they began their seminary education; while, on the other hand, 31 per cent of those thirty-five and under and 23 per cent of those over fifty-five entered when they were fourteen or younger. Thus, some of the apparent relationship between resignation and youthful entry to the seminary among diocesan priests may be the result of age. Resignees are younger than active priests, and younger priests are more likely to have entered the seminary in their early teens.

Resigned priests are also more likely to have had advanced education since ordination (Table 3.5). Thus, 70 per cent of the active diocesan priests have no additional degree while only 47 per cent of the resigned

TABLE 3.1

EDUCATION OF THE CLERGY

(Per Cent)

Education	Diocesan			Religious		
	Bishops	Active Priests	Resigned Priests	Major Superiors	Active Priests	Resigned Priests
Had at least graduated from high school before entering seminary	58	62	—[a]	60	63	—[a]
Had all pre-seminary education in Catholic schools	65	65	68	64	64	61
Had a degree at time of ordination	71	67	83	58	67	88

[a] Not asked of resigned priests.

TABLE 3.2

EDUCATION OF THE CLERGY, BY AGE
(Per Cent of Active Diocesan and Religious Priests)

Education	Age			
	26-35	36-45	46-55	Over 55
Had at least graduated from high school before entering the seminary	60	62	64	63
Had all pre-seminary education in Catholic schools	67	63	66	64
Had a degree at the time of ordination	74	68	65	64

TABLE 3.3

AGE AT ENTRY TO SEMINARY, BY CLERICAL STATUS
(Per Cent)

Age at Entry to Seminary	Diocesan			Religious		
	Bishops	Active Priests	Resigned Priests	Major Superiors	Active Priests	Resigned Priests
14 and under	30	27	35	29	27	24
15-17	15	18	22	23	18	21
18	15	17	19	15	17	21
19-21	30	23	18	24	23	23
Over 21	9	15	6	9	15	11
Total	99 [a]	100	100	100	100	100

[a] Not 100 per cent because of rounding.

TABLE 3.4

AGE AT ENTRY TO SEMINARY, BY AGE
(Per Cent of Active Diocesan and Religious Priests)

Age at Entry to Seminary	Age			
	26-35	36-45	46-55	Over 55
14 and under	31	28	26	23
15-17	17	19	18	18
18	21	17	14	16
19-21	23	21	25	25
Over 21	8	15	18	18
Total	100	100	101 [a]	100

[a] Not 100 per cent because of rounding.

diocesan priests have no additional degree. The principal difference among diocesan priests is in those who have master's degrees. Thus, 34 per cent of the resigned diocesan priests have master's degrees and only 14 per cent of the active diocesan priests have this degree. Among religious priests, 75 per cent of the actives have no additional degree and 24 per cent of the resignees have no such degree. The distribution of master's degrees among the religious priests is comparable to that among diocesan priests, with 31 per cent of the resignees and only 14 per cent of the actives having M.A.'s. Resigned religious priests are also more likely than the actives to have Ph.D.'s (16 per cent versus 3 per cent).

The apparently higher education of the resignees cannot be explained by youthfulness because, as we note in Table 3.6, there is no correlation between age and advanced education. There are a number of possible explanations for the better education of the resignees. It may be that the fact of an advanced education facilitates resignation for those who know that they will be able to support themselves after they leave the priesthood. Possibly those who go on for graduate work have wider experience with the world beyond the Church and hence greater self-confidence about their capacity to operate in such a world. Some men may pursue advanced training before resignation precisely so that they can support themselves after they leave. Finally, those who have advanced education may be more likely to ask serious questions about their role in the priesthood.

TABLE 3.5

EDUCATION SINCE ORDINATION, BY CLERICAL STATUS

(Per Cent)

Education	Diocesan			Religious		
	Bishops	Active Priests	Resigned Priests	Major Superiors	Active Priests	Resigned Priests
Theological degree less than doctorate	11	4	5	13	3	16
Theological doctorate	34	5	4	17	3	4
Master's degree	10	14	34	28	14	31
Ph.D.	8	4	3	9	3	16
Other	6	3	7	4	2	8
No additional degree	31	70	47	30	75	24
Total	100	100	100	101[a]	100	99[a]

[a] Not 100 per cent because of rounding.

TABLE 3.6

EDUCATION SINCE ORDINATION, BY AGE
(Per Cent of Active Diocesan and Religious Priests)

Education	Age			
	26-35	36-45	46-55	Over 55
Theological degree less than doctorate	5	2	3	3
Theological doctorate	3	5	5	4
Master's degree	12	17	14	12
Ph.D.	3	3	3	4
Other	3	3	4	3
No additional degree	74	70	71	74
Total	100	100	100	100

However, even though there is a difference in the amount of advanced education between the resigned priests and the actives, we could find no correlation between higher education and inclination to leave the priesthood among those who are active. Thus, advanced education was not one of the variables that entered into the model that we shall discuss in Chapter 13. It may, of course, be that in the first wave of resignations advanced education did play a causal role, but at the present time it no longer plays such a role.

Table 3.7 shows that 2 per cent of the active priests are engaged in full-time study, and another 10 per cent of the diocesan and 11 per cent of the religious priests are engaged in part-time study. Theology is the most likely field of study, involving 37 per cent of the diocesan and 38 per cent of the religious priests. Counseling holds second place, with 25 per cent of the diocesan and 20 per cent of the religious pursuing courses in that discipline. As one might expect, priests thirty-five and under are the most likely to be involved in study, with 19 per cent of them either in full-time or part-time study (Table 3.8). In all four age groups of students, theology is the most popular field for advanced work, with counseling taking second place with priests forty-five and under. Among those between thirty-six and forty-five, counseling is just behind theology in popularity, with 34 per cent engaged in advanced study in theology and 30 per cent studying counseling. However, among those between forty-six and fifty-five, the social sciences, education, and humanities are slightly more popular than counseling, and among those over fifty-five,

TABLE 3.7

CURRENT STUDIES BY CLERICAL STATUS
(Per Cent)

Current Studies	Active Diocesan Priests	Active Religious Priests
In studies:		
Full-time	2	2
Part-time	10	11
Field of study:		
Humanities	6	5
Social sciences	10	13
Education	12	12
Counseling	25	20
Theology	37	38
Other	10	11

TABLE 3.8

CURRENT STUDIES BY AGE
(Per Cent of Active Diocesan and Religious Priests)

Current Studies	Age			
	26-35	36-45	46-55	Over 55
In studies:				
Full-time	3	2	2	1
Part-time	16	11	8	5
Field of study:				
Humanities	5	1	11	9
Social sciences	9	11	15	7
Education	10	12	15	15
Counseling	25	30	10	15
Theology	39	34	42	41
Other	12	12	6	12

counseling ties for second in popularity with education, with both fields of study claiming the attention of 15 per cent of the respondents in that age category.

Active priests are ambivalent in their evaluation of their seminary training (Table 3.9). Sixty-six per cent of the active diocesan priests assert that their seminaries prepared them at least moderately well for priestly work, as do 93 per cent of the bishops. On the other hand, 58 per cent of the diocesan priests think seminary courses were too theoretical, 48 per cent think the course presentation was too superficial, 64 per cent think the courses were irrelevant to pastoral needs, 72 per cent think few attempts were made to help the seminarian learn how to deal with people, and 64 per cent think the seminary was too sheltered from the mainstream of life. Religious priests and major superiors are in substantial agreement with this evaluation. On the other hand, a majority of the bishops reject all the criticisms of their seminary training. Furthermore, 60 per cent of the bishops and 49 per cent of the major superiors approve of high school seminaries, as opposed to 32 per cent of the diocesan priests and 31 per cent of the religious. Bishops, thus, have both more favorable recollections of their seminaries and more sympathy for a comprehensive seminary education.

The resignees are less likely to think that they were well prepared by their seminary for priestly work. Only 35 per cent of the diocesan resignees and 54 per cent of the religious resignees agree with such a statement. The resignees are more likely to be critical even than the youngest age group of the active priests since 61 per cent of those thirty-five and under think the seminary prepared them at least moderately well for priestly work (Table 3.10). There is a considerable correlation with age in the criticisms of seminary training save on the matter of helping seminarians to learn how to deal with people. Here only four percentage points separate those over fifty-five from those thirty-five and under. On the other hand, the oldest group of priests is more likely (38 as opposed to 26 per cent) to approve the preparatory seminary. Given the common assumption that apparently the most effective vocational recruiting is done by priests under thirty-five, one can see the paradox contained in the phenomenon that three-fifths of the bishops approve of the preparatory seminaries and only one-fourth of the priests thirty-five and under approve of them. In other words, the men who are responsible for funding, building, and administering the preparatory seminaries are favorably disposed to them while the men most likely to win students for them are not favorably disposed to the high school seminary.

TABLE 3.9

OPINION OF SEMINARY EDUCATION, BY CLERICAL STATUS

(Per Cent)

Opinion	Diocesan			Religious		
	Bishops	Active Priests	Resigned Priests	Major Superiors	Active Priests	Resigned Priests
Seminary prepared them very well or moderately well for priestly work	93	66	35	75	68	54
Seminary courses too theoretical	38	58	—[a]	49	59	—[a]
Course presentation too superficial	29	48	—[a]	44	49	—[a]
Courses irrelevant to pastoral needs	42	64	—[a]	61	66	—[a]
Few attempts made to help learn how to deal with people	54	72	—[a]	69	72	—[a]
Too sheltered from the mainstream of life	41	64	—[a]	59	67	—[a]
Approve of prep seminary	60	32	—[a]	49	31	—[a]

[a] Not asked of resigned priests.

TABLE 3.10

OPINION OF SEMINARY EDUCATION, BY AGE
(Per Cent of Active Diocesan and Religious Priests)

Opinion	Age			
	26-35	36-45	46-55	Over 55
Seminary prepared them very well or moderately well for priestly work	61	64	72	76
Seminary courses too theoretical	64	61	55	52
Course presentation too superficial	56	50	47	42
Courses irrelevant to pastoral needs	73	68	62	57
Few attempts made to help learn how to deal with people	74	75	70	70
Too sheltered from the mainstream of life	69	69	62	60
Approve of prep seminary	26	31	33	38

Despite the existence of the seminary system, however, we can see from Table 3.11 that a majority of American clergy had some dating experience before they made the decision to enter a seminary; thus, 24 per cent of the active priests report that they dated two or three times a month or more before they entered the seminary and 36 per cent say they dated at least several times a year. Only 40 per cent of the active priests had no dating experience *before* entering the seminary. However, only a handful (about 15 per cent) dated *after* they entered the seminary. Bishops (though not major superiors) are less likely to have dated, with exactly one-half of the bishops saying that they had no dating experience before becoming seminarians. Approximately two-fifths of the priests in all four age categories never dated (Table 3.12). Those over fifty-five are somewhat less likely to report that before they entered the seminary they dated two or three times a month or more.

We are unable, of course, to evaluate through survey data the contribution that dating experience made to the development of the priests' personal insights and social skills, but there is no evidence in our tables for the widespread assumption that priests had little dating experience before their seminary training began.

The most frequently mentioned sources of strong encouragement in becoming a priest among all active clergy are one's mother and a priest (Table 3.13). Thirty-three per cent of the bishops, 28 per cent of the diocesan priests, 24 per cent of the major superiors, and 29 per cent of

TABLE 3.11

DATING IN YOUTH, BY CLERICAL STATUS

(Per Cent)

Dating	Diocesan			Religious		
	Bishops	Active Priests	Resigned Priests	Major Superiors	Active Priests	Resigned Priests
Before seminary:						
Two or three times a month or more	20	24	29	22	24	39
Several times a year	30	36	29	41	36	30
Never	50	40	42	37	40	32
Total	100	100	100	100	100	101[a]
During seminary:						
Two or three times a month or more	0	1	0	0	1	1
Several times a year	7	14	13	11	15	7
Never	93	85	87	89	84	92
Total	100	100	100	100	100	100

[a] Not 100 per cent because of rounding.

TABLE 3.12

DATING IN YOUTH, BY AGE
(Per Cent of Active Diocesan and Religious Priests)

Dating	Age			
	26-35	36-45	46-55	Over 55
Before seminary:				
Two or three times a month or more	25	26	25	19
Several times a year	37	36	33	38
Never	38	37	42	43
Total	100	99 [a]	100	100
During seminary:				
Two or three times a month or more	1	1	1	1
Several times a year	15	15	13	14
Never	83	84	86	86
Total	99 [a]	100	100	101 [a]

[a] Not 100 per cent because of rounding.

TABLE 3.13

ENCOURAGEMENT FOR VOCATION, BY CLERICAL STATUS
(Per Cent "Encouraged Strongly" by Each Individual To Become a Priest)

Individual	Diocesan		Religious	
	Bishops	Active Priests	Major Superiors	Active Priests
Mother	33	28	24	29
Father	21	15	10	16
Other member of family	14	11	6	11
Priest	40	32	32	32
Nun	32	21	30	19
Brother	11	4	2	4

the religious priests mention their mothers as influential; and 40 per cent, 32 per cent, 32 per cent, and 32 per cent, respectively, mention a priest. Nuns, fathers, and other members of the family are mentioned less frequently. However, one-third of the bishops mention nuns, which is the same proportion that mention their mothers, so it can apparently be said that nuns seem to have played a somewhat more important role in the vocational decision of bishops (and of major superiors too) than they did for other priests.

Interestingly enough, Table 3.14 shows that there is no decline in the reporting of strong encouragement among the younger clergy, no matter who the source of encouragement might be. Thus, priests thirty-five and under are no less likely than their older confreres to report that each individual strongly encouraged them.

Analysis

The analytic findings concerning time of entry to the seminary and dating before entering can be summarized briefly. The two variables relate to each other at a .4 level, apparently indicating that the younger one was when entering the seminary, the less likely one was to have dated before entering. Dating — but not time of entry — relates at a .2 level with one's score on the inner-directed personality scale, which will be discussed in the next chapter, but there are no other significant relationships between either of these two variables and any of the other more than eighty variables considered in our analysis. The most significant finding

TABLE 3.14

ENCOURAGEMENT FOR VOCATION, BY AGE

(Per Cent of Active Diocesan and Religious Priests "Encouraged Strongly" by Each Individual To Become a Priest)

Individual	Age			
	26-35	36-45	46-55	Over 55
Mother	28	26	30	30
Father	15	13	17	17
Other member of family	10	10	10	13
Priest	32	29	34	33
Nun	20	19	22	20
Brother	4	3	5	4

then, as it frequently is in social research, is a "non-finding." Seminary education and dating experience relate neither positively nor negatively with any of the vast array of aspects of the clerical life that we are studying. The time at which one *entered the seminary* and one's dating experience before entering do not effect one's religious values, view of the priesthood, relationship with colleagues, attitude toward ecclesiastical structures, experience with problems, fulfillment and satisfactions, morale, or even the decision whether to stay a priest or to resign from the priesthood. The time of entry to the seminary does not even influence one's score on the personality scale, although dating experience does.

This finding runs contrary to an immense amount of clerical folklore. Critics of the seminary system describe all its negative effects on the life of the clergy, and defenders of the system point to all the positive effects that the seminary system supposedly has. One does not doubt, of course, that there may be many positive and negative effects of the seminary that the measures used in this study do not record. It also might be persuasively argued that the important impact of the seminary is quite independent of when one enters it. Thus, whether one becomes a seminarian at fourteen or twenty is much less important than the fact that one does indeed go through at least four years, if not more, in the seminary environment. Under such circumstances, the absence of correlations could be explained by the argument that the impact of the seminary is not increased by the amount of time one spends in it or by the early age at which one enters it.

But even if one is prepared to go as far as one can in conceding the plausibility of such an argument, it still must be admitted that it is surprising indeed to have to report that there are no correlations between the age at which one entered the seminary and subsequent attitudes and behavior and that there is only one quite moderate correlation between one's dating experience and subsequent variables. It is not the purpose of the present project to attempt an analysis of the American Catholic seminary system. Nevertheless, it is to be hoped that those who do engage in research on the impact of seminaries will want to investigate more fully this rather astonishing "non-finding."

Not only does the age at which one entered the seminary not relate to subsequent variables, the amount of one's post-ordination education does not predict one's personality score, religious values, desire to marry, or future plans in the priesthood. In view of the frequently heard comment that it is those with the better education who are most likely to have problems in the priesthood, this "non-finding" constitutes an important point in our research.

Conclusion

We may summarize the present chapter by responding to a number of hypothetical questions:

1. *Is it true that most American priests have entered the seminary in early adolescence with practically no social experience with women?* About three-fifths of the American priests had at least graduated from high school before entering the seminary. The majority of priests had some dating experience, and one-quarter of those fifty-five and under had dated two or three times a month or more before they entered the seminary.

2. *Are resigned priests likely to have more education than those who remain in the priesthood?* Those who have already left the priesthood have had more advanced education than those who remain in it, a phenomenon that cannot be explained by age. However, the amount of advanced education does not predict a propensity to plan to leave the priesthood among those who are presently active priests.

3. *What do priests think of their seminary experience?* Most priests think that the seminary prepared them at least moderately well for their work as priests, though substantial majorities are critical of the seminaries in a number of important matters. There is widespread agreement in all age groups that the seminary failed to prepare them for the task of dealing with people.

4. *Does the age at which a young man entered the seminary, or the dating experience he had before he entered, predict any of the attitudes and behavior he exhibits in later life?* There is no correlation between age at entry and any of the subsequent variables considered in our study, and there is only one moderate correlation between dating experience and subsequent attitudes and behavior.

CHAPTER 4

THE PERSONALITY OF THE PRIEST

In this chapter we consider the scores of the American clergy on certain personality measurements. On the one hand, it might be assumed that, given the selectivity and the long period of training for Roman Catholic priests and the very special kind of dedication and work required of a priest, the Catholic clergy ought to manifest a high degree of emotional maturity. But, on the other hand, it has been argued recently that the nature of the seminary training which most priests experience, the hierarchical organization of the structure of the Church, and the celibate life required of Catholic priests, would produce men whose emotional maturation had been seriously impeded. From the former point of view the priest *ought* to be a very mature man because of the challenges of his work while in fact he may be a considerably less mature man because of the institutional structures in which he was trained and in which he must live and work.

The question of the personality development of the clergy is the primary focus of a companion study being conducted by the Department of Psychology at Loyola University of Chicago. Nevertheless, in consultation with the Loyola project it was decided that NORC would administer a personality inventory to one-fifth of the respondents in its sample. Upon the recommendation of the Loyola project, the Personal Orientation Inventory (POI) developed by Everett L. Shostrom (1966) was the instrument chosen for use at NORC.[1]

The inventory purports to measure psychologist Abraham Maslow's concept of the self-actualizing person:

A person who is more fully functioning and lives a more enriched life than does the average person. Such an individual is seen as developing and utilizing all of his unique capabilities or potentialities, free of the inhibitions and emotional turmoil of those less self-actualized (Shostrom, 1966, p. 5).[2]

53

The POI consists of 150 items in which the respondent is asked to choose which of two opposite statements more closely represents his own attitude. The 150 items are divided into two principal scales — "time competent" and "inner-directed." Shostrom describes the time-competent person as follows:

> The self-actualized person is primarily Time Competent and thus appears to live more fully in the here-and-now. He is able to tie the past and the future to the present in meaningful continuity. He appears to be less burdened by guilts, regrets, and resentments from the past than is the non-self-actualized person and his aspirations are tied meaningfully to present working goals. He has faith in the future without rigid or over-idealistic goals. . . . The self-actualized individual's past and future orientations are depicted as reflecting positive mental health to the extent that his past is used for reflective thought and the future is tied to present goals (p. 15).

The notion of inner-direction was first introduced into American social science by the distinguished sociologist, David Riesman, in his book, *The Lonely Crowd* (1950). Shostrom describes the inner-directed man in the following words:

> The inner-directed person appears to have incorporated a psychic "gyroscope" which is started by parental influences and later on is further influenced by other authority figures. The inner-directed man goes through life apparently independent, but still obeying this internal piloting. The source of inner-direction seems to be implanted early in life and the direction is guided by a small number of principles. The source of direction for the individual is inner in the sense that he is guided by internal motivations rather than external influences. This source of direction becomes generalized as an inner core of principles and character traits (p. 17).[3]

In addition to being scored for these two principal scales, items are also scored for ten sub-scales, described by Shostrom (1966, p. 6) as follows:

Self-Actualizing Value — measures affirmation of a primary value of self-actualizing people.

Existentiality — measures ability to situationally or existentially react without rigid adherence to principles.

Feeling Reactivity — measures sensitivity of responsiveness to one's own needs and feelings.

Spontaneity — measures freedom to react spontaneously or to be oneself.

Self-Regard — measures affirmation of self because of worth or strength.

Self-Acceptance — measures affirmation or acceptance of self in spite of weaknesses or deficiencies.

Nature of Man — measures degree of the constructive view of the nature of man, masculinity, femininity.

Synergy — measures ability to be synergistic, to transcend dichotomies.

Acceptance of Aggression — measures ability to accept one's natural aggressiveness as opposed to defensiveness, denial, and repression of aggression.

Capacity for Intimate Contact — measures ability to develop contactful intimate relationships with other human beings, unencumbered by expectations and obligations.

To understand the analysis in terms of this chapter, the reader must grasp the fact that the word "normal" is not used in the sense of "typical." Shostrom and his associates, with the help of colleagues in clinical psychology, located three groups of people to whom to administer the test. The first group was rated by the clinicians as "relatively self-actualized"; that is, they would be the kinds of persons expected to score rather high on an instrument which measured that aspect of emotional maturity. The "relatively non-self-actualized" group, on the other hand, would be expected to score rather low on such measures; while the third group, the so-called "normal" respondents, were certified as likely to fall somewhere in between the other two groups. The self-actualized group had 29 members, the non-self-actualized group, 34, and the normal adult group, 158. It is to be noted that Maslow's theory on which the Personal Orientation Inventory is based expects that a relatively small proportion of the population will, in fact, be highly self-actualized. Thus, most respondents in any typical sample population could be expected to fall either in the normal or the relatively non-self-actualized categories.

Description

The following are the principal findings on "self-actualization" among American Catholic clergy to be reported in this first section of this chapter:

1. Active priests fall between the normal and the non-self-actualized groups on most scale measures when age is not taken into account.

2. Resigned priests score slightly higher than active priests on most of the scales.

3. Lower scores among the active clergy are to be found on measures of "self-actualizing value," "feeling reactivity," "existentiality," "acceptance of aggression," and "capacity for intimate contact." Only on the measure of "feeling reactivity" do they fall below the score of the non-self-actualized group.

4. Active priests forty-five and under are extremely close to the "norm" on virtually all measures on the POI scales.

5. All the personality scores decline with age of the priests.

6. After standardizing for age, priests' scores on measures of self-actualization are higher than the scores of most comparison groups on which data are available.

If one looks at the scores of active priests as presented in Table 4.1 and graphically depicted in Figure 4.1, one can see that on most of the scales the scores of the active priests are somewhere between the normal group and the non-self-actualized group and that the resigned priests are consistently somewhat higher than the active priests. As a matter of fact, on nature of man, the resigned priests score .8 *higher* than the self-actualized group. Active priests are lower than the non-self-actualized on feeling reactivity, which suggests that the clergy may be rather low on sensitivity of response to their own needs and feelings. In addition, on measures of self-actualizing value, existentiality, acceptance of aggression, and capacity for intimate contact their scores are rather low, though the same as or above the non-self-actualized group. This would indicate that the clergy may find it somewhat difficult to react without rigid adherence to principles, to accept their own natural aggressiveness, and to be able to develop intimate relationships with others. On the other hand, they are the same as the self-actualized group in their constructive view of the nature of man and within the norm on their self-regard, their self-acceptance, and their capacity to see the opposites of life as meaningfully related (synergy).

The low score of the clergy on the existentiality scale may be a function of a number of questions that would present special problems for priests. Two of the items that would lead to a high score on the existentiality scale are "I am not orthodoxly religious" and "I have no problem in fusing sex with love." However, the relatively low scores on self-actualizing value, feeling reactivity, acceptance of aggression, and capacity for intimate contact do represent some possible confirmation for the argument that seminary training does inhibit the development of

TABLE 4.1

PERSONALITY SCALES

(Mean Scores)

Scale	Self-Actualized Group	Normal Adult Group	Non-Self-Actualized Group	Active Priests	Resigned Priests
Time competent	18.9	17.7	15.8	17.2	17.8
Inner-directed	92.9	87.2	75.8	81.0	89.4
Self-actualizing value	20.7	20.2	18.0	18.9	20.3
Existentiality	24.8	21.8	18.8	18.8	22.0
Feeling reactivity	16.3	15.7	14.3	13.5	15.4
Spontaneity	12.7	11.6	9.8	10.8	12.3
Self-regard	12.9	12.0	10.2	11.8	12.7
Self-acceptance	18.9	17.1	14.2	16.3	17.3
Nature of man	12.3	12.4	11.3	12.3	13.1
Synergy	7.6	7.3	6.2	6.8	7.3
Acceptance of aggression	17.6	16.6	14.7	14.9	16.0
Capacity for intimate contact	20.2	18.8	16.5	16.9	19.4
N	(29)	(158)	(34)	(917)	(270)

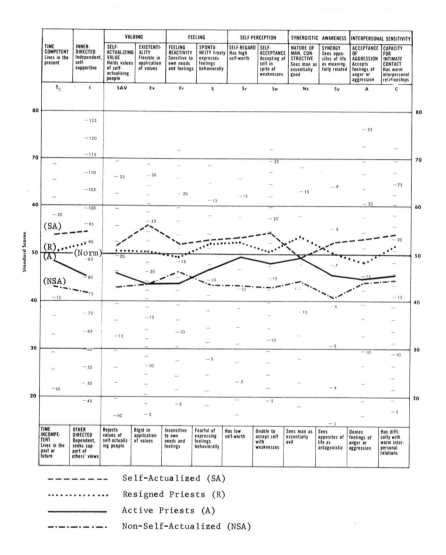

Fig. 4.1.—POI profiles for sample groups and for priests.

a capacity to respond to one's own emotions and also limits somewhat the development of a capacity for intimate contact. However, if one looks through the profiles in Figure 4.2, one notes that the scores of the active clergy forty-five and under on capacity for intimate contact is virtually the same as that of all other groups on which data are available. Relatively low scores, then, on feeling reactivity and acceptance of aggression seem to indicate the sort of personality problems that one might expect to be special to the clergy. It is worth emphasizing once again that the scores on these two scales are not *abnormally* low. The mean scores in the clergy, for example, are not nearly as low as the scores reported by Shostrom for respondents with neurotic problems.

In humanistic psychology the capacity to show love and the capacity to be angry are seen as manifestations of the same basic personality component. It is argued that both capacities demonstrate contact with one's emotions, confidence in basic healthfulness, and the ability to express feelings in appropriate ways. A man who scores in the normal range on the capacity for intimacy and lower on the capacity to deal with his aggressive emotions is, according to this perspective, caught in the difficult bind of being able to release some of his emotions but not being able to cope with other powerful and closely related emotions. According to Shostrom, such a person will manifest the "nice guy" syndrome — a form of passive aggressive behavior in which one uses affection and service of others as a means of controlling and punishing them. We are not saying, of course, that all priests are "nice guys" in the sense meant here, but it does seem that there may be a somewhat higher proportion of "nice guys" in the priesthood than in comparable groups.

One of the most striking things about the personality scores of the Catholic clergy is that there is apparently a strong correlation between self-actualization and youthfulness. As Table 4.2 indicates, on each of the scales there is a consistent decline in the mean score as one moves from the younger to the older age groups. There are a number of possible explanations for this difference: (1) There may have been a steady change over the past decades in the type of person recruited in the priesthood. (2) There may have been changes in seminary training, changes that have been relatively consistent through the last several decades. (3) The lower scores in the older age brackets may indicate an attrition caused by the resignation of men who would score high on the self-actualization measures. (4) There may also be a wearing effect by which the ecclesiastical institution slowly depresses the level of self-actualization in a priest's personality.

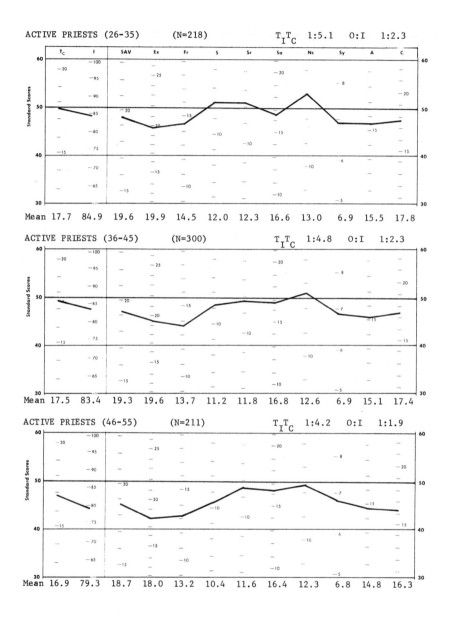

Fig. 4.2.—POI profiles for priests.

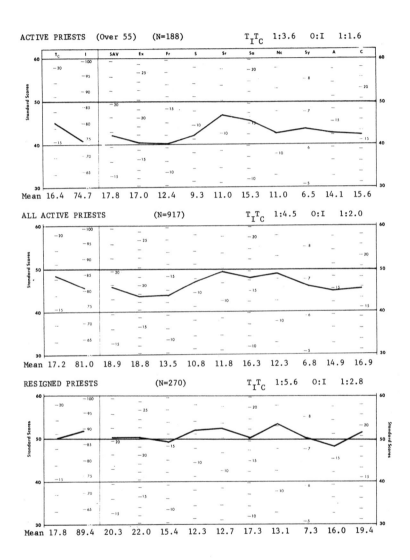

Fig. 4.2.—POI profiles for priests (cont.).

TABLE 4.2

PERSONALITY SCALES BY AGE OF ACTIVE DIOCESAN
AND RELIGIOUS PRIESTS
(Mean Scores)

Scale	Age			
	26-35	36-45	46-55	Over 55
Time competent	17.7	17.5	16.9	16.4
Inner-directed	84.9	83.4	79.3	74.7
Self-actualizing value	19.6	19.3	18.7	17.8
Existentiality	19.9	19.6	18.0	17.0
Feeling reactivity	14.5	13.7	13.2	12.4
Spontaneity	12.0	11.2	10.4	9.3
Self-regard	12.3	11.8	11.6	11.0
Self-acceptance	16.6	16.8	16.4	15.3
Nature of man	13.0	12.6	12.3	11.0
Synergy	6.9	6.9	6.8	6.5
Acceptance of aggression	15.5	15.1	14.8	14.1
Capacity for intimate contact	17.8	17.4	16.3	15.6

Explanation (3) is most unlikely since there have been very few resignations among priests over forty-five years old. Explanation (2) is also rather unlikely because the real changes in seminary training have apparently occurred in the last decade. Explanations (1) and (4) cannot be evaluated unless there is longitudinal research, with tests administered to men at various times in the course of their career in the priesthood.

One can theorize that self-actualization may decline with age (save among those who are in the top 1 per cent — to use Shostrom's phrase — of the self-actualized). Weariness, waning of energy, and poor health could easily lead to lower scores on the test scales. In conversation with Dr. Shostrom, we learned that no correlations between the test scores and aging have yet been made. However, he did say that he assumed that there would be a decline with age and that meaningful comparisons between the clergy and other groups should be limited to younger priests. The mean age of his normative groups was 39; that of the clergy in our sample was 46.6. Hence standardization for age is necessary if one is to evaluate the relative self-actualization of Catholic priests. If one inspects the graphs in Figure 4.2 showing the personality profiles for priests between 26 and 35 and between 36 and 45, one can see that on most of the scales priests in these age categories are close to the norm. Without attempting to settle definitively the question of lower scores for older priests, one can still say that with regard to younger priests, who can be logically compared with the norms, there is no evidence of poor personality development.

A comparison between the resigned priests and the youngest active priests, who come from roughly the same age bracket as the resignees, reveals that the differences between the actives and the resignees decline somewhat. Indeed, on the time-competent measure, there is virtually no difference between the youngest actives and the resignees, while a difference of 4.5 points on the inner-directed scale still persists between the youngest actives and the resignees. It may be that it requires a certain amount of inner-direction to take the step that is necessary to break with the priesthood.

Dr. Shostrom has advanced for us another explanation for the relatively higher scores among the resignees. "Inner-directedness" is conceptualized as a form of relative independence from others. Humanistic psychologists take it to be a sign of health for a man to be able to operate in relative autonomy and with relative freedom from others. But just as they think too little autonomy is unhealthy, so they think that too much autonomy is also unhealthy. One can be neurotically autonomous as well as neurotically dependent. Shostrom is inclined to think of a score of over 100 on the inner-directed scale as showing signs of this "pathological freedom" — or alternately, of a feeling that one must get the "best possible" score on self-actualization. Table 4.3 shows a distribution of both active and resigned priests on a typology of inner-directed scores that Shostrom considers a useful measure not only of self-actualization and non-self-actualization but also of "hyper-self-actualization" and "hypo-self-actualization." While 4 per cent of all active clergy fall into the "hyper" category (that is, have scores higher than the self-actualization group), some 17 per cent of the resignees do so. On the other hand, only 6 per cent of the resignees are in the "hypo" group (that is, have scores lower than the non-self-actualization group), while 20 per cent of all actives are in this group. It must be emphasized that both extremes represent inappropriate autonomy. Thus, far more of the resignees are likely to be "excessively autonomous" and far more of the actives are likely to be "overdependent."

These differences may well be an effect rather than a cause of resignation. The exhilaration and excitement (and here we follow Shostrom's speculation) that follow a difficult and painful decision to free oneself

The Catholic Priest in the United States

TABLE 4.3

"HYPER" AND "HYPO" SELF-ACTUALIZATION FOR ACTIVE PRIESTS
AND RESIGNEES ON INNER-DIRECTED SCALE
(Per Cent)

Inner-Directed Scale	Active Priests		Resigned Priests
	All	45 and Under	
Hyper-self-actualized (score above 100)	4	7	17
Self-actualized (score between 91 and 100)	10	12	18
Normal (score between 88 and 90)	11	15	18
Non-self-actualized (score between 73 and 87)	55	52	40
Hypo-self-actualized (score under 73)	20	14	6
Total	100	100	99 [a]

[a] Not 100 per cent because of rounding.

from a situation in which one has not been happy is likely to produce a burst of well-being and euphoria that might bias scale response upward. A member of the Loyola staff has commented to us that we may be dealing with a phenomenon that Karen Horney described as going on a "binge of health." Certainly we shall see in Chapter 11 on morale that there seems to be an extremely high level of positive emotional affect, or feeling of well-being, among the resignees.

This speculation, of course, is not meant to be criticism of resignees, but rather an attempt to understand why so many of them would fall into the excessively autonomous category. The alternative to seeing this over-autonomy as an effect of resignation is to view it as a cause and to conclude that some of the resignees left because of an incapacity to accept normal dependence in their relationships.

On the other hand, one might note that the exact opposite problem can be found among the active priests. One-fifth of them are hypo-self-actualized, that is, very passive and not likely to assert themselves in a way that would be conducive to a healthy reaction to reality. We can see from Table 4.3 that some of the respondents in the "hypo" group are older men, since the proportion of priests forty-five and under in the "hypo" category is smaller than the proportion of all priests in this category. Hence one could say that their scores are the result of the ordinary impact of the aging process. Others may simply have been worn down by the frustrations that they have encountered in life, and still others may have personalities that are not fundamentally assertive. One might speculate that *some* of the resignees have left the priesthood because they could not accept healthy dependence, and that *some* of the actives stay because they are not inclined to seek healthy independence.

If the Roman Catholic clergy are not highly self-actualized, it does not necessarily follow that they are less self-actualized than most other humans. Quite the contrary. As the mean scores in Table 4.4 and Figure 4.3 indicate, the scores of the Catholic priests thirty-five and under on the two principal components of the POI compare favorably with most other groups on which data are available. Only Peace Corps volunteers and divinity students have higher scores on the time-competent scale, and there is virtually no difference between the younger clergy and either the Peace Corps volunteers or the divinity students on the inner-directed scale. Interestingly enough, the scores of all the active priests are the same as the scores of the supervisors in a large electronics company, who are presumably about the same age and have the same

TABLE 4.4

ACTIVE PRIESTS AND OTHERS ON SELF-ACTUALIZING SCALES
(Mean Scores)

Group	Time Competent	Inner- Directed	N
Normal adult group	17.7	87.2	—
All active priests	17.2	81.0	917
Active priests 35 years of age and under	17.7	84.9	218
College juniors and seniors [a]	15.8	79.9	150
College freshmen [a]	15.1	75.6	2,046
Peace Corps volunteers [a]	19.4	84.2	62
Supervisors in electronics company [a]	17.2	81.1	66
College freshmen (graduates of public high schools) [b]	16.0	83.1	72
College freshmen (graduates of Catholic high schools) [b]	16.1	82.5	99
Protestant clergy: [c]			
Colgate-Rochester divinity students	18.8	85.0	—
New Zealand Baptist ministers	17.7	67.5	—

[a] Data from Shostrom (1966).
[b] Data from Krump (1970).
[c] Data from Webster and Stewart (1969); no case bases given.

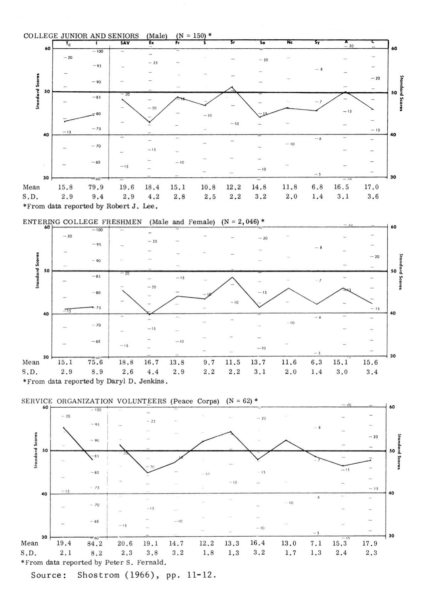

COLLEGE JUNIOR AND SENIORS   (Male)   (N = 150) *

	Tc	I	SAV	Ex	Fr	S	Sr	Sa	Nc	Sy	A	C
Mean	15.8	79.9	19.6	18.4	15.1	10.8	12.2	14.8	11.8	6.8	16.5	17.0
S.D.	2.9	9.4	2.9	4.2	2.8	2.5	2.2	3.2	2.0	1.4	3.1	3.6

*From data reported by Robert J. Lee.

ENTERING COLLEGE FRESHMEN   (Male and Female)   (N = 2,046) *

Mean	15.1	75.6	18.8	16.7	13.8	9.7	11.5	13.7	11.6	6.3	15.1	15.6
S.D.	2.9	8.9	2.6	4.4	2.9	2.2	2.2	3.1	2.0	1.4	3.0	3.4

*From data reported by Daryl D. Jenkins.

SERVICE ORGANIZATION VOLUNTEERS (Peace Corps)   (N = 62) *

Mean	19.4	84.2	20.6	19.1	14.7	12.2	13.3	16.4	13.0	7.1	15.3	17.9
S.D.	2.1	8.2	2.3	3.8	3.2	1.8	1.3	3.2	1.7	1.3	2.4	2.3

*From data reported by Peter S. Fernald.

Source: Shostrom (1966), pp. 11-12.

Fig. 4.3.—POI profiles for selected reference groups.

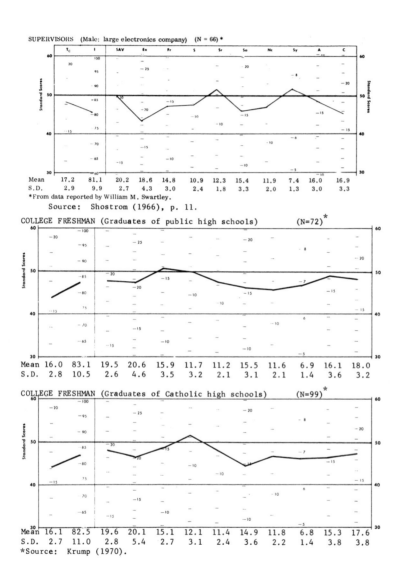

Fig. 4.3.—POI profiles for selected reference groups (cont.).

degree of responsibility as the clergy. Finally, the scores of Catholic clergy are substantially higher than the scores of the various student population groups to whom the POI has been administered. One could summarize the findings in Table 4.4 and Figure 4.3 by saying that priests don't seem very different in their self-actualization from anyone else.

The scores of Catholic priests on the Personal Orientation Inventory represent a set of findings that are rather unspectacular. Priests are not a highly self-actualized group, but neither are they a non-self-actualized group. The personality problems that seem special to them seem to involve their capacity to respond to their own feelings and especially their feelings of aggression. The amount of self-actualization present in the clergy decreases with age; and those with high scores on the self-actualization measures are also slightly more likely to resign from the priesthood, though the full implications of this will have to await further analysis in the concluding chapters of this report.

We can conclude this descriptive section of Chapter 4 by responding to a number of hypothetical questions:

1. *Has the priesthood interfered with the emotional development of the men who have entered it?* There is no evidence to support such a conclusion. Young priests score higher on measures of self-actualization than college students and compare favorably with Peace Corps volunteers. Might these younger clergy have had even more development toward self-actualization if they had not entered the priesthood? In the absence of data collected on them before they entered the seminary it is impossible to answer this question.

2. *Have the "self-actualizers" left the priesthood, as has been asserted in the popular press?* Not all those who have left have high scores on self-actualization and not all those who have high self-actualization scores have left. There are many with rather low scores on the POI who have departed from the priesthood and many with rather high scores who are still in it. However, it must still be said, subject to further analysis, that there is a correlation between a high score on the inner-directed scale and resignations from the priesthood even when a comparison is made between resignees and actives in their own age category.

3. *Are there certain special emotional problems in the priesthood?* Insofar as the rather limited analysis in this report can testify, the principal emotional problems that are distinctive to the priest are the inability to be sensitive to one's own needs and feelings and particularly the capacity to accept one's own aggressive impulses.

4. *Are there certain special strengths in the personalities of priests?*

One very definite strength is apparently the priest's capacity to take a constructive view of the nature of man. In addition, priests demonstrate relative strength in their ability to affirm their own self-worth and to accept themselves for what they are in spite of weaknesses and deficiencies.

5. *Do priests have excessively dependent personalities?* We could find no evidence of excessive dependency among priests when we compared priests forty-five and under with test norms (leaving aside the moot point of whether test scores can be expected to decline with age). When mean scores of priests of the same age as the normative groups were compared with the mean norms, there were only minor differences, most of which suggest that, if anything, the problem of the priest is lack of a capacity to cope with aggressive feelings rather than an excessive need for dependency.

6. *Do the data in this chapter indicate that priests are the kind of men who can provide confident and vigorous leadership in times of crisis and change?* Between one-tenth and one-fifth of the clergy could be said to be "self-actualized" persons (Table 4.3), a proportion that is probably not very different from that to be found in the general American population of college-educated males. The clergy are not neurotic misfits, but neither by and large do they seem to be the kind of men who would make charismatic leaders.

7. *Are the resignees more self-actualized than those who remain in the priesthood?* When age is held constant, the scores on every one of the personality sub-scales are slightly higher for the resigned priests than they are for active priests. However, there is some tendency for the resigned priests to be hyper-self-actualized and the active priests to be hypo-self-actualized; that is, some of the former display an abnormal need for independence and some of the latter tend to display an abnormal lack of independence.

8. *What are the factors in the background and training of a priest that lead to the development of the self-actualizing personality and what are the factors that impede such development?* For the answers to these questions, it is necessary to turn to the second section of this chapter to determine what factors correlate with the self-actualizing priestly personality.

9. *Did seminary training cause a diminution of the capacity of priests to have intimate friendships?* It would be hard on the basis of our data to respond in the affirmative to this question. While the mean score of the Catholic clergy on capacity for intimate contact is only somewhat above that of the non-self-actualized group, so are the mean scores of

every comparison group on which we have data; and the mean score of young priests is actually higher than that of young Catholics in colleges.

Analysis

Correlations were computed between the two principal POI scales (time competence and inner-directedness) and age, education of parents, occupation, ethnicity, religious devotion of parents, age at entering the seminary, encouragement to become a priest, and own education after ordination. The only correlation above .2 to emerge from these computations was a −.34 relationship between age and inner-directedness. Since time competence did not relate with any subsequent variables in our model, it was dropped from further analysis. We conclude, then, that one's "inner-directedness" is largely idiosyncratic, that is, relatively independent of demographic, socioeconomic, social psychological, and educational background variables—at least insofar as we are able to measure these variables.

The following questions may be asked to summarize the analytic section of this chapter:

1. *Is it true that those who entered the seminary later or who had more education since ordination are more likely to be emotionally mature?* There is no evidence in our data to support either of these possibilities.

2. *Did the priesthood attract young men whose social class, family background, or childhood experiences made them less likely to be autonomous than the typical American male?* There is no evidence in our data that this has occurred.

---

1. We acknowledge with thanks permission to use material from the *EITS Manual* granted by Everett L. Shostrom of Educational and Industrial Testing Service.

2. The reader interested in investigating further the implications of Maslow's definition is referred to Maslow (1962).

3. It should be noted that "humanistic psychology," the tradition in which Maslow worked and which is represented by the POI test, has emerged as a reaction against both Behaviorism and Freudianism. Many of the humanistic psychologists, including both Maslow and Shostrom, will argue that they are much closer to religion than they are to psychoanalysis.

CHAPTER 5

THE SPIRITUAL LIFE OF PRIESTS

Traditional Catholic teaching has ascertained that the priest is a man who stands between the ultimate and the mundane. He enjoys special contact with the sacred through the Church's sacramental system and he also is expected to preach the Church's basic interpretive scheme — its basic explanation of the meaning and purpose of reality. On the other hand, he is also expected to possess skills in dealing with the most ordinary human problems — growth, marriage, sickness, suffering, and death. It has been argued by traditional Catholic spirituality that systematic and regular contact with the transcendent through prayer and meditation, spiritual reading, and private devotions, as well as through public worship at Mass, is absolutely essential for the priest if he is to bridge successfully the chasm between the sacred and the profane, between the transcendent and the ordinary, between the ultimate and the mundane.

Description

Two principal findings are reported in the descriptive section of this chapter:

1. There is still considerable support for traditional practices of spirituality and piety in the Catholic clergy in the United States, though this support is somewhat lower among the clergy.

2. The Roman breviary is said today by only a minority of priests, at least as far as daily recitation of the whole breviary is concerned.

We see in Table 5.1 that more than eight-tenths of American Catholic priests say Mass every day and more than nine-tenths consider the Mass as an important form of prayer for them. Approximately three-fifths (53 per cent of the active diocesan and 62 per cent of the active religious priests) read the Bible at least once a week in addition to the readings required by the liturgy, and approximately half (46 per cent of the active

71

TABLE 5.1

SPIRITUAL ACTIVITIES BY CLERICAL STATUS

(Per Cent)

Spiritual Activity	Diocesan			Religious		
	Bishops	Active Priests	Resigned Priests	Major Superiors	Active Priests	Resigned Priests
Celebrate Mass every day	98	85	—[a]	96	82	—[a]
Read the Bible once a week or more	66	53	—[a]	63	62	—[a]
Pray or meditate privately every day	71	46	26	70	57	30
Feel that celebrating Mass is a very important form of prayer and worship	99	92	—[a]	96	92	—[a]

[a] Not asked of resigned priests.

diocesan and 57 per cent of the active religious) report that they pray or meditate privately every day. Bishops and major superiors are more likely than the active priests to report frequent participation in all these spiritual activities.

Table 5.2 shows that fewer young priests say Mass every day or pray or meditate privately every day. There is very little difference in the proportion who think that Mass is important, and practically no difference in the percentage saying that they read the Bible frequently. The younger clergy are also more likely than the resignees to report daily prayer or meditation (38 per cent vs. 26 and 30 per cent). The traditional practices of piety, therefore, are not being ignored, but there is some sign that the younger clergy are less likely to pursue them.

There is no social scientific evidence on the proportion of the American clergy who daily recited each hour of the Roman breviary ten or fifteen years ago. However, the impression seems to be widespread that almost all priests were extremely careful in fulfilling this obligation to the letter. If this impression is accurate, data in Table 5.3 represent a dramatic change, for only 43 per cent of the diocesan priests and 42 per cent of the religious priests report that they say all Hours of the breviary every day (as opposed to 86 per cent of the bishops), and 30 per cent of the diocesan priests and 25 per cent of the religious priests report that they do not say the breviary at all. In Table 5.4 we see that 50 per cent of those thirty-five and under and 36 per cent of those between thirty-six and forty-five report that they never say the breviary. Only 15 per cent and 30 per cent of these two age categories, respectively, say that they recite the whole breviary every day. It is interesting to compare the differences between the youngest and oldest age groups:

TABLE 5.2

SPIRITUAL ACTIVITIES BY AGE
(Per Cent of Active Diocesan and Religious Priests)

Spiritual Activity	Age			
	26-35	36-45	46-55	Over 55
Celebrate Mass every day	72	78	89	95
Read the Bible once a week or more	61	55	55	58
Pray or meditate privately every day	38	42	53	69
Feel that celebrating Mass is a very important form of prayer and worship	88	90	93	96

TABLE 5.3

RECITATION OF BREVIARY, BY CLERICAL STATUS
(Per Cent)

Frequency of Recitation	Diocesan		Religious	
	Bishops	Active Priests	Major Superiors	Active Priests
Daily for all of the Hours	86	43	60	42
Daily for some of the Hours	10	11	24	19
All or some of the Hours several times a week	2	9	5	9
All or some of the Hours several times a month	1	7	5	5
Not at all	1	30	5	25
Total	100	100	99 [a]	100

[a] Not 100 per cent because of rounding.

73 per cent of the older priests say that they recite the divine office in its entirety every day, while 50 per cent of the younger priests say that they never recite the divine office. Given the fact that the theoretical obligation to say the office still exists, the widespread disregard of the obligation of the breviary is rather a striking phenomenon.

TABLE 5.4

RECITATION OF BREVIARY, BY AGE
(Per Cent of Active Diocesan and Religious Priests)

Frequency of Recitation	Age			
	26-35	36-45	46-55	Over 55
Daily for all of the Hours	15	30	51	73
Daily for some of the Hours	13	17	16	13
All or some of the Hours several times a week	12	10	10	4
All or some of the Hours several times a month	10	7	4	2
Not at all	50	36	20	8
Total	100	100	101 [a]	100

[a] Not 100 per cent because of rounding.

We also made an attempt to determine the extent of "religious experience" among the clergy (Table 5.5). Fifty-six per cent of the active priests report that they frequently experienced the sense of being in the presence of God and 47 per cent think that they frequently have a deep experience of being personally loved by Christ. Approximately one-quarter even report frequently experiencing an overwhelming feeling of being at one with God. Only a very small proportion report negative feelings of being afraid of God or of being abandoned by God. The dark night of the soul, in other words, does not seem to be a characteristic experience for American priests. The bishops are somewhat more likely than active priests to report religious experiences, while the resignees in most instances are less likely to have had frequent religious experiences.

Religious experience is also less likely among the younger clergy (Table 5.6); indeed, only one-fifth of the younger priests report a "frequent overwhelming feeling" that might be roughly described as a mystical experience. Thus, both adherence to the traditional exercises of piety and a sensation of religious experience are less likely among younger clergy than among older clergy.

Analysis

We were forced to make a decision on whether frequency of prayer or frequency of sense of contact with God in prayer would be a better indicator in our causal model. We chose the latter both because one can assume that the experience of mystical contact would likely have a more lasting effect than prayer without such mystical experience and because in fact an index based on mystical or religious experience was more likely to relate with variables to the right of it in the model. The "religious-experience" index was composed of responses to the first three items in Table 5.5. The average intercorrelation of the responses to these three items was .44, indicating a clear response pattern.

Only one prior variable in our whole battery of demographic, socio-economic, religious, educational, and social psychological variables correlates at an important level with this index; there is a relationship of $-.20$ between family tension and religious experience. In other words, those who come from tense families are somewhat less likely to have experienced a feeling of some kind of personal contact with God. One may speculate that a combination of the image of God as a parent and relatively unsatisfactory relationships with one's parents may contribute to this relationship.

TABLE 5.5

RELIGIOUS EXPERIENCES BY CLERICAL STATUS

(Per Cent Reporting Having Had Each Experience "Frequently" During Past Two or Three Years)

Religious Experience	Diocesan			Religious		
	Bishops	Active Priests	Resigned Priests	Major Superiors	Active Priests	Resigned Priests
An overwhelming feeling of being at one with God or Christ	35	26	17	23	23	23
A sense of being in the presence of God	75	56	37	56	56	42
A deep feeling of being personally loved by Christ here and now	63	47	30	46	47	32
A feeling of being afraid of God	3	4	1	1	4	1
A feeling of being tempted by the devil	10	16	0	13	12	0
A feeling of being abandoned by God	1	2	0	0	1	1

TABLE 5.6

RELIGIOUS EXPERIENCES BY AGE
(Per Cent of Active Diocesan and Religious Priests Reporting Having
Had Experience "Frequently" During Past Two or Three Years)

Religious Experience	Age			
	26-35	36-45	46-55	Over 55
An overwhelming feeling of being at one with God or Christ	20	23	22	34
A sense of being in the presence of God	46	52	56	69
A deep feeling of being personally loved by Christ here and now	40	43	48	56
A feeling of being afraid of God	2	3	4	5
A feeling of being tempted by the devil	11	15	16	15
A feeling of being abandoned by God	2	2	1	1

It is now appropriate for us to put the first path coefficients into our model. Figure 5.1 shows standardized coefficients (*betas*) of —.34 between age and inner-directedness, .10 between age and religious experience, and —.18 between family tension and religious experience.[1] The difference between the *r* of —.20 and the *beta* of —.18 for this last relationship means that when the influence of age is held constant, the relationship declines slightly.

In our path model we follow the convention of not showing coefficients that are lower than .09. The relationship between age and religious experience just makes this level. In other words, there is a very slight relationship between age and some kind of mystical contact. Older priests are a little more likely than younger priests to have such experiences. However, given the different prayer habits of the young and the old and the very different sets of values (as we shall see in the next chapter), the small size of this relationship is very surprising. We conclude that mysticism is distributed fairly evenly in the clerical population and is less present only among those who come from tense families.

However, as the two residual coefficients of .94 for inner-directedness and .98 for religious experience indicate, we are not able to explain much of the variance in either of these indicators (12 per cent of the variance on inner-directed and 5 per cent on religious experience). Of this latter 5 per cent, about 3 per cent is accounted for by family tension. So family tension has a rather small explanatory power; however, the

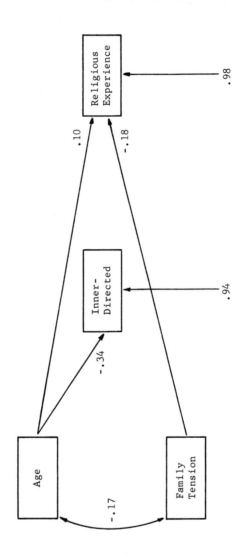

NOTE: All paths with coefficients less than .09 have been omitted from this figure.

Fig. 5.1.—Path diagram relating religious experience to prior variables. Active priests only.

relationship is not uninteresting, given the "soft" nature of the retrospective question about family tension and the inability of any other variable to tell us anything about what causes mystical (or quasi-mystical) experiences.

Both the descriptive and analytic sections of this chapter can be summarized in one set of questions:

1. *Do priests still pray?* Most priests still pray, though the young pray less than the old, a phenomenon that may have been true of the young at any time in the history of the priesthood and not unique to the present time.

2. *Do most priests still say the breviary?* Only about two-fifths of them still honor the complete obligation, with the older priests more likely to do so than the younger.

3. *Do priests still have religious experiences of mystical or quasi-mystical contact with God?* More than half report a frequent sense of being in the presence of God. This religious experience is only slightly related to age and seems fairly equally distributed in all groups of the clergy, save for those who come from tense family backgrounds.

4. *Is there a relationship between frequency of prayer and frequency of mystical experience?* Given the fact that one would expect these two variables to be closely related, it is surprising to report that the positive correlation is only a modest .29. In other words, only about 9 per cent of the variance in the frequency of mystical experience can be explained by the frequency of prayer. The traditional theological position that mysticism is a "given" which cannot be directly pursued receives some confirmation from this finding.

1. All the multiple regression problems executed for this report employ pair-wise deletion of missing cases. In the final stage of the analysis the definitive models were rerun using list-wise deletion. A careful comparison of the two sets of coefficients revealed only minor discrepancies between the different techniques for handling missing cases in our data.

CHAPTER 6

ATTITUDES AND VALUES AMONG THE CATHOLIC CLERGY

In this chapter we attempt to present an overview of the attitudes of the American Catholic priesthood on religious, moral, ecumenical, and social issues. A number of qualifications are in order at the beginning of the chapter:

1. There is considerable room for improvement in the art of surveying religious attitudes and values. The attitudinal items used in the present chapter have been very carefully developed. Some of them are based on other research and all have been criticized, modified, and pretested. Nonetheless, no claim can be made that any individual item precisely reflects the attitudes and values of the respondents; however, it is possible to have a high degree of confidence that constellations and patterns of responses do indeed tell us something important about those who have answered the questions. Thus, the attitudinal indices used in the second part of this chapter do represent, albeit somewhat crudely, patterns of attitudes that actually exist in the minds of our respondents.

2. On those items referring to attitudes about the priesthood and about religion, no attempt was made to assess theological orthodoxy. Experience of other research and of our own pretest indicates that there is nearly unanimous agreement on items which are statements of doctrinal position. Our principal effort was to discover differences in emphases, which we have chosen to call "traditional" versus "modern." By using these labels, no judgment is made that "traditional" is inferior or superior to "modern." The former category is composed of items that tend to stress the essentialist and unchanging aspects of Catholic doctrine, and the latter is made up of items that tend to represent more the existentialist and open-ended aspects of doctrine. There was an expectation that response patterns would emerge from the use of these different kinds of items, partly based on the fact that similar items had produced response patterns in other research.

3. Since one set of items emphasizes the "new" vocabulary of Catholic doctrine and the other set the "old," the age correlation that is constant in this chapter is not at all unexpected. Quite the contrary, the absence of an age correlation would have called into serious question the effectiveness of the items.

4. Part of the difference between those who endorse "traditional" and those who endorse "modern" values and attitudes may be the vocabularies from the different cultural experiences of generations and from different kinds of seminary education.

5. However, it also seems likely that different response patterns also represent rather different—if not quite fundamentally opposed—notions of what the priesthood, Church, and religion are supposed to be.

This may be the appropriate place to make certain remarks about the age correlation to be described in this and subsequent chapters. In discussions of research on the professions, one frequently gets the impression that some observers think that the only ones who really ought to be studied are the younger members of a profession. The reaction of a whole profession can easily be brushed aside with the observation that things are different among the young. The implicit assumption in such an approach is a conviction, which is certainly widespread in American society, that young people represent the wave of the future, and that what they are now is what everyone will be in the next twenty, thirty, or fifty years. It is not our intention to minimize the importance of the patterns to be observed among the most youthful respondents, but there are a number of cautionary remarks that ought to be noted:

1. Any cross-sectional research such as the present effort cannot say conclusively that differences between the young and the old are indeed a generational change. In principle there is no evidence that when the older respondents were young they did not think the same things the young do now. Only longitudinal research, which interviews the same people at different points in time, can exclude the possibility that what we are observing is not generational change (that is, differences among varying age cohorts) but change with age (that is, changes in the attitudes of specific individuals as they move through the life cycle). In this particular project it is extremely unlikely that, for example, priests over fifty-five had the same opinion on birth control when they were under thirty-five that those of that age do today. Nonetheless, one must be cautious in postulating a comprehensive generation gap.

2. Even in the assumption of generational change, the best we can do on the basis of comparison between youth and age is project trends into

the future. If a given attitude is endorsed by smaller proportions of people as we move down the age categories, we can safely say that if the trend indicated by our data continues, then the number supporting a given value will become smaller and smaller. However, it is important to note that trends have a way of changing, and one must be cautious about projecting present trends into the future.

3. No human organization with any intelligence dismisses all of its membership over thirty-five. Even if one can make the extremely drastic assumption that the older half of a profession has nothing important to contribute, to act on that assumption would be utterly destructive to the morale of the organization. It would also serve notice to those who are presently still relatively young that their days of importance and relevance are numbered.

4. Any human organization that is willing to wipe out its values completely in the name of youth may find that it has to start with a clean slate every ten or fifteen years, because those ideas that are most fashionable with one generation of youth have a way of being rather dramatically rejected by the next.

It must be emphasized that the above comments are made by way of a corrective; all issues are not settled when it is said, "But the young think differently." On the other hand, realistic appraisal of a situation must recognize the very strong likelihood that the trends represented by youthful respondents will grow stronger before they grow weaker.

Description

The following principal findings will be reported in the descriptive section of the present chapter:

1. While there is strong support for those attitudes that come closest to being an expression of orthodoxy, there is also strong support for new and more flexible attitudes toward the priesthood and religion. The latter attitudes are especially prevalent among the young.

2. Substantial proportions of the Catholic priesthood in the United States do not accept the Church's official teachings on divorce and birth control, nor do they support the traditional attitude toward masturbation. However, there still is overwhelming support for the Church's official position on abortion and pre-marital sex.

3. Since the issuance of the encyclical letter *Humanae Vitae,* there has been a deterioration of support for the Church's official position on artificial contraception. The official teaching no longer commands the support of the majority of American priests.

4. Bishops are more "conservative" than active priests in their religious and moral attitudes; they are more "liberal" on matters of race and welfare and are more strongly committed to ecumenism.

Attitudes toward the Priesthood and Religion

Table 6.1 presents the responses of the clergy to items in a battery designed to measure their attitudes toward the priesthood. The first thing to be observed about the table is that 88 per cent of the diocesan priests think of the priest as a man who proclaims God's word and administers the sacraments and 74 per cent feel that they are most a priest when they are saying Mass and hearing confessions. Furthermore, 71 per cent see a "permanent character" in the priesthood that makes a priest essentially different from the laity, and 61 per cent agree that when a priest is doing work of which the bishop approves, he is doing priestly work. Finally, a little over half of the diocesan priests (54 per cent) are willing to say that there is almost never a good reason for leaving the priesthood.

On the other hand, 52 per cent of the diocesan priests are willing to concede that a decision to resign from the priesthood may be a wise and mature choice in some circumstances, and 56 per cent are willing to support the idea of a part-time ministry. Only minority support is available for those items that represent rather strong departures from "traditional" thinking about the priesthood: only 30 per cent of the diocesan priests think it would be good if Christian communities were to choose their own priests from among available ordained priests; 34 per cent think that the notion of a priest as "a man set apart" is a barrier to Christian community; 28 per cent think of the priesthood as a transitory institutional role; and 18 per cent think there is no ontological difference between the laity and the clergy. In summary, most of the "traditional" items receive majority support and most of the "modern" emphases do not.

There are virtually no differences between the religious priests and the diocesan priests in their responses to the questions in Table 6.1. The bishops, however, are more likely than the active priests to endorse the "traditional" items and less likely to endorse the "modern" ones. Resignees, on the other hand, are less likely to endorse the "traditional" ones and more likely to endorse the "modern" ones.

At this point it is perhaps necessary to say something about the attitudes of resigned priests to be reported in this chapter and elsewhere in the present report. There can be no doubt—as will become obvious in this and subsequent chapters—that the resignees have very different

TABLE 6.1

ATTITUDES ON THE PRIESTHOOD, BY CLERICAL STATUS

(Per Cent Agreeing "Strongly" or "Somewhat")

Attitude	Diocesan			Religious		
	Bishops	Active Priests	Resigned Priests	Major Superiors	Active Priests	Resigned Priests
Since the priesthood is a lifelong commitment, there is almost never a good reason for leaving	86	54	—[a]	60	55	—[a]
I think it would be a good idea if Christian communities such as parishes were to choose their own priest from among available ordained priests	8	30	69	24	32	64
Ordination confers on the priest a new status or a permanent character which makes him essentially different from the laity within the church	92	71	28	77	72	31
The idea that the priest is a "man set apart" is a barrier to the full realization of true Christian community	5	34	80	24	32	77
Whatever else is said about the humanitarian preoccupations and interpersonal relationships of priests, we must remember that the priest is *the* man in society who proclaims God's Word and provides for sacramental encounter with God in Chirst	98	88	—[a]	96	87	—[a]
I feel that I am most a priest when I am saying Mass and hearing confessions	84	74	45	76	70	47
In many cases a decision to resign from the priesthood is a wise and mature choice	27	52	—[a]	50	49	—[a]

TABLE 6.1—Continued

Attitude	Diocesan			Religious		
	Bishops	Active Priests	Resigned Priests	Major Superiors	Active Priests	Resigned Priests
The priesthood as we know it is a transitory institutional role which will eventually be modified so that there will be much less difference between Christians who have Holy Orders and those who do not	7	28	78	27	28	77
If being on the picket line alienates a priest from most Catholics in an area, a priest should not engage in social protest movements	49	40	8	41	36	11
I think it would be a good idea if Christian communities such as parishes were to choose their own priest from among the parishioners. Such a man would acquire the proper training and then be ordained to act as the priest of the parish for some period of time	3	17	55	17	21	51
For some men being a priest could be a part-time job. Some ordained priests could earn their living at some other employment, and help out on weekends, while others would work full time in the parish and other ministries	24	56	—[a]	65	62	—[a]
As a priest, I feel that I am a member of the bishop's team. When I am doing a job that has the local bishop's approval, I am doing priestly work	87	61	—[a]	60	55	—[a]
Nowadays, you can hardly be an effective priest if you are assigned to a conventional parish	1	14	55	10	15	54
There is no ontological difference between the priest and the laity, since all share in the common priesthood of Christ given at baptism; the difference is mainly one of assigned duties in the church	4	18	65	10	19	57

[a] Not asked of resigned priests.

kinds of attitudes and values from the active priests. But we are unable to say whether their different attitudes are a cause or an effect of their resignation. They may have had their different attitudes before they left the priesthood and found their values incompatible with those of their colleagues in the clergy, or the experience of resigning from the priesthood may have led to a drastic attitudinal change, or these two factors might be involved in some combination. Since, however, we do not have information on the resignees' attitudes before resignation, we are unable to choose among these three alternatives. We can, of course, compare resignees with those in the priesthood who are about to resign, and this comparison will be the basis of our analysis of the causality of resignation in Chapter 13. However, even this comparison will leave something to be desired because men leaving the priesthood at the present time may have different attitude constellations from those who left in the past. The only way in which one could determine with confidence whether attitude differences precede or follow resignation would be to interview the same men before and after. In the present state of our data, then, we can only assert the difference between the resignees and the actives without being able to determine whether these differences are a cause or an effect of the resignation experience or a combination of both.

As might be expected, attitudes toward the priesthood correlate strongly with age (Table 6.2). While 97 per cent of the older clergy (those over fifty-five) agree that the priest is one who proclaims God's word and administers the sacraments, 75 per cent of those thirty-five and under endorse the same statement; and while 89 per cent of those over fifty-five think they are most a priest when they are saying Mass and hearing confessions, 56 per cent of those thirty-five and under would agree. The "traditional" formulations, then, have not been abandoned by the younger clergy, but they do not enjoy nearly as strong support as they do among the older clergy.

On the other hand, 46 per cent of the younger clergy think it would be a good idea if Christian communities chose their own priests, 79 per cent approve the concept of a part-time priesthood, 50 per cent feel that the idea of a priest set apart is a barrier to the realization of Christian community, 45 per cent think of the priesthood as a transitional institutional role in the Church, and 32 per cent think that the principle difference between the clergy and the laity is one of assigned duties in the Church. On some matters, then, the "traditional" emphasis triumphs over the "modern" even among the younger clergy. But the margin of triumph is much thinner than it is among the older clergy.

TABLE 6.2

ATTITUDES ON THE PRIESTHOOD, BY AGE
(Per Cent of Active Diocesan and Religious Priests
Agreeing "Strongly" or "Somewhat")

Attitude	Age			
	26-35	36-45	46-55	Over 55
Since the priesthood is a lifelong commitment, there is almost never a good reason for leaving	24	40	66	86
I think it would be a good idea if Christian communities such as parishes were to choose their own priest from among available ordained priests	46	39	26	13
Ordination confers on the priest a new status or permanent character which makes him essentially different from the laity within the church	52	63	78	91
The idea that the priest is a "man set apart" is a barrier to the full realization of true Christian community	50	40	27	16
Whatever else is said about the humanitarian preoccupations and interpersonal relationshops of priests, we must remember that the priest is *the* man in society who proclaims God's Word and provides for sacramental encounter with God in Christ	75	86	91	97
I feel that I am most a priest when I am saying Mass and hearing confessions	56	65	76	89
In many cases a decision to resign from the priesthood is a wise and mature choice	71	62	42	29
The priesthood as we know it is a transitory institutional role which will eventually be modified so that there will be much less difference between Christians who have Holy Orders and those who do not	45	34	21	13
If being on the picket line alienates a priest from most Catholics in an area, a priest should not engage in social protest movements	19	28	44	61
I think it would be a good idea if Christian communities such as parishes were to choose their own priest from among the parishioners. Such a man would acquire the proper training and then be ordained to act as the priest of the parish for some period of time	31	24	15	6

TABLE 6.2—Continued

Attitude	Age			
	26-35	36-45	46-55	Over 55
For some men being a priest could be a part-time job. Some ordained priests could earn their living at some other employment, and help out on weekends, while others would work full time in the parish and other ministries	79	70	54	33
As a priest, I feel that I am a member of the bishop's team. When I am doing a job that has the local bishop's approval, I am doing priestly work	36	47	68	83
Nowadays, you can hardly be an effective priest if you are assigned to a conventional parish	19	18	12	8
There is no ontological difference between the priest and the laity, since all share in the common priesthood of Christ given at baptism; the difference is mainly one of assigned duties in the church	32	22	13	8

A number of items were included in the questionnaire to measure the respondents' perception of the situation that manifests what the social scientists call "anomie." This is a situation of "normlessness"; that is, disorganization and confusion caused by the loss of one set of values in a transition to a new set of values. We observe in Table 6.3 that the majority of priests (70 per cent or more) agree that it is important in the Church that people are examining what has meaning for them. More than 80 per cent feel that the basic values of the Church remain the same, even though their expression is changing. Slightly better than half (52 per cent) think that the relationships between priests and laity are better today than they were in the past. On the other hand, 58 per cent of the diocesan priests and 44 per cent of the religious priests believe that "what is lacking today is that closeness among priests that used to be so evident."

Only one-third agree that relationships between the laity and the clergy before Vatican II were much better than they are today, and only two-fifths report that they have trouble deciding which of the new liturgical rules to follow. Less than one-fifth think that today "most people really don't believe in anything."

TABLE 6.3

"ANOMIC" ATTITUDES BY CLERICAL STATUS

(Per Cent Agreeing "Strongly" or "Somewhat")

Attitude	Diocesan			Religious		
	Bishops	Active Priests	Resigned Priests	Major Superiors	Active Priests	Resigned Priests
The important thing in the Church today is that people are really examining what has meaning for them	58	70	—[a]	76	74	—[a]
What is lacking today is that closeness among priests that used to be so evident	70	58	—[a]	46	44	—[a]
The basic values of the Church remain the same, but their expression is changing	94	84	—[a]	91	85	—[a]
The relationship between laity and priests was much better before Vatican II when everyone knew just how he was expected to act	46	34	16	24	30	12
With the new roles for everyone in the Church that have developed since Vatican II, the relationships between priests and laity are much better	44	52	—[a]	48	52	—[a]
Everything changes so quickly in the liturgy these days that I often have trouble deciding what rules to follow	41	40	—[a]	32	40	—[a]
The trouble with the Church today is that most people really don't believe in anything	10	19	13	11	17	15

[a] Not asked of resigned priests.

There are some indications that bishops perceive more anomie in the present ecclesiastical situation than do priests. Of the bishops, 46 per cent think that the relationship between the clergy and the laity was better before the Vatican Council, and 70 per cent lament the decline of closeness among priests.

There is also a strong correlation between perception of anomie and age, with the older priests being more likely to give an anomic response than the younger priests to every item in Table 6.4. For example, 58 per cent of those over fifty-five think that relationships between laity and priests were better before the Vatican Council than they are today, while only 9 per cent of those thirty-five and under agree with this statement. One could summarize Tables 6.3 and 6.4 by saying that while there is evidence of concern about confusion in the Church, particularly among those over forty-five, this confusion could not be said to be pervasive.

TABLE 6.4

"ANOMIC" ATTITUDES BY AGE
(Per Cent of Active Diocesan and Religious Priests
Agreeing "Strongly" or "Somewhat")

Attitude	Age			
	26-35	36-45	46-55	Over 55
The important thing in the Church today is that people are really examining what has meaning for them	83	79	66	59
What is lacking today is that closeness among priests that used to be so evident	36	47	56	67
The basic values of the Church remain the same, but their expression is changing	77	82	89	91
The relationship between laity and priests was much better before Vatican II when everyone knew just how he was expected to act	9	21	39	58
With the new roles for everyone in the Church that have developed since Vatican II, the relationships between priests and laity are much better	68	58	46	37
Everything changes so quickly in the liturgy these days that I often have trouble deciding what rules to follow	14	32	49	63
The trouble with the Church today is that most people really don't believe in anything	15	16	19	22

The attitude items in Table 6.5 were designed to tap "traditional" religious attitudes in the Catholic clergy. We observe that 88 per cent of the diocesan priests think of Jesus Christ as God and 87 per cent think of the Catholic Church as "the one true Church." Sixty-six per cent assert both that they think of heaven as "Beatific Vision" and that they feel the sacraments are "channels for receiving grace." Sixty-two per cent think of God primarily as the Supreme Being and the Creator of the universe, and 52 per cent accept the notion that the primary task of the Church is to encourage its members to live Christian lives. Exactly half of the diocesan priests endorse the idea that the only response to the mystery of the Trinity is humble acceptance; however, only 29 per cent would describe the Church as "a place of refuge and quiet reflection away from the world," and only 26 per cent agree with the item suggesting that one's faith may be jeopardized by studying Protestant theologians. In other words, those "traditional" items that come closest to being a restatement of orthodox doctrinal formulations are endorsed by substantial segments of the clergy, while those that seem to advocate withdrawal from the world receive only minority support.

On virtually all of the "traditional" items, there is more agreement from the bishops than from the priests. Thus, 58 per cent of the bishops see a danger to the faith from studying Protestant theologians. On the other hand, bishops are no more likely than their priests to advocate the Church as a place of refuge and quiet reflection away from the world.

There is little in the way of important differences between religious priests and diocesan priests. It is of some interest to note, however, that the resigned priests are far less likely than the currently active priests to endorse the "traditional" doctrines, although 43 per cent of the diocesan resignees and 52 per cent of the religious resignees are willing to admit that the Catholic Church is the one true Church.

Given the fact that the questions were designed to tap traditional religious attitudes, it is not surprising that there is a strong correlation between age and every item in Table 6.6. Nonetheless, a majority of the priests thirty-five and under are likely to endorse only two of the "traditional" items — the traditional formularies about the Catholic Church being the one true Church and about Jesus Christ being the God who became man to die for our sins. Those items received the support of three-quarters of those in the youngest age category. However, only minorities, and in most instances rather small minorities, of priests thirty-five and under are willing to accept other "traditional" statements contained in Table 6.6.

TABLE 6.5

"TRADITIONAL" RELIGIOUS ATTITUDES BY CLERICAL STATUS

(Per Cent Agreeing "Strongly" or "Somewhat")

Attitude	Diocesan			Religious		
	Bishops	Active Priests	Resigned Priests	Major Superiors	Active Priests	Resigned Priests
The mystery of the Trinity is so profound and so central that I feel I should humbly accept it as given and not seek to plumb its depths	56	50	15	56	44	18
I think of God primarily as the Supreme Being, immutable, all-powerful, and the Creator of the universe	69	62	34	55	54	40
The Catholic Church is the one true Church established by Christ with St. Peter and his successors as its head	97	87	43	96	88	52
The important thing to stress when teaching about Jesus is that He is truly God, and, therefore, adoration should be directed toward Him	73	54	21	58	52	27
The principal meaning of Christ's resurrection for me is that it proved His Divinity	73	61	29	61	58	35
I think of Jesus Christ as the God who humbled Himself by becoming man and dying for my sins	96	88	—[a]	91	87	—[a]
To doubt one article of faith that is de fide is to question the whole of revealed truth	72	47	—[a]	51	48	—[a]
I think of heaven as the state in which my soul will rest in blissful possession of the Beatific Vision	80	66	—[a]	72	64	—[a]

TABLE 6.5—Continued

Attitude	Diocesan			Religious		
	Bishops	Active Priests	Resigned Priests	Major Superiors	Active Priests	Resigned Priests
I feel that the most important thing to recognize about the sacraments is that they are channels for receiving grace	83	66	—[a]	68	67	—[a]
A Christian should look first to the salvation of his soul; then he should be concerned about helping others	59	48	13	45	48	17
The Church should be a place of refuge and quiet reflection away from the world	30	29	—[a]	25	27	—[a]
The primary task of the Church is to encourage its members to live the Christian life rather than to try to reform the world	55	52	31	50	52	37
Faith means essentially belief in the doctrines of the Catholic Church	69	45	7	49	42	15
One's faith may be jeopardized by studying Protestant theologians	58	26	—[a]	36	30	—[a]

[a] Not asked of resigned priests.

TABLE 6.6

"TRADITIONAL" RELIGIOUS ATTITUDES BY AGE
(Per Cent of Active Diocesan and Religious Priests
Agreeing "Strongly" or "Somewhat")

Attitude	Age			
	26-35	36-45	46-55	Over 55
The mystery of the Trinity is so profound and so central that I feel I should humbly accept it as given and not seek to plumb its depths	23	37	54	74
I think of God primarily as the Supreme Being, immutable, all-powerful, and the Creator of the universe	31	48	67	84
The Catholic Church is the one true Church established by Christ with St. Peter and his successors as its head	74	84	93	98
The important thing to stress when teaching about Jesus is that He is truly God, and, therefore, adoration should be directed toward Him	26	42	62	82
The principal meaning of Christ's resurrection for me is that it proved His Divinity	33	50	70	84
I think of Jesus Christ as the God who humbled Himself by becoming man and dying for my sins	75	84	92	98
To doubt one article of faith that is *de fide* is to question the whole of revealed truth	18	35	57	78
I think of heaven as the state in which my soul will rest in blissful possession of the Beatific Vision	36	56	75	90
I feel that the most important thing to recognize about the sacraments is that they are channels for receiving grace	37	56	77	91
A Christian should look to the salvation of his soul; then he should be concerned about helping others	22	38	56	75
The Church should be a place of refuge and of quiet reflection away from the world	12	20	32	48
The primary task of the Church is to encourage its members to live the Christian life rather than to try to reform the world	29	43	60	74
Faith means essentially belief in the doctrines of the Catholic Church	16	32	52	74
One's faith may be jeopardized by studying Protestant theologians	6	16	34	53

But if the "traditional" formulations that come closest to being orthodox doctrine are accepted by most priests, this does not mean that the more "modern" religious attitudes are rejected. Quite the contrary, as we see from inspecting percentages in Table 6.7. All of the "modern" statements are accepted by a majority of active priests, whether they are religious or diocesan. Among the diocesan priests, 60 per cent agree that God is found principally in relationships with people, 58 per cent see God's word coming through prophetic men such as Gandhi or King, 65 per cent believe that the Christian must emphasize openness to the Spirit, 65 per cent approve of priests marching on picket lines, 66 per cent think that in deep communication and union with other persons is "a taste of what heaven will be like," 70 per cent agree that the Church has been inadequate in facing up to civil rights issues, 69 per cent are willing to describe faith as "primarily an encounter with God in Christ Jesus, rather than an assent to a coherent set of defined truths," and 52 per cent are willing to agree that there are times when a person must put conscience above the Church's teaching. There is very little difference between the diocesan and religious priests on these items. As one might imagine, the resignees are even more likely to consent to such "modern" statements.

The bishops, on the other hand, are apparently somewhat less in sympathy with such "modern" expressions of religious values. Majority support among the bishops is found for the notion that the priests who feel called to do so may march in picket lines or speak out on controversial issues (54 per cent). Furthermore, 54 per cent of the bishops also are in agreement with the proposition that the Church has been inadequate in facing up to civil rights issues — only 16 percentage points behind their priests on this rather strong position. While 60 per cent of the active diocesan priests think that God is found principally in relationships with people, only 22 per cent of the bishops agree. Forty-six per cent of the bishops think of faith as an encounter with God, but 69 per cent of their priests support this opinion. Active priests are between three and four times more likely than bishops (52 per cent versus 15 per cent) to say that one must put personal conscience above the Church's teachings on certain occasions.

We discover in Table 6.8 the expected correlation between age and response to items measuring "modern" religious attitudes. A majority of priests under forty-six endorse all the items by very substantial margins, and only two items — God found primarily in relationships with people and conscience over Church teaching — fail to win majority support of those between forty-six and fifty-five. Even among those over

TABLE 6.7

"MODERN" RELIGIOUS ATTITUDES BY CLERICAL STATUS

(Per Cent Agreeing "Strongly" or "Somewhat")

Attitude	Diocesan			Religious		
	Bishops	Active Priests	Resigned Priests	Major Superiors	Active Priests	Resigned Priests
For me, God is found principally in my relationships with people	22	60	82	51	56	79
God's Word comes to us through some of the great prophetic men of our times, such as Mahatma Gandhi and Martin Luther King	37	58	86	64	62	80
Today's Christian must emphasize more than ever openness to the Spirit rather than dependence on traditional ecclesiastical structures	38	65	—[a]	70	66	—[a]
I think that priests who feel called to do so ought to be witnessing to Christ on the picket line or speaking out on controversial issues	54	65	—[a]	65	66	—[a]
When I experience moments of deep communication and union with other persons, these sometimes strike me as a taste of what heaven will be like	45	66	—[a]	67	68	—[a]
For the most part, the Church has been inadequate in facing up to the civil rights issues	54	70	—[a]	76	70	—[a]
Faith is primarily an encounter with God in Christ Jesus, rather than an assent to a coherent set of defined truths	46	69	89	74	72	90
There are times when a person has to put his personal conscience above the Church's teaching	15	52	98	44	51	93

[a] Not asked of resigned priests.

TABLE 6.8

"MODERN" RELIGIOUS ATTITUDES BY AGE
(Per Cent of Active Diocesan and Religious Priests
Agreeing "Strongly" or "Somewhat")

Attitude	Age			
	26-35	36-45	46-55	Over 55
For me, God is found principally in my relationships with people	78	64	47	44
God's Word comes to us through some of the great prophetic men of our times, such as Mahatma Gandhi and Martin Luther King	88	69	52	33
Today's Christian must emphasize more than ever openness to the Spirit rather than dependence on traditional ecclesiastical structures	89	75	55	42
I think that priests who feel called to do so ought to be witnessing to Christ on the picket line or speaking out on controversial issues	88	75	59	42
When I experience moments of deep communication and union with other persons, these sometimes strike me as a taste of what heaven will be like	81	73	60	53
For the most part, the Church has been inadequate in facing up to the civil rights issues	83	75	67	55
Faith is primarily an encounter with God in Christ Jesus, rather than an assent to a coherent set of defined truths	92	79	61	49
There are times when a person has to put his personal conscience above the Church's teaching	80	64	42	22

fifty-five, more than half agree with the "modern" positions on the nature of heaven (53 per cent) and the Church's inadequacy on civil rights matters (55 per cent). Just under half feel that faith is an encounter with God (49 per cent). Finally, there is more sympathy for the "modern" position among priests over fifty-five than among bishops.

It can be said in summary of the first eight tables that a substantial number of priests are able to combine both "traditional" formulations and more "modern" statements of religious values. The younger clergy are more likely to emphasize the newer values, while the older clergy emphasize more "traditional" values. The bishops are somewhat less attached to the "traditional" statements than are priests in the oldest age category, but they are generally less likely than the oldest priests to sympathize with the "modern" values. There are, then, rather sharp differences of opinion on religious values between bishops and priests.

Attitudes toward Sexual Morality

Tables 6.9 through 6.28 present data concerning the attitude of the Catholic clergy regarding the Church's position on sexual morality. Because of the delicate, controversial, and important nature of these attitudes, considerable effort was expended in the wording of the questions. The implications of each question were carefully discussed with members of the Ad Hoc Committee for the Study of the Life and Ministry of the Priest before the final draft of the questionnaire was prepared. In this section of the chapter we shall abandon our usual strategy of

TABLE 6.9

ATTITUDES ON MASTURBATION, BY CLERICAL STATUS
(Per Cent)

Attitude	Diocesan		Religious	
	Bishops	Active Priests	Major Supe- riors	Active Priests
Adolescent masturbation is a normal developmental phase in a person's maturing sexuality and among adults occasional masturbation is usually the result of stress or conflict, hence in most cases it is not sinful	17	43	40	40
For both adolescents and adults, in most cases deliberate masturbation is sinful but no more than venially	18	22	22	23
For both adolescents and adults, in most cases deliberate masturbation is a mortal sin	55	29	31	29
Other	11	6	7	9
Total	101 [a]	100	100	101 [a]

[a] Not 100 per cent because of rounding.

compressing as much data as possible into one table and instead give the full range of responses to each question.

Only 29 per cent of the Catholic priests in the country are presently willing to agree with the statement, "For both adolescents and adults, in most cases deliberate masturbation is a mortal sin" (Table 6.9). Sixty-five per cent of the diocesan priests and 63 per cent of the religious say that it is at most a venial sin or that it is no sin at all. But a majority of the bishops (55 per cent) still feel that in most cases masturbation *is* a mortal sin. To the extent that the "traditional" teaching of the moral theology manuals was most reluctant to think of masturbation as anything but a grave sin, one can observe in Table 6.9 a drastic turning away from the traditional teaching. Indeed, two-fifths of the diocesan priests are willing to accept the statement that explains masturbation largely in psychological rather than moral terms.

Support for the "psychological" interpretation of masturbation is even stronger among the younger priests (Table 6.10). Thus, 52 per cent of those between thirty-six and forty-five and 64 per cent of those thirty-five and under endorse the "psychological" explanation. An idea of the strongly divergent values between the young and the old can be obtained

TABLE 6.10

ATTITUDES ON MASTURBATION, BY AGE
(Per Cent of Active Diocesan and Religious Priests)

Attitude	Age			
	26-35	36-45	46-55	Over 55
Adolescent masturbation is a normal developmental phase in a person's maturing sexuality and among adults occasional masturbation is usually the result of stress or conflict, hence in most cases it is not sinful	64	52	36	15
For both adolescents and adults, in most cases deliberate masturbation is sinful but no more than venially	20	23	25	21
For both adolescents and adults, in most cases deliberate masturbation is a mortal sin	8	17	32	59
Other	8	8	7	5
Total	100	100	100	100

by comparing the 64 per cent of the young who think that in most cases masturbation is not sinful at all with the 59 per cent of those over fifty-five who think that in most cases it is a grave sin. This is but the first example of a phenomenon that we shall discover consistently repeated in subsequent tables: there are very sharp disagreements between the older and the younger clergy on matters of sexual morality.

However, while a more "liberal" [1] position on masturbation seems to have become rather commonplace among the Catholic clergy, no such change is observed in their thinkings on premarital sex (Table 6.11). Four-fifths of the active priests reject intercourse between people who are not married. However a substantial proportion of the resignees are willing to approve of it: 18 per cent of the diocesan resignees and 16 per cent of the religious order resignees approve of premarital sexual intercourse, even for those who merely share affection. The younger priests are also more willing to give their approval (Table 6.12). Thus, 25 per cent of those thirty-five and under and 19 per cent of those between thirty-six and forty-five do not object to premarital intercourse in certain circumstances. Although the majority in these age categories reject premarital intercourse, one can see the beginning of erosion of support for the "traditional" position.

In Table 6.13 we turn to perhaps the most controversial issue of all: the attitude of the clergy toward birth control, particularly in light of the encyclical letter *Humanae Vitae*. It was decided to ask questions about the opinion of the clergy both before the issuance of that encyclical and since its promulgation with the intention of attempting to determine whether the encyclical and changing opinion as a result of it have had any important impact on other areas of the life and ministry of the priest.

If the first two opinions in Table 6.13 — that all artificial conception is morally wrong, or that even if it is not certainly all morally wrong, the faithful may still not practice it — are taken to represent the official Catholic teaching, one can see that based on their own reports, even before the issuance of the encyclical letter only a bare majority (51 per cent) of active American Catholic priests were willing to accept such a position. Of their episcopal leaders, 84 per cent supported the official position (as did 59 per cent of the major superiors). Furthermore, Table 6.14 shows that much of the support for the official position was concentrated in the older clergy; only 21 per cent of those thirty-five and under and 41 per cent of those between thirty-six and forty-five supported the official teaching even before the encyclical, compared to 63 per cent of those between forty-six and fifty-five and 79 per cent of those over

TABLE 6.11

ATTITUDES ON PREMARITAL SEX, BY CLERICAL STATUS

(Per Cent)

Attitude	Diocesan			Religious		
	Bishops	Active Priests	Resigned Priests	Major Superiors	Active Priests	Resigned Priests
It is morally acceptable for couples who share affection	0	2	18	1	2	16
It is morally acceptable for couples who are in love	0	6	30	4	5	26
It is morally acceptable for couples who are engaged	0	7	16	5	8	16
It is never morally acceptable: couples should wait until they are married	100	80	16	87	78	22
Other	0	6	20	3	7	20
Total	100	101 [a]	100	100	100	100

[a] Not 100 per cent because of rounding.

TABLE 6.12

ATTITUDES ON PREMARITAL SEX, BY AGE
(Per Cent of Active Diocesan and Religious Priests)

Attitude	Age			
	26-35	36-45	46-55	Over 55
It is morally acceptable for couples who share affection	2	2	1	1
It is morally acceptable for couples who are in love	10	8	4	1
It is morally acceptable for couples who are engaged	13	9	6	3
It is never morally acceptable: couples should wait until they are married	62	72	86	94
Other	13	9	3	1
Total	100	100	100	100

fifty-five. Half of those thirty-five and under and one-third of those between thirty-six and forty-five were either taking a position that would leave birth control decisions to the conscience of the individuals involved or actively supporting all methods of artificial contraception.

But in the years since the issuance of the encyclical, the erosion has apparently continued (Table 6.15), though whether the encyclical "caused" the further erosion is a judgment that our data do not enable us to make. When our data were collected in the winter of 1969-70, about 40 per cent of American priests (an increase of about 11 percentage points) were willing to support the traditional position, but roughly another 40 per cent (a decrease of about 10 percentage points) were taking stands that were diametrically opposed to that position. In the same period of time there was very little change in the bishops' stand, with 70 per cent of the hierarchy (down 5 percentage points) still insisting that all artificial contraception is morally wrong because it is forbidden by the natural law and 13 per cent (up 4 per cent) insisting that whatever theoretical position might be taken, the faithful are still bound to avoid all methods of artificial contraception.

Looking at the change by age (Table 6.16), we see that there is almost no support left for the official position among the priests thirty-five and under, with a mere 13 per cent endorsing it (down 8 percentage points). There is also waning support among those between thirty-six and forty-

TABLE 6.13

BIRTH CONTROL ATTITUDES BEFORE *HUMANAE VITAE*, BY CLERICAL STATUS

(Per Cent)

Attitude	Diocesan			Religious		
	Bishops	Active Priests	Resigned Priests	Major Superiors	Active Priests	Resigned Priests
All artificial contraception is morally wrong because it is clearly forbidden by the natural law and by the Church's teaching	75	40	4	46	39	5
It is not certain that all artificial contraception is morally wrong; still, the faithful are bound to follow the guidance of the teaching of the Church and avoid all methods of artificial contraception	9	11	2	13	12	5
It is not certain that all artificial contraception is morally wrong; therefore, the faithful are morally justified in using *at least some methods* of artificial contraception when they have adequate reasons for avoiding more children	5	15	11	20	15	14
There is no doubt that the responsible use of at least *some* methods of artificial contraception is morally acceptable, while the use of other methods may be morally wrong	1	5	9	3	6	10
Judgment concerning the morality of artificial contraception should be left to the responsibly formed consciences of the individuals involved	7	22	53	14	20	47
Given adequate reasons for avoiding children, all methods of artificial contraception are morally acceptable	2	5	19	3	6	17
Other	1	2	2	1	2	3
Total	100	100	100	100	100	101 [a]

[a] Not 100 per cent because of rounding.

TABLE 6.14

BIRTH CONTROL ATTITUDES BEFORE *HUMANAE VITAE,* BY AGE
(Per Cent of Active Diocesan and Religious Priests)

Attitude	Age			
	26-35	36-45	46-55	Over 55
All artificial contraception is morally wrong because it is clearly forbidden by the natural law and by the Church's teaching	11	27	51	68
It is not certain that all artificial contraception is morally wrong; still, the faithful are bound to follow the guidance of the teaching of the Church and avoid all methods of artificial contraception	10	14	12	11
It is not certain that all artificial contraception is morally wrong; therefore, the faithful are morally justified in using *at least some methods* of artificial contraception when they have adequate reasons for avoiding more children	21	19	14	7
There is no doubt that the responsible use of at least *some* methods of artificial contraception is morally acceptable, while the use of other methods may be morally wrong	8	6	4	3
Judgment concerning the morality of artificial contraception should be left to the responsibly formed consciences of the individuals involved	38	26	14	8
Given adequate reasons for avoiding children, all methods of artificial contraception are morally acceptable	10	6	4	2
Other	2	2	2	1
Total	100	100	101 [a]	100

[a] Not 100 per cent because of rounding.

five, with 30 per cent supporting the official position (down 11 percentage points). But among all age categories, support for the position taken in the encyclical letter *Humanae Vitae* has declined since the encyclical was issued. While it cannot be said that the encyclical caused the decline (at least on the basis of the data available to us), it must still be observed as an objective fact that insofar as it was designed to obtain the consent of

TABLE 6.15
BIRTH CONTROL ATTITUDES AFTER *HUMANAE VITAE*, BY CLERICAL STATUS
(Per Cent)

Attitude	Diocesan			Religious		
	Bishops	Active Priests	Resigned Priests	Major Superiors	Active Priests	Resigned Priests
All artificial contraception is morally wrong because it is clearly forbidden by the natural law and by the Church's teaching	70	29	1	34	29	2
It is not certain that all artificial contraception is morally wrong; still, the faithful are bound to follow the guidance of the teaching of the Church and avoid all methods of artificial contraception	13	11	1	14	13	2
It is not certain that all artificial contraception is morally wrong; therefore, the faithful are morally justified in using *at least some* methods of artificial contraception when they have adequate reasons for avoiding more children	3	13	5	15	14	8
There is no doubt that the responsible use of at least *some* methods of artificial contraception is morally acceptable, while the use of other methods may be morally wrong	1	4	6	3	4	7
Judgment concerning the morality of artificial contraception should be left to the responsibly formed consciences of the individuals involved	11	32	56	28	30	54
Given adequate reasons for avoiding children, all methods of artificial contraception are morally acceptable	2	7	28	3	7	24
Other	1	3	3	3	3	3
Total	101[a]	99[a]	100	100	100	100

[a] Not 100 per cent because of rounding.

TABLE 6.16

BIRTH CONTROL ATTITUDES AFTER *HUMANAE VITAE,* BY AGE
(Per Cent of Active Diocesan and Religious Priests)

Attitude	Age			
	26-35	36-45	46-55	Over 55
All artificial contraception is morally wrong because it is clearly forbidden by the natural law and by the Church's teaching	7	17	34	59
It is not certain that all artificial contraception is morally wrong; still, the faithful are bound to follow the guidance of the teaching of the Church and avoid all methods of artificial contraception	6	13	15	13
It is not certain that all artificial contraception is morally wrong; therefore, the faithful are morally justified in using *at least some methods* of artificial contraception when they have adequate reasons for avoiding more children	16	17	13	8
There is no doubt that the responsible use of at least *some* methods of artificial contraception is morally acceptable, while the use of other methods may be morally wrong	5	4	5	3
Judgment concerning the morality of artificial contraception should be left to the responsibly formed consciences of the individuals involved	50	37	25	13
Given adequate reasons for avoiding children, all methods of artificial contraception are morally acceptable	13	9	5	3
Other	3	3	3	2
Total	100	100	100	101[a]

[a] Not 100 per cent because of rounding.

the American clergy in moral teaching, the encyclical letter was apparently not successful.

In Table 6.17 we examine the direction of change in birth control attitudes since the encyclical letter. The responses on the diagonal — running from left top to right bottom — represent those respondents who said that their positions were the same both before the encyclical and

The Catholic Priest in the United States

TABLE 6.17

BIRTH CONTROL ATTITUDES BEFORE AND AFTER *HUMANAE VITAE*
(Per Cent of Active Diocesan and Religious Priests)

Before *Humanae Vitae*	After *Humanae Vitae*						
	A	B	C	D	E	F	Other
A. All artificial contraception is morally wrong because it is clearly forbidden by the natural law and by the Church's teaching	27	4	3	1	4	0	1
B. It is not certain that all artificial contraception is morally wrong; still, the faithful are bound to follow the guidance of the teaching of the Church and avoid all methods of artificial contraception	1	6	2	0	2	0	0
C. It is not certain that all artificial contraception is morally wrong; therefore, the faithful are morally justified in using *at least some methods* of artificial contraception when they have adequate reasons for avoiding more children	0	1	8	1	4	1	0
D. There is no doubt that the responsible use of at least *some* methods of artificial contraception is morally acceptable, while the use of other methods may be morally wrong	0	0	0	3	2	0	0
E. Judgment concerning the morality of artificial contraception should be left to the responsibly formed consciences of the individuals involved	0	0	0	0	19	1	0
F. Given adequate reasons for avoiding children, all methods of artificial contraception are morally acceptable	0	0	0	0	1	5	1
Other	0	0	0	0	0	0	2

Diagonal (no change)	=	70
Above ("liberal" change)	=	27
Below ("conservative" change)	=	3
Total	=	100

after (70 per cent). The per cents above the diagonal represent a change in favor of a more "lenient" position; 27 per cent of the respondents have moved in this direction. The per cents below the diagonal represent change in the direction of a stricter position since *Humanae Vitae;* 3 per cent of the respondents changed in this direction. The gross change, then, is 30 per cent — 3 per cent to a more "conservative" position and 27 per cent to a more "liberal" position — and the net loss of support for the official position is 24 per cent.

Most of the respondents are still clustered around the diagonal, indicating that the extent of their movement from an old position to a new one is not great. However, 6 per cent of all the priests in the country have moved from a position that would impose the official teaching on all Catholics to a position that would leave the decision entirely in the hands of responsible married people.

There also has been a deterioration in support for the official position in confessional practice on birth control (Table 6.18). Before the encyclical some 36 per cent of the diocesan priests and 35 per cent of the religious were willing either to leave moral judgment to the con-

TABLE 6.18

BIRTH CONTROL PROCEDURE IN CONFESSION BEFORE
HUMANAE VITAE, BY CLERICAL STATUS
(Per Cent)

Procedure	Diocesan		Religious	
	Bishops	Active Priests	Major Superiors	Active Priests
Discourage the use of artificial contraception under pain of denial of absolution to a penitent who refused even to try to avoid the use of contraceptives	59	26	29	27
Discourage the use of artificial contraception, but not deny absolution to a penitent who was convinced of his moral justification in using contraceptives	32	36	40	35
Neither discourage nor encourage the use of artificial contraception, but accept the moral judgment of the responsibly formed conscience of the penitent who chooses to use contraceptives	5	31	25	31
Encourage the penitent who has adequate reasons in a responsible use of artificial contraception	0	5	5	4
Other	4	2	1	3
Total	100	100	100	100

science of the penitent or even occasionally to actively support a birth control decision, though only 5 per cent of the bishops would have taken such a "liberal" stand. It was among the younger clergy that the most support for the "liberal" position was found, with 63 per cent of those under thirty-six taking a tolerant attitude toward birth control in the confessional, as opposed to 14 per cent of those over fifty-five (Table 6.19). But at the present time (Table 6.20), 51 per cent of the diocesan priests and 49 per cent of the religious priests take the "liberal" position in the confessional, an increase of 15 percentage points among the diocesan priests and 14 percentage points among the religious priests. Only 9 per cent of the bishops (an increase of 4 percentage points) are willing to take the "liberal" stand, and 42 per cent still think that absolution should be refused to penitents who will not promise to try to avoid

TABLE 6.19

BIRTH CONTROL PROCEDURE IN CONFESSION
BEFORE *HUMANAE VITAE,* BY AGE
(Per Cent of Active Diocesan and Religious Priests)

Procedure	Age			
	26-35	36-45	46-55	Over 55
Discourage the use of artificial contraception under pain of denial of absolution to a penitent who refused even to try to avoid the use of contraceptives	6	21	33	45
Discourage the use of artificial contraception, but not deny absolution to a penitent who was convinced of his moral justification in using contraceptives	27	35	38	40
Neither discourage nor encourage the use of artificial contraception, but accept the moral judgment of the responsibly formed conscience of the penitent who chooses to use contraceptives	53	37	24	13
Encourage the penitent who has adequate reasons in a responsible use of artificial contraception	10	5	3	1
Other	4	2	2	2
Total	100	100	100	101 [a]

[a] Not 100 per cent because of rounding.

TABLE 6.20

BIRTH CONTROL PROCEDURE IN CONFESSION AFTER
HUMANAE VITAE, BY CLERICAL STATUS
(Per Cent)

Procedure	Diocesan		Religious	
	Bishops	Active Priests	Major Superiors	Active Priests
Discourage the use of artificial contraception under pain of denial of absolution to a penitent who refused even to try to avoid the use of contraceptives	42	13	14	13
Discourage the use of artificial contraception, but not deny absolution to a penitent who was convinced of his moral justification in using contraceptives	45	33	36	34
Neither discourage nor encourage the use of artificial contraception, but accept the moral judgment of the responsibly formed conscience of the penitent who chooses to use contraceptives	8	44	44	42
Encourage the penitent who has adequate reasons in a responsible use of artificial contraception	1	7	4	7
Other	4	3	2	4
Total	100	100	100	100

the use of contraceptives. Only 13 per cent of the priests (diocesan and religious) will take this stand. Finally, in Table 6.21 we see that 76 per cent of the priests between twenty-six and thirty-five, 57 per cent of those between thirty-six and forty-five, and 45 per cent of those between forty-six and fifty-five vote for the more "liberal" position in the confessional. Even among those over fifty-five, there has been an increase of 9 percentage points (from 14 to 23 per cent) in support for the "liberal" position. Thus, in every age group of the priests, confessional practice on the subject of birth control has grown more "liberal" since the issuance of *Humanae Vitae*.

TABLE 6.21

BIRTH CONTROL PROCEDURE IN CONFESSION
AFTER *HUMANAE VITAE*, BY AGE
(Per Cent of Active Diocesan and Religious Priests)

Procedure	Age			
	26-35	36-45	46-55	Over 55
Discourage the use of artificial contraception under pain of denial of absolution to a penitent who refused even to try to avoid the use of contraceptives	3	8	14	28
Discourage the use of artificial contraception, but not deny absolution to a penitent who was convinced of his moral justification in using contraceptives	18	31	38	46
Neither discourage nor encourage the use of artificial contraception, but accept the moral judgment of the responsibly formed conscience of the penitent who chooses to use contraceptives	62	50	40	21
Encourage the penitent who has adequate reasons in a responsible use of artificial contraception	14	7	5	2
Other	3	4	3	3
Total	100	100	100	100

As might be expected, the change in confessional practice corresponds to the change in theoretical position (Table 6.22). Sixty-six per cent of the respondents are on the diagonal in Table 6.22, which means that their position has not changed in the last five years. Of the 33 per cent who have changed their position, 29 per cent are above the diagonal, meaning that they have moved in the "liberal" direction, and 4 per cent are below the diagonal, indicating that they have moved in the "conservative" direction. Once again, most changes are clustered along the diagonal, though 3 per cent of all the priests in the sample (approximately 2,000 priests, if we project from our sample to the total priest population) have moved from a stand in which they would refuse absolution to those who practice birth control to a position of accepting the moral judgment of married persons, whatever that judgment might be. In both theory and practice, then, the last several years have witnessed a deterioration of support for the official position.

TABLE 6.22

BIRTH CONTROL PROCEDURE IN CONFESSION
BEFORE AND AFTER *HUMANAE VITAE*
(Per Cent of Active Diocesan and Religious Priests)

Before *Humanae Vitae*	After *Humanae Vitae*				
	A	B	C	D	Other
A. Discourage the use of artificial contraception under pain of denial of absolution to a penitent who refused even to try to avoid the use of contraceptives	12	10	3	0	1
B. Discourage the use of artificial contraception, but not deny absolution to a penitent who was convinced of his moral justification in using contraceptives	1	21	12	1	0
C. Neither discourage nor encourage the use of artificial contraception, but accept the moral judgment of the responsibly formed conscience of the penitent who chooses to use contraceptives	0	2	27	2	0
D. Encourage the penitent who has adequate reasons in a responsible use of artificial contraception	0	0	1	4	0
Other	0	0	0	0	2

Diagonal (no change)   = 66
Above ("liberal" change)   = 29
Below ("conservative" change) = 4
Total = 99[a]

[a] Not 100 per cent because of rounding.

One of the reasons for the apparent inability of the encyclical letter *Humanae Vitae* to prevent a continuing deterioration of clerical support for the official birth control position is that a substantial segment of the clergy do not feel that it was a legitimate exercise of authority.[2] Table 6.23 shows that 9 per cent of the diocesan priests argue that the Pope is incompetent to use his teaching authority in this way and 33 per cent more feel that *Humanae Vitae* was a misuse of the Pope's authority because of the absence of collegiality. Only 36 per cent of the diocesan priests and 37 per cent of the religious assert that *Humanae Vitae* was a competent and appropriate exercise of the Papal teaching authority. Of the bishops, 72 per cent — just twice as high a proportion as for the diocesan priests — agree that *Humanae Vitae* was a competent and appropriate use of authority.

TABLE 6.23

ATTITUDE TOWARD *HUMANAE VITAE,* BY CLERICAL STATUS
(Per Cent)

Attitude	Diocesan		Religious	
	Bishops	Active Priests	Major Superiors	Active Priests
The issuance of *Humanae Vitae* was a competent and appropriate use of Papal teaching authority	72	36	42	37
In issuing *Humanae Vitae* the Pope acted within his authority to teach, but the encyclical was issued at an inappropriate time	14	18	22	19
The Pope is competent to teach concrete directives of the natural law as he did in *Humanae Vitae,* but *Humanae Vitae* was a misuse of that authority because he failed to act with sufficient collegiality	9	33	25	28
The Pope is incompetent to use his teaching authority in this way because he cannot *impose* concrete universal directives of the natural law	2	9	7	10
Other	3	4	4	6
Total	100	100	100	100

The younger priests are more likely than the older priests to disapprove of *Humanae Vitae* (Table 6.24). Thus, 64 per cent of those thirty-five and under and 49 per cent of those between thirty-six and forty-five think it was either a misuse of authority or an exercise of authority that the Pope did not possess; compared to 32 per cent of those between forty-six and fifty-five and 16 per cent of those over fifty-five. Even the priests over fifty-five are somewhat less likely than the bishops to agree that the encyclical was both competent and appropriate (65 per cent compared to 72 per cent). The American clergy, then, insofar as they are represented by our sample, have not only become more "liberal" on the matter of birth control since the issuance of the encyclical, but only a minority are willing to accept the encyclical as a competent and appropriate use of the teaching authority of the papacy.

TABLE 6.24

ATTITUDE TOWARD *HUMANAE VITAE*, BY AGE
(Per Cent of Active Diocesan and Religious Priests)

Item	Age			
	26-35	36-45	46-55	Over 55
The issuance of *Humanae Vitae* was a competent and appropriate use of Papal teaching authority	14	23	43	65
In issuing *Humanae Vitae* the Pope acted within his authority to teach, but the encyclical was issued at an inappropriate time	16	21	20	17
The Pope is competent to teach concrete directives of the natural law as he did in *Humanae Vitae*, but *Humanae Vitae* was a misuse of that authority because he failed to act with sufficient collegiality	47	38	25	13
The Pope is incompetent to use his teaching authority in this way because he cannot *impose* concrete universal directives of the natural law	17	11	7	3
Other	6	7	5	1
Total	100	100	100	99[a]

[a] Not 100 per cent because of rounding.

There is also no longer majority support for the official teaching on divorce (Table 6.25). Only 40 per cent of the active diocesan priests and 42 per cent of the active religious priests are willing to exclude all possibility of divorce. About 30 per cent of the active priests are willing to grant divorce even if the cases where it might be appropriate would turn out to be numerous. On the other hand, 82 per cent of the bishops (and 53 per cent of the major superiors) support the "traditional" position, and only 3 per cent are willing to contemplate the possibility of numerous cases of divorce. Turning to divorce attitudes by age (Table 6.26), 45 per cent of the active priests under thirty-six, 37 per cent of the group between thirty-six and forty-five, 25 per cent of those between forty-six and fifty-five, and 12 per cent of those over fifty-five are willing to permit divorces in cases that might turn out to be frequent. The older clergy are again somewhat more sympathetic than the bishops to the "liberal" position and somewhat less likely to endorse the most "traditional" statements of the old position.

TABLE 6.25

ATTITUDES ON DIVORCE, BY CLERICAL STATUS

(Per Cent)

Attitude	Diocesan			Religious		
	Bishops	Active Priests	Resigned Priests	Major Superiors	Active Priests	Resigned Priests
Divorce with freedom to remarry in the case of a marriage *ratum et consummatum* is forbidden by divine law and can never be permitted by the Church	58	32	2	41	33	3
Divorce with the freedom to remarry in the case of *ratum et consummatum* marriages should continue to be forbidden by the Church *without exception*, but this is not clearly a matter of divine law	24	8	1	12	9	1
In some few extreme cases, divorce with freedom to remarry can and should be granted even though the marriage is *ratum et consummatum*	12	26	10	20	23	9
Divorce with freedom to remarry should be granted even in *ratum et consummatum* marriages if a divorce would alleviate a situation obviously damaging to the couple and their children (if any), and this even if such cases were to be fairly numerous	3	29	79	22	30	79
Other	3	5	8	5	5	8
Total	100	100	100	100	100	100

TABLE 6.26

ATTITUDES ON DIVORCE, BY AGE
(Per Cent of Active Diocesan and Religious Priests)

Attitude	Age			
	26-35	36-45	46-55	Over 55
Divorce with freedom to remarry in the case of a marriage *ratum et consummatum* is forbidden by divine law and can never be permitted by the Church	14	22	38	55
Divorce with the freedom to remarry in the case of *ratum et consummatum* marriages should continue to be forbidden by the Church *without exception,* but this is not clearly a matter of divine law	5	8	10	11
In some few extreme cases, divorce with freedom to remarry can and should be granted even though the marriage is *ratum et consummatum*	29	28	23	19
Divorce with freedom to remarry should be granted even in *ratum et consummatum* marriages if a divorce would alleviate a situation obviously damaging to the couple and their children (if any), and this even if such cases were to be fairly numerous	45	37	25	12
Other	7	5	4	3
Total	100	100	100	100

If there have been considerable departures from the "traditional" teaching of the Church on matters of birth control and divorce, however, there do not seem to be such changes on the question of abortion (Table 6.27). Only approximately 10 per cent of the active priests think that abortion may be morally permissible in certain cases, though 40 per cent more are at least willing to permit investigation of the issue. (But only 24 per cent of the bishops are in favor of such investigation.) Furthermore, Table 6.28 shows that the younger priests are not much more in sympathy with abortion than are the older priests: only 14 per cent of those thirty-five and under think that abortion may in some cases be morally permissible. However, the young are somewhat more likely to want to see the issue investigated (56 per cent). It is worth noting in

Table 6.27, incidentally, that only 23 per cent of the resignees approve of abortion.

It can be said, in summarizing the data on attitudes toward sexual morality, that the overwhelming majority of the clergy still support the Church's teaching on premarital sex and abortion, but that substantial segments no longer support the official teaching on birth control and divorce.

Attitudes toward Ecumenism and Social Problems

The final two sets of attitudes to be considered in this chapter are concerned with ecumenism and social problems. The most striking finding in Table 6.29 is that bishops are more likely than other priests to attend ecumenical gatherings, to have social and work contact with Protestant and Jewish clergy, and to be strongly committed to ecumenism. The pattern of response may have something to do with the fact that a bishop, as head of a diocese, is in a position to associate with non-Catholic clergy on many civic and ceremonial projects and events that are not part of the life of the ordinary priest. Only a bare majority of diocesan priests (53 per cent) attend ecumenical gatherings several times a year or more, 49 per cent have social contact with Protestant clergy, and 60 per cent report working with Protestant clergy several times a year or more. Only 34 per cent describe themselves as strongly committed to ecumenism.

There is more ecumenical participation, more social and work contact with Protestant clergy, and more commitment to ecumenism among the younger clergy than among the older (Table 6.30). Nevertheless, bishops are more likely to engage in ecumenical contact and to be strongly committed to ecumenism than are even the youngest clergy in the sample. For reasons of structure or obligation or conviction, it would appear that ecumenism is higher on the bishops' lists of priorities than it is on those of the younger clergy.

One should perhaps note in passing the rather small amount of contact between the Catholic clergy and Jewish rabbis. This may very well be explained by the fact that the Jewish population in the country tends to be concentrated in a few large cities, whereas the Catholic population and the Catholic clergy are more widely dispersed. Many priests may be in parishes and cities where there simply is no Jewish rabbi available for social contact or work cooperation.

The bishops are not only more committed to ecumenism, they are also more likely to take a "liberal" stand on matters of race and welfare policy

TABLE 6.27

ATTITUDES ON ABORTION, BY CLERICAL STATUS

(Per Cent)

Attitude	Diocesan			Religious		
	Bishops	Active Priests	Resigned Priests	Major Superiors	Active Priests	Resigned Priests
There is no need of theological development in the direction of change in the Church's teaching, since direct abortion is always wrong	73	49	10	42	46	10
The Church has to allow open investigation of the issue, not only on moral, but also on medical and social grounds	24	40	58	43	40	55
In certain well-defined circumstances, especially when the mother's life is endangered, direct abortion can be morally permissible	2	9	23	10	12	23
Other	1	2	9	5	2	11
Total	100	100	100	100	100	99[a]

[a] Not 100 per cent because of rounding.

TABLE 6.28

ATTITUDES ON ABORTION, BY AGE

(Per Cent of Active Diocesan and Religious Priests)

Attitude	Age			
	26-35	36-45	46-55	Over 55
There is no need of theological development in the direction of change in the Church's teaching, since direct abortion is always wrong	27	37	52	71
The Church has to allow open investigation of the issue, not only on moral, but also on medical and social grounds	56	51	37	18
In certain well-defined circumstances, especially when the mother's life is endangered, direct abortion can be morally permissible	14	10	10	9
Other	3	2	1	2
Total	100	100	100	100

TABLE 6.29

ECUMENISM BY CLERICAL STATUS

(Per Cent)

Item	Diocesan		Religious	
	Bishops	Active Priests	Major Superiors	Active Priests
Took part in ecumenical gatherings several times a year or more during past year	79	53	39	35
Had social contact with Protestant clergy several times or more during past year	58	49	35	42
Had social contact with rabbis several times or more during past year	34	11	10	11
Worked with Protestant clergy several times or more during past year	84	60	34	37
Worked with rabbis several times or more during past year	62	18	9	13
Strongly committed to the goals of the movement toward Christian unity	56	34	30	31

TABLE 6.30

ECUMENISM BY AGE
(Per Cent of Active Diocesan and Religious Priests)

Item	Age			
	26-35	36-45	46-55	Over 55
Took part in ecumenical gatherings several times or more during past year	54	48	44	35
Had social contact with Protestant clergy several times or more during past year	51	49	47	36
Had social contact with rabbis several times or more during past year	7	12	14	9
Worked with Protestant clergy several times or more during past year	55	53	51	40
Worked with rabbis several times or more during past year	13	18	20	13
Strongly committed to the goals of the movement toward Christian unity	44	35	27	25

(Table 6.31). Thus, 68 per cent of the bishops, as opposed to 52 per cent of the active diocesan priests, are willing to endorse the guaranteed annual wage; and 67 per cent of the bishops, as opposed to 55 per cent of the priests, think that urban riots are understandable in the light of the slow progress toward equality for American Negroes. On both these issues the opinion of the bishops is much closer to that of the resignees than it is to the active priests. And on the matter of guaranteed annual wage, the bishops are even more likely than the younger clergy to endorse the "liberal" position and only slightly less likely to understand urban riots (Table 6.32).

One item on each of these two sets of questions was designed to tap a "radical" position, advocating on the one hand the elimination of the capitalist system, and on the other hand, a revolutionary posture for American blacks. Only 2 per cent of the bishops, about 7 per cent of the active clergy, approximately 16 per cent of the resignees, and 12 per cent of those under thirty-six take a "radical" position on the need to overthrow capitalism. Four per cent of the bishops, approximately 11 per cent of the active priests, about 19 per cent of the resignees, and 17 per cent of those under thirty-six take a "radical" position on race.

Sister Marie Augusta Neal, S.N.D., of Emmanuel College, Boston, has made available to us data on the response to these two questions of a

TABLE 6.31

SOCIAL ATTITUDES BY CLERICAL STATUS

(Per Cent)

Attitude	Diocesan			Religious			Catholic Adults[a]
	Bishops	Active Priests	Resigned Priests	Major Superiors	Active Priests	Resigned Priests	
Opinion on a guaranteed annual income for poor families:							
It is a good way to make some progress in dealing with the problem of poverty	68	52	69	65	54	64	28
It is not a good idea, for it would encourage people who would otherwise work for a living to do less work or none at all, and simply rely on other people's money to support them	30	42	16	29	38	19	62
It is simply a surface reform, since poverty stems from the nature of the capitalistic system itself. The only way to wipe out poverty really is to get rid of capitalism and replace it with some other economic system	2	6	15	6	8	17	10
Total	100	100	100	100	100	100	100

TABLE 6.31—Continued

Attitude	Diocesan			Religious			Catholic Adults[a]
	Bishops	Active Priests	Resigned Priests	Major Superiors	Active Priests	Resigned Priests	
Opinion of riots by urban Negroes:							
They are understandable in the light of very slow progress of the movement to provide Negro Americans with equality	67	55	71	70	62	69	35
They constitute a revolutionary response that is right, given the current condition of Negroes in American society	4	12	21	11	10	17	12
They are wrong. Negroes who riot are going too far. Law and order must be preserved	29	33	8	19	28	14	53
Total	100	100	100	100	100	100	100

[a] Based on data made available to us by Sister Marie Augusta Neal, S.N.D.

non-random sample of 898 Catholic adults.[3] As we can see in Table 6.31, all groups of the clergy are more likely than the laity to endorse the "liberal" position. Indeed, the bishops are 40 percentage points more likely to approve the guaranteed annual wage than are the laity and 32 percentage points more likely to be understanding on the subject of urban riots. Data on a religious community of women (not presented in the tables) indicate that their responses are roughly comparable to those of the clergy.

A number of comments on Tables 6.31 and 6.32 are in order. First of all, they reveal a good deal more social liberalism and even radicalism than one can reasonably expect to find in the American Catholic population, or even in the American population in general. There is among the American clergy a long tradition of social concern. Grounded in the social encyclicals of the Popes, reinforced by social statements of the American hierarchy, and insisted upon in the repeated pronouncements of national social action leaders such as the late Monsignor John Ryan and the presently active Monsignor George Higgins, the "liberalism" depicted in Tables 6.31 and 6.32 corresponds to a concern that has been part of the historic tradition of American Catholicism for the last seventy years.

This tradition may also explain the more "liberal" position of those in the present hierarchy. Their predecessors were involved in developing the tradition, sponsored the Social Action Department of the National Catholic Welfare Conference and now the U.S. Catholic Conference, and have supported the work of men such as Ryan and Higgins. It may also be that in their position as heads of dioceses, the bishops are more likely to see the implications of social problems in the needs of deprived peoples with whom the ordinary priest does not normally come in contact. These explanations are, of course, sheer speculation, but the fact does remain that insofar as our measures tap social action attitudes, bishops do display more sympathy for the guaranteed annual wage and for the Negro riots than do typical American Catholic clergymen.

We turn now as usual to a set of questions as a means of summarizing this chapter:

1. *Are the clergy turning away from orthodox Catholicism?* There is little evidence that doctrinal orthodoxy is being abandoned by priests, though some formulations are less enthusiastically endorsed by the younger clergy. What seems to be happening, rather, is a turn toward new emphases, with the traditional ones being maintained, though to a lesser extent among the younger clergy.

2. *Is there a perception of confusion and uncertainty within the*

TABLE 6.32

SOCIAL ATTITUDES BY AGE
(Per Cent of Active Diocesan and Religious Priests)

Attitude	Age			
	26-35	36-45	46-55	Over 55
Opinion on a guaranteed annual income for poor families:				
It is a good way to make some progress in dealing with the problem of poverty	60	55	52	44
It is not a good idea, for it would encourage people who would otherwise work for a living to do less or none at all, and simply rely on other people's money to support them	28	36	42	53
It is simply a surface reform, since poverty stems from the nature of the capitalistic system itself. The only way to wipe out poverty really is to get rid of capitalism and replace it with some other economic system	12	9	6	3
Total	100	100	100	100
Opinion of riots by urban Negroes:				
They are understandable in the light of very slow progress of the movement to provide Negro Americans with equality	70	65	57	43
They constitute a revolutionary response that is right given the current condition of Negroes in American society	17	13	8	6
They are wrong. Negroes who riot are going too far. Law and order must be preserved	13	22	35	51
Total	100	100	100	100

Church? There is some feeling of confusion and uncertainty — perceived more by the bishops than by the clergy. But it would not be appropriate to say that anomie is seen as being widespread in the Church.

3. *Is support for the Church's position on sexual morality deteriorating?* There seems little reason to doubt that support among the clergy for the Church's teaching on birth control and divorce is waning. The change in birth control attitudes can be documented by our data, and the position on divorce is remarkably different from the traditional one.

On the other hand, there is little evidence of a change in position on either premarital sex or abortion, though the younger clergy are somewhat more sympathetic to premarital sex and a substantial segment of priests think that the abortion issue ought to be carefully investigated.

4. *Did the encyclical letter* Humanae Vitae *obtain the consent of the majority of the American priests?* The overwhelming evidence is that it did not.

5. *Are bishops more "conservative" than their priests?* Insofar as the labels "conservative" and "liberal" have any meaning at all, we can say that on matters of religious attitudes and sexual morality, bishops tend to be even more "conservative" than the clergy over fifty-five, while on matters of ecumenism and social action, bishops tend to be even more "liberal" than the clergy under thirty-six.

Analysis

The various attitudinal items were combined into seven indices, the components of which are described in Appendix C. Table 6.33 presents the relations of these indices with the prior variables in our causal model. The "modern-church" index is composed of items indicating a "modern" attitude toward matters of church, theology, and religion, and positive correlations with the "modern-church" and "modern-priest" indices indicate a high score on the modernity dimension. Positive correlations with the anomie, sexual morality, and acceptance of *Humanae Vitae* indices (the last of which is an item rather than an index) indicate, respectively, a high anomie score, departure from traditional sexual morality, and a positive response to the birth control encyclical. Positive scores on the social problems and ecumenical indices indicate "liberal" positions on social problems and ecumenism.

We observe in Table 6.33 that younger priests are substantially more likely to endorse "modern" values and less likely to accept traditional sexual morality. Younger priests are also less inclined to support *Humanae Vitae*. Finally, they are "liberal" on social and ecumenical issues. Those from more tense family backgrounds are also more likely to be "modern" in their religious and moral attitudes, perhaps because a tense family situation has disposed them to be ready to take issue with traditional positions. A higher score on the "inner-directed" personality scale predicts both "modern" religious values and "liberal" sexual attitudes and also, though not as strongly, "liberal" social and ecumenical positions. Finally, those with less religious experience are somewhat

TABLE 6.33

CORRELATES OF RELIGIOUS ATTITUDE INDICES

(Pearson r)

Variable	Modern Priest	Modern Church	Anomie	Sexual Morality	*Humanae Vitae*	Social Problems	Ecumenism
Age	-.55	-.63	.46	-.51	.43	-.37	-.16
Family tension	.24	.21	-.11	.22	-.20	.17	.02
Inner-directed	.41	.46	-.39	.43	-.35	.36	.24
Religious experience	-.19	-.13	-.02	-.16	.14	-.09	.08

more likely to hold "modern" values and to disagree with the traditional position on sexual morality.

In other words, the young, those from tense families, the "inner-directed," and those with less religious experience are the priests most likely to disagree with traditional religious formulations and to reject official positions on sexual morality.

We observe that there is a very high level of intercorrelation among all seven indices (Table 6.34). Since they tend to correlate with one another and with the same prior variables, we decided to select one, the "modern-church" index, for inclusion in our causal model. (We shall henceforth refer to it as "modern" values.) This index was chosen in part because it had high relationships with subsequent variables and in part because one's attitude on God, religion, and Church can easily be conceptualized and is logically prior to one's attitudes on the priesthood, sexual morality, social problems, and ecumenism.

We can explain 49 per cent of the variance in "modern" values about the Church (Table 6.35). The principal explanatory component, as one might well imagine, is age: 40 per cent of the variance is explained by age, 1 per cent by family tension, 7 per cent by the score on the "inner-directed" scale, and 1 per cent by religious experience. The standardized regression weights (*betas*) in Figure 6.1 indicate how the influence of age is exercised on "modern" values. The direct path between the two is $-.50$; and the indirect path through "inner-directedness" is $(-.34 \times .29) = -.10$. Thus, the younger priests are likely to have more "modern" values both because they are younger and because they are more inner-directed.

To summarize the analytic section of this chapter:

1. *Is there a generation gap among the clergy?* If by generation gap one means a clean break that divides the clergy into two separate groups, there is no such gap. What we find, rather, is a generation "slope" with each ten-year age category being more "modern" in its religious attitudes and more "liberal" in its sexual morality than its immediate elders. If one just compares those under thirty-six with those over fifty-five, there is obviously a gap and not a slope, but the priesthood as it exists in reality is not made up of just these two groups.[4]

2. *Is age by itself the main cause of attitudinal differences among the clergy?* We are not able to explain variation on the "modern" values index by demographic, educational, or socioeconomic backgrounds. Hence, insofar as our measures allow us to find other explanations besides age, we must say that age seems to be the principal cause of differing attitudes.

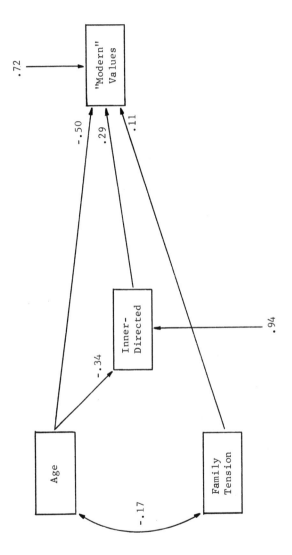

NOTE: All paths with coefficients less than .09 and all variables without significant paths have been omitted from this figure.

Fig. 6.1.—Path diagram relating "modern" values to prior variables. Active priests only.

TABLE 6.34

INTERCORRELATIONS OF RELIGIOUS ATTITUDE INDICES

(Pearson *r*)

Variable	Modern Priest	Modern Church	Anomie	Sexual Morality	*Humanae Vitae*	Social Problems	Ecumenism
Modern priest	—	.80	−.58	.79	−.70	.58	.27
Modern church	—	—	−.68	.74	−.68	.62	.31
Anomie	—	—	—	−.54	.49	−.48	−.29
Sexual morality	—	—	—	—	−.75	.53	.27
Humanae Vitae	—	—	—	—	—	−.49	−.24
Social problems	—	—	—	—	—	—	.24
Ecumenism	—	—	—	—	—	—	—

TABLE 6.35
EXPLANATION OF VARIANCE ON "MODERN" VALUES INDEX

Variable	R^2	R^2 Change
Age	.40	.40
Family tension	.41	.01
Inner-directed	.48	.07
Religious experience	.49	.01

Some explanation can be found in the greater tendency to "inner-directedness" among the young but the direct path between age and "modern" values is —.50, while the indirect path through "inner-directedness" is only —.10. Whether the more conservative attitudes of older priests result from growing old biologically or from different kinds of cultural and generational experiences is not a question that we can answer with certainty from our data. However, if the former explanation is the case, one would then predict that as they grow older, the young clergy will assume the same attitudes that the old have now. As this seems rather unlikely, the second explanation may well be preferable.

1. We use the word "liberal" in this context for lack of a better word. It is used to denote a position that is to some lesser or greater extent deviant from the "traditional" teachings of Catholic morality. Its use should not be interpreted as an approval by the NORC study of the moral position represented. Much less should it be interpreted as an argument in favor of a modification of the Church's official position.

2. It is perhaps appropriate to note that NORC herein makes no judgment on the correctness or the wisdom of the issuance of the encyclical, but merely reports factual data describing the reactions of the Catholic clergy to that encyclical.

3. We are grateful to Sister Neal for making these data available to us.

4. Much of the talk that one hears today about a "generation gap" is not documented by research data. The work of our colleagues Joe L. Spaeth, John Johnstone, and William McCready at NORC, and the repeated studies of young people by the Survey Research Center, University of Michigan, find little evidence of such a gap. The much publicized "youth culture" is, in fact, a very tiny proportion of even the college-educated population. The generation "slope" found in our study of the priesthood is thus an exception to the general tendency of survey findings. However, it must be noted that "young" as it is used in the present report does not mean quite the same thing as "young" does in the field of "youth" studies. Half of our "youngest" group of clergy are over thirty.

Those who argue for a "generation gap" by comparing the youngest and the oldest clergy not only commit the fallacy of ignoring the middle groups, they also overlook the fact that some of the older clergy have "young" values and some of the young clergy have "old" values.

CHAPTER 7

STRUCTURE AND POWER IN THE LIFE OF A PRIEST

The Roman Catholic Church has traditionally been an organization with both a firm institutional structure and strong concentration of power in the hands of the Pope and the bishops. Considerable discussion has occurred in the wake of the Second Vatican Council on the feasibility and desirability of modifying both the shape of ecclesiastical structures and the distribution of power in the Church. In the present chapter we attempt to assess the opinion of the American Catholic clergy on the organizational structure and the distribution of power in the Church and to discover what background factors, if any, affect the attitude of the clergy on questions of ecclesiastical power.

Description

In the descriptive section of this chapter, the following six findings are reported:

1. There is substantial agreement among the clergy on the actual distribution of power in the Church.

2. There is substantial agreement among the clergy on the need for a greater distribution of power in theory to groups that are now perceived as not having much power.

3. There is substantial agreement among all groups of clergy on the need for a strong bishop.

4. But there is widespread disagreement between priests and bishops about the distribution of power to make specific decisions on matters of both ecclesiastical administration and liturgical practice.

5. There is also great disagreement between priests and bishops on the helpfulness of certain frequently discussed structural reforms of the Church.

6. There is considerable tendency among the clergy to violate those regulations that are felt to be inappropriate.

There is relatively little disagreement among bishops, active priests, and major superiors about the actual distribution of power in a Roman Catholic diocese (Table 7.1). When asked how much influence certain persons or groups have in determining policies and actions in the diocese, 99 per cent of the bishops, 96 per cent of the diocesan priests, 96 per cent of the major superiors, and 95 per cent of the religious priests thought that the bishop has "a very great deal" or "a great deal" of power. The only other persons whom a majority of the respondents consider to have this much power are chancery officials. About one-fifth of the priests think of auxiliary bishops as having a great deal of power, and a slightly smaller proportion consider pastors to have such power. Very few of the respondents think of deans, other priests, or laity as having considerable power.

While the bishops realize that they have a great deal of power, they are also more likely than priests to think that others have power. For example, more bishops than priests see the auxiliary bishops, deans or vicars, and even pastors, other priests, and laity as having "a very great deal" or "a great deal" of power. The most striking difference, however, is that half the bishops see the priests' senate as having power, while only about one-fifth of the priests see the senate as powerful. To sum

TABLE 7.1

ACTUAL DISTRIBUTION OF POWER IN DIOCESE,
BY CLERICAL STATUS

(Per Cent Thinking Each Group Has "A Very Great Deal" or "A Great Deal"
of Influence in Determining Policies and Actions in the Diocese)

Group	Diocesan		Religious	
	Bishops	Active Priests	Major Superiors	Active Priests
Bishop	99	96	96	95
Auxiliary bishops	28	19	17	23
Chancery officials	57	50	58	56
Deans or vicars	16	7	11	14
Priests' senate	50	23	26	19
Pastors	28	16	16	22
Other priests	13	4	2	5
Laity	13	4	4	4

up the data in Table 7.1, the American clergy is pretty well agreed that the principal loci of power are the bishop and the chancery office and that there is relatively little power elsewhere, though the bishops are somewhat more likely to think that others also have power. (Perhaps no man is quite convinced that he has as much power as others think he has; he thinks he can see limitations on his own exercise of authority that others cannot see.) The most striking difference of opinion between priests and bishops is that far more bishops are likely to think of the priests' senate as powerful.

Nor is there much disagreement among the various age groups of the clergy about the *de facto* distribution of power (Table 7.2). The older clergy are somewhat less likely to think that the chancery and pastors have power, but no age group doubts that the bishop has a great deal of power and that non-pastoral priests and laity do not.

There is, however, considerable sentiment in the hierarchy for a redistribution of power. We see in Table 7.3 that considerably more bishops say that auxiliary bishops, deans, and lay people *should* have power than are willing to say that these groups in fact *do* have power. As a matter of fact, for a number of the groups the proportions wanting to see them have a great deal of power do not differ notably between priests and bishops. Approximately the same proportions of the hierarchy and the diocesan clergy think that the bishops, auxiliary bishops, pastors,

TABLE 7.2

ACTUAL DISTRIBUTION OF POWER IN DIOCESE, BY AGE

(Per Cent of Active Diocesan and Religious Priests Thinking Each Group Has "A Very Great Deal" or "A Great Deal" of Influence in Determining Policies and Actions in the Diocese)

Group	Age			
	26-35	36-45	46-55	Over 55
Bishop	95	95	96	95
Auxiliary bishops	22	19	20	23
Chancery officials	62	52	52	46
Deans or vicars	11	7	9	12
Priests' senate	20	20	23	23
Pastors	27	22	14	12
Other priests	5	5	4	3
Laity	3	3	5	4

TABLE 7.3

IDEAL DISTRIBUTION OF POWER IN DIOCESE,
BY CLERICAL STATUS

(Per Cent Thinking Each Group *Should* Have "A Very Great Deal" or "A Great
Deal" of Influence in Determining Policies and Actions in the Diocese)

Group	Diocesan		Religious	
	Bishops	Active Priests	Major Superiors	Active Priests
Bishop	96	90	96	88
Auxiliary bishops	49	42	54	45
Chancery officials	63	32	36	37
Deans or vicars	38	26	27	26
Priests' senate	53	61	61	65
Pastors	37	34	32	34
Other priests	23	24	18	23
Laity	32	34	38	38

other priests, and laity should have a great deal of power (nine-tenths, two-fifths, one-third, one-quarter, and one-third, respectively). Bishops are more likely than their priests to endorse greater influence in decision-making for chancery officials and deans. On the other hand, priests are more likely than bishops to want to see a great deal of power in the hands of the priests' senate (61 per cent versus 53 per cent). But interestingly enough, this 53 per cent of the bishops is approximately the same as the proportion of bishops who believe that the priests' senate actually *already has* a great deal of power. The situation, thus, is extremely interesting, for one-fifth of the priests think the priests' senate has a great deal of power at the present time while three-fifths think that it should have a great deal of power. There is, then, a strong sentiment in the clergy for increasing the power of the priests' senate. On the other hand, approximately half the bishops think both that the priests' senate *has* a great deal of power and that it *should* have a great deal of power. Apparently there is not strong sentiment among bishops for increasing the level of influence of the priests' senate. In other words, the institutional change to redistribute power that the priests are most likely to want is the one the bishops are least likely to support.

It should be noted, however, that no case can be made from the data in Table 7.3 for the proposition that priests wish to strip powers from the bishops, for nine-tenths of the priests in the sample think that bishops should have "a very great deal" or "a great deal" of power. Instead of wanting to cut up in a different way a limited power pie, the clergy apparently believe in the possibility of making a bigger pie in which more groups can have a great deal of power than is possible in the present ecclesiastical structure.

There are not very many dissimilarities among active diocesan priests, active religious priests, and major superiors. However, the major superiors are a little less likely to want to see the non-pastoral clergy have a great deal of power and a little more likely to want to see auxiliary bishops have power.

Despite the fact that there is little disagreement among the different age groups of the clergy about where ecclesiastical power actually is, there is, nonetheless, substantial disagreement about where it *ought* to be (Table 7.4). While the older priests are not much more likely than the younger to endorse the notion of great power and influence for the bishop and for the chancery officials, the younger priests are more likely to emphasize power for priests' senates, pastors, other priests, and laity. But enthusiasm for the priests' senate is high even among priests over fifty-five, with 42 per cent of them saying that the priests' senate ought to have a great deal of power. (While 91 per cent of them say that the bishop ought to have a great deal of power, 43 per cent say that the

TABLE 7.4

IDEAL DISTRIBUTION OF POWER IN DIOCESE, BY AGE

(Per Cent of Active Diocesan and Religious Priests Thinking Each Group
Should Have "A Very Great Deal" or "A Great Deal" of Influence
in Determining Policies and Actions in the Diocese)

Group	Age			
	26-35	36-45	46-55	Over 55
Bishop	85	88	91	91
Auxiliary bishops	42	42	47	43
Chancery officials	29	34	36	39
Deans or vicars	25	27	26	24
Priests' senate	80	71	57	42
Pastors	39	36	34	26
Other priests	38	28	20	8
Laity	60	44	28	14

auxiliary bishop ought to and 39 per cent say the chancery office ought to.) Similarly, the priests' senate is the second most popular locus of power after the bishop in the minds of priests of all ages. One can conclude from the first four tables of this chapter that the priests' senate is likely to be the subject of controversy and conflict in the Roman Catholic Church in the years to come.

Just as there is agreement among priests about the distribution of power in the Church, so there is considerable agreement about who has the influence on specific decisions. Of the eight decisions considered in Table 7.5 — home Mass, assignment of priests, clerical living quarters, expenditure of funds, appointment of pastors, establishment of new parishes, construction of parish facilities, and retirement of pastors — in general 70 per cent or more of the respondents agree that the bishop or the chancery office does indeed have the authority to make the decisions. The proportions in agreement on the nature of decision-making decline below 70 per cent only on the subject of home Mass, where 59 per cent of the bishops and 65 per cent of the priests think that the bishop or the chancery have the decision-making power, and on the subjects of assigning priests and authorizing expenditures, where approximately 66 per

TABLE 7.5

ACTUAL CENTRALIZATION OF AUTHORITY, BY CLERICAL STATUS

(Per Cent Saying Bishop or Chancery Has the Authority or the Most
Influence in Making Each Type of Decision)

Decision	Diocesan		Religious	
	Bishops	Active Priests	Major Supe- riors	Active Priests
Authorize Mass in homes or apartments	59	65	75	65
Determine where a priest is assigned	67	72	76	85
Determine where a priest has his living quarters	82	76	82	73
Authorize an expenditure of more than $500 from parish funds	66	70	85	71
Appoint pastors	86	88	91	94
Establish new parishes	86	97	97	98
Authorize construction	88	95	97	94
Retire pastors	80	89	92	92

cent of the bishops think that they or the chancery have the most influence in decision-making.

There are a number of other items — the appointment of pastors, the establishment of new parishes, the authorization of construction, and the retirement of pastors — where bishops are a little less likely than priests to think of themselves or the chancery as having the most influence in making decisions. Nonetheless, the overwhelming majority of bishops do think that they have the most influence in these areas. On determining clerical living quarters, bishops are more likely than diocesan priests to think of themselves as having great influence.

Interestingly enough, the major superiors are the most likely of all to see the bishop or chancery as the primary decision-maker, a phenomenon that may well be a function of the special kind of relationship that exists in a diocese between major superiors and bishops, with the former having obligations both to the bishops and to their own religious communities, which transcend diocesan boundaries.

There is also considerable agreement among age groups on who has the principal influence on decision-making in specific matters. On the last four items in Table 7.6 there is little difference between the youngest priests and the oldest priests in the unanimity with which they assign decision-making influence to the bishops or chancery. However, on the

TABLE 7.6

ACTUAL CENTRALIZATION OF AUTHORITY, BY AGE

(Per Cent of Active Diocesan and Religious Priests Saying Bishop
or Chancery Has the Authority or the Most Influence
in Making Each Type of Decision)

Decision	Age			
	26-35	36-45	46-55	Over 55
Authorize Mass in homes or apartments	47	62	71	77
Determine where a priest is assigned	70	75	79	84
Determine where a priest has his living quarters	70	73	76	79
Authorize an expenditure of more than $500 from parish funds	60	67	75	80
Appoint pastors	88	90	90	94
Establish new parishes	97	97	97	98
Authorize construction	95	94	95	94
Retire pastors	89	90	90	91

first three items — authorization of Mass in homes, determination of where a priest is assigned, and determination of living quarters of a priest — the older clergy are somewhat more likely to see the bishop and his chancery as the principal decision-makers. Only on the subject of home Masses and only among the clergy thirty-five and under do less than a majority (47 per cent) say that the bishop or the chancery has the most influence in decision-making.

Furthermore, the hierarchy apparently does not see the need for a change in the present decision-making patterns, even though, as we noted earlier, there is some tendency for bishops to endorse wider distribution of power in theory. Table 7.7 presents little evidence to indicate that bishops think a change needs to be made in the present decision-making processes on the specific issues represented in the table. There is little difference between the first column in Table 7.5 and the first column in Table 7.7. The overwhelming majority of the hierarchy, then, are endorsing a position which asserts that they or their chancery offices have the most influence in making these specific decisions and that they should continue to have the most influence in making these decisions.

TABLE 7.7

IDEAL CENTRALIZATION OF AUTHORITY, BY CLERICAL STATUS

(Per Cent Thinking Bishop or Chancery *Ought* To Have the
Authority To Make Each Type of Decision)

Decision	Diocesan		Religious	
	Bishops	Active Priests	Major Superiors	Active Priests
Authorize Mass in homes or apartments	53	29	24	24
Determine where a priest is assigned	67	41	56	44
Determine where a priest has his living quarters	73	36	44	31
Authorize an expenditure of more than $500 from parish funds	59	32	35	33
Appoint pastors	84	51	69	53
Establish new parishes	83	62	71	64
Authorize construction	80	60	66	58
Retire pastors	73	47	64	51

Priests, on the other hand, strongly indicate that they believe change is in order. If one compares the second column of Table 7.5 with the second column of Table 7.7, one can see a drop of 30 to 40 percentage points from the way active diocesan priests see the decisions actually being made to the way they think the decisions ought to be made. Thus, 88 per cent of the active priests see bishops or chancery officials as the principal decision-makers in the appointment of pastors, but only 51 per cent think they ought to be the principal decision-makers; and 97 per cent of the diocesan priests think the bishops or their staffs should be the principal decision-makers on the establishment of new parishes, while 62 per cent think that the bishops or the chancery officials ought to be the principal decision-makers. Furthermore, 72 per cent of the diocesan priests think that bishops or their chanceries have the most influence in deciding where a priest is assigned and 76 per cent think that the bishop or chancery has the most influence in determining where he lives. However, the comparable figures for thinking that this is the way things should be are only 41 per cent on the matter of assignments and only 36 per cent on the matter of living quarters. To put the matter somewhat differently, on the very important questions of where a priest is assigned and where he should live, there is no indication among the bishops of sympathy for a change in the decision-making process, but very strong evidence of a desire among the priests for a change in the process. There is little difference between diocesan and religious priests on the subject of the ideal distribution of decision-making authority in a diocese, though major superiors are somewhat more likely than their colleagues in the religious communities to approve of a strong centralization of decision-making in the hands of the bishop and his chancery.

The demand for decentralization of decision-making power is much stronger among the younger priests than it is among the older priests (Table 7.8). Thus, 69 per cent of priests over fifty-five think that the bishop or the chancery should have the most influence in making the decision on where a priest is assigned, and 63 per cent think that centralization is appropriate in the determination of a priest's living quarters. On the other hand, only 16 per cent and 9 per cent, respectively, of the priests thirty-five and under agree with this centralization of decision-making. Furthermore, 80 per cent of the priests over fifty-five approve of the bishop or the chancery appointing new pastors, but only 24 per cent of those thirty-five and under approve. Nevertheless, priests over fifty-five still show some sympathy for change in decision-making;

TABLE 7.8

IDEAL CENTRALIZATION OF AUTHORITY, BY AGE

(Per Cent of Active Diocesan and Religious Priests Thinking Bishop or
Chancery *Ought* To Have the Authority To Make Each Type of Decision)

Decision	Age			
	26-35	36-45	46-55	Over 55
Authorize Mass in homes or apartments	6	16	31	54
Determine where a priest is assigned	16	30	51	69
Determine where a priest has his living quarters	9	21	43	63
Authorize an expenditure of more than $500 from parish funds	13	22	38	58
Appoint pastors	24	39	62	80
Establish new parishes	45	53	56	83
Authorize construction	44	49	65	79
Retire pastors	28	37	55	74

on each item the proportion who say that the bishop or the chancery
should have the principal decision-making power is smaller than the
proportion who say that the bishop or the chancery actually *does* have
the power. In other words, there is sympathy for change in specific
decision-making at all age levels of the clergy, although the degree of
sympathy varies.

Given the dissatisfaction with the distribution of power and influence
in Roman Catholic dioceses, one might well wonder whether there is a
tendency to break rules and regulations that are deemed unpopular or
inappropriate. Table 7.9 indicates that there is indeed a rather strong
tendency in this direction. Half of the active priests have said Mass in a
home or apartment on their own initiative, although in many dioceses
this decision on one's own initiative is not legal. Even 38 per cent of the
bishops have said Mass in this fashion. Furthermore, 44 per cent of
the diocesan priests and 48 per cent of the religious priests have modified
the rubrics of the Mass to fit the occasion, 33 per cent of the diocesan
and 46 per cent of the religious have said Mass without the proper
vestments, 21 per cent and 24 per cent, respectively, have apparently
violated Rome's clear injunction against giving Communion to non-
Catholics, and 16 per cent of the diocesan priests and 13 per cent of the
religious priests have given the sacraments to people who are in marriages
that the Church deems invalid.

TABLE 7.9

ACTUAL EXERCISE OF PERSONAL INITIATIVE,
BY CLERICAL STATUS

(Per Cent Having Done Each Activity on Their Own Authority)

Activity	Diocesan		Religious	
	Bishops	Active Priests	Major Supe- riors	Active Priests
Said Mass in a home or apartment	38	48	44	50
Notably modified the rubrics to fit the occasion	7	44	42	48
Said Mass without the proper vestments ..	4	33	33	46
Given Communion to non-Catholics	4	21	18	24
Given sacraments to those who are divorced and remarried	2	16	8	13

As might be expected, this exercise of initiative correlates with age (Table 7.10). The majority of priests forty-five and under said Mass in a home, modified rubrics, and said Mass without proper vestments. Forty per cent of those thirty-five and under and 28 per cent of those between thirty-six and forty-five have given Communion to non-Catholics, and 24 per cent of those thirty-five and under and 19 per cent of

TABLE 7.10

ACTUAL EXERCISE OF INITIATIVE, BY AGE

(Per Cent of Active Diocesan and Religious Priests Having Done
Each Activity on Their Own Authority)

Activity	Age			
	26-35	36-45	46-55	Over 55
Said Mass in a home or apartment	75	61	42	20
Notably modified the rubrics to fit the occasion	77	58	34	13
Said Mass without the proper vestments	65	51	28	12
Given Communion to non-Catholics	40	28	15	6
Given sacraments to those who are divorced and remarried	24	19	11	4

those between thirty-six and forty-five have given the sacraments to people in invalid marriages. It is interesting to note that bishops are almost twice as likely (38 per cent compared to 20 per cent) to have said Mass in the home as are priests over fifty-five.

Table 7.11 shows that approximately half the priests in the country think they ought to have the power to modify Mass rubrics or vestments, while about three-quarters think they ought to have the authority to say home Masses. About one-third think they ought to have the power to give Communion to non-Catholics and to Catholics who are in invalid marriages. However, except for saying Mass in a home, only a handful of bishops are willing to endorse such changes. If we compare the first column of Table 7.11 with the first column of Table 7.9, we see that with the exception of the home Mass situation, there is little sympathy among bishops for any change in the regulations regarding the exercise of initiative on these liturgical matters. But if one compares the second column of the two tables, one sees that in each instance more diocesan priests think they should have the power to exercise the initiatives in question than have in fact exercised such initiative. Again, the religious priests are similar to the diocesan priests in their thinking. Even without the power, it is clear that substantial numbers of the clergy are not hesitant about violating clearly specified liturgical regulations.

Finally, it is the younger clergy who are the most likely to think they ought to have the authority to make these liturgical decisions (Table

TABLE 7.11

IDEAL EXERCISE OF INITIATIVE, BY CLERICAL STATUS

(Per Cent Thinking They *Ought* To Have the Authority To Do Each Activity)

Activity	Diocesan		Religious	
	Bishops	Active Priests	Major Supe- riors	Active Priests
Say Mass in a home or apartment	55	78	81	73
Notably modify the rubrics to fit the occasion	8	54	55	56
Say Mass without the proper vestments	6	46	49	54
Give Communion to non-Catholics	3	32	31	35
Give sacraments to those who are divorced and remarried	4	34	24	33

TABLE 7.12

IDEAL EXERCISE OF INITIATIVE, BY AGE

(Per Cent of Active Diocesan and Religious Priests Thinking They
Ought To Have the Authority To Do Each Activity)

Activity	Age			
	26-35	36-45	46-55	Over 55
Say Mass in a home or apartment	94	87	71	53
Notably modify the rubrics to fit the occasion	84	69	45	22
Say Mass without the proper vestments	79	64	38	20
Give Communion to non-Catholics	56	43	25	11
Give sacraments to those who are divorced and remarried	59	43	26	10

7.12). Thus, 94 per cent of priests thirty-five and under and 87 per cent of those between thirty-six and forty-five think they ought to have the power to make these decisions, compared to 53 per cent of those over fifty-five. Furthermore, of those between thirty-six and forty-five, approximately two-thirds think they ought to have authority on modifying both rubrics and vestments and about two-fifths feel they ought to have the authority to give the sacraments both to non-Catholics and to those in invalid marriages. Those thirty-five and under feel more strongly on these matters, while those over fifty do not have much sympathy for change. We have once again a clear pattern: the bishops see no particular need for change, the priests display strong sympathy for change, and the younger priests are the ones most likely to endorse change.

But it is not merely decision-making in dioceses or initiative on liturgical matters that gives rise to differences of opinion between the priests and the hierarchy. There is also very considerable disagreement about what more general reforms would help the Church. Thus the majority of active diocesan priests endorse eight of the twelve possible changes listed in Table 7.13, while the majority of bishops support only three of the changes. The most popular change with the priests and the second most popular with the hierarchy is the institution of the married diaconate, with 86 and 80 per cent, respectively, supporting such an innovation. The next most important change from the priests' viewpoint is the institution of a court of appeals distinct from the hierarchy. But while 78 per cent of the diocesan clergy recommend this as a helpful change for the Church, only 58 per cent of the bishops support it.

TABLE 7.13

REFORMS IN THE CHURCH, BY CLERICAL STATUS

(Per Cent Thinking Each Possible Change Would Help
"Very Much" or "Somewhat")

Possible Change	Diocesan		Religious	
	Bishops	Active Priests	Major Superiors	Active Priests
Associate pastors choosing to live where they wish	9	41	25	36
All priests living in community when this is possible	83	57	86	74
A parish lay advisory board having some say in the transfer and selection of priests	21	46	58	56
Wider approval of household ministries, "small group parishes within a parish," and floating parishes	32	64	73	71
Elimination of Catholic school systems	0	20	9	17
Some priests holding secular jobs during the week	16	46	41	48
A court of appeals for all members of the Church distinct from the hierarchy guaranteeing them due process of law	58	78	81	75
Some married priests working in a variety of ministries	39	70	59	69
Election of the Pope by the Synod of Bishops	43	70	72	69
Introduction of the married diaconate whenever and however the local church chooses	80	86	87	86
Election of bishops by the priests of the diocese	24	70	68	74
Election of bishops by the priests, religious, and laity of the diocese	24	65	64	69

Furthermore, 70 per cent of the clergy are in favor of some married priests working in the ministry, election of the Pope by the Synod of Bishops, and election of bishops by priests in their own dioceses. However, comparable figures for the bishops are only 39 per cent, 43 per cent, and 24 per cent. It is worth noting that two-fifths of the bishops favor the election of the Pope by bishops but only one-quarter of them favor the election of bishops by their priests. The most important change from the bishops' viewpoint is priests living in the community when this is possible (83 per cent), though this is much less popular with the priests (57 per cent). In other words, those changes that the majority of priests support are by and large opposed by the majority of bishops (with the exception of the married diaconate and the court of appeals). The single change that a large majority of the bishops endorse — priests living together — arouses considerably less enthusiasm among the clergy.

Turning to those changes that receive less than majority support from the priests, about two-fifths of the diocesan priests are willing to support the notion of associate pastors choosing their own dwelling, of a lay board helping to select priests, and of some priests holding secular jobs. Only one-fifth think the Church would be helped by the closing of parochial schools. (Support for parochial education is very strong among all four groups represented in Table 7.13.)

With the exception of much more enthusiasm for community life, religious priests are in substantial agreement with diocesan priests about which institutional reforms would be most helpful for the Church. When we consider the viewpoints by age in Table 7.14, we see that support for the institutional reforms correlates with age on all items except community life for priests.

We summarize the descriptive section of this chapter by responding to a number of questions:

1. *Do priests want to abolish the institution of a strong bishop?* All the evidence is that they do not. Even the younger priests cast a majority vote for a strong bishop.

2. *Do the clergy want a considerable decentralization of power and decision-making influence in the Church?* There can be very little doubt that they do. Hence, one must conclude that priests view ecclesiastical power as an expandable rather than a fixed pie—giving someone a larger piece does not mean that others must get smaller pieces.

3. *What is the most popular new locus of power?* The priests' senate seems to be the one most frequently mentioned.

4. *What is the bishops' view of the centralization of power?* On a theoretical level, some bishops, who are aware of their own very great power, are apparently willing to agree with decentralization of decision-making. However, on the specific topics considered, there is little change from the proportion describing the actual centralization to the proportion

The Catholic Priest in the United States

TABLE 7.14

REFORMS IN THE CHURCH, BY AGE

(Per Cent of Active Diocesan and Religious Priests Thinking Each
Possible Change Would Help "Very Much" or "Somewhat")

Possible Change	Age			
	26-35	36-45	46-55	Over 55
Associate pastors choosing to live where they wish	65	48	28	15
All priests living in community when this is possible	61	62	63	73
A parish lay advisory board having some say in the transfer and selection of priests	72	63	42	27
Wider approval of household ministries, "small group parishes within a parish," and floating parishes	84	77	55	44
Elimination of Catholic school systems	31	23	14	8
Some priests holding secular jobs during the week	62	51	40	24
A court of appeals for all members of the Church distinct from the hierarchy guaranteeing them due process of law	90	82	74	62
Some married priests working in a variety of ministries	86	76	61	45
Election of the Pope by the Synod of Bishops	88	78	67	48
Introduction of the married diaconate whenever and however the local church chooses	94	88	84	80
Election of bishops by the priests of the diocese	90	80	68	50
Election of bishops by the priests, religious, and laity of the diocese	83	73	60	45

describing what might be an ideal centralization. In practice, then, bishops do not seem to be greatly dissatisfied with the way decisions are made in the Church.

5. *Is there serious conflict potential between bishops and priests?* Given a situation where there is disagreement between leadership and followers on both the practical distribution of power and the helpfulness of structural reform, in which there is in fact a heavy concentration of power in the hands of leadership, and, finally, in which there seems to be a widespread tendency to ignore unpopular regulations, it would be a mistake not to see considerable potential for serious conflict.

6. *Is there any particular institution that might be the subject of conflict?* The priests' senate seems to be a highly controversial institution. Priests think it has little power and ought to have more; bishops as a group seem to think that it has quite enough power.

7. *Is there a tendency for priests to ignore rules they don't like?* At least on liturgical matters, there does seem to be such a tendency.

8. *What reforms in the Church are most popular with priests?* A married diaconate is the change that receives the most support; 70 per cent or more of the priests also favor an impartial system of appeals, some married priests, election of the Pope by bishops, and election of bishops by priests.

9. *Are priests in favor of closing Catholic schools?* They are not. A very large majority do not think this would be a helpful change. Even among the younger clergy, there is majority support for parochial schools.

Analysis

We constructed three indices for use in the analytic section of this chapter: a measure of the experience of power conflict, which was composed of the difference between the way priests see the actual distribution of power in their dioceses and the way they think power ought to be distributed; an index composed of the amount of initiative in liturgical matters that a priest reported; and a "church-reform" index, which was composed of highly intercorrelated answers to what reforms would be most helpful to the Church. (For full details on the construction of these indices, see Appendix C.)

Table 7.15 indicates that all three indices have the same pattern of correlations. Younger priests are more likely to experience power conflict, to act on their own, and to advocate major structural reform in the Church. Those who come from tense family backgrounds are also consistently likely to experience power conflict, to have exercised their own liturgical initiative, and to support church reform. Having a high score on the inner-directed scale is also correlated with all three indices. Religious experience has small negative correlations (−.13) with both the power-conflict and church-reform indices, and an even smaller negative correlation (−.07) with taking the initiative in liturgical matters. Finally, there are very high positive correlations between "modern" religious values and these three indices — .56, .72, and .76, respectively.

Furthermore, all three indices are rather highly intercorrelated (Table 7.16). Those who dislike the distribution of power, who act on their own initiative in liturgical matters, and who want ecclesiastical reform

TABLE 7.15

CORRELATES OF POWER AND STRUCTURE INDICES
(Pearson *r*)

Variable	Power Conflict	Initiative in Liturgical Matters	Church Reform
Age	−.41	−.50	−.52
Family tension	.18	.19	.21
Inner-directed	.27	.41	.38
Religious experience	−.13	−.07	−.13
"Modern" values	.56	.72	.76

are rather likely to be the same people. Therefore, we chose for inclusion in our model one of the three measures — the experience of conflict between the way power is distributed and the way it is felt that it ought to be distributed.

We observe in Table 7.17 that 32 per cent of the variance in the experience of power conflict can be explained by variables prior to it. Age accounts for 17 per cent of the variance, family tension for 1 per cent, inner-directed for 2 per cent, religious experience for 1 per cent, and "modern" values for 11 per cent. Figure 7.1 presents graphically these relationships and demonstrates very clearly how age influences the experience of power conflict. (Family tension and religious experience have been omitted from the figure because of their low correlations with power conflict.) The direct path between age and conflict is only −.10 but the indirect path through "modern" values is $(-.50 \times .47) = -.24$. In other words, the major reason why the young experience power con-

TABLE 7.16

INTERCORRELATIONS OF POWER AND STRUCTURE INDICES
(Pearson *r*)

Variable	Power Conflict	Initiative in Liturgical Matters	Church Reform
Power conflict	—	.48	.57
Initiative in liturgical matters	—	—	.64
Church reform	—	—	—

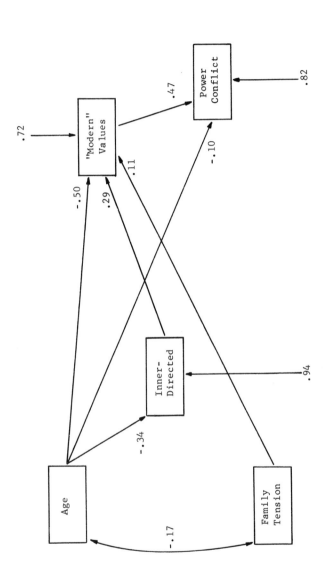

NOTE: All paths with coefficients less than .09 and all variables without significant paths have been omitted from this figure. Active priests only.

Fig. 7.1.—Path diagram relating power conflict to prior variables.

TABLE 7.17

EXPLANATION OF VARIANCE ON POWER-CONFLICT INDEX

Variable	R^2	R^2 Change
Age	.17	.17
Family tension	.18	.01
Inner-directed	.20	.02
Religious experience	.21	.01
"Modern" values	.32	.11

flict in the Church is because their values regarding the Church and religion differ from those of their elders.

Table 7.18 provides another way of viewing this phenomenon. The figures in the first column are the simple correlations presented in Table 7.15. The figures in subsequent columns represent the net coefficients when each new variable is taken into account. Thus, if one reads across the first row of the table, one sees that the relationship between age and the experience of conflict changes from −.41 to −.39 when one takes into account the fact that the young are more likely to come from tense families. There is a further change to −.34 when we consider that the young are also likely to be more inner-directed, a change to −.33 when we allow for the impact of religious experience, and finally a change to −.10 when we take into account the fact that the young have more modern values. Thus, the young experience conflict over the distribution of power not simply because they are young but because they are more likely to come from tense families, to be inner-directed, and especially because they are more likely to have "modern" values. Similarly, the size of the correlation between family tension and power conflict goes from .18 to .05 when we have successively considered that those from tense families are more likely to be younger and to have modern values. (Inner-direction is not linked to power conflict in Figure 7.1 because the path coefficient of .02 is substantially under the .09 level.)

It is worth noting that Figure 7.1 and Table 7.18 point to a serious problem for Church leaders. Older priests and those in a position of leadership are not likely to be able to understand or sympathize with the younger clergy's dissatisfaction over the distribution of power precisely because this dissatisfaction is partly caused by values that the leadership and the older clergy do not share with the younger clergy. The "generation gap" or "generation slope" is in fact a "value gap" or "value slope."

TABLE 7.18

SIMPLE CORRELATIONS AND TOTAL INDEPENDENT EFFECTS OF SELECTED VARIABLES
ON POWER-CONFLICT INDEX

Variable	Simple Correlation (Pearson r)	Independent Effects of Added Variable (Standardized Net Regression Weights)				
		Age	Family Tension	Inner-Directed	Religious Experience	"Modern" Values
Age	−.41	−.41	−.39	−.34	−.33	−.10
Family tension	.18	—	.11	.11	.10	.05
Inner-directed	.27	—	—	.15	.16	.02
Religious experience	−.13	—	—	—	−.08	−.05
"Modern" values	.56	—	—	—	—	.47

By way of summary, we may ask the following questions:

1. *Who are most likely to be dissatisfied with the present state of Church structure?* The young, those from tense families, those with inner-directed personalities, those with low scores on religious experience, and those with "modern" religious values are the ones most likely to be dissatisfied.

2. *Is it merely the fact of being young that makes the young unhappy with the power and structural situation?* The relationship between youth and dissatisfaction seems to be the result of different attitudes and values about what the Church and religion are.

3. *Does the dissatisfaction of the young with the distribution of power indicate trouble for the Church?* It apparently does, precisely because the difference seems to be rooted in quite different values about the nature of the Church and the nature of Christianity. What we are witnessing is not merely a disagreement between those who have power and those who do not, but a disagreement among those with opposing ideologies about the nature of the reality whose power structure is the subject of disagreement. Power conflicts that are rooted in ideological differences tend to be much more serious than power conflicts among those who share the same ideologies.

CHAPTER 8

THE CLERICAL CULTURE

In recent years it has been repeatedly asserted that the Roman Catholic clergy comprise a separate "caste" or a separate "subculture." Most of those who use these terms do not intend them to be taken in a strict literal sense. The clergy are not cut off from the laity as are the Brahmins from the Untouchables, and the values and behavior of the clergy do not really arise from cultures that are distinct from that of the laity, as are, for example, the cultures of the French and British in Canada. In this chapter we address ourselves to questions about the personal relationships of the clergy and their satisfactions with some of these relationships. In the analytic section of the chapter, we attempt to discover what the predictors are of a clergyman's involvement in the "clerical subculture."

Description

In this section, we report data which indicate that very considerable numbers of the clergy apparently do not think of themselves as lonely, as cut off from the laity, or as living in difficult, if not intolerable, circumstances.

Respondents were asked to think about all the people whom they considered to be "really close friends — people you feel free to talk with about personal things." Then they were asked whether they had many such friends. Table 8.1 shows that about one-third of the priests and about two-fifths of the bishops and major superiors think that they have many close friends. In Table 8.2 we can see little variation among the age groups in the proportion saying they have many such friends.

That such a proportion of the clergy do consider themselves as having many of the kinds of friends that they can talk to "about personal things" may well be taken as a sign that there is still considerable capacity for intimacy in the clergy, despite their seminary training and despite the celibate state — especially when one realizes that only a small proportion (2 per cent) say that they have no such friends at all.

155

TABLE 8.1

FRIENDSHIPS BY CLERICAL STATUS

	Diocesan		Religious	
	Bishops	Active Priests	Major Superiors	Active Priests
Per cent having many close friends	41	31	43	36

TABLE 8.2

FRIENDSHIPS BY AGE
(Active Diocesan and Religious Priests)

	Age			
	26-35	36-45	46-55	Over 55
Per cent having many close friends	34	37	32	27

It is very possible, of course, that people overestimate both the number of their close friends and the degree of closeness. However, the fact that they define themselves as having close friends is itself a reality quite independent of whether it is accurate or not. In other words, the clergy do not perceive themselves as cut off from human contact.

When we classify these friends by group (Table 8.3), we see that beyond the limits of their own family, the most frequently reported friendships for diocesan priests are with other priests they knew in the seminary (69 per cent) and with priests they have met since ordination (68 per cent). Only 46 per cent say they have close friendships with laymen in their present work and 32 per cent with laywomen in their present work. Finally, although 51 per cent report having close friends among laymen not involved in their present work, only 37 per cent report such friendships with laywomen not involved in their present work and 24 per cent with women religious.

Religious priests, for their part, are the most likely to report close friends among members of their religious order or congregation (86 per cent) and less likely than diocesan priests to report close friends among the laity. Bishops are also less likely than diocesan priests to mention laity as friends.

TABLE 8.3

CLASSIFICATION OF CLOSE FRIENDS, BY CLERICAL STATUS
(Per Cent Having Close Friends in Each Group)

Group	Diocesan		Religious	
	Bishops	Active Priests	Major Supe-riors	Active Priests
Members of my immediate family or other relatives	76	70	77	70
Fellow priests with whom I was in the seminary	79	69	49	52
Fellow priests from my religious order or congregation	—[a]	—[a]	97	86
Fellow priests whom I met after leaving the seminary	88	68	43	44
Laymen from the parish where I am now, or connected with my present work	32	46	27	39
Laywomen from the parish where I am now, or connected with my present work	18	32	17	28
Laymen from outside my present parish, or whom I met while involved in other work	46	51	50	44
Laywomen from outside my present parish, or whom I met while involved in other work	32	37	30	35
Women religious	27	24	35	29
Ministers from a Protestant church	5	11	8	10

[a] Not applicable.

Table 8.4 shows that the younger clergy are more likely than their older confreres to see themselves as having close friends among laymen and laywomen, both those involved in their present work and those not connected with their present work. They are also more inclined to report close friendships with women religious.

One can summarize the findings of the first four tables by saying that while most priests perceive themselves as having close friends among their colleagues in the clergy, a very considerable number also think of themselves as having close personal friendships with people who are not clergy.

TABLE 8.4

CLASSIFICATION OF CLOSE FRIENDS, BY AGE

(Per Cent of Active Diocesan and Religious Priests
Having Close Friends in Each Group)

Group	Age			
	26-35	36-45	46-55	Over 55
Members of my immediate family or other relatives	70	72	70	67
Fellow priests with whom I was in the seminary	75	63	57	52
Fellow priests from my religious order or congregation	32	41	42	46
Fellow priests whom I met after leaving the seminary	55	60	58	56
Laymen from the parish where I am now, or connected with my present work	51	45	40	36
Laywomen from the parish where I am now, or connected with my present work	39	32	28	22
Laymen from outside my present parish, or whom I met while involved in other work	51	53	48	38
Laywomen from outside my present parish or whom I met while involved in other work	41	42	35	25
Women religious	33	32	22	19
Ministers from a Protestant church	14	12	9	7

When one pushes the matter a little further and asks them which of their closest friends they associate with most often (Table 8.5), one sees that priests are inclined to report more frequent close associations with other priests than with laity. Thus, 45 per cent of the diocesan priests say that one of their most frequent associations is with close friends who were at the seminary with them, and 50 per cent report such an association with close friends whom they met after leaving the seminary. Only 31 per cent mention laymen from their parish and 20 per cent mention laywomen. Among the religious priests, almost three-quarters say that their most frequent associations are with members of their own order or congregation, only about one-quarter think of themselves as having frequent associations with close friends who are laymen, and about one-fifth consider themselves as having frequent associations with close friends who are laywomen.

However, there is some evidence in Table 8.6 that frequency of association with lay friends is higher among the younger clergy. Thus, as

TABLE 8.5

FREQUENT ASSOCIATES BY CLERICAL STATUS
(Per Cent Associating Most Often with Each Group as Close Friends)

Group	Diocesan		Religious	
	Bishops	Active Priests	Major Supe-riors	Active Priests
Members of my immediate family or other relatives	44	46	40	32
Fellow priests with whom I was in the seminary	46	45	19	23
Fellow priests from my religious order or congregation	—[a]	—[a]	89	72
Fellow priests whom I met after leaving the seminary	76	50	27	26
Laymen from the parish where I am now, or connected with my present work	19	31	19	28
Laywomen from the parish where I am now, or connected with my present work	10	20	8	18
Laymen from outside my present parish, or whom I met while involved in other work	23	28	27	24
Laywomen from outside my present parish, or whom I met while involved in other work	12	19	16	19
Women religious	12	11	14	12
Ministers from a Protestant church	3	5	3	4

[a] Not applicable.

one moves across the table from those thirty-five and under to those over fifty-five, one can see that in general there is a decrease in the proportion reporting frequent association with laymen and laywomen (and with women religious, too, for that matter).

Table 8.7 merely confirms the emerging pattern of considerable investment of friendship resources among one's clerical colleagues. Thus, 50 per cent of the diocesan priests and 62 per cent of the religious priests say that they have six or more close friends among the clergy, and 41 per cent of the diocesan and 73 per cent of the religious say that they have at least one close friend among those living in the same residence

TABLE 8.6

FREQUENT ASSOCIATES BY AGE

(Per Cent of Active Diocesan and Religious Priests Associating
Most Often with Each Group as Close Friends)

Group	Age			
	26-35	36-45	46-55	Over 55
Members of my immediate family or other relatives	40	42	41	38
Fellow priests with whom I was in the seminary	45	35	35	28
Fellow priests from my religious order or congregation	26	35	35	37
Fellow priests whom I met after leaving the seminary	35	42	42	37
Laymen from the parish where I am now, or connected with my present work	36	32	29	23
Laywomen from the parish where I am now, or connected with my present work	26	21	17	13
Laymen from outside my present parish, or whom I met while involved in other work	27	30	26	20
Laywomen from outside my present parish, or whom I met while involved in other work	22	23	17	13
Women religious	16	13	9	8
Ministers from a Protestant church	5	5	4	3

TABLE 8.7

FRIENDSHIPS WITH PRIESTS, BY CLERICAL STATUS
(Per Cent)

Item	Diocesan		Religious	
	Bishops	Active Priests	Major Superiors	Active Priests
Six or more good friends are priests	82	50	76	62
One or more close friends among those living in same residence	53	41	89	73
Spent last vacation with priests	65	41	38	31

with them. (The higher proportion among the religious may be a function of the spirit in a religious community or simply of larger numbers of people in the residences of religious communities.) Finally, 41 per cent of the diocesan priests and 31 per cent of the religious priests spent their last vacation with other priests. It should be noted, incidentally, that 35 per cent of diocesan priests and 48 per cent of religious priests spent their vacations with their families. Furthermore, priests may not be completely cut off from relationships with the world beyond the clergy. Indeed, 16 per cent of the diocesan priests and 11 per cent of the religious spent their last vacation with lay people. However, there does exist, nonetheless, a very strong tendency for priests to enter into friendships with other priests. This tendency is even more powerful among bishops and major superiors.

These patterns are not greatly affected by age (Table 8.8). However, the youngest priests are less likely than the older priests to have at least six good friends among their confreres.

As hardly needs to be said, most priests live in the same residences with other priests (Table 8.9). Over 90 per cent of the priests in the country, in fact, live in either rectories or religious houses. Only bishops seem likely to have quarters of their own, and even then 74 per cent of them consider themselves to be living in rectories or religious houses.

Nor is there evidence of grave dissatisfaction with their living situation — despite the support among many priests for letting priests decide themselves where to live. Thus, 74 per cent of the diocesan priests and 80 per cent of the religious priests say that they consider the place they live to be their own home — "a place where you can be yourself, relax, or entertain if you wish."

TABLE 8.8

FRIENDSHIPS WITH PRIESTS, BY AGE
(Per Cent of Active Diocesan and Religious Priests)

Item	Age			
	26-35	36-45	46-55	Over 55
Six or more good friends are priests	45	52	59	64
One or more close friends among those living in same residence	57	54	56	57
Spent last vacation with priests	38	34	37	38

TABLE 8.9

LIVING SITUATION BY CLERICAL STATUS
(Per Cent)

Living Situation	Diocesan		Religious	
	Bishops	Active Priests	Major Superiors	Active Priests
Location of private quarters:				
In rectory or religious house	74	92	98	94
With relatives	1	1	0	0
In own private home or apartment	25	6	2	4
Other arrangements	—	1	—	1
Total	100	100	100	99 [a]
Consider residence to be own "home"	97	74	90	80

[a] Not 100 per cent because of rounding.

However, this satisfaction with living situation declines somewhat with age (Table 8.10). Thus, 88 per cent of those over fifty-five, 82 per cent of those between forty-six and fifty-five, 72 per cent of those between thirty-six and forty-five, and 64 per cent of those between twenty-six and thirty-five consider their residence a "home." We can see that al-

TABLE 8.10

LIVING SITUATION BY AGE
(Per Cent of Active Diocesan and Religious Priests)

Living Situation	Age			
	26-35	36-45	46-55	Over 55
Location of private quarters:				
In rectory or religious house	95	92	93	94
With relatives	0	0	0	1
In own private house or apartment	4	6	6	5
Other arrangements	1	2	1	1
Total	100	100	100	101 [a]
Consider residence to be own "home"	64	72	82	88

[a] Not 100 per cent because of rounding.

though dissatisfaction with their residence is more frequent among the younger clergy, most of them still consider the place where they live to be satisfactory enough to call it "home."

The priests also seem to be reasonably satisfied with the personal relationships they have with those with whom they work and live (Table 8.11). About one-third of the diocesan priests, for example, think that they have "excellent" relationships with their pastor, their fellow assistants, residents in the rectory, and even with the housekeeper. Two-fifths think that they have "excellent" relationships with the assistants. Furthermore, only 15 per cent report "poor" or "very poor" relationships with their pastors and 4 per cent report "poor" or "very poor" relationships with housekeepers. The tyrannical pastor and the autocratic housekeeper so dearly beloved in fiction and folklore do not seem to be typical of the reality in which most of the clergy find themselves.

However, satisfaction with relationships in the parish setting declines with youthfulness as far as relationships with the pastor and the housekeeper are concerned (Table 8.12). Thus, while 44 per cent of those over fifty-five think that they have "excellent" relationships with their pastors, 29 per cent of those thirty-five and under think this. Also, 39 per cent of the priests over fifty-five say that they have "excellent" relationships with their housekeepers, compared to 28 per cent of those thirty-five and under. There is, however, no appreciable change in the proportion reporting "excellent" relationships with their fellow assistants,

TABLE 8.11

RELATIONS WITH COLLEAGUES IN PARISH SETTING,
BY CLERICAL STATUS

(Per Cent of Active Diocesan Priests Having Personal
Relationships with Each Type of Colleague)

Colleague	Personal Relationships	
	Excellent	Poor or Very Poor
Pastor	30	15
Assistant(s)	43	3
Fellow assistant(s)	37	4
Resident priest(s)	37	4
Housekeeper/cook	34	4

TABLE 8.12

RELATIONS WITH COLLEAGUES IN PARISH SETTING, BY AGE

(Per Cent of Active Diocesan and Religious Priests Having "Excellent"
Personal Relationships with Each Type of Colleague)

Colleague	Age			
	26-35	36-45	46-55	Over 55
Pastor	29	32	37	44
Assistant(s)	41	33	41	40
Fellow assistant(s)	34	34	35	34
Resident priest(s)	29	32	35	37
Housekeeper/cook	28	33	40	39

and little change in the proportion reporting such relationships with assistants or other residents in the rectory.

The religious priests apparently perceive their colleague relationships as being even less of a problem than do diocesan priests (Table 8.13). Thus, only 4 per cent of the religious think of their relationship with the person in charge of their house as being "poor" or "very poor," while 44 per cent consider it "excellent." The religious are, however, slightly less likely than diocesan priests to report their relationships with other colleagues in their residential setting as being "excellent."

TABLE 8.13

RELATIONS WITH COLLEAGUES IN "NON-PARISH"
SETTING, BY CLERICAL STATUS

(Per Cent of Active Religious Priests Having Personal
Relationships with Each Type of Colleague)

Colleague	Personal Relationships	
	Excellent	Poor or Very Poor
Person in charge	44	4
Priests	28	2
Brothers	31	1
Students	25	2
Lay Help	32	1

Among those living in "non-parish" settings, there is also a decline in level of satisfactions as one moves from the older to the younger priests (Table 8.14). While 53 per cent of those over fifty-five say their relationship with the person in charge is "excellent," only 36 per cent of those thirty-five and under report this. There is even a decline from 36 per cent to 26 per cent in the proportion of those saying that their relationships with their priest colleagues in the residential situation are "excellent." Thus, in both the parish and the non-parish settings, the younger priests are less likely to be satisfied with the relationship patterns than the older priests.

In the descriptive tables presented in this chapter, the Roman Catholic clergy in the United States do not emerge as men who perceive themselves as being lonely or in intolerable situations. There are some who have no friends and others who find that the relationships with those with whom they live are very bad, but most priests perceive themselves as reasonably satisfied with their living circumstances and enjoying close personal relationships. Many see themselves as having close personal relationships beyond the limitations of the clerical world.

The descriptive section of the present chapter can be summarized by the responses to the following four questions:

1. *Is there a "clerical culture?"* In the strict sense of the word, of course there is not, though no research was required to demonstrate this. Nevertheless, there is in our data considerable evidence to indicate strong tendencies in the direction of something that would resemble a "clerical culture." Priests are not cut off or isolated from the laity the way real subcultures are isolated from main cultures. Nevertheless, there is a

TABLE 8.14

RELATIONS WITH COLLEAGUES IN "NON-PARISH" SETTING, BY AGE
(Per Cent of Active Diocesan and Religious Priests Having "Excellent"
Personal Relationships with Each Type of Colleague)

Colleague	Age			
	26-35	36-45	46-55	Over 55
Person in charge	36	46	41	53
Priests	26	27	28	36
Brothers	28	26	28	42
Students	28	23	24	26
Lay help	26	28	34	42

strong tendency among the clergy to associate in their friendship and recreational patterns with other clergy — a tendency that is reinforced by the fact that most clergy live in houses with other clergy.

2. *Are priests without friends?* Some certainly are and others may very well be, but most priests see themselves as having close personal friends, and a substantial proportion see themselves as having many such friends, with some even among the laity. It would be a mistake to think of the clergy as entirely composed of a group of men who think of themselves as lonely and isolated, although, as we shall see, loneliness is a serious problem for some priests.

3. *Are the priests' relationships within the "clerical culture" intolerable?* Insofar as one can judge from information on priests' relationships with those with whom they live and their attitudes toward the place where they live, one must respond "no" to this question. Very small proportions, for example, report bad relationships with the pastor or the person in charge of the house where they live, but substantial proportions report "excellent" relationships with these ecclesiastical superiors. It is clearly not our intention to suggest that there is no room for improvement in the residential relationships of the clergy. Nevertheless, the fact that approximately three-quarters of the priests in the country consider the place where they live to be a "home" raises the question of whether one could reasonably expect that proportion to go much higher, given the imperfection of the human condition.

4. *Is there pressure toward change in the patterns of the so-called "clerical culture?"* There apparently is such pressure building up among the younger clergy, who are more likely both to have friends who are not priests and to be dissatisfied with the residential situation in which they find themselves. Nevertheless, a majority of the younger priests still think of the residence in which they live as a place where they can be themselves, relax, or entertain. They also report that some of their most frequent associations with close friends are with other priests. If the so-called "clerical culture" — understood here as a strong tendency for priests to associate with other priests — is breaking up, then, at least by the measures available in this chapter, it is breaking up slowly.

Analysis

Two indices were derived from the question on living situation and personal relationships (Question 69). One index, which we somewhat romantically called the "lonely-cleric" index, was designed to measure isolation from friendship relations. However, it correlated with no other variable and was discarded. The second index measures the respondent's perception of the quality of his relationships with the colleagues with whom he lives. It is called the "colleague-relationship" index. (See Appendix C for details on the composition of this index.) Unfortunately, Table 8.15 shows no very strong relationship with this index, but as we can see that older priests are more likely to be satisfied with their colleague relationships, and those from tense family backgrounds and those with "modern" religious values are less likely to be satisfied with their relationships. However, only 7 per cent of the variance on the colleague-relationship index can be explained, and 5 per cent of that is a function of age (Table 8.16).

The relationships of age and family tension with colleague relationships are expressed graphically in Figure 8.1, in which one can see that only two paths converge on the colleague-relationship box — a path of .19 from age and a path of .09 from family tension. Since values, personality, and religious experience have no important relationship with whether a priest perceives that he has good relationships with his colleagues, these variables have been omitted from the figure. Only age

TABLE 8.15

CORRELATES OF COLLEAGUE-RELATIONSHIP INDEX

Variable	Pearson r
Age	.22
Family tension	−.14
Inner-directed	−.01
Religious experience	.11
"Modern" values	−.16

TABLE 8.16

EXPLANATION OF VARIANCE ON COLLEAGUE-RELATIONSHIP INDEX

Variable	R^2	R^2 Change
Age	.05	.05
Family tension	.06	.01
Inner-directed	.06	.00
Religious experience	.07	.01
"Modern" values	.07	.00

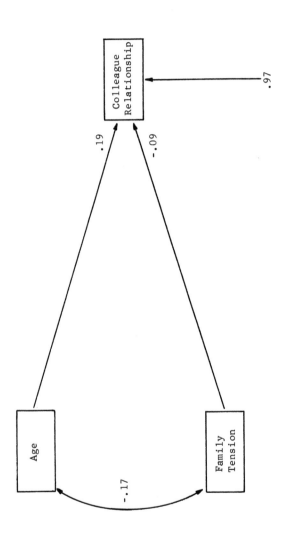

NOTE: All paths with coefficients less than .09 and all variables without significant paths have been omitted from this figure.

Fig. 8.1—Path diagram relating colleague support to prior variables. Active priests only.

and less family tension are conducive to satisfaction with colleague relationships.

In addition to the correlations described above, there is a $-.23$ relationship between being an associate pastor and colleague relationships. (Since "associate pastor" did not correlate at a consistently high level with other variables in our model, it was dropped as a variable from our analysis.) However, in subsequent chapters we shall occasionally discuss it and mention its relationship to other variables.

We summarize this quite brief analytical section by asking only one question:

What priests are most likely to feel that the relationships with the colleagues with whom they live are unsatisfactory? The young are more likely to be dissatisfied with their colleague relationships than the old, but age explains only 5 per cent of the variance in satisfaction with colleague relationships.

CHAPTER 9

THE WORK OF PRIESTS

The priesthood is a profession because it possesses the dominant attributes generally ascribed to a profession: expertise, autonomy, responsibility, and commitment to serving people. The priest's expertise flows from a special body of knowledge and skills acquired through a long training process; he exercises autonomy and responsibility in his undertakings within the hierarchical structure of the Church (though the extent of this exercise will depend on his status and type of affiliation; a Trappist monk, for example, exercises less autonomy and responsibility than the pastor of a large urban parish); and his various pastoral and intellectual activities are predominantly people-oriented.

Two special characteristics, however, mark off the priest from other professionals and make the priesthood somewhat of a profession *sui generis*. These distinguishing marks are the transcendant motivation that underlies the priest's work and the all-embracing nature of that work. The priest works within a transcendental context wherein he is concerned basically with his own and other people's religious needs, and traditionally he has been seen as a man whose whole life, both professional and personal, is dedicated to his vocation. Hence, the study of the work of priests and their professional attitudes must be seen within this unique context. While it is legitimate to compare priests with other professionals, it must be borne in mind that there are other criteria besides professional standards by which to judge the relevance and effectiveness of the work.

In this chapter we ask some questions about the occupations and the professional standards of the Catholic clergy. We consider not only their actual satisfaction with their work and how they compare it with other professions but how these relate to other factors in their priestly life.

Description

In the descriptive section of this chapter we report the following principal findings:

171

1. Priests work moderately long hours — in excess of fifty hours per week.

2. Religious priests are more satisfied with their jobs than diocesan priests.

3. Older priests are in general more satisfied with their jobs than are younger priests.

4. Job satisfactions of associate pastors are not only lower than that of other priests but are also lower than that of a sample of unskilled American industrial workers.

5. Priests compare themselves favorably with other professionals such as doctors and lawyers on the general characteristics of professionalism.

6. The majority of American priests see themselves in need of professional updating.

7. Many priests are rather regular readers of serious authors and journals.

Among the younger diocesan clergy, the most frequent current position is that of associate pastor, while among the older clergy the most frequent position is pastor (Table 9.1). Among active diocesan priests, 83 per cent describe themselves as engaged in parish work (Table 9.2). The next highest proportion (18 per cent) describe themselves as teaching high

TABLE 9.1

CURRENT POSITION FOR PRIESTS BY AGE
(Per Cent)

Current Position	Age			
	26-35	36-45	46-55	Over 55
Diocesan administration	1	2	0	0
Pastor	3	15	32	35
Associate pastor	47	23	11	2
Special diocesan work	13	15	11	5
Retired diocesan	0	0	0	7
Major superior	2	8	11	8
Local superior or religious staff	2	8	11	8
Religious member	31	33	33	39
Religious on special assignment	3	5	4	4
Total[a]	102	109	113	108

[a] Totals add to more than 100 per cent because some respondents reported more than one position.

TABLE 9.2

CURRENT MAIN JOBS BY CLERICAL STATUS
(Per Cent of Priests)

Current Main Job	Diocesan		Religious	
	Active Priests	Resigned Priests[a]	Active Priests	Resigned Priests[a]
Diocesan administration	3	4	1	4
Religious administration	0	4	11	4
Educational administration	6	4	13	6
Parish work	83	58	46	25
Counseling work	16	4	25	2
Chancery or tribunal work	4	4	1	4
Retreat work, mission band	1	0	8	7
Pious groups	0	0	2	7
Home missions	1	0	2	7
Religious instruction	14	2	12	1
Campus ministry	3	5	6	7
Institutional chaplaincies	10	5	10	7
Military chaplaincies	4	5	2	7
Social work	8	4	6	5
Publications, press	1	1	2	4
Monastic observances	0	0	11	0
University and college teaching	3	3	14	12
High school and grade school teaching	18	6	17	7
Major seminary work (college level and above)	2	5	8	8
Minor seminary work (high school)	1	5	3	8
Writing and research	2	1	8	4
Further studies	5	2	10	8
Mass media	1	1	1	4
Arts	1	1	2	4
Experimental ministry	1	4	3	5

[a] Position at time of resignation.

school or grade school, while 16 per cent consider counseling as one of their current main jobs and 14 per cent view religious instruction as one of their main jobs.[1] Parish work is also the most frequently mentioned main job of active religious priests, although the 46 per cent reporting this sort of activity is considerably lower than the 83 per cent among diocesan priests. The next most frequently mentioned main job among active religious is counseling (25 per cent). Others view as their current main jobs teaching in high school and grade school (17 per cent), teaching in higher education (14 per cent), and religious instruction (12 per cent). Resignees also report parish work most frequently as their main job before resignation, though far fewer of them are willing to describe it as their main job than are active priests. Among the rather surprising findings in Table 9.2 are that diocesan priests are as likely as religious order priests to be involved in some sort of high school or grade school teaching (although such teaching by diocesan priests is much more on a part-time basis), and that resignees from religious orders seem to come disproportionately from both missionaries and military chaplains. Finally, Table 9.3 shows that younger clergy are more likely than the older clergy to consider counseling, religious instruction, teaching in high schools or grade schools, and parish work as their main job. Since the older clergy do not mention any main job more frequently than the younger priests, one presumes that what we have reported in Table 9.3 is the existence of a considerable number of double assignments among the clergy under forty-five.

Priests work moderately long hours. Bishops report a work week of 61 hours, major superiors of about 58 hours, and active priests of about 52 hours (Table 9.4). Even priests over fifty-five estimate that their average work week involves about 50 hours (Table 9.5), which is only 5 hours less than that reported by the youngest clergy in the sample.

What sort of satisfactions do the clergy obtain from their jobs? To answer this question we used a series of scales developed by Patricia C. Smith (Smith, *et al.,* 1969). These scales are designed to measure the satisfaction of respondents to their work, pay, supervision, and opportunities for promotion on their jobs. Workers are asked to rate their job on a list of fifty-one adjectives, such as "fascinating," "routine," "satisfying" for the work itself; "impolite," "tactful," and "intelligent" for supervision; "adequate" and "highly paid" for pay; "promotion on ability" and "dead-end assignment" for opportunities for promotion.[2]

It would appear from Table 9.6 that religious priests find their jobs more satisfactory on each of the four scales than do diocesan priests. The diocesan score on work satisfaction is 34.6, while the religious score is 37.0. On supervision, diocesan priests score 36.9, religious priests, 42.0. On pay, the diocesan score is 28.5 and the religious is 30.5; and on promotion, the diocesans score 21.0 and the religious, 26.2. It may be that the community life among the religious priests provides more social support, higher morale, and greater job satisfaction than is available to diocesan priests. Indeed, the typical religious order priest seems to have

TABLE 9.3

CURRENT MAIN JOBS BY AGE
(Per Cent of Active Diocesan and Religious Priests)

Current Main Job	Age			
	26-35	36-45	46-55	Over 55
Diocesan administration	1	3	2	1
Religious administration	2	5	7	4
Educational administration	5	12	11	7
Parish work	75	64	66	63
Counseling	26	25	18	12
Chancery work	2	4	2	2
Retreat work, mission band	3	5	3	5
Pious groups	1	1	2	1
Home missions	1	2	1	2
Religious instruction	22	13	11	8
Campus ministry	6	7	4	2
Institutional chaplaincies	11	9	10	10
Military chaplaincies	2	5	4	1
Social work	11	8	6	3
Publications, press	1	2	2	2
Monastic observances	3	4	6	6
University and college teaching	5	8	9	8
High school and grade school teaching	32	19	12	9
Major seminary work (college level and above)	5	6	5	2
Minor seminary work (high school)	4	3	1	1
Writing and research	4	5	5	5
Further studies	18	9	4	1
Mass media	1	1	1	0
Arts	2	2	1	1

TABLE 9.4

WORKING HOURS BY CLERICAL STATUS

	Diocesan		Religious	
	Bishops	Active Priests	Major Superiors	Active Priests
Mean hours of work per week	61.1	52.4	58.5	52.3

The Catholic Priest in the United States

TABLE 9.5

WORKING HOURS BY AGE
(Active Diocesan and Religious Priests)

	Age			
	26-35	36-45	46-55	Over 55
Mean hours of work per week	54.5	53.6	51.9	49.2

TABLE 9.6

JOB SATISFACTION BY CLERICAL STATUS
(Mean Scores)

Job Satisfaction	Diocesan		Religious	
	Bishops	Active Priests	Major Superiors	Active Priests
Work	38.5	34.6	37.6	37.0
Supervision	42.0	36.9	41.4	42.0
Pay	33.2	28.5	32.4	30.5
Promotion	26.6	21.0	25.0	26.2

a level of job satisfaction not very different from that of bishops or, for that matter, from that of his own superiors. On the other hand, there are differences in levels of job satisfaction between active diocesan priests and their bishops; in each case there is a difference of more than four points on the Smith scales in favor of the bishops.

Table 9.7 shows that older priests are more satisfied with their work, supervision, and pay than are younger priests. However, the latter are much more satisfied with the opportunity for promotion, perhaps because they simply see more future ahead of them than do older priests.

In Table 9.8, median job satisfaction scores are presented for a somewhat more detailed breakdown of the Catholic clergy, together with a comparison between the clergy and approximately 2,000 adult male employees in American industries.[3] The most striking finding in Table 9.8 is that associate pastors not only are lower than any of the other clergy on all four scales, they are also lower on all four scales than professionals and middle managers in industry and even lower than un-

TABLE 9.7

JOB SATISFACTION BY AGE

(Mean Score of Active Diocesan and Religious Priests)

Job Satisfaction	Age			
	26-35	36-45	46-55	Over 55
Work	34.5	35.8	36.7	35.7
Supervision	37.9	39.7	41.0	39.8
Pay	27.9	29.4	30.3	29.8
Promotion	24.2	24.2	16.0	13.2

skilled manual workers on two out of the four scales. Only in the area of pay are associate pastors more satisfied with their work situation than are the lowest category of workers in American industry. Given the fact that 47 per cent of the priests thirty-five and under and 23 per cent of the priests between thirty-six and forty-five are associate pastors, this very low level of job satisfaction ought to be considered a serious problem for the American Catholic priesthood.

The highest levels of job satisfaction among diocesan priests (other than bishops) are to be found among those working in the chancery office or doing special work, with the chancery office staff being especially high in their anticipation of the possibilities of promotion in their job (fully 8 points higher on the promotion-satisfaction scale than associate pastors). Chancery office staff (herein including other diocesan administrators) and those in special work have scores that generally fall between professionals and middle managers in industrial plants; pastors compare favorably with the middle managers represented in the table, scoring somewhat lower in their satisfaction with work, slightly ahead in their satisfaction with supervision and pay, and the same in their satisfaction with promotion. All four categories of religious priests, on the other hand, outscore the middle managers in three out of the four scales. In the area of satisfaction with their work, however, only religious order "specialists" have scores equal to those of middle managers, while the other three types of religious priests have scores that are one or two points lower.

The supervision, pay, and promotion measures might be of debatable value when applied to a profession *sui generis,* but after consultation with Professor Smith, we are persuaded that the work-satisfaction scale (the first column in Table 9.8) is a useful measure for evaluating priests'

TABLE 9.8

JOB SATISFACTION BY CURRENT POSITION FOR PRIESTS AND MALE INDUSTRIAL EMPLOYEES

(Median Scores)[a]

Current Position	Job Satisfaction			
	Work	Supervision	Pay	Promotion
Active diocesan priests:				
Bishop	40	45	34	22
Chancery official	39	48	34	23
Pastor	37	43	33	19
Associate pastor	34	36	29	15
Special assignment and other diocesan priests	39	45	32	20
Active religious priests:				
Major religious superior	39	47	34	21
Assistant to major superior and local superior	38	47	34	24
Member priest	39	45	34	21
Religious order "specialist"[b]	40	46	33	24
Male employees in 21 industrial plants:				
Professional[c]	45	47	37	25
Middle manager	40	42	32	19
Unskilled worker	34	42	25	16

[a] Median scores are presented to make the two sets of data comparable.

[b] E.g., military chaplains, professors in secular universities.

[c] Ph.D. and M.A. level managers.

reactions to their work. We shall therefore use this scale in our analyses in subsequent chapters.

Work satisfaction relates strongly to the current main job of priests. As we see in Table 9.9, the highest level of work satisfaction is found among those engaged in higher educational or literary activities — all the groups in these categories having a mean score above 38, with the top places going to those in writing and research (39.9) and in major seminary work (39.8). On the other hand, some of the lowest scores (35 and under) are reported by those who engage in the jobs that are most typical of the priestly life — high school and grade school teaching (35.1), religious instruction (35.0), and parish work (34.7). The intermediate ranges of work satisfaction are occupied for the most part by administrators, chaplains, counselors, and social workers.

In other words, the jobs that provide the highest levels of satisfactions are occupied by relatively few priests and those with the lowest levels of satisfactions are occupied by the greatest number of priests. The rather low satisfaction of those whose main job is parish work probably represents a fairly serious problem since we saw in Table 9.2 that parish work is what the largest number of priests do.

Whatever their dissatisfactions may be, most American priests say they would be willing to become priests again (Table 9.10); 99 per cent of the bishops, 78 per cent of the diocesan priests, 86 per cent of the major superiors, and 79 per cent of the religious priests make this assertion. And while there is some correlation with age (Table 9.11), it is still worth noting that there is only a 6 percentage point difference between priests thirty-five and under and priests between forty-six and fifty-five who say they would enter the priesthood again. Table 9.10 also shows that 35 per cent of the active diocesan priests and 45 per cent of the active religious priests feel their talents are being used "a great deal"— as do 78 per cent of the bishops and 56 per cent of the major superiors. The resignees, on the other hand, are considerably less likely to think that their talents were utilized "a great deal" when they were priests (25 per cent of the diocesan resignees and 34 per cent of the religious resignees make this assertion). Just as the religious reported more job satisfaction, so they are 10 percentage points more likely to say that their talents are being utilized "a great deal." Older priests are also more likely than younger priests to think that their talents are being used extensively.

Table 9.10 shows that large majorities of the active priests think that they compare favorably with other professionals. Nine-tenths of them think that they have as much, if not more, commitment to serving the

TABLE 9.9

WORK SATISFACTION BY CURRENT MAIN JOB
(Active Diocesan and Religious Priests)

Current Main Job	Mean Scores
Writing and research	39.9
Major seminary work	39.8
University and college teaching	39.2
Publications, press	38.6
Educational administration	38.3
Campus ministry	38.2
Mass media	38.2
Retreat work, mission band	37.8
Religious administration	37.5
Diocesan administration	37.3
Counseling	37.2
Experimental ministry	36.8
Home missions	36.8
Further studies	36.6
Chancery	36.5
Institutional chaplaincies	36.5
Monastic observances	36.3
Social work	36.3
Military chaplaincies	36.2
High school and grade school teaching	35.1
Religious instruction	35.0
Parish work	34.7
Pious groups	34.2
Arts	33.6

needs of people as do other professionals. Three-quarters think that they compare favorably with other professionals on the depth of knowledge and skills and on responsibility for an undertaking; and almost three-fifths see themselves as comparable in autonomy to make decisions. Resignees, on the other hand, are much less likely than the active priests to think that when they were active they compared as favorably with other professionals on autonomy and responsibility. However, on the matter of commitment to serving the needs of people, even the resignees feel that they compared favorably with other professionals when they were priests.

Bishops are even more inclined than the active priests to make favorable comparisons between themselves and other professionals, as are major superiors. And Table 9.11 shows that on autonomy and responsi-

TABLE 9.10

JOB REACTIONS BY CLERICAL STATUS
(Per Cent)

Reactions	Diocesan			Religious		
	Bishops	Active Priests	Resigned[a] Priests	Major Superiors	Active Priests	Resigned[a] Priests
Would enter priesthood again	99	78	—[b]	86	79	—[b]
Feel talents are utilized "a great deal"	78	35	25	56	45	34
More or about the same as other professionals:						
Depth of knowledge and skill	88	76	74	79	76	76
Autonomy to make decisions	88	55	21	80	61	29
Responsibility for an undertaking	94	73	38	94	76	45
Commitment to serving needs of people	98	94	91	93	90	86

[a] Answers refer to when the resignees were still in the ministry.
[b] Not asked of resigned priests.

bility, younger priests are less likely to see themselves in a favorable light in comparison with other professionals that are older priests.

The greatest hesitation about making a favorable comparison seems to be on the question of autonomy in decision-making. It is interesting to note that religious priests, even though they have a vow of obedience, are somewhat more likely to perceive themselves as having decision-making autonomy than do diocesan priests, who have no such vow. Finally, only among the younger active clergy are less than a majority willing to make a favorable comparison on the subject of autonomy in decision-making. There is, then, every reason to conclude on the basis of Tables 9.10 and 9.11 that the majority of Catholic clergy in the United States do not see their profession *sui generis* as deficient in a number of important qualifications when compared to other professionals.

Furthermore, if a recognition of a need for higher training is a mark of high professional standards, then the American Catholic priests do quite well by this measure (Table 9.12). Approximately 65 per cent of them view themselves as needing to study ways to relate Christian faith to a changing society; about 58 per cent want updating in Biblical, theological, and related fields; about 44 per cent are desirous of training in planning and evaluating the Church's work; 40 per cent of diocesan priests and 33 per cent of the religious priests see a need for the development of skills in preaching and counseling; and about 36 per cent would like more training in how to be agents of change in the community and in the Church. Furthermore, in Table 9.13 we see that the younger clergy, presumably fresh from the most recent theological instruction in their

TABLE 9.11

JOB REACTIONS BY AGE
(Per Cent of Active Diocesan and Religious Priests)

Reactions	Age			
	26-35	36-45	46-55	Over 55
Would enter priesthood again	74	71	80	89
Feel talents are utilized "a great deal"	26	38	44	47
More or about the same as other professionals:				
Depth of knowledge and skill	71	76	79	79
Autonomy to make decisions	45	52	65	68
Responsibility for an undertaking	64	71	79	83
Commitment to serving needs of people	92	93	92	90

TABLE 9.12

FURTHER TRAINING NEEDED, BY CLERICAL STATUS
(Per Cent Feeling a "Need" for Each Item)

Item	Diocesan		Religious	
	Bishops	Active Priests	Major Superiors	Active Priests
Training in how to plan and evaluate the Church's work	46	46	51	42
Preparation for another occupation	1	10	4	9
Time to reflect on and evaluate the direction of my ministry	29	35	33	34
Training in ministerial skills (preaching, counseling, etc.)	16	40	30	33
Learning how to be a change agent in Church and community	29	36	50	37
Updating in Biblical, theological, and related fields	54	58	66	59
Study to relate Christian faith to our rapidly changing society	62	65	74	66

seminaries, are no more—but no less—interested in theological updating than anyone else, but are more likely than the older groups to want further training in other areas and time to reflect and evaluate the direction of their ministry. There is no evidence at all in either of the last two tables to indicate that as professional men the Catholic clergy are willing to rest on their laurels.

Furthermore, substantial proportions of them keep in touch with the Catholic periodical literature (Table 9.14). All active clergy list their local diocesan newspaper as the publication they read the most. Among the bishops the next most popular journals are *The Priest* (54 per cent), *America* (52 per cent), and *Worship* (36 per cent). The other most popular journals among active diocesan priests are: *The National Catholic Reporter* (40 per cent), *The Priest* (31 per cent), *Homiletic and Pastoral Review* (25 per cent), *America* (24 per cent), and *The Critic* (22 per cent). Major superiors vote for *The National Catholic Reporter* (51 per cent), *America* (42 per cent), *The Priest* (30 per cent), *The Critic* and *Homiletic and Pastoral Review* (29 per cent each), and *Theological Studies* (21 per cent). Active religious priests also give top billing to *The National Catholic Reporter* (39 per cent), followed by *America* (28

TABLE 9.13

FURTHER TRAINING NEEDED, BY AGE
(Per Cent of Active Diocesan and Religious Priests
Feeling a "Need" for Each Item)

Item	Age			
	26-35	36-45	46-55	Over 55
Training in how to plan and evaluate the Church's work	48	46	45	38
Preparation for another occupation	15	12	6	4
Time to reflect on and evaluate the direction of my ministry	45	38	33	23
Training in ministerial skills (preaching, counseling, etc.)	50	37	33	28
Learning how to be a change agent in Church and community	49	41	32	24
Updating in Biblical, theological, and related fields	54	62	63	54
Study to relate Christian faith to our rapidly changing society	72	68	64	58

per cent), *The Critic* and *Homiletic and Pastoral Review* (21 per cent each), and *The Priest* (19 per cent). The "liberal" journal, *Commonweal,* is read by 15 per cent among both the diocesan and the religious priests, and the "conservative" *The Wanderer* is read by 8 per cent of the diocesan and 6 per cent of the religious priests. It is interesting to note that with the exception of *The National Catholic Reporter* and *The Critic,* the bishops are more likely to report reading every one of the journals listed than are the active diocesan priests. Perhaps the episcopal office involves some sense of responsibility that one ought to "keep up" with as much Catholic periodical literature as possible.

Most of the journals listed in Table 9.14 would be characterized as "middlebrow," but *Theology Digest, Theological Studies, Concilium,* and *The Catholic Biblical Quarterly* are serious scholarly journals, and one-tenth of the American Catholic priests report that they read most issues of these magazines. There are no data available on the reading of professional journals by members of other professions, but one must say on the basis of Table 9.14 that one would be hard put to make a case against the proposition that important segments of the Catholic clergy do indeed strive to keep abreast of current developments in their profession.

TABLE 9.14

PUBLICATIONS READ, BY CLERICAL STATUS

(Per Cent Who Read "Most Issues" of Each Publication)

Publication	Diocesan			Religious		
	Bishops	Active Priests	Resigned Priests	Major Superiors	Active Priests	Resigned Priests
Cross Currents	7	6	—a	8	5	—a
Homiletic and Pastoral Review	30	25	12	29	21	13
The National Catholic Reporter	24	40	76	51	39	70
American Ecclesiastical Review	30	8	—a	16	12	—a
The Priest	54	31	11	30	19	7
Commonweal	28	15	—a	21	15	—a
America	52	24	34	42	28	33
The Critic	20	22	—a	29	21	—a
Concilium	10	9	13	13	10	16
The Wanderer	18	8	—a	6	6	—a
The Catholic Mind	23	5	—a	10	7	—a
Worship	36	16	25	19	15	22
Theology Digest	24	12	23	18	17	28
Theological Studies	24	12	—a	21	14	—a
Local diocesan newspaper	95	83	—a	80	61	—a
The Way	8	3	—a	10	4	—a
The Catholic Biblical Quarterly	13	3	—a	6	6	—a

a Not asked of resigned priests.

Among the young clergy (Table 9.15), *The National Catholic Reporter* continues to be the most popular journal (54 per cent) after the local diocesan newspaper. *The Critic* (31 per cent) takes second place, followed by *America* (24 per cent) and *Commonweal* (20 per cent). Among priests over fifty-five, *The Priest* is the most frequently mentioned journal (39 per cent), followed by *Homiletic and Pastoral Review* (36 per cent), *America* (26 per cent), and *The National Catholic Reporter* (22 per cent). One notes in Table 9.15 that the younger clergy and the older clergy seem to read rather different journals; *Commonweal,* for example, is twice as popular among the younger clergy, as is *The National Catholic Reporter. America,* on the other hand, is read by approximately one-quarter of all age groups.

There is also considerable interest among Catholic priests in some of the more important Catholic writers of the last decade (Table 9.16). If one notes in passing the fact that the overwhelming majority of priests and bishops alike report themselves as "greatly influenced" by the docu-

TABLE 9.15

PUBLICATIONS READ, BY AGE
(Per Cent of Active Diocesan and Religious Priests Who
Read "Most Issues" of Each Publication)

Publication	Age			
	26-35	36-45	46-55	Over 55
Cross Currents	6	5	5	6
Homiletic and Pastoral Review	9	18	30	36
The National Catholic Reporter	54	46	34	22
American Ecclesiastical Review	4	7	10	19
The Priest	15	19	30	39
Commonweal	20	16	12	10
America	24	27	27	26
The Critic	31	24	17	11
Concilium	11	10	8	7
The Wanderer	1	2	7	18
The Catholic Mind	2	4	8	11
Worship	19	15	14	13
Theology Digest	19	14	13	12
Theological Studies	14	12	13	13
Local diocesan newspaper	63	69	78	84
The Way	3	3	4	5
The Catholic Biblical Quarterly	4	4	5	6

TABLE 9.16

INFLUENTIAL AUTHORS READ, BY CLERICAL STATUS

(Per Cent Reporting Each Author Has Influenced Their Thinking "Greatly")

Author	Diocesan			Religious		
	Bishops	Active Priests	Resigned Priests	Major Superiors	Active Priests	Resigned Priests
Gregory Baum	2	8	—[a]	6	6	—[a]
Cardinal Bea	23	7	—[a]	12	8	—[a]
Dietrich Bonhoeffer	0	9	15	8	9	15
Robert McAfee Brown	0	2	—[a]	4	2	—[a]
Daniel Callahan	0	3	—[a]	3	3	—[a]
Yves Congar	18	10	—[a]	18	13	—[a]
Harvey Cox	1	10	—[a]	9	11	—[a]
Teilhard de Chardin	5	23	32	21	25	35
Henri de Lubac	15	7	—[a]	14	11	—[a]
Avery Dulles	11	6	—[a]	6	9	—[a]
Louis Evely	16	24	14	20	18	12
Bernard Häring	18	29	26	33	26	21
Eugene Kennedy	16	28	—[a]	23	20	—[a]
Hans Küng	6	23	39	15	20	33
Jacques Maritain	20	9	—[a]	23	12	—[a]
Martin Marty	0	2	—[a]	3	2	—[a]

TABLE 9.16—Continued

Author	Diocesan			Religious		
	Bishops	Active Priests	Resigned Priests	Major Superiors	Active Priests	Resigned Priests
John L. McKenzie	9	26	40	18	22	30
Gabriel Moran	4	14	—[a]	16	15	—[a]
John Courtney Murray	36	16	—[a]	25	21	—[a]
Marc Oraison	1	10	—[a]	6	12	—[a]
Pope Paul VI	74	33	13	43	34	7
Karl Rahner	41	26	25	36	32	24
Rosemary Reuther	0	2	—[a]	2	1	—[a]
Edward Schillebeeckx	11	24	32	19	24	25
Cardinal Suenens	20	23	29	23	20	30
Documents of Vatican II	94	63	42	81	68	40

[a] Not asked of resigned priests.

ments of Vatican II, and if one also notes the importance of the writings of Pope Paul VI to all categories of active clergy, then one can say that for the bishops the most popular of the theological writers is Karl Rahner (41 per cent) and the second most popular is the great American theologian John Courtney Murray (36 per cent). Twenty-three per cent of the bishops mention Cardinal Bea as having greatly influenced their thinking, and 20 per cent mention both Jacques Maritain and Cardinal Suenens of Brussels. Active diocesan priests are most likely to report that they were influenced by the European theologian Bernard Häring (29 per cent) and the American psychologist Eugene Kennedy (28 per cent). Other popular authors with the diocesan clergy are John L. McKenzie (26 per cent), Karl Rahner (26 per cent), Louis Evely (24 per cent), Edward Schillebeeckx (24 per cent), Teilhard de Chardin (23 per cent), and Hans Küng (23 per cent). Karl Rahner is the most popular of the influential authors among the major superiors (36 per cent) and among active religious priests (32 per cent).

In Table 9.17 we see that Bernard Häring leads the list among the clergy thirty-five and under (49 per cent), but we note that 41 per cent of the young clergy report that they were greatly influenced by Teilhard de Chardin and Eugene Kennedy, and about 35 per cent report they were influenced by Louis Evely, Hans Küng, and John L. McKenzie. The Catholic writers read most infrequently by all groups are Daniel Callahan (4 per cent by the youngest priests) and Rosemary Reuther (2 per cent by the youngest priests).

Rahner, Schillebeeckx, Küng, Häring, and Cardinal Suenens are some of the most important European leaders of the intellectual movements in the Church since the Vatican Council. Murray, McKenzie, and Kennedy are major intellectual figures in the American Catholic environment. The fact that considerable proportions of the American priesthood are willing to say that these writers have greatly influenced their thinking indicates that very serious effort has been put into the attempt to keep up with the most recent developments in the Church. About one-tenth of the priests over fifty-five, for example, say that they have been greatly influenced by the work of Cardinal Suenens, and one-fifth of these older priests say the same thing about Karl Rahner. Given the extreme depth and complexity of Professor Rahner's thought, one is forced to conclude that those older priests who have pursued his work vigorously enough to be greatly influenced by him have shown an impressive level of professional commitment.

Since we do not have comparable data about other professional

TABLE 9.17

INFLUENTIAL AUTHORS READ, BY AGE

(Per Cent of Active Diocesan and Religious Priests Reporting
Each Author Has Influenced Their Thinking "Greatly")

Author	Age			
	26-35	36-45	46-55	Over 55
Gregory Baum	10	7	6	3
Cardinal Bea	6	6	7	10
Dietrich Bonhoeffer	19	8	4	2
Robert McAfee Brown	4	2	2	1
Daniel Callahan	4	3	2	1
Yves Congar	16	12	9	8
Harvey Cox	22	10	5	2
Teilhard de Chardin	41	27	15	8
Henri de Lubac	12	8	7	7
Avery Dulles	11	7	6	5
Louis Evely	35	21	16	10
Bernard Häring	49	28	17	12
Eugene Kennedy	41	26	17	6
Hans Küng	34	25	14	8
Jacques Maritain	5	7	13	18
Martin Marty	3	2	1	2
John L. McKenzie	36	28	17	12
Gabriel Moran	26	16	8	3
John Courtney Murray	18	18	21	17
Marc Oraison	20	12	7	3
Pope Paul VI	15	24	40	57
Karl Rahner	41	29	22	21
Rosemary Reuther	2	1	2	1
Edward Schillebeeckx	46	24	13	8
Cardinal Suenens	27	27	18	12
Documents of Vatican II	68	66	63	64

groups, it is impossible to assess how well the American Catholic clergy measures up to professional standards. Nevertheless, one must say in summarizing the data reported in this chapter that the Catholic priests do not look unimpressive. They work moderately long hours and evaluate themselves rather highly in comparison with other professional groups. Substantial proportions of them keep in contact with the periodical literature in their field and read the most serious and most important professional scholars. Whether the counterparts of Karl Rahner would be as popular in other professions or whether journals such as *Concilium* would be as widely read cannot be estimated with absolute confidence, but until data become available, it can be safely said that in absolute terms the Catholic clergy look rather good.

We conclude the descriptive section of the present chapter by asking a number of hypothetical questions:

1. *How do Catholic priests evaluate themselves in comparison with other professionals?* Priests evaluate themselves quite highly in comparison with other professionals, although the smallest majority is found among those who think that the amount of autonomy which priests have in decision-making is comparable to the amount which other professionals have.

2. *Do priests work hard?* This is an extremely difficult question to answer since it is practically impossible to define what hard work is, but at least they work moderately long hours, with the mean hours per week in excess of 50.

3. *Do priests get satisfaction out of their work?* Religious priests are more satisfied with their jobs than diocesan priests; and among diocesan priests, the lowest level of job satisfaction is found among associate pastors, who are lower even than comparison groups in the American population. Since the associate pastors represent about half of the priests thirty-five and under and a quarter of the priests between thirty-six and forty-five, the fact that their job satisfaction is even lower than that of unskilled manual workers represents an extremely serious problem for the clergy as a profession.

4. *Are priests interested in maintaining their professional skills?* The majority of priests want updating in theological and religious studies, and a fairly good proportion keep in touch with the best in periodical and scholarly literature. Not all priests read, of course; nowhere near a majority read the most serious journals such as *Concilium* or *Theological Studies,* but there is still considerable evidence that many priests do make serious efforts to stay well informed in the areas of their professional responsibility.

Analysis

Two indices are used in the analytic section of this chapter: one is the work-satisfaction index of Patricia Smith that we have already used in our descriptive tables, and the other is an index of "professional comparison" prepared by combining responses to the question of how a priest evaluates his professional position vis-à-vis other professionals.

As can be seen from Table 9.18, the index measuring the priest's comparative evaluation of his profession is more sensitive to prior variables than is the index measuring his absolute satisfaction with his work. Older priests, those who come from less tense families, those who report mystical experiences, and those with traditional values are more likely than other priests to evaluate their professional activity highly in comparison with other professionals.

Table 9.19 shows that these variables, together with "inner-directedness," account for only 15 per cent of the variance, though given the fact that none of them directly relate to the work the priest is doing, such an explanatory power is not unsatisfactory. In other words, at least 15 per cent of the variance in a priest's comparison of himself with other professionals can be accounted for by his age, his family background, his personality, his religious experience, and his values, quite independently of what he is actually doing in his work.

We are able to explain only 6 per cent of the variance on the work-satisfaction index with our analytic model (Table 9.20). Thus coming from a tense family, having an inner-directed personality, and possessing a record of religious experiences each adds 2 per cent to the explanation of whether a priest likes his work. Interestingly enough, neither age nor religious values have any explanatory power with regard to work satisfaction. Neither the young nor the "modern" are any less likely to be satisfied with their work, nor are they likely to be more satisfied.

Since professional comparison and work satisfaction are phenomena for which it is impossible to postulate a direction of causal flow, separate path diagrams were prepared for each of them (Figures 9.1 and 9.2).

TABLE 9.18

CORRELATES OF WORK-SATISFACTION AND
PROFESSIONAL-COMPARISON INDICES
(Pearson r)

Variable	Work Satisfaction	Professional Comparison
Age	.05	.25
Family tension	−.12	−.15
Inner-directed	.12	.08
Religious experience	.19	.20
"Modern" values	−.02	−.25

TABLE 9.19

EXPLANATION OF VARIANCE ON PROFESSIONAL-
COMPARISON INDEX

Variable	R^2	R^2 Change
Age	.06	.06
Family tension	.07	.01
Inner-directed	.10	.03
Religious experience	.12	.02
"Modern" values	.15	.03

TABLE 9.20

EXPLANATION OF VARIANCE ON WORK-SATISFACTION INDEX

Variable	R^2	R^2 Change
Age	.00	.00
Family tension	.02	.02
Inner-directed	.04	.02
Religious experience	.06	.02
"Modern" values	.06	.00

The decision was made to use work satisfaction in subsequent development of the model because even though we can explain less of the variation on the work-satisfaction scale, it is a somewhat stronger predictor of other variables "further down" the model, such as loneliness and future plans in the priesthood. It also makes some intuitive sense to think of a man's basic satisfaction with his work as being more important than his comparison of his work with the work of others.

An especially interesting phenomenon emerges in Figure 9.1. Even though the correlation between an inner-directed personality and a high professional comparison score is only .08, we observe that when age is held constant, the standardized regression coefficient goes up to .23. In other words, among those in the same age groups, those with higher inner-direction scores are more likely to be satisfied with their professional status in comparison with others than are those with lower inner-direction scores. While age accounts for 6 per cent of the variance in professional comparison, the absence of family tension, an inner-directed

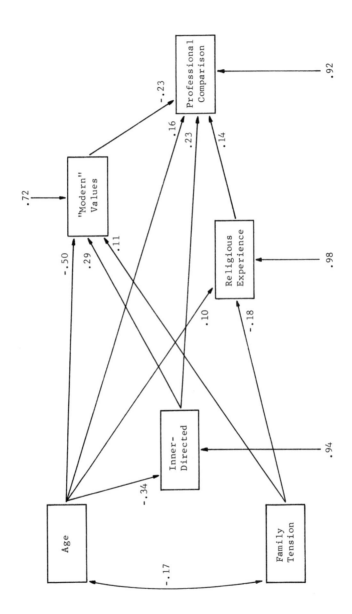

Fig. 9.1.—Path diagram relating professional comparison to prior variables. Active priests only.

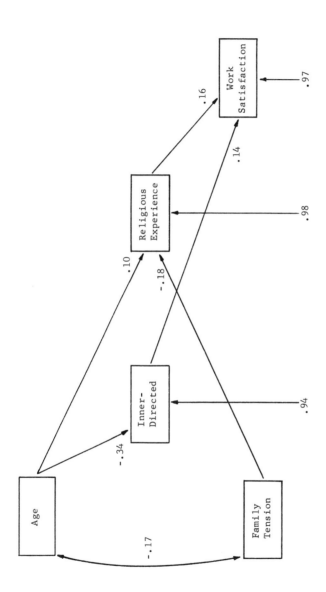

Fig. 9.2.—Path diagram relating work satisfaction to prior variables. Active priests only.

NOTE: All paths with coefficients less than .09 and all variables without significant paths have been omitted from this figure.

personality, and the experience of the mystical also contribute in combination 6 per cent of the explanation of the variance.

Even if the relationships are rather small, it is still interesting that family background, personality orientation, and religious experience can make a contribution to professional comparison — especially since the measures of both family tension and mystical experience are quite crude.

We note in Figure 9.2 that there are only two direct paths leading to the work-satisfaction box — a .16 coefficient from religious experience and a .14 from inner-direction. Thus, the basic model that we are using in this report does not tell us much about the reasons for being satisfied or dissatisfied with one's work. Of course, the technical problems of building the model make it impossible for us to include the specific work that a priest is doing in this analytic framework. What the model as it presently exists tells us is that quite independently of what specific work a man does, his level of satisfaction with it is shaped in part by whether he has had quasi-mystical experiences and in part by whether he is a "self-actualizing" person.

Feeling that one's talent is being used has a —.23 correlation with being an associate pastor and a .26 correlation with the number of hours worked per week. The latter correlation gives some hint of the willingness of the priests to work. The more they work, the more likely they are to think that their talents are being used. Given the fact that the work week seems relatively long, this relationship between satisfaction over the use of one's talent and the amount of time one works is some indication of the very high level of commitment that exists among many Catholic priests.

One of the variables in our correlation matrix was whether a priest was a member of a religious community or not. Even though there was an indication in the descriptive section of this chapter of a higher level of work satisfaction among the religious, this higher level of satisfaction produces a correlation with being a religious of only .12. Furthermore, no correlation in excess of .2 was found between being a religious and any of the other variables in our analytic model. We conclude that as far as the variables in our model are concerned, there is little difference between diocesan and religious priests, and therefore this variable was dropped from our model. (For a further discussion of the differences that do exist, see Appendix E.) Whether there are differences among religious communities is a question that merits further analysis after the completion of the present report.

There is also no important correlation between size of one's professional group (diocese or religious community) and work satisfaction (the actual correlation is .02). Size of community or diocese also did not turn out to be an important predictor of any of the variables in our model, including future plans in the priesthood. Hence, it too was dropped from our model.

Four questions will serve as a summary of our analytic findings:

1. *Which priests are most likely to be satisfied in their work?* Even though it is hard to explain satisfaction, those most likely to be favorably disposed toward their profession are the older priests, those with more "traditional" values, those who have had mystical experiences, those who come from less tense families, and those who have inner-directed personalities.

2. *Is dissatisfaction in the priesthood caused by long work hours?* On the contrary, the opposite seems to be the case. There is a positive relationship between number of hours worked and the feeling that one's talent is being used.

3. *Are there any important differences between religious and diocesan priests?* Although there is a somewhat higher level of work satisfaction among the religious, this difference produced a correlation of only .12. On the other variables used in our causal model, no differences even this large emerged.

4. *Is work satisfaction more likely in small dioceses or communities than in large?* We could discover no relationship of this kind.

1. The figures add to more than 100 per cent because many priests report more than one main job.

2. The four checklists can be found in Questions 20, 21, 25, and 26 of the main questionnaire (Appendix F).

3. We are grateful to Patricia C. Smith for making the data on industrial employees available to us.

CHAPTER 10

SATISFACTIONS AND FRUSTRATIONS IN THE PRIESTHOOD

Thus far we have considered how a priest, coming to the ministry with his family background and his personality, undergoing certain religious experiences, and accepting certain values, perceives the general ecclesiastical structure, his relationships with his most immediate colleagues, and his work. We now turn to the question of how this mix of background, experiences, values, perceptions, and work affects his satisfaction or dissatisfaction with the position in which he finds himself and the problems that he feels he encounters as a priest.

Description

Two principal findings are reported in the descriptive section of this chapter:

1. There are very considerable differences between active priests and resignees in what activities are perceived as being rewarding in the clerical life.

2. According to our respondents, the most serious problem that priests experience is the "way authority is exercised in the Church." Celibacy is mentioned rather far down the list of serious problems — even by the youngest age group of the clergy.

It is not merely from formal prayer that a priest is expected to develop his spiritual life. His work also is supposed to be part of his spiritual and personal development. Many priests do report that certain kinds of work are very valuable as contributions to their personal and spiritual fulfillment (Table 10.1). Among active diocesan priests, 67 per cent think that visiting the sick is very valuable, 62 per cent report that preparing sermons is very valuable, 57 per cent say that helping poor people is valuable, 54 per cent see value in spiritual reading, 50 per cent in small group discussions of spiritual concerns, 43 per cent find great value

TABLE 10.1

SPIRITUAL AND PERSONAL FULFILLMENT BY CLERICAL STATUS

(Per Cent Reporting Each Activity As "Very Valuable")

Activity	Diocesan			Religious		
	Bishops	Active Priests	Resigned Priests	Major Superiors	Active Priests	Resigned Priests
Visiting the sick	81	67	23	57	54	27
Helping people who are poor	77	57	49	55	48	54
Participating in some significant social action such as a rally or demonstration	11	8	14	6	7	14
Private devotion to Mary, e.g., rosary	74	43	6	51	46	8
Small group discussions of spiritual concerns	42	50	30	64	51	35
Supporting the causes of minority peoples	50	32	36	38	31	43
Preparing sermons	70	62	—[a]	62	62	—[a]
Active concern for mentally ill or retarded	40	30	26	18	23	25
Regular confession (at least monthly)	80	50	5	56	50	6
Working for better political leadership	15	14	18	13	14	21
Spiritual reading	79	54	15	72	62	21
Providing recreational facilities for the young or the deprived	28	24	14	18	18	15
Having a good time at a social gathering	21	28	24	21	24	22
Personal donations of money to worthy causes	53	42	12	30	17	12
Literature, drama, film, art	14	26	30	24	30	34

[a] Not applicable.

in private devotion to Mary, and 42 per cent say that making personal donations of money to worthy causes is very valuable to their personal and spiritual fulfillment. Although all these percentages are for diocesan priests, the patterns for the religious priests are similar. Bishops are even more likely than the active priests to find fulfillment in most of the activities listed in Table 10.1.

Table 10.2 shows significant patterns of change with age in spiritual and personal fulfillment. The value for fulfillment is less among the younger clergy than among the older in visiting the sick, in helping the poor, in private devotion to Mary (a decline from 79 per cent among those over fifty-five to 13 per cent among those thirty-five and under), in preparing sermons, in regular confession, and in reading spiritual books. On the other hand, the younger clergy find more value in small group discussions, in supporting the causes of minority peoples, in having a good time at social gatherings, and in literature, film, drama, and art.

TABLE 10.2

SPIRITUAL AND PERSONAL FULFILLMENT BY AGE

(Per Cent of Active Diocesan and Religious Priests Reporting
Each Activity As "Very Valuable")

Activity	Age			
	26-35	36-45	46-55	Over 55
Visiting the sick	51	56	64	73
Helping people who are poor	48	49	56	60
Participating in some significant social action such as a rally or demonstration	13	9	5	3
Private devotion to Mary, e.g., rosary	13	31	54	79
Small group discussions of spiritual concerns	61	57	47	35
Supporting the causes of minority peoples	38	33	30	27
Preparing sermons	56	58	66	70
Active concern for mentally ill or retarded	22	25	30	32
Regular confession (at least monthly)	26	41	57	74
Working for better political leadership	15	14	14	13
Spiritual reading	47	53	60	69
Providing recreational facilities for the young or the deprived	21	19	21	24
Having a good time at a social gathering	35	28	25	18
Personal donations of money to worthy causes	23	24	35	41
Literature, drama, film, art	37	29	23	21

This is not to imply that none of the younger clergy find value in either visiting the sick or preparing sermons, for 51 per cent of those thirty-five and under report that the former is very valuable for their fulfillment and 56 per cent report that the latter is very valuable.

We should note that the resigned priests were asked about their present fulfillments and not about those while they were in the active ministry. Except for preparing sermons, all the activities listed in Table 10.1 can apply to Christians in general. Without being in an official ministry, resignees are as likely or more likely than active priests under forty-six to find value in helping the poor, participating in significant social action, supporting the causes of minority groups, being concerned for the mentally ill, and enjoying literature, film, drama, and art. Like younger priests, few resignees highly value private devotion to Mary. Only a small minority still value other traditional forms of spiritual fulfillment, and about one-fourth value visiting the sick, small group discussions of spiritual concerns, and having a good time at social gatherings. Sixty-five per cent of the married resignees report "relating to my wife" as valuable to their spiritual and personal fulfillment.

A related question asked respondents to indicate the importance of various activities as sources of satisfaction in their lives. Table 10.3 shows that 83 per cent of the active diocesan priests find the administration of the sacraments and the liturgy of great importance as a source of satisfaction. Seventy-three per cent find great satisfaction in working with people and 60 per cent in being a part of a community of Christians. A little less than half of the active diocesan priests also report of great importance as a source of satisfaction the opportunity to exercise intellectual and creative abilities, the spiritual security that results from responding to the divine call, and the challenge of being a leader of a Christian community. Active religious priests are somewhat less likely than diocesan priests to find satisfaction in the liturgy and in the Christian community but more likely to find it in exercising intellectual and creative abilities.

For bishops, the greatest source of satisfaction is the liturgy (94 per cent), second is working with people (69 per cent), third is spiritual security from the divine call (67 per cent), and fourth is the satisfaction that comes from organizing and administering the work of the Church (64 per cent). The bishops are thus considerably more likely than active diocesan priests (a 30-percentage-point difference) to find satisfaction in administration, a phenomenon which may be a function of the

TABLE 10.3

SOURCES OF SATISFACTION, BY CLERICAL STATUS

(Per Cent Reporting That Each Item Is of "Great Importance" As a Source of Satisfaction)

Item	Diocesan			Religious		
	Bishops	Active Priests	Resigned Priests	Major Superiors	Active Priests	Resigned Priests
Joy of administering the sacraments and presiding over the liturgy	94	83	54	83	76	47
Respect that comes to the priestly office	37	25	5	15	21	3
Satisfaction in organizing and administering work of the Church	64	34	14	45	26	12
Opportunity to exercise intellectual and creative abilities	48	48	54	52	58	54
Spiritual security that results from responding to the divine call	67	43	8	50	48	9
Challenge of being the leader of the Christian community	57	41	31	55	33	25
Engaging in efforts at social reform	27	21	41	19	23	43
Being part of a community of Christians who are working together to share the good news of the gospel	60	60	49	79	67	46
Opportunity to work with many people and be a part of their lives	69	73	72	78	71	64
The well-being that comes from living the common life with like-minded confreres	48	36	19	76	62	22

fact that bishops have more opportunity for administration and also probably somewhat more challenging administrative responsibilities.

The resigned priests, on the other hand, are less likely than the active priests to report satisfying experiences while they were in the ministry. Fifty-four per cent of the resignees, as opposed to 83 per cent of the active diocesan priests, found great satisfaction in the liturgy; 8 per cent, as opposed to 43 per cent, found great satisfaction in the spiritual security that results from responding to the divine call; 31 per cent, as opposed to 41 per cent, found great satisfaction in exercising the role of leader of the Christian community; 49 per cent, as opposed to 60 per cent, found great satisfaction in working with a Christian community to spread the gospel; and 19 per cent, as opposed to 36 per cent, enjoyed the common life with like-minded confreres. A pattern is now beginning to emerge with regard to the resignees. Not only did they have fewer sources of satisfaction when they were in the ministry than active priests have, but also they found less reward in precisely those things which most active priests find rewarding, and also in which most active priests must spend most of their time. However, they were as likely as other priests to enjoy working with people and more likely to enjoy exercising intellectual and creative abilities and engaging in efforts at social reform. The resignees, in other words, got less satisfaction than active priests from the religious and spiritual dimensions of the priestly role and more satisfactions from the social, intellectual, and cultural aspects of the role.

In this respect, they are even different from the youngest members of the active clergy (Table 10.4). While those thirty-five and under are less likely than older priests to report satisfactions from the liturgy, they are still 21 percentage points more likely than the diocesan resignees to report it. The younger clergy are also more likely than both the older clergy and the resignees to say that they get satisfaction out of working with people, working with a Christian community to spread the gospel, and serving as a leader of a Christian community. Only on the matter of social reform are more resignees than clergy thirty-five and under likely to report greater satisfaction.

In other words, even if the younger clergy find less reward in some of the traditional activities required of the priest (they find little reward in the respect that comes to the priestly office or in spiritual security), they are still very likely to make up for lack of satisfaction in some areas by increased satisfaction in working with a Christian community, leading the Christian community, working with people, and exercising intellectual and creative abilities. The resignees apparently were unable to

TABLE 10.4

SOURCES OF SATISFACTION, BY AGE

(Per Cent of Active Diocesan and Religious Priests Reporting That Each
Item Is of "Great Importance" As a Source of Satisfaction)

Item	Age			
	26-35	36-45	46-55	Over 55
Joy of administering the sacraments and pre-siding over the liturgy	75	76	82	88
Respect that comes to the priestly office	8	17	24	42
Satisfaction in organizing and administering work of the Church	18	25	33	47
Opportunity to exercise intellectual and crea-tive abilities	61	56	49	44
Spiritual security that results from responding to the divine call	19	34	53	73
Challenge of being the leader of the Christian community	42	36	34	38
Engaging in efforts of social reform	29	22	19	17
Being part of a community of Christians who are working together to share the good news of the gospel	71	64	58	60
Opportunity to work with many people and be a part of their lives	81	73	70	64
The well-being that comes from living the com-mon life with like-minded confreres	42	41	47	62

compensate quite as well. Far fewer of them report satisfaction from presiding over the liturgy. Only on working for social reform do more resignees than the younger clergy report satisfaction. We can conclude tentatively, therefore, that the younger clergy who remain in the priesthood have been able to obtain a "mix" of satisfaction by blending the two dimensions of the priestly role — religious and social — in a combination that has proved rewarding. The resignees, on the other hand, were less likely to enjoy the religious role. Presumably the opportunities to engage in the social role are relatively limited. One might even guess, therefore, that the resignees' tendency to place such strong emphasis on the social role created for many of them situations in which there was relatively little satisfaction in their everyday work.

The other side of the coin of fulfillment and satisfaction is problems. We learn from Table 10.5 that the most frequently mentioned "great

TABLE 10.5

PROBLEMS IN THE PRIESTHOOD FOR SELF, BY CLERICAL STATUS

(Per Cent Reporting Each As "A Great Problem to Me Personally")

Problem	Diocesan			Religious		
	Bishops	Active Priests	Resigned Priests	Major Superiors	Active Priests	Resigned Priests
Lack of clear idea of what a priest is	0	7	25	0	5	23
Theological change in the concept of the priesthood	1	8	19	3	6	21
Absence of challenge in priestly work	1	9	32	3	5	22
The way authority is exercised in the Church	2	29	73	12	21	62
Relationships with superiors or pastor	1	15	41	2	8	22
Celibacy	1	12	58	4	9	55
Relevance of the work that priests do	1	10	54	1	8	51
Uncertainty about the future of the Church	3	10	19	5	7	23
Unrealistic demands and expectations of lay people	2	8	13	1	5	13
Loneliness of priestly life	1	16	51	8	13	52
Too little work	4	4	13	4	3	11
Too much work	8	9	7	7	7	8
Conflict with parishioners or laity about issues of the day	1	6	8	3	4	8
Lack of opportunity for personal fulfillment	0	10	50	3	6	41
Difficulty of really reaching people today	9	17	23	10	15	20

problem" is the way authority is exercised in the Church, with 29 per cent of the active diocesan priests and 21 per cent of the active religious priests indicating that this is a great problem to them personally. The second most frequently mentioned problem is the difficulty of really reaching people (17 per cent and 15 per cent), and the third is the loneliness of the priestly life (16 per cent and 13 per cent). The fourth most frequently mentioned problem among the diocesan priests is relationship with superiors or pastors (15 per cent), and the fifth is celibacy (12 per cent). Among the religious priests, celibacy is the fourth most frequently mentioned problem (9 per cent). Approximately one-tenth of the active diocesan priests mention as great problems lack of opportunity for personal fulfillment, relevance of the work that priests do, and too much work. In the light of the data in Table 10.5, it is difficult to argue that celibacy is the most serious problem facing active priests in the American Church. They are more than twice as likely to describe authority as a great problem than they are to so describe celibacy. It is worth noting, incidentally, that the way authority is exercised is also twice as likely to be mentioned as a problem than relationships with one's own superiors.

Bishops are not inclined to report great problems for themselves. The most serious one that they as a group experience is the difficulty of really reaching people (9 per cent). Major superiors are less likely than the active priests to report problems, though for them the one most frequently mentioned is also authority (12 per cent), followed by the difficulty of reaching people (10 per cent).

The resigned priests are much more likely to report problems. The most frequently mentioned one for them is also authority (73 per cent for the resigned diocesans and 62 per cent for the resigned religious), with celibacy mentioned second most frequently (58 per cent for the diocesans and 55 per cent for the religious). Other problems mentioned by more than half of the resignees are the relevance of the work the priest does, the loneliness of priestly life, and the lack of opportunity for personal fulfillment. Both active and resigned priests mention some of the same problems, but except for placing authority first on the list and loneliness third, the order varies. Thus, while the active priests mention celibacy fourth or fifth, the resignees place this second on their list of great problems to them personally. Relationships with superiors, the relevance of one's work, the lack of opportunity for personal fulfillment, and the difficulty of reaching people are also mentioned as principal problems by both resignees and actives but with varying degrees of emphasis.

Younger priests, like resignees, are more likely to have "great problems" (Table 10.6). Comparing those thirty-five and under to those over fifty-five, authority is a more serious problem (44 per cent versus 10 per cent), as is loneliness (23 per cent versus 6 per cent), difficulty in getting through to people (23 per cent versus 9 per cent), dealing with superiors (22 per cent versus 5 per cent), and celibacy and irrelevance of priestly work, each of which is mentioned by 18 per cent of the younger priests compared to 3 per cent of the older priests. However, two points must be made: (1) the younger clergy are less likely than the resignees to report any of these as great problems, and (2) celibacy is in fifth place in the list of problems among priests under thirty-six, as it is for active priests in general. It ought *not* to be concluded, therefore,

TABLE 10.6

PROBLEMS IN THE PRIESTHOOD FOR SELF, BY AGE

(Per Cent of Active Diocesan and Religious Priests Reporting Each
As "A Great Problem to Me Personally")

Problem	Age			
	26-35	36-45	46-55	Over 55
Lack of clear idea of what a priest is	9	8	4	2
Theological change in the concept of the priesthood	5	7	8	8
Absence of challenge in priestly work	10	10	5	3
The way authority is exercised in the Church	44	31	18	10
Relationships with superiors or pastor	22	14	7	5
Celibacy	18	15	8	3
Relevance of the work that priests do	18	12	5	3
Uncertainty about the future of the Church	10	9	8	7
Unrealistic demands and expectations of lay people	8	7	6	5
Loneliness of priestly life	23	20	10	6
Too little work	3	4	3	4
Too much work	12	9	8	5
Conflict with parishioners or laity about issues of the day	7	5	4	4
Lack of opportunity for personal fulfillment	13	11	6	4
Difficulty of really reaching people today	23	17	15	9

that the celibacy issue is not a problem for active priests, but it seems to us that one can legitimately argue from the data available in the study that it is not the only problem, nor even necessarily the most important problem. If it is a problem to be dealt with, it is one that presumably could be most effectively dealt with in a context of solutions to other problems that more priests are likely to feel are great problems for them personally.

Although priests over forty-five are much less likely than the younger clergy to have great problems, 18 per cent of those between forty-six and fifty-five mention authority as a serious problem, 15 per cent mention the difficulty of reaching people, and 10 per cent mention loneliness.

The final two descriptive tables in Chapter 10 deal with the respondents' perception not of their own problems but of the problems existing among most of the priests they know. If one looks at the active diocesan priests in Table 10.7, one notes that 35 per cent of them think that authority is a great problem for other priests, 27 per cent see relationships with superiors as a great problem, and 14 per cent mention theological change, the absence of challenge in priestly work, the loneliness of priestly life, and the difficulty of reaching people. Only 12 per cent mention the lack of personal fulfillment and 10 per cent mention celibacy. The list of problems in the order of importance is roughly the same whether one is describing one's own problems or the problems of others in the priesthood. In most cases, authority looms as the most frequently mentioned problem and celibacy is rather far down the list. Again, we are not asserting that the celibacy issue is not an important one for the Church and for its priesthood, but we are saying that on the basis of our data it would seem that priests perceive authority to be a more serious problem both for themselves and for other priests.

There are considerable differences among the age groups in perceptions of other priests' problems (Table 10.8), with the most obvious difference being that the younger a priest is, the more likely he is to perceive his colleagues as having problems. However, in all four age groups authority is the most frequently mentioned problem, with 19 per cent of those over fifty-five, 27 per cent of those between forty-six and fifty-five, 39 per cent of those between thirty-six and forty-five, and 45 per cent of those thirty-five and under mentioning it as a great problem for priests they know. Relationships with superiors is the second most frequently listed problem in each age group, with the range running from 14 per cent for those over fifty-five to 33 per cent for those thirty-five or younger. In other words, there is agreement on what the two

TABLE 10.7

PROBLEMS IN THE PRIESTHOOD FOR OTHERS, BY CLERICAL STATUS

(Per Cent Reporting Each As "A Great Problem to Most Priests I Know")

Item	Diocesan			Religious		
	Bishops	Active Priests	Resigned Priests	Major Superiors	Active Priests	Resigned Priests
Lack of clear idea of what a priest is	3	13	17	10	11	18
Theological change in the concept of the priesthood	3	14	16	11	13	14
Absence of challenge in priestly work	5	14	16	13	10	13
The way authority is exercised in the Church	9	35	47	29	29	34
Relationships with superiors or pastor	9	27	37	18	20	24
Celibacy	1	10	22	4	8	22
Relevance of the work that priests do	2	10	20	9	10	22
Uncertainty about the future of the Church	6	13	13	10	10	16
Unrealistic demands and expectations of lay people	2	7	5	2	5	5
Loneliness of priestly life	4	14	24	12	14	26
Too little work	2	4	6	3	3	5
Too much work	1	6	5	2	7	6
Conflict with parishioners or laity about issues of the day	3	7	7	3	6	6
Lack of opportunity for personal fulfillment	4	12	19	7	9	20
Difficulty of really reaching people today	6	14	15	10	14	13

TABLE 10.8

PROBLEMS IN THE PRIESTHOOD FOR OTHERS, BY AGE

(Per Cent of Active Diocesan and Religious Priests Reporting Each As
"A Great Problem to Most Priests I Know")

Item	Age			
	26-35	36-45	46-55	Over 55
Lack of clear idea of what a priest is	17	16	8	5
Theological change in the concept of the priesthood	17	15	11	10
Absence of challenge in priestly work	16	15	10	7
The way authority is exercised in the Church	45	39	27	19
Relationships with superiors or pastor	33	29	18	14
Celibacy	13	11	7	4
Relevance of the work that priests do	15	13	7	5
Uncertainty about the future of the Church	14	13	11	8
Unrealistic demands and expectations of lay people	6	7	6	6
Loneliness of priestly life	20	17	12	6
Too little work	4	4	3	3
Too much work	8	6	6	6
Conflict with parishioners or laity about issues of the day	8	7	6	6
Lack of opportunity for personal fulfillment	13	14	8	6
Difficulty of really reaching people today	18	17	12	8

main problems are, though the younger priests see these problems as much more widespread among their colleagues than do older priests. Even among the youngest, celibacy is low on the list, taking tenth place, with 13 per cent seeing it as a great problem for their colleagues, as opposed to 11, 7, and 4 per cent, respectively, for the older three age categories.

We summarize this section of the chapter by asking certain questions:

1. *What are the principal satisfactions in the life of the priest?* Presiding over the liturgy, working with people, and being a part of a Christian community seem to be the principal sources of satisfaction.

2. *What are the principal problems of the priesthood?* Authority is the most frequently mentioned problem, with the difficulty of reaching people, loneliness, relations with superiors, and celibacy coming next.

Analysis

In this analytic section we attempt to offer an explanation for the "loneliness" problem, which, as we shall see in subsequent chapters, is a powerful predictor of future plans in the priesthood. We observe in Table 10.9 that the younger clergy ($-.37$), those from tense families ($.22$), the inner-directed ($.11$), and those with "modern" values ($.37$) are more likely to have problems with loneliness, while those with higher work satisfaction ($-.26$) and a record of religious experience ($-.21$) are less likely to think of loneliness as a serious problem.

As Table 10.10 indicates, 25 per cent of the variance on loneliness can be accounted for in our causal model, with age accounting for 14 per cent of the variance, family tension and religious experience each accounting for 2 per cent, the value scale taking care of 3 per cent more, and work satisfaction accounting for 4 per cent. The remaining three-fourths of the variance must be attributed to factors not measured in our model. However, it must be said that given a problem as amorphous as loneliness, an explanation of one-fourth of the variance is highly acceptable.

If we look at Figure 10.1, we note that there are three direct paths over .10 leading to loneliness — from age ($-.21$), from "modern" values ($.22$), and from work satisfaction ($-.21$) — as well as paths of .10 from family tensions and $-.10$ from religious experience. Age also exercises an indirect influence through "modern" values of $(-.50 \times .22) = -.11$.

There is an overlap between the problem of the way authority is used and the problem of loneliness; but problems with authority explain only 2 percent of the variance on desire to marry while loneliness explains 7 per cent of the variance when the two variables are considered simultaneously (the model is not shown in our tables and figures). In other

TABLE 10.9

CORRELATES OF REPORTING THAT "LONELINESS
OF PRIESTLY LIFE" IS A PROBLEM

Variable	*Pearson* r
Age	$-.37$
Family tension	$.22$
Inner-directed	$.11$
Religious experience	$-.21$
"Modern" values	$.37$
Work satisfaction	$-.26$

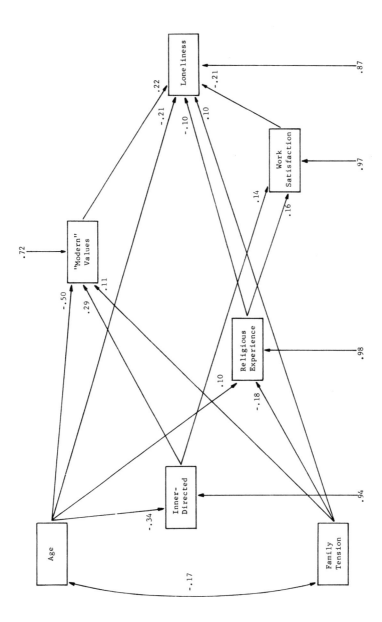

Fig. 10.1. — Path diagram relating loneliness to prior variables. Active priests only.

NOTE: All paths with coefficients less than .09 have been omitted from this figure.

TABLE 10.10

EXPLANATION OF VARIANCE ON LONELINESS

Variable	R^2	R^2 Change
Age	.14	.14
Family tension	.16	.03
Inner-directed	.16	.00
Religious experience	.18	.02
"Modern" values	.21	.02
Work satisfaction	.25	.04

words, there is a notable impact of loneliness that is quite independent of problems with authority. (The *beta* coefficients with desire to marry when all prior variables are held constant and the influence of these two problems on each other is also held constant is .33 for loneliness and .12 for problems with authority.) The authority problem and the loneliness problem then are not altogether independent of one another, but there is a substantial amount of independence, with the latter problem much more likely than the former to be a strong predictor of the desire to marry, which in its turn is a strong predictor of plans to leave the priesthood. Because of these relationships to subsequent variables in our analysis, we have added loneliness to our model.

We summarize with four questions:

1. *Why do some men experience more loneliness than others?* Young priests are more lonely than older priests, and those with less work satisfaction are more lonely than those with high work satisfaction, but a good deal of the loneliness must still be considered unexplained.

2. *Does what we know of the personality of priests from our personality scales enable us to explain much of the loneliness?* It does not.

3. *If priests liked their work better, would they be less lonely?* There is only a relatively moderate net effect of work satisfaction on loneliness, suggesting that an increase in the amount of work satisfaction would decrease the amount of loneliness only to a very moderate extent.

4. *Does difficulty with authority contribute to loneliness?* It is impossible to postulate one as a cause of the other, but when the mutual influence of loneliness and problems with authority are held constant, loneliness contributes much more of an explanation to the desire to marry than does authority.

CHAPTER 11

THE MORALE OF THE CLERGY

It is frequently said that the Catholic clergy in the United States are going through a very serious morale crisis. That assertion can probably be made of any profession in contemporary American society, though the startling increase in the number of resignations among Catholic priests and the impression that considerable confusion has been generated in the wake of the Second Vatican Council raise the possibility that the morale crisis may be especially severe among priests.

In this chapter we propose to use three measures of psychological well-being developed by Norman M. Bradburn. In Bradburn's theorizing about psychological well-being (or "happiness"), a "hydraulic model" is used. It is assumed that psychological well-being results not so much from the absence of negative feelings or the presence of positive feelings but from a satisfactory "balance of payments" between positive and negative feelings. Thus, a man may be "happy" if there is a rather low level of positive feeling in his life, as long as the level of negative feelings is even lower. Similarly, he may be "happy" even though there is much negative feeling in his life as long as there are also strong positive feelings that outweigh the negative ones. On the other hand, he may be "unhappy" despite having much positive emotional "payoff" in his life if the frustrations and dissatisfactions outweigh this "payoff." To put the matter statistically, Bradburn's model assumes that there is no correlation between positive and negative feelings — that is, the absence of the former does not predict the presence of the latter and vice versa.

Hence, the three scales that are used in accordance with the model are the following: a positive affect scale, which attempts to measure the feelings of satisfaction and emotional reward in a person's life; a negative affect scale, which is designed to record the feelings of frustration and dissatisfaction that a person experiences; and an affect balance scale, which is merely the difference between the other two scales. These three measures, or scales, are derived from items in the following questions:

215

During the past few weeks, did you ever feel —

A. Particularly excited or interested in something?
B. So restless that you couldn't sit long in a chair?
C. Proud because someone complimented you on something you had done?
D. Very lonely or remote from other people?
E. Pleased about having accomplished something?
F. Bored?
G. On top of the world?
H. Depressed or very unhappy?
I. That things were going your way?
J. Upset because someone criticized you?

These items may seem deceptively simple, but the reader who is interested in the theoretical and empirical rationale for the selection of these items and wishes to investigate their utility at greater length will discover in the work of Professor Bradburn (1969) that the three scales turn out to be extremely effective measures of psychological well-being.

Description

In the descriptive section of this chapter we report the following findings:

1. The mean score of American priests on the positive affect scale is probably the same as that of college-educated American males of the same age category who are married and higher than that of such males who are not married.

2. On the negative affect scale, scores of priests are lower than that of comparable American married males and much lower than that of unmarried males.

3. Therefore, on the affect balance scale, which measures the balance of psychological well-being, priests are higher than comparable American males who are married and much higher than unmarried males.

4. There is an apparent decline in morale as a priest approaches a decision to resign, then a burst of euphoria after such a decision, followed by an apparent slight tapering off of this euphoria in the succeeding years.

In Table 11.1 we note that bishops show a slightly lower level of positive affect than do diocesan priests and a much lower level of negative affect, so that on the affect balance scale bishops score 2.6 and active priests 2.0. Insofar as this scale measures psychological well-

TABLE 11.1

AFFECT SCALE SCORES BY CLERICAL STATUS

(Mean Scores)

Scale	Diocesan		Religious	
	Bishops	Active Priests	Major Supe-riors	Active Priests
Positive affect scale	3.2	3.3	3.1	3.3
Negative affect scale	.6	1.3	1.1	1.2
Affect balance scale	2.6	2.0	2.0	2.1

being, then, the morale of bishops can be said to be somewhat higher than that of diocesan priests. However, there is little difference between the diocesan priests and religious priests on the affect scales.

Since scores on the affect balance scale are the differences between scores on the positive and negative affect scales and can run from -5 to $+5$, one can conclude from Table 11.1 that Catholic priests enjoy a reasonable "balance-of-payments" surplus in their psychological well-being. Interestingly enough, psychological well-being, as measured by the affect balance scale, does not vary much by age, although the youngest priests are slightly lower than the older priests on the scale (Table 11.2). However, the similarity in balance is caused by the fact that both positive and negative affect decline with age. On positive affect the scores range from 3.7 for the youngest to 2.7 for the oldest, and on negative affect the range is from 1.9 for the youngest to .7 for the oldest.

TABLE 11.2

AFFECT SCALE SCORES BY AGE

(Mean Scores of Active Diocesan and Religious Priests)

Scale	Age			
	26-35	36-45	46-55	Over 55
Positive affect scale	3.7	3.4	3.2	2.7
Negative affect scale	1.9	1.4	1.0	.7
Affect balance scale	1.8	2.0	2.2	2.0

Older priests have somewhat fewer satisfactions than younger priests but also somewhat fewer emotional problems.

But the critical question for our purposes is how the American clergy compare with other males in the population in terms of psychological well-being. Through the courtesy of Professor Bradburn, data from a national sample study were made available for comparative purposes. It was decided that the only meaningful comparison was between priests and college-educated males in the same age categories. We observe in Table 11.3 that there are virtually no differences in positive affect, as measured by the Bradburn scales, between priests and married males who graduated from college and are in the same age group. The only difference is among respondents over fifty-five, and the fact that there are but ten respondents in the national sample who are over fifty-five makes this comparison meaningless.

Even though they are not married and even though they are in a profession that has considerable frustrations and is presently going through a serious crisis, the positive affect of priests is no lower than that of married college graduates who are the same age as the priests and indeed it is somewhat higher than the positive affect of unmarried males who graduated from college.

Although priests are virtually the same as married college-educated males in positive affect, they have *less* in the way of emotional problems as represented by the negative affect scale. Indeed, the lower scores of the clergy on this scale are considerable. Thus, priests are .7 lower in the twenty-six to thirty-five category and .7 lower in the thirty-six to forty-five category, although only .2 lower in the forty-six to fifty-five bracket.

Since the affect balance scale is the difference between the positive affect scale and the negative affect scale, we are prepared for the finding that Catholic priests score substantially higher than their age and education peers in the national population in terms of psychological well-being — at least as that variable is measured by our scale. The total score for priests is six times higher than that for unmarried college-educated males.

It is surely not the intention of this report to deny the existence of a morale crisis in the Catholic clergy. However, it is worth observing that however critical things may be for priests, their psychological well-being, as measured by the indicators available to us, is not only not worse than that of other men of comparable age and education but is better — better even than that of married men and much better than that of unmarried men.

TABLE 11.3

AFFECT SCALE SCORES OF PRIESTS AND COLLEGE-EDUCATED
MALES, BY AGE

(Mean Scores)

Age	Active Priests	College-educated Males[a] (Non-Priests)	
		Married	Unmarried
Positive Affect Scale			
26-35	$3.7_{(1,094)}$	$3.7_{(58)}$	—
36-45	$3.4_{(1,526)}$	$3.5_{(41)}$	—
46-55	$3.2_{(1,155)}$	$3.2_{(32)}$	—
Over 55	$2.7_{(1,313)}$	$3.2_{(10)}$	—
Total	$3.4_{(5,088)}$	$3.5_{(141)}$	$3.2^{b}_{(20)}$
Negative Affect Scale			
26-35	$1.9_{(1,094)}$	$2.6_{(58)}$	—
36-45	$1.5_{(1,526)}$	$2.2_{(41)}$	—
46-55	$1.1_{(1,155)}$	$1.3_{(32)}$	—
Over 55	$.7_{(1,313)}$	$1.9_{(10)}$	—
Total	$1.0_{(5,088)}$	$2.2_{(141)}$	$2.8^{b}_{(20)}$
Affect Balance Scale			
26-35	$1.8_{(1,094)}$	$1.1_{(58)}$	—
36-45	$2.0_{(1,526)}$	$1.3_{(41)}$	—
46-55	$2.2_{(1,155)}$	$1.0_{(32)}$	—
Over 55	$2.0_{(1,313)}$	$.3_{(10)}$	—
Total	$2.4_{(5,088)}$	$1.3_{(141)}$	$.4^{b}_{(20)}$

[a] Data from NORC Happiness Study, 1963.
[b] Not enough cases for breakdown by age.

It would be very helpful if one could study the change in psychological well-being that occurs in a man as he approaches resignation from the priesthood, decides to resign, and then begins his new life in the world beyond the priesthood. On the basis of clinical interviews with people contemplating resignation, Dr. James J. Gill, the prominent Jesuit psychiatrist, has suggested that resignation is preceded by a notable increase in depression (*Medical Insight,* 1969). When the decision to resign is finally made, there follows a burst of euphoria that Gill suggests, on the basis of psychoanalytic theory, will gradually ebb away to be replaced eventually by more depression.

We do not have data available to test Gill's hypothesis, but it is possible to create a "dummy" model that will enable us at least to speculate on his hypothesis. Our model (contained in Table 11.4) is *not* a longitudinal model, that is, it does not follow one man through eleven points in time. Instead it looks at eleven groups of men who at the present time are in different positions on the continuum of certainly staying in the priesthood to being out of the priesthood for five or six years. As one runs down the first column in Table 11.4, one can see that there is a steady decline of positive affect from a 3.2 score among those who are committed to the priesthood to a 2.8 score among those who will probably leave. But then among those who have definitely decided to leave, positive affect increases to a score of 3.4, which is higher than that of

TABLE 11.4

AFFECT SCALE SCORES OF ACTIVE PRIESTS AND RESIGNEES

(Mean Scores)

Item	Positive Affect Scale	Negative Affect Scale	Affect Balance Scale	N
Active priests (by future plans in priesthood):				
Definitely will not leave	3.2	.9	2.3	2,933
Probably will not leave	3.4	1.6	1.8	1,553
Uncertain	3.0	2.3	.7	447
Probably will leave	2.8	2.2	.6	97
Definitely decided to leave	3.4	2.1	1.3	59
Resigned priests (by year of resignation):				
1970	4.1	1.7	2.4	24
1969	4.2	1.3	2.9	301
1968	4.2	1.2	3.0	228
1967	4.2	1.4	2.8	123
1966	4.0	1.5	2.5	47
1964-65	4.0	1.7	2.3	16

those who are definitely committed to the priesthood. Then after resignation positive affect increases even more to a very high level (fluctuating around 4.1), which can only be characterized as euphoria. If one compares the positive affect scores of resignees in the first column of Table 11.4 with those of typical college-educated married American males in Table 11.3, one can see that in terms of positive affect the resigned priests are not only as well off as typical American males but much better off.

Similarly, on the negative affect scale there is a fairly steady increase in negative affect up to the time a decision has been made to resign. There is a decrease in negative affect in the years after resignation until one has been away from the priesthood for a half decade, when negative affect increases once again. In most of the time points after resignation, however, resigned priests are lower in negative affect than that of the typical college-educated American males represented in Table 11.3.

Finally, in the last column of Table 11.4 we see that psychological well-being as measured by the affect balance scale declines from 2.3 to .6 as one progresses from a definite commitment to stay to a probable decision to leave. Then affect balance moves up again to 1.3 when a decision has been made, and climbs back to 2.4 immediately after resignation. It climbs once again to a euphoric 3.0 several years after resignation, only to begin a decline again to 2.3 five or six years after resignation, which is the same level as active priests who have definitely decided to stay in the priesthood.

There is, then, in Table 11.4 some evidence in support of one element of Gill's hypothesis. Psychological well-being goes down as one approaches resignation, begins to move up when one makes the decision to resign, and then moves up quite high in the years immediately after resignation, only to decline somewhat in later years. *However,* two things must be noted about the psychological well-being of the clergy who resigned five or six years ago: (1) it is the same (2.3) as the psychological well-being of those who definitely are not leaving the priesthood and (2) it is substantially *higher* than that of typical college-educated American males as recorded in Table 11.3. There is, therefore, no reason to believe, at least on the basis of our data, that resignees have any less psychological well-being than committed active priests. Nor is there any reason to believe that they are less capable of happy lives than typical American males.

Many of our colleagues at NORC have observed that the scores of the resigned priests on the positive affect scale smack of euphoria. There may be a very simple explanation for this. As we have pointed out in earlier chapters, many men in the priesthood apparently do not like their work. They find many frustrations and dissatisfactions in the life of a priest. If a man is caught in a situation that comes close to being intolerable, and then is able to break out of the situation at considerable pain, there is every reason to expect that his sense of well-being will go up and stay up for a considerable period of time, if not indefinitely. Euphoric they may be, but that euphoria may be neither forced nor unauthentic.

To conclude the descriptive section of this chapter briefly, we observe in Table 11.5 that about three-fifths of the active diocesan priests, two-fifths of the religious priests, one-third of the bishops, and one-fifth of the major superiors have at least one day off almost every week. Approximately 80 per cent of all clergy except the major superiors had a vacation within the past year, while 64 per cent of the latter had one. Most priests, then, manage to have vacations, and three-fifths of the diocesan priests also have at least a day off every week. Furthermore, Table 11.6 shows that the youngest priests are more likely both to have a day off and to have a vacation.

To summarize the descriptive section of this chapter through the usual series of questions, we ask:

1. *Are priests unhappy?* Quite the contrary, they seem to be happier than comparable groups of men — at least insofar as happiness is measured by our indicators of psychological well-being.

2. *Is the decision to resign preceded by a decline in psychological well-being and followed by an increase in it?* This pattern does indeed seem to occur, at least insofar as our "dummy" model is able to indicate.

TABLE 11.5

RECREATION BY CLERICAL STATUS

(Per Cent)

	Diocesan		Religious	
Recreation	Bishops	Active Priests	Major Superiors	Active Priests
One day or more off almost every week	31	63	23	41
Last vacation within a year	79	84	64	80

TABLE 11.6

RECREATION BY AGE

(Per Cent of Active Diocesan and Religious Priests)

Recreation	Age			
	26-35	36-45	46-55	Over 55
One day or more off every week	60	54	55	46
Last vacation within a year	92	86	81	72

There is also some evidence of a return to more normal levels of psychological well-being several years after resignation.

3. *Are resigned priests less happy than those who remain in the priesthood?* Again, insofar as our indicators are valid measures, they are not any less happy, and indeed are more happy, than typical American males of the same educational background and age.

Analysis

In reading the analysis section of this chapter, one must keep in mind the fact that the positive and negative affect scales do not correlate with one another. A person can score high on both scales or low on both scales. In Professor Bradburn's theorizing, happiness is the result of having a positive scale score that is higher than the negative scale score. A person can thus be "happy" with a low score on the positive scale, as long as his score on the negative scale is even lower.

In Table 11.7 we see that the principal explanations of positive affect are youthfulness, a high score on the inner-directed scale, an experience of mystical feelings, having "modern" values, and high work satisfaction. This particular combination of predictive variables is not often found in our report. Men who score high on positive affect are younger, inner-directed in their personality, and modern in their theological thinking, but have had religious experiences and are highly satisfied with their work.

Table 11.7 show that negative affect is more likely to be found among the young and among those who come from tense family backgrounds. Those with negative affect also are less likely to have had religious experiences, have high scores on the "modern" scale, have low professional comparison scores, and are more likely to have low work satis-

TABLE 11.7

CORRELATES OF POSITIVE AFFECT, NEGATIVE AFFECT,
AND AFFECT BALANCE SCALES

(Pearson *r*)

Variable	Positive Affect Scale	Negative Affect Scale	Affect Balance Scale
Age	−.32	−.33	.01
Family tension	−.02	.20	−.16
Inner-directed	.26	.05	.15
Religious experience	.17	−.17	.24
"Modern" values	.28	.29	−.01
Professional comparison	.09	−.25	.25
Work satisfaction	.31	−.30	.43
Loneliness	.00	.45	−.33

faction scores. The strongest predictor of negative affect, however, is the experience of loneliness as a problem — a correlation of .45. There is, however, little correlation between negative affect and one's score on the inner-directed personality scale. Negative affect in the clergy, then, results from loneliness, youthfulness, little satisfaction from one's work, more "modern" religious values, a low evaluation of the priesthood in comparison with other occupations, a tense family background, and a low level of religious experience.

Psychological well-being as measured by the affect balance scale correlates with having religious experiences, seeing loneliness as a problem, a high professional evaluation of the ministry, and high work satisfaction. It does not, interestingly enough, correlate with age. Happiness is no monopoly of either the young or the old in the clergy; it is to be found among those who like their work, are not lonely, rate the priesthood rather high in comparison with other professions, and have had some experiences of contact with God. There is a relationship between psychological well-being as measured by the affect balance scale and a propensity to stay in the priesthood (a correlation of .23).

Since age correlates negatively with both the positive and negative affect scales, it has no correlation with the affect balance scale. Similarly, having "modern" values predicts both high positive affect and high negative affect but has no relationship with the affect balance scale. The positive and negative relationships thus cancel each other out. On the other hand, work satisfaction correlates positively with high positive affect (.31) and negatively with high negative affect (−.30) and hence becomes a very strong predictor of a high score on the affect balance scale (.43). If one asks how Roman Catholic priests could be made more happy (in the sense of having a higher "balance of payments" between positive and negative affect), an obvious response would be that one must increase the level of their work satisfaction score.

It is possible to explain a respectable 24 per cent of the variance on the positive affect scale with our predictor variables — with age and work satisfaction making most of the contribution to the explanation (Table 11.8). Twenty-nine per cent of the variance on the negative scale can be explained, with age, work satisfaction, and loneliness having the main explanatory power (Table 11.9). (When the influence of all other factors is held constant, loneliness adds 7 percentage points to the explanatory power of our model.)

TABLE 11.8

EXPLANATION OF VARIANCE ON POSITIVE AFFECT SCALE

Variable	R^2	R^2 Change
Age	.10	.10
Family tension	.11	.01
Inner-directed	.13	.02
Religious experience	.16	.03
"Modern" values	.17	.01
Work satisfaction	.24	.07

TABLE 11.9

EXPLANATION OF VARIANCE ON NEGATIVE AFFECT SCALE

Variable	R^2	R^2 Change
Age	.11	.11
Family tension	.13	.02
Inner-directed	.13	.00
Religious experience	.15	.02
"Modern" values	.16	.01
Work satisfaction	.22	.06
Loneliness	.29	.07

We note from the first row of Table 11.10 that the young are higher in positive affect in part because they are more inner-directed (a change of .06 from −.33 to −.27) and in part because they are more "modern" (a change of .06 from −.29 to −.23). From the third row we see that the inner-directed have higher morale in part because they are more "modern" and in part because they like their work better. Further, those who have religious experiences have higher morale in part because they too like their work better.

On the other hand, in Table 11.11 we see that the young have higher negative affect in part because they are more "modern" (a change of .08) and in part because they see loneliness as a problem (a change of .06). Those from tense families have higher negative affect in part because they have fewer religious experiences, in part because they have more "modern" values, and in part because they have less work satisfaction. Those who have not had religious experiences are inclined to higher negative affect in part because they are more "modern," in part because they like their work less, and in part because they see loneliness as a problem.

Figures 11.1 and 11.2 enable us to examine graphically the causes of positive and negative affect. The principal direct paths to positive affect in Figure 11.1 are age (−.25) and work satisfaction (.28), with religious experience (.15), modern values (.11), and inner-directedness (.09) making smaller direct contributions to positive affect.

In Figure 11.2 loneliness dominates the paths leading to negative affect (.30), though work satisfaction (−.19) and age (−.17) also have a direct impact on negative affect. Age thus has a negative influence on both positive and negative affect (both go down as you get older) while work satisfaction has a negative influence on negative affect and a positive influence on positive affect (the more you like your work, the more positive feelings go up and negative feelings go down).

We can summarize with the following questions:

1. *Why are some priests happy and others not happy?* Religious experience, work satisfaction, and favorable comparisons with other professionals seem to be the principal components of high morale for priests. Thus, if a priest feels that he is in contact with God and likes his work, then his morale "balance of payments" is likely to be very satisfactory.

2. *Are young priests more or less happy than older priests?* Younger priests have both higher positive affect and higher negative affect but the

TABLE 11.10

SIMPLE CORRELATIONS AND TOTAL INDEPENDENT EFFECTS OF SELECTED VARIABLES ON NEGATIVE AFFECT

Variable	Simple Correlation (Pearson r)	Independent Effects of Added Variable (Standardized Net Regression Weights)					
		Age	Family Tension	Inner-Directed	Religious Experience	"Modern" Values	Work Satisfaction
Age	−.32	−.32	−.33	−.27	−.29	−.23	−.25
Family tension	−.02	—	−.08	−.07	−.04	−.05	−.03
Inner-directed	.26	—	—	.17	.16	.13	.09
Religious experience	.17	—	—	—	.18	.19	.15
"Modern" values	.28	—	—	—	—	.11	.11
Work satisfaction	.31	—	—	—	—	—	.28

TABLE 11.11

SIMPLE CORRELATIONS AND TOTAL INDEPENDENT EFFECTS OF SELECTED VARIABLES ON POSITIVE AFFECT

Variable	Simple Correlation (Pearson r)	Independent Effects of Added Variable (Standardized Net Regression Weights)						
		Age	Family Tension	Inner-Directed	Religious Experience	"Modern" Values	Work Satis-faction	Loneli-ness
Age	−.33	−.33	−.31	−.33	−.32	−.24	−.23	−.17
Family tension	.20	—	.14	.14	.12	.11	.09	.06
Inner-directed	.05	—	—	−.06	−.06	−.10	−.07	−.06
Religious experience	−.17	—	—	—	−.11	−.09	−.06	−.03
"Modern" values	.29	—	—	—	—	.15	.15	.08
Work satisfaction	−.30	—	—	—	—	—	−.25	−.19
Loneliness	.45	—	—	—	—	—	—	.30

"balance of payments" for both young and old is such that there is no correlation between the affect balance scale and age.

3. *Is loneliness an important cause of low morale among priests?* It appears to be. When all other variables are held constant, the "pure" contribution of loneliness to negative affect explains 7 per cent of the variance.

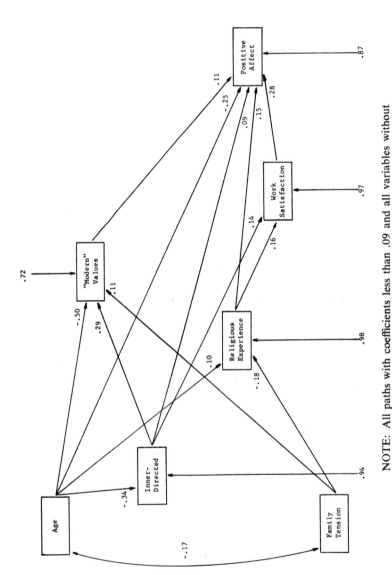

NOTE: All paths with coefficients less than .09 and all variables without significant paths have been omitted from this figure.

Fig. 11.1 — Path diagram relating positive affect to prior variables. Active priests only.

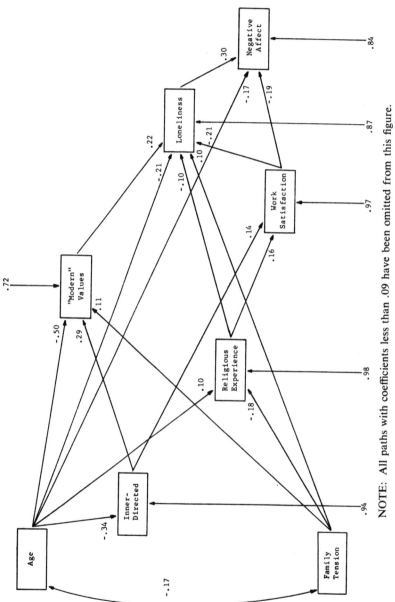

NOTE: All paths with coefficients less than .09 have been omitted from this figure.

Fig. 11.2 — Path diagram relating negative affect to prior variables. Active priests only.

CHAPTER 12

THE CELIBACY ISSUE

It would be very difficult to be unaware that the Roman Catholic Church is involved in a serious controversy on the issue of obligatory celibacy for its clergy. The Vatican has given repeated indications that a change in this discipline is not to be expected, and the hierarchies of the world have, generally speaking, endorsed the Vatican stand. Nevertheless, the controversy and agitation over the issue continue. In the present chapter we report the direct reactions of the clergy to certain questions that relate to the celibacy issue.

Description

The principal findings to be reported in the descriptive section of this chapter are that a slight majority of priests support a change in the celibacy discipline, and that most priests would not marry if they could — indeed, even most *young* priests would not marry if they were free to do so. Most priests value celibacy as a means for facilitating their work, but they also expect a change in the discipline rather soon. The hierarchy, however, seems firmly opposed to change.

Table 12.1 shows that approximately a third of the American priests "strongly" support celibacy as a matter of *personal choice* for diocesan priests, and another fifth agree "somewhat" with such a proposal. Thus, 56 per cent of the diocesan priests and 53 per cent of the religious priests agree either strongly or somewhat that celibacy should be a matter of personal choice for diocesan priests. But while 52 per cent of the religious superiors are also in favor of such a change, only 11 per cent of the bishops are willing to agree. To look at the matter from the other end of the scale, 28 per cent in each category of active priests disagree strongly with optional celibacy, while 73 per cent of the hierarchy disagree strongly with such a proposal.

There are, in addition, sharp differences among age groups. If we inspect the upper-left-hand and lower-right-hand corners of Table 12.2,

233

TABLE 12.1

ATTITUDE ON OPTIONAL CELIBACY, BY CLERICAL STATUS

(Per Cent Giving Each Response to the Statement, "Celibacy Should Be a
Matter of Personal Choice for Diocesan Priests")

Response	Diocesan		Religious	
	Bishops	Active Priests	Major Superiors	Active Priests
Agree strongly	3	37	30	32
Agree somewhat	8	19	22	21
Uncertain	4	7	13	9
Disagree somewhat	12	10	12	10
Disagree strongly	73	28	24	28
Total	100	101[a]	101[a]	100

[a] Not 100 per cent because of rounding.

we discover that three-fifths of the priests thirty-five and under strongly support optional celibacy, while three-fifths of the priests over fifty-five strongly oppose it. A majority of those under forty-six are either strongly or somewhat in favor of a change, and almost half of those between forty-six and fifty-five support a personal choice with regard to celibacy. It is also clear from comparing the last column of Table 12.2 with the first column of Table 12.1 that priests over fifty-five are somewhat more disposed to change than are bishops, with 21 per cent of the priests over fifty-five willing to express at least some support for optional celibacy, as opposed to 11 per cent of the bishops.

As Table 12.3 indicates, the differences between the priests and the bishops persist in their expectations of whether in fact there will be a change in the celibacy discipline. More than three-fifths of the priests expect such a change, but less than one-fifth of the bishops anticipate it. Of those bishops who expect a change, only 59 per cent think the change will occur within the next ten years, while about 75 per cent of the priests who expect a change think that it will be within ten years. There is, then, not only a strong disagreement over whether a change in the celibacy regulation is desirable, there are also very different expectations about whether such a change will occur.

TABLE 12.2

ATTITUDE ON OPTIONAL CELIBACY, BY AGE

(Per Cent of Active Diocesan and Religious Priests Giving Each Response
to the Statement, "Celibacy Should Be a Matter of Personal
Choice for Diocesan Priests")

Response	Age			
	26-35	36-45	46-55	Over 55
Agree strongly	61	43	25	10
Agree somewhat	23	24	20	11
Uncertain	4	8	10	8
Disagree somewhat	6	10	13	11
Disagree strongly	5	15	32	60
Total	99[a]	100	100	100

[a] Not 100 per cent because of rounding.

But while more than half the priests in the country would approve of the change and over three-fifths expect a change, only one-fifth of the diocesan priests and one-tenth of the religious say that they would "certainly" or "probably" marry in the event of a change. The celibacy change, then, is apparently advocated as a matter of principle more than as something that has a direct relationship with the personal plans and inclinations of most priests.

Table 12.3 also shows that a little more than half of the diocesan priests and a little less than half of the religious priests agree that those who have left the priesthood should be invited to return; but less than one-tenth of the bishops agree with this stance.

When we look at expectations by age (Table 12.4), we see that almost nine-tenths of those thirty-five and under expect a change, while only one-third of those over fifty-five expect it. Furthermore, only 4 per cent of those over fifty-five think they would "certainly" or "probably" marry, compared to 33 per cent of those under thirty-six. One could perhaps write two different newspaper stories from that portion of Table 12.4 which depicts the percentages of those under thirty-six who would marry if they were free to do so. One story would have the headline, "One-third of younger priests would marry," and the other, "Two-thirds of younger priests would not marry." Both headlines, of course, would be true, and which emphasis one selects is largely a matter of personal

TABLE 12.3

FUTURE OF CELIBACY, BY CLERICAL STATUS

(Per Cent)

Item	Diocesan			Religious		
	Bishops	Active Priests	Resigned Priests	Major Superiors	Active Priests	Resigned Priests
Expect change in law of celibacy	18	65	92	67	61	93
Expect change in law of celibacy within 10 years[a]	59	75	73	69	74	74
Would certainly or probably marry if celibacy for priests became optional	1	22	—[b]	6	13	—[b]
Would certainly or probably transfer to a diocese in order to marry	—[c]	—[c]	—[b]	3	9	—[b]
Agree strongly or somewhat that priests who have resigned from the priesthood should be invited to reapply for permission to function as priests again, whether they are married or single	9	54	—[b]	44	48	—[b]

[a] Of those who expect change.
[b] Not asked of resigned priests.
[c] Not applicable.

TABLE 12.4

FUTURE OF CELIBACY, BY AGE

(Per Cent of Active Diocesan and Religious Priests)

Item	Age			
	26-35	36-45	46-55	Over 55
Expect change in law of celibacy	88	76	58	33
Expect change within 10 years[a]	76	78	75	66
Would certainly or probably marry if celibacy for priests became optional	33	24	13	4
Would certainly or probably transfer to a diocese in order to marry	14	13	7	2
Agree somewhat or strongly that priests who have resigned from the priesthood should be invited to reapply for permission to function as priests again, whether they are married or single	76	62	42	25

[a] Of those who expect change.

choice. Whatever choice is made, the point must still be emphasized that even among the younger clergy (who are most in favor of a change in the celibacy regulation), a large majority at the present time do not see themselves as either certainly or probably relinquishing their commitment to celibacy.

There are dramatic differences among the age groups about the question of inviting the resigned priests to return. One-quarter of those over fifty, two-fifths of those between forty-six and fifty-five, three-fifths of those between thirty-six and forty-five, and three-quarters of those thirty-five and under are in sympathy with the return of the resignees.

One is forced, then, to ask what advantages priests see in the unmarried state. We observe in Table 12.5 that 78 per cent of the diocesan priests think that celibacy is an advantage for doing their work better. Furthermore, 56 per cent see it as a means of developing their love of God and 56 per cent also describe it as a means of relating more fully to other people. Finally, 52 per cent endorse it as a means of personal growth and development. Support for each of these advantages is somewhat higher among the religious clergy, indicating perhaps that the formal "vow" of celibacy may strengthen one's commitments to the advantages of the celibate state.

TABLE 12.5

ATTITUDES TOWARD VALUE OF CELIBACY, BY CLERICAL STATUS

(Per Cent Feeling that Celibacy Is "Very Much" or "Somewhat"
of an Advantage for Each Aspect)

Aspect	Diocesan		Religious	
	Bishops	Active Priests	Major Superiors	Active Priests
For doing my work better	96	78	90	85
For my personal growth and development	82	52	68	62
For the development of my love of God	89	56	77	70
For relating more fully to other people	86	56	72	68

The proportion agreeing with each of the positive aspects of celibacy increases with age (Table 12.6). A majority of all those over thirty-five endorse all of the positive functions of celibacy with the exception of those between thirty-six and forty-five on the matter of celibacy promoting personal growth and development — only 43 per cent in that age category agree with such an assertion. However, majority support among those thirty-five and under can be found only for the statement that celibacy is an asset for doing their work better (73 per cent).

TABLE 12.6

ATTITUDES TOWARD VALUE OF CELIBACY, BY AGE

(Per Cent of Active Diocesan and Religious Priests Feeling that Celibacy
Is "Very Much" or "Somewhat" of an Advantage for Each Aspect)

Aspect	Age			
	26-35	36-45	46-55	Over 55
For doing my work better	73	75	83	92
For my personal growth and development	37	43	64	81
For the development of my love of God	39	52	71	86
For relating more fully to other people	45	52	66	82

Yet the clergy do tend to support a change in the celibacy regulations. We must look to Table 12.7 to see the reasons. First of all, although more than 80 per cent of the active priests agree that "the celibate life allows more time for the priest to be available to the people," only 44 per cent of the diocesan and 49 per cent of the religious priests agree that "celibacy is essential in order to realize the full potential of the priesthood," and 55 per cent of the diocesan and 48 per cent of the religious agree that "the present requirement of celibacy keeps many men from entering the priesthood who would actually make excellent priests." Somewhat more than half of the priests agree that today's deeper understanding of the person is helping us to realize that celibacy is in fact harmful for some priests." Finally, about one-third of the priests think that "a married clergy would better understand the problems of the laity," and also one-third think that "priestly companionship with God" ought to "exclude companionship with another in marriage."

Piecing these responses together, we can see that the overwhelming majority of the priests agree that celibacy provides a priest with more time to be available to the people, but slightly less than half think that celibacy is essential to fulfill the potential of the priesthood, and only one-third think that the nature of the priest's relationship with God excludes companionship with another in marriage. On the other hand, approximately half think that celibacy may be harmful to some priests and half also think that many men are kept from the priesthood by the requirement of celibacy. Only a third, however, think that married men could more deeply understand the problems of the laity. Celibacy, in other words, is perceived to be useful, important, valuable, but not absolutely essential. The obligation is seen as standing in the way of some men's happiness in the priesthood and of other men joining it.

We also discover in Table 12.7 that about half the priests in the country think it unwise for priests to have women as close friends, and about three-fifths think that there are many women who like to chase after priests. On the other hand, about half think that "a warm friendship between a priest and a woman may help him become more fully human."

There are also rather dramatic correlates between attitudes on celibacy and women and the age of priests, although there is only some difference between old and young in their agreement that celibacy does allow more time for the priest to be available to the people (Table 12.8). However, 77 per cent of those over fifty-five think it is unwise for priests to have women as close friends, as opposed to 24 per cent of those thirty-five and under. Seventy-eight per cent of the upper age group think that

TABLE 12.7

ATTITUDES TOWARD SEXUALITY, BY CLERICAL STATUS

(Per Cent Agreeing Strongly or Somewhat with Each Statement)

Statement	Diocesan			Religious		
	Bishops	Active Priests	Resigned Priests	Major Superiors	Active Priests	Resigned Priests
Usually, it is unwise for priests to have women as close friends	76	51	—[a]	51	48	—[a]
Celibacy is essential in order to realize the full potential of the priesthood	83	44	4	52	49	2
When a priest has a warm friendship with a woman, it usually helps him become more fully human	23	50	91	55	53	87
Priestly companionship with God means an experiential union so close and so strong as to exclude companionship with another in marriage	54	30	2	35	34	1
The present requirement of celibacy keeps many men from entering the priesthood who would actually make excellent priests	24	55	—[a]	45	48	—[a]
A married clergy would better understand the problems of the laity	6	32	87	24	32	86
Today's deeper understanding of the person is helping us to realize that celibacy is in fact harmful for some priests	19	53	93	55	54	91
The celibate life allows more time for the priest to be available to the people	94	82	—[a]	90	86	—[a]

TABLE 12.7 — Continued

Statement	Diocesan			Religious		
	Bishops	Active Priests	Resigned Priests	Major Superiors	Active Priests	Resigned Priests
There are quite a few women who like to chase after priests	64	61	—[a]	60	58	—[a]
Marriage contributes to the fullness of human life and therefore can contribute to the fullness of priestly life	10	48	96	40	44	93
The *primary* reason for celibacy is that it witnesses to the future life with God	53	36	14	55	41	15
Temptations to impurity are the most serious temptations in the lives of most priests	20	30	—[a]	26	28	—[a]

[a] Not asked of resigned priests.

TABLE 12.8

ATTITUDES TOWARD SEXUALITY, BY AGE

(Per Cent of Active Diocesan and Religious Priests Agreeing Strongly
or Somewhat with Each Statement)

Statement	Age			
	26-35	36-45	46-55	Over 55
Usually it is unwise for priests to have women as close friends	25	38	58	77
Celibacy is essential in order to realize the full potential of the priesthood	18	33	53	78
When a priest has a warm friendship with a woman, it usually helps him become more fully human	72	63	43	28
Priestly companionship with God means an experiential union so close and so strong as to exclude companionship with another in marriage	11	21	35	59
The present requirement of celibacy keeps many men from entering the priesthood who would actually make excellent priests	72	61	46	33
A married clergy would better understand the problems of the laity	46	39	27	18
Today's deeper understanding of the person is helping us to realize that celibacy is in fact harmful for some priests	73	64	48	29
The celibate life allows more time for the priest to be available to the people	79	79	85	93
There are quite a few women who like to chase after priests	52	54	60	72
Marriage contributes to the fullness of human life and therefore can contribute to the fullness of priestly life	74	59	35	16
The *primary* reason for celibacy is that it witnesses to the future life with God	38	33	38	45
Temptations to impurity are the most serious temptations in the lives of most priests	16	25	33	41

celibacy is essential for the full potential of the priesthood, compared to only 18 per cent of the younger age group. Thirty-three per cent of those over fifty-five think the present requirement keeps excellent men out of the priesthood, while 72 per cent of those thirty-five and under think so. In other words, while there is an agreement among older and younger priests that there are certain advantages of celibacy to priestly work, there is strong disagreement about whether celibacy is essential and whether there might also be an advantage in having a married clergy in addition to a celibate clergy.

In the figures reported in Table 12.7, there is little difference between the active diocesan and religious priests. However, as one might expect, the resignees are much more sympathetic to positions that indicate a change in the celibacy regulations and the bishops much less sympathetic. For example, only about a fifth of the bishops think that celibacy may be harmful for some priests while over half the active priests and nine-tenths of the resignees think so. On the other hand, 54 per cent of the bishops think that the priesthood excludes companionship with a woman in marriage, while only 30 per cent of the diocesan actives and only 2 per cent of the resignees agree.

What is the nature of the relationship between men who are committed to the celibate life and women? The answer goes far beyond the scope of the present survey, though perhaps one can expect somewhat more clarification on this question from the Loyola report. However, the respondents to the NORC questionnaire were asked, "How often do you . . . go out with women socially — other than for necessary professional reasons?" The responses are shown in Table 12.9. A little over 50 per cent of the active priests in the country say that they never go out socially with women; about 35 per cent say that they do so several times a year; approximately 10 per cent report doing so several times a month; and 4 per cent say that they do so weekly.

But most of those who report that they go out with women socially say they do so in groups and not in couples; only about 10 per cent of the priests in the country report going out with women "as a couple."

Table 12.10 shows that there are some differences between the younger and the older priests in their patterns of going out with women. Thus, 68 per cent of the older priests say that they never go out with women socially, while only 36 per cent of the younger say that they never do. However, most of the socializing by the younger clergy is still done only several times a year (42 per cent). The younger clergy are also somewhat more likely to go out with women "as a couple" (14 per cent), but nonetheless, 50 per cent of them report that their social interaction with women is in a group.

There is little in Tables 12.9 and 12.10 to indicate that the Catholic clergy are engaged in feverish courtship relationships in preparation for a change in the celibacy regulation. On the other hand, whatever is to

TABLE 12.9

GOING OUT WITH WOMEN SOCIALLY, BY CLERICAL STATUS

(Per Cent)

Going Out with Women Socially	Diocesan		Religious	
	Bishops	Active Priests	Major Superiors	Active Priests
Frequency:				
Several times a year	22	34	38	37
Several times a month	3	10	5	8
One or more times a week	0	4	0	4
Never	75	52	57	51
Total	100	100	100	100
Mode:				
With a group	24	39	36	39
As a couple	0	10	5	9
Never	76	52	59	52
Total	100	101[a]	100	100

[a] Not 100 per cent because of rounding.

be said about the nature of their relationships with women, it is clear that many of them do not fail to have at least occasional social companionship with women. Indeed, over one-fifth of the bishops and almost two-fifths of the major superiors report going out socially with women several times a year. However, none of the bishops and only 5 per cent of the major superiors report that they go out with women "as a couple."

The style of social interaction with women and the frequency are combined in Table 12.11. By far the largest proportion of the American priests who associate socially with women limit their relationships to several times a year and then in groups. Thus, 82 per cent of the active priests either never go out with women or do so rarely and then only in groups. Among the rest, 2 per cent go out weekly as a couple and 2 per cent more go out several times a month as a couple, while 5 per cent go out as a couple several times a year.

There are, however, generally positive feelings among priests on the matter of some social relations with women. In response to an open-ended question (which permitted them to respond in their own words),

TABLE 12.10

GOING OUT WITH WOMEN SOCIALLY, BY AGE
(Per Cent of Diocesan and Religious Priests)

Going Out with Women Socially	Age			
	26-35	36-45	46-55	Over 55
Frequency:				
Several times a year	42	39	34	27
Several times a month	15	12	8	3
One or more times a week	7	4	4	2
Never	36	46	54	68
Total	100	101[a]	100	100
Mode:				
With a group	50	42	37	27
As a couple	14	12	8	5
Never	36	46	55	68
Total	100	100	100	100

[a] Not 100 per cent because of rounding.

TABLE 12.11

PATTERNS OF SOCIAL INTERACTION WITH WOMEN

Social Interaction with Women	*Per Cent of Active Priests*
Never go out with them	52
Several times a year in a group	30
Several times a year as a couple	5
Several times a month in a group	7
Several times a month as a couple	2
Weekly or more in a group	2
Weekly or more as a couple	2
	100

more than 71 per cent of the sample approved either strongly or moderately of some social relations with women, and 47 per cent of the bishops expressed some approval (Table 12.12). On the other hand, 35 per cent of the bishops, as opposed to 15 per cent of the diocesan priests, 13 per cent of the religious priests, and 18 per cent of the major superiors, disapproved of such social relations. Among the age categories in Table 12.13, older priests are most likely to disapprove (23 per cent of those over fifty-five). On the other hand, 83 per cent of those thirty-five and under expressed approval.

We can summarize the picture that emerges of the Catholic clergy's attitude on the celibacy issue as depicted in the descriptive section of this chapter by responding to five questions:

1. *Is there a strong desire among the Roman Catholic clergy to marry?* The answer to this question is in the negative. Only about one-fifth of the diocesan priests and one-tenth of the religious priests say that they would either certainly or probably marry if they could. Even among those under thirty-six, two-thirds indicate that they would not either certainly or probably marry if they could do so.

2. *Do priests strongly support and expect change in the celibacy regulations?* The answer to this question is a clear affirmative. More than half the priests are at least somewhat in favor of the change, and approximately three-fifths expect the change. Three-quarters of those expecting a change think it will occur within the next decade.

TABLE 12.12

OPINIONS ON SOCIAL RELATIONS WITH WOMEN,
BY CLERICAL STATUS

(Per Cent)

Opinion	Diocesan		Religious	
	Bishops	Active Priests	Major Superiors	Active Priests
Strongly positive	12	41	33	42
Moderately positive	35	30	37	34
Neither positive nor negative	18	14	12	10
Moderately negative	28	11	15	8
Strongly negative	7	4	3	5

TABLE 12.13

OPINIONS ON SOCIAL RELATIONS WITH WOMEN, BY AGE

(Per Cent of Active Diocesan and Religious Priests)

Opinion	Age			
	26-35	36-45	46-55	Over 55
Strongly positive	56	46	35	26
Moderately positive	27	30	34	37
Neither positive nor negative	9	13	13	14
Moderately negative	3	7	14	16
Strongly negative	5	4	3	7

3. *Is the celibate state valued by the Catholic clergy?* Here the answer must be "yes." The overwhelming majority of priests see it as an advantage in their work and a considerable proportion also see it as an advantage for having fuller relationships with other people. The younger clergy, who see more disadvantages in celibacy and are more strongly in favor of a change, are less likely to endorse some of the reasons advanced for celibacy. Nevertheless, they tend to be in agreement with their older colleagues on the fundamental advantage of celibacy in assisting the priest in his work.

4. *If most priests would not marry and if most see a definite advantage in celibacy, why is there support for a change?* Apparently, many of those who support a change do so because they are not convinced that celibacy is essential to the priesthood and because they think that celibacy can be harmful for some priests and is keeping many men out of the priesthood. In other words, a change in the celibacy regulation is perceived as being desirable for the Church, if not necessarily desirable for oneself.

5. *Are substantial numbers of priests actively engaged in courtship in preparation for marriage when the celibacy regulation is changed?* There is no evidence presently that they are.

Analysis

Two variables were chosen for the analytic section of this chapter — social interaction with women and desire to marry. As we see in Table 12.14, there are only three strong predictors of the former — age (−.24), "modern" values (.32), and loneliness (.24). However, most

TABLE 12.14

CORRELATES OF SOCIAL INTERACTION WITH WOMEN AND
DESIRE TO MARRY

(Pearson *r*)

Variable	Social Interaction with Women	Would Marry If Free To Do So
Age	−.24	−.46
Family tension	.10	.15
Inner-directed	.22	.26
Religious experience	−.07	−.16
"Modern" values	.32	.44
Professional comparison	−.11	−.24
Work satisfaction	−.02	−.19
Loneliness	.24	.51
Negative affect	.15	.27

of the variables in our model correlate near to or above .2 with the desire to marry. Young priests, those from tense family backgrounds, those with inner-directed personalities, those with "modern" values, and those with high negative affect are more likely than their opposite numbers to desire marriage if it were possible for them. On the other hand, those with a high sense of professional comparison, high work satisfaction, and some record of religious experience are less likely than their opposites to want to marry. Loneliness is the strongest predictor of the desire to marry, with a correlation of .51.

Our causal model permits us to cope with a most respectable 38 per cent of the variance on plans to marry if it were possible (Table 12.15). Age accounts for 21 per cent of the variance; but when age, tension, personality, religious experiences, values, and work satisfaction are all held constant, the addition of loneliness to the model improves its explanatory power considerably (8 per cent). Negative affect adds little to the predictive power of the model and will be dropped from our path diagrams in the rest of this report. An inspection of Figure 12.1 shows that the desire to marry acts somewhat like a magnet, attracting lines from all over the page. Age, "modern" values, inner-directedness, work satisfaction, and loneliness all have direct paths converging on the desire to marry — with the path of .35 from loneliness being the largest. In other words, many of the problems of the priesthood that we have discussed so far in this report focus on the desire to marry.

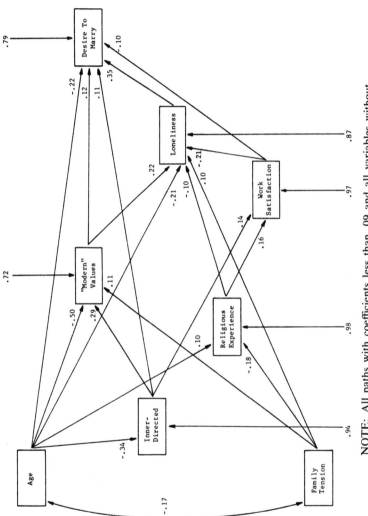

NOTE: All paths with coefficients less than .09 and all variables without significant paths have been omitted from this figure.

Fig. 12.1.—Path diagram relating desire to marry to prior variables. Active priests only.

The Catholic Priest in the United States

TABLE 12.15

EXPLANATION OF VARIANCE ON DESIRE TO MARRY

Variable	R^2	R^2 Change
Age	.21	.21
Family tension	.22	.01
Inner-directed	.23	.01
Religious experience	.24	.01
"Modern" values	.26	.02
Work satisfaction	.29	.03
Loneliness	.37	.08
Negative affect	.38	.01

Table 12.16 enables us to make some further comments on the desire to marry. The younger clergy are likely to want to marry in part because of their personality orientation, their more "modern" values, and their greater loneliness. Those from tense families are more likely to want to marry in part because of their lower level of religious experience, their more "modern" values, and their higher level of loneliness. Those with inner-directed personalities are more likely to want to marry in part because of their "modern" values. Those who have had religious experiences are less likely to want to marry in part because their values are somewhat less "modern," because their work satisfaction is higher, and because their loneliness is lower. Those with high work satisfaction are less likely to want to marry in part because they are less apt to be lonely.

Perceiving loneliness as a personal problem, therefore, is an extremely important factor in the desire of many priests to marry, but it is not the only factor. Values, work satisfaction, personality, and sheer age are also involved.

By way of a summary question, we ask:

What are the principal explanations for the desire of some priests to marry? Loneliness and youthfulness both separately and in combination provide us with a substantial amount of the explanation for the desire to marry. Values, personality, and lack of work satisfaction are also factors to be considered.

TABLE 12.16

SIMPLE CORRELATIONS AND TOTAL INDEPENDENT EFFECTS OF SELECTED VARIABLES ON DESIRE TO MARRY

Variable	Simple Correlation (Pearson r)	Independent Effects of Added Variable (Standardized Net Regression Weights)							
		Age	Family Tension	Inner-Directed	Religious Experience	"Modern" Values	Work Satisfaction	Loneliness	Negative Affect
Age	-.46	-.46	-.45	-.40	-.39	-.30	-.28	-.21	-.22
Family tension	.15	—	.08	.08	.06	.04	.03	-.01	-.01
Inner-directed	.25	—	—	.12	.13	.08	.10	.11	.11
Religious experience	-.16	—	—	—	-.12	-.10	-.08	-.04	-.04
"Modern" values	.44	—	—	—	—	.19	.19	.12	.12
Work satisfaction	-.19	—	—	—	—	—	-.17	-.09	-.10
Loneliness	.51	—	—	—	—	—	—	.34	.35
Negative affect	.27	—	—	—	—	—	—	—	-.04

CHAPTER 13

FUTURE PLANS

While no good data exist about resignations from the Catholic priesthood in the United States before 1966, there is a widespread impression, which seems to be solidly grounded, that resignations were rather rare. As we shall point out in Chapter 15, slightly less than 5 per cent of the diocesan clergy in the United States resigned in the four-year period from 1966 through 1969. In this chapter, we shall present rather briefly some descriptive information about resignations at the present time and then analyze the resignation phenomenon. We shall also complete the causal model that we have been developing with resignation in mind. While in this chapter we principally discuss those who are still active priests and examine their plans and attitudes toward resigning, in Chapter 15 we shall report on those men who have already resigned from the priesthood.

Description

There are five principal findings to be recorded in the descriptive section of this chapter:

1. At the time the data in this report were collected, about 3 per cent of the priests in the sample were definitely or probably going to leave the priesthood in the near future.

2. About 22 per cent of the priests thirty-five and under were either going to leave or were at least uncertain about their future in the ministry.

3. A large proportion of American priests have rethought their own position because of the departure of friends from the priesthood.

4. The main reasons given for staying in the priesthood are the sense of vocation and happiness in the work.

5. The main reasons given for leaving the priesthood are desire to marry, desire for personal growth, and inability to live within the structure of the Church.

Table 13.1 shows that 55 per cent of the diocesan priests and 62 per

253

TABLE 13.1

FUTURE PLANS IN THE PRIESTHOOD, BY CLERICAL STATUS

(Per Cent)

Future Plans in the Priesthood	Diocesan		Religious	
	Bishops	Active Priests	Major Superiors	Active Priests
Definitely will not leave	99	55	77	62
Probably will not leave	1	32	21	28
Uncertain	0	10	2	7
Probably will leave	0	2	0	2
Definitely decided to leave	0	1	0	1
Total	100	100	100	100

cent of the religious order priests in the United States say that they will definitely stay in the priesthood, and 32 per cent of the diocesan and 28 per cent of the religious say that they will probably not leave. This leaves 13 per cent of the diocesan and 10 per cent of the religious who are uncertain about their future or who are probably or definitely leaving. Of these, 10 per cent of the diocesan and 7 per cent of the religious are in the uncertain category. We can see in Table 13.2, as might be ex-

TABLE 13.2

FUTURE PLANS IN THE PRIESTHOOD, BY AGE

(Per Cent of Active Diocesan and Religious Priests)

Future Plans in the Priesthood	Age			
	26-35	36-45	46-55	Over 55
Definitely will not leave	25	44	71	92
Probably will not leave	53	40	22	7
Uncertain	17	11	5	1
Probably will leave	3	3	1	0
Definitely decided to leave	2	2	0	0
Total	100	100	99 [a]	100

[a] Not 100 per cent because of rounding.

pected, that those most likely to be uncertain or planning on leaving are those thiry-five and under (22 per cent). However, 16 per cent of those between thirty-six and forty-five are also either uncertain or planning to leave, as are 6 per cent of those between forty-six and fifty-five.

One can once again write newspaper headlines either way. One can stress the fact that 3 per cent say that they are likely to leave or one can stress the fact that 55 per cent of the diocesan priests are definitely not leaving. However, given the fact that approximately 5 per cent of the diocesan clergy resigned between 1966 and 1969 and another 3 per cent are likely to have resigned in 1970 or will do so shortly, a net loss of 10 per cent from the ranks of the active diocesan ministry does not seem at all unlikely, and this percentage is likely to be even higher among clergy under forty-five. Thus, there is no evidence in Tables 13.1 and 13.2 to suggest that the resignation crisis in the Catholic priesthood is over.

More than 70 per cent of the active diocesan priests and more than 80 per cent of the active religious priests have friends who have left the priesthood since the beginning of 1966, and approximately half of those with friends who have left have three or more such friends (Table 13.3). Forty-five per cent of the diocesan priests and 39 per cent of the religious priests report that they have rethought their own status because of friends leaving. Hence, it is reasonable to conclude that many Catholic priests have been jolted by the resignations of their confreres. This jolt seems to be particularly severe among the younger priests (Table 13.4), with 50 per cent of those between thirty-six and forty-five and 64 per cent of those thirty-five and under saying that they have rethought their own position because of their friends' leaving.

TABLE 13.3

FRIENDS LEAVING THE PRIESTHOOD, BY CLERICAL STATUS

(Per Cent)

Item	Active Diocesan Priests	Active Religious Priests
Have friends who have left the priesthood since 1966	73	83
More than 3 friends have left[a]	53	47
Have rethought own status because of a friend's leaving[a]	45	39

[a] Of those with friends who have left the priesthood.

TABLE 13.4

FRIENDS LEAVING THE PRIESTHOOD, BY AGE

(Per Cent of Active Diocesan and Religious Priests)

Item	Age			
	26-35	36-45	46-55	Over 55
Have friends who have left the priesthood since 1966	89	87	74	59
More than 3 friends have left[a]	44	44	58	60
Have rethought own status because of a friend's leaving	64	50	32	11

[a] Of those with friends who have left the priesthood.

Those still in the priesthood were asked to indicate the two most important reasons for staying, and those uncertain or planning to leave were asked to give the two most important reasons for leaving. The resignees were also asked the second question. We learn from Table 13.5 that among active diocesan priests the most frequently mentioned reasons for staying are a sense of vocation (60 per cent) and happiness in work (43 per cent). Giving witness to Christ in the modern world (32 per cent)

TABLE 13.5

REASONS FOR STAYING IN THE PRIESTHOOD,
BY CLERICAL STATUS

(Per Cent Giving Each as First or Second Most Important Reason)

Reason	Active Diocesan Priests	Active Religious Priests
Sense of vocation	60	65
Happiness in priestly work	43	38
To give witness to Christ	32	37
To save soul	26	24
To try to renew structures of the Church	9	6
Other	30	30
Total[a]	200	200

[a] Totals equal 200 per cent because of combined categories.

and saving one's soul (26 per cent) are the other two reasons receiving most frequent mention. The basic pattern of response is the same for active religious priests, with some slight percentage differences.

Table 13.6 shows that a sense of vocation and happiness are also the two principal reasons among the priests under forty-six, although giving witness to Christ is more important than happiness in work for those thirty-five and under. The younger priests are also more likely than the older ones to mention renewing the structures of the Church as a reason for staying (16 per cent versus 1 per cent) and less likely to mention the salvation of their souls (6 per cent versus 46 per cent).

The principal reason given for resignation by both the active priests and the resignees is the desire to marry (Table 13.7). Thus, 51 per cent of the active diocesan priests and 44 per cent of the resigned diocesan priests give this as their first or second most important reason. The second most frequently mentioned reason by the active diocesan priests who are likely to leave is that they can no longer live within the structure of the Church (34 per cent), and the third most frequently mentioned reason is personal development and growth (18 per cent). Religious priests who are still active mention personal development more frequently than the structure of the Church (36 per cent and 22 per cent, respectively).

Although desire to marry is the most frequently mentioned reason for

TABLE 13.6

REASONS FOR STAYING IN THE PRIESTHOOD, BY AGE

(Per Cent of Active Diocesan and Religious Priests Giving Each
as First or Second Most Important Reason)

Reason	Age			
	26-35	36-45	46-55	Over 55
Sense of vocation	57	59	66	66
Happiness in priestly work	41	41	40	40
To give witness to Christ	45	35	32	26
To save soul	6	16	31	46
To try to renew structures of the Church	16	10	4	1
Other	35	38	27	20
Total[a]	200	199[b]	200	199[b]

[a] Totals equal 200 per cent because of combined categories.
[b] Not 200 per cent because of rounding.

TABLE 13.7

REASONS FOR LEAVING THE PRIESTHOOD,
BY CLERICAL STATUS

(Per Cent Giving Each as First or Second Most Important Reason)

Reason	Diocesan		Religious	
	Active Priests[a]	Resigned Priests	Active Priests[a]	Resigned Priests
Desire to marry	51	44	44	44
Personal development and growth	18	27	36	25
No longer believe it is one's vocation	10	7	18	15
Can no longer live within the structure of the Church as a priest	34	26	22	28
Emotional problems make a change necessary	9	9	12	13
No longer get the satisfaction there used to be from being a priest	14	3	11	4
No longer agree with some of the ethical and moral teachings of the Church	7	19	5	14
Talents are not being used sufficiently	13	6	6	4
The work of a churchman seems relevant	10	8	7	6
The Church is not facing the relevant questions of the day	12	18	20	19
Other	22	33	19	28
Total[b]	200	200	200	200

[a] Of those uncertain, probable, or definite about leaving the priesthood.
[b] Totals equal 200 per cent because of combined categories.

leaving, just under half of the diocesan actives do not mention it as either the first or second reason and more than half of the other three groups in Table 13.7 do not mention it as the first or second reason. In other words, if one combines inability to live any longer within the structure of the Church, decline of satisfaction in the priestly office, dissatisfaction with the ethical and moral teachings of the Church, the lack of use of talents, and the seeming irrelevancy of the Church and its work, one discovers that 90 per cent of the active diocesan priests who are thinking of resigning mention one of these as their first or second reason, while only 51 per cent mention desire to marry as a first or second reason. Furthermore, 80 per cent of the diocesan resignees mention at least one of these problems as their first or second reason for leaving, while only 44 per cent mention desire to marry.

We summarize the descriptive section of the chapter by responding to the following hypothetical questions:

1. *Is the present resignation rate among priests likely to persist?* There is no evidence in the present data to suggest that, at least on a national level, resignation rates are likely to decline.

2. *How many more priests are likely to resign?* If only that 3 per cent who responded to our questionnaire by saying that they were probably or definitely going to leave should in fact resign, there will be 2,000 more resignees in the reasonably near future. If substantial numbers of those who are uncertain, or even who say they probably will not leave, should in fact decide to resign, the numbers could be very much higher.

3. *Are many priests shaken by the resignations of their friends?* It seems obvious that many are and that a substantial number of American priests have been forced to rethink their position in the priesthood because of the rising resignation rates.

4. *Why do men resign from the priesthood?* The most frequently mentioned reason is the desire to marry. However, various aspects of frustration in the priestly work in *combination* are mentioned even more frequently than the desire to marry.

5. *Why do men stay in the priesthood?* The principal reasons for staying are a sense of vocation and happiness in the work. Younger priests also mention a desire to give witness to Christ and to reform the structures of the Church.

Analysis

It should be kept in mind while reading the analytic section of this chapter that we are not attempting to explain a decision to resign but rather a position on a five-point scale running from having made a definite decision to leave to having made a definite decision to stay. It should also be recalled once again that we are dealing with partial causality. Thus, when we say that there is a negative correlation between having "modern" values and one's place on the "future-plans" scale, we do not mean that all those with "modern" values are inclined to leave, but merely that they are more likely to consider doing so than those with more traditional values.

We note in Table 13.8 that those who are most likely to stay in the priesthood are older priests (.44), those who have had religious experiences (.20), those who perceive strong colleague relationships (.23),

TABLE 13.8

CORRELATES OF FUTURE PLANS TO STAY IN THE PRIESTHOOD

Variable	Pearson r
Age	.44
Family tension	−.20
Inner-directed	−.28
Religious experience	.20
"Modern" values	−.47
Power conflict	−.39
Colleague relationship	.23
Work satisfaction	.23
Professional comparison	.29
Positive affect	−.02
Loneliness	−.48
Negative affect	−.34
Desire to marry	−.66

those with high work satisfaction (.23), and those who compare themselves favorably with other professionals (.29). Those who are most likely to incline toward leaving the priesthood are those from tense families (−.20), those with high inner-directed scores (−.28), those with "modern" values (−.47), those who experience conflict over the distribution of power (−.39), those who perceive loneliness as a problem (−.48), those with high negative affect (−.34), and those with a desire to marry (−.66).

A combination of nine of these variables enables us to explain more than half of the variance (.52) in future plans with regard to the priesthood — a very high level of explanatory power in the kind of research that this study represents. Table 13.9 shows that 19 per cent of the variance is accounted for by youth, with family tension, inner-direction, and religious experience each adding 2 per cent more to the predictive power of the model. Next, "modern" values and work satisfaction in their turn each add 4 per cent more to the explanation. Loneliness accounts for an additional 6 per cent, and the desire to marry explains the final 13 per cent of predictive power in the model.

Figure 13.1, which completes the model that we have been developing throughout this report, shows that there are only four direct paths leading to future plans: .09 from work satisfaction, −.10 from loneliness, −.14 from "modern" values, and −.47 from desire to marry. The reason for this phenomenon is the "converging" of so many paths on the

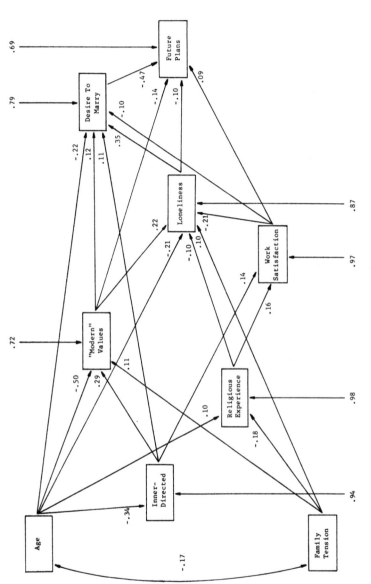

NOTE: All paths with coefficients less than .09 and all variables without significant paths have been omitted from this figure.

Fig. 13.1.—Path diagram relating future plans in priesthood to prior variables. Active priests only.

TABLE 13.9

EXPLANATION OF VARIANCE ON FUTURE PLANS
TO STAY IN THE PRIESTHOOD

Variable	R^2	R^2 Change
Age	.19	.19
Family tension	.21	.02
Inner-directed	.23	.02
Religious experience	.25	.02
"Modern" values	.29	.03
Work satisfaction	.33	.04
Loneliness	.39	.06
Negative affect	.39	.00
Desire to marry	.52	.13

desire to marry, which we described in the previous chapter. Therefore, a good deal of the predictive power of our model operates through the desire to marry. If one asked why men are inclined to resign from the priesthood, we would answer by saying that the chief explanation is the desire to marry — the chief explanation, be it noted, but not the only one. Then the next appropriate question is why people wish to marry. The chief explanation, though not the only one, is that they are lonely. And why are they lonely? The chief explanations for loneliness, though not the only ones, are low work satisfaction, "modern" religious values, and youthfulness.

It all sounds very complicated when it is described in words, and perhaps looks even more complicated as it is graphically represented in Figure 13.1, which is the closest thing in this report to an answer to the question of why priests resign. But it must be emphasized that this figure is in effect a simplification of reality. The actual "real-life" situation in which a man makes up his mind whether to stay in the priesthood or leave it is in fact more complicated rather than less complicated than the model presented in Figure 13.1.

We can clarify the model somewhat by examining Table 13.10. First of all, it should be noted that the model reduces the relationship between age and future plans from .44 to .04, indicating that we are able to explain most of this relationship. If we are asked why older priests are more likely than younger priests to plan to stay in the priesthood, we would say that the principal explanations for this phenomenon are that older priests are less inner-directed, have more "traditional" values, are

TABLE 13.10

SIMPLE CORRELATIONS AND TOTAL INDEPENDENT EFFECTS OF SELECTED VARIABLES ON FUTURE PLANS TO STAY IN THE PRIESTHOOD

Variable	Simple Correlation (Pearson r)	Independent Effects of Added Variable (Standardized Net Regression Weights)								
		Age	Family Tension	Inner-Directed	Religious Experience	"Modern" Values	Work Satisfaction	Loneliness	Negative Effect	Desire To Marry
Age	.44	.44	.42	.37	.35	.22	.21	.15	.14	.04
Family tension	−.20	—	−.12	−.13	−.10	−.07	−.06	−.03	−.03	−.03
Inner-directed	−.28	—	—	−.15	−.16	−.09	−.11	−.12	−.13	−.08
Religious experience	.20	—	—	—	.15	.13	.09	.07	.07	.05
"Modern" values	−.47	—	—	—	—	−.26	−.26	−.20	−.19	−.14
Work satisfaction	.23	—	—	—	—	—	.21	.15	.14	.09
Loneliness	−.48	—	—	—	—	—	—	−.28	−.26	−.10
Negative affect	−.34	—	—	—	—	—	—	—	−.05	−.07
Desire to marry	−.66	—	—	—	—	—	—	—	—	−.47

less lonely, and are less likely to want to marry. Secondary explanations are that the older priests are somewhat more likely to have had religious experiences and to be satisfied with their jobs and somewhat less likely to come from tense families and to have high scores on the negative affect scale. If, on the other hand, the question is reversed and we are asked why younger priests are more likely to leave, we would reply that the principal explanations for this phenomenon are that younger priests are more inner-directed, have more "modern" values, are more lonely, and are more likely to want to marry. Secondary explanations for the relationship are that the younger are somewhat more likely to come from tense families and to have high negative affect scores and somewhat less likely to have had religious experiences and to be satisfied with their jobs.

We can also account for more than three-fourths of the relationship between family tension and future plans. Those who come from tense families are more likely to think of leaving the priesthood because they have had fewer religious experiences, endorse more "modern" values, and are more likely to be lonely.

The inner-directed are more likely to leave the priesthood in part because they are more likely to have "modern" values and in part because they want to marry. Those with "modern" values are more likely to think of leaving in part because they are more lonely and in part because they are more likely to want to marry. Those with low work satisfaction are more inclined to leave because they are lonely and because they want to marry. Finally, almost all of the impact of negative affect is the result of loneliness.

We have chosen to use regression coefficients throughout the analytic section of this report because they are the only feasible way to handle a multivariable model. One can use percentage tables up to three or four variables, but beyond that number the use of percentage tables becomes hopelessly confusing. Each simple correlation, for example, represents a whole table of percentages. However, it seems appropriate at this point to introduce one percentage table (Table 13.11) to illustrate the relationship between the desire to marry and future plans with regard to the priesthood. (The whole table is summed up in the r of $-.66$ that we saw in Table 13.8.)

One notes first of all that those who will definitely or probably leave are all concentrated in the two groups who would certainly or probably marry sometime if they could. Furthermore, even the percentages for those uncertain about leaving are much lower in the remaining three categories concerning possible marriage. Looking at the possibilities of mar-

TABLE 13.11

FUTURE PLANS IN THE PRIESTHOOD BY DESIRE TO MARRY

(Per Cent of Active Diocesan and Religious Priests)

Future Plans in Priesthood	"If celibacy for priests became optional, do you think you would ever get married?"				
	Certainly Yes	Probably Yes	Uncertain	Probably No	Certainly No
Definitely will not leave	11	16	31	55	93
Probably will not leave	19	48	55	43	6
Uncertain	35	29	13	2	1
Probably will leave	17	6	0	0	0
Definitely decided to leave ..	18	1	0	0	0
Total	100	100	99ᵃ	100	100
Weighted N	(3,644)	(7,830)	(10,176)	(17,548)	(24,033)

ᵃ Not 100 per cent because of rounding.

riage, among those who would certainly marry, 70 per cent are either uncertain or planning on leaving, and among those who would probably marry, 36 per cent are uncertain or leaving. Among the remaining three categories, those who are uncertain or leaving are 13 per cent, 2 per cent, and 1 per cent, respectively. There cannot be the slightest doubt of the power of this relationship.

It would appear, then, from the analysis above and in the preceding chapter that the desire to marry is the main (though not the only) explanation of the inclination to leave the priesthood and that loneliness is the main (though not the only) explanation for the desire to marry. We have much less success in predicting loneliness than we do future plans and the desire to marry, though loneliness is something much less specific than either of the other two. Apparently some men are better able to cope with the celibate life without encountering loneliness and hence without being so desirous of marriage and without being as likely to contemplate leaving. Whatever the hidden causes of this ability to cope with celibacy without being lonely, they are not related to the personality variables measured by the POI scale. We must be content, therefore, with saying that some men find themselves much more lonely in the priestly life than others; these are the ones most likely to want to marry and most likely to think seriously about leaving the priesthood.

It should be noted that in order to determine whether other variables would provide more powerful explanatory force, three other variables were put into the position occupied in the model by work satisfaction — colleague relationship, professional comparison, and experience of power conflict. They did not improve the predictability of the model over the level provided by work satisfaction. Then all three of these variables were put into the model together with work satisfaction, but there was still no improvement in predictive power. In other words, we are not missing any relationships by using work satisfaction in the model instead of these other indicators.

By the way of concluding questions, we can ask the following:

1. *What is the explanation of future plans with regard to staying in or leaving the priesthood?* There is no single explanation, but the desire to marry is the strongest predictor of plans to leave, in part because it acts as a channel for other causes.

2. *What, then, is the explanation of priests' desiring to marry?* There are a number of causes, but the principal one appears to be the loneliness that some men experience in the priesthood.

3. *Why are young priests more likely than old to think of resigning?* Most of this relationship can be explained by different personalities, different religious values, a higher level of loneliness, and a greater desire to marry.

4. *How could resignation rates be lowered?* It is not our purpose to make recommendations, but in terms of the statistics in our model, a notable reduction in the rate would occur if there were less of a desire to marry and less loneliness.

CHAPTER 14

RECRUITING FOR THE PRIESTHOOD

The resignations from the priesthood are not the only or even necessarily the most critical problem that the Catholic priesthood in the United States faces today. It is generally agreed that there has been a dramatic slump in the number of young men entering the seminaries to study for the priesthood, and perhaps even a greater slump in the numbers of those finally ordained. The problem is made even more serious by the fact that the age cohorts currently of seminary age are much bigger than age cohorts in the past. In other words, the proportionate drop in enrollment is even greater than the absolute drop. Many reasons could be advanced to explain this decline, but only one falls within the competence of this study: It may be likely that priests, who — as data in previous chapters have demonstrated — are extremely important in the encouragement of a priestly vocation, are no longer deeply committed to recruiting colleagues and successors. In this chapter, we shall ask whether in fact such a decline in enthusiasm for vocational recruiting has occurred. Then we shall investigate whether the same variables that explain resignation from the priesthood also explain current recruiting attitudes.

A comparison of the percentages in Table 14.1 with those in Table 14.2 indicates how drastic the change in vocational recruiting attitudes is as perceived by the clergy. Thus, 64 per cent of the diocesan priests say that five years ago they actively encouraged boys to enter the seminary, as opposed to 33 per cent at the present time. Furthermore, 56 per cent of the religious priests offered such encouragement five years ago and only 27 per cent do today. Even among the bishops there has been a decline from 89 per cent to 75 per cent, and among the major superiors, from 72 per cent to 42 per cent. The shift in attitudes is not toward discouraging young men from entering the seminary but rather toward encouraging them while apprising them of the uncertainties that afflict the priesthood, or toward allowing them to make up their own minds without encouragement or discouragement. A great many priests (36 per cent,

TABLE 14.1

VOCATIONAL RECRUITING ATTITUDE FOUR OR FIVE
YEARS AGO, BY CLERICAL STATUS

(Per Cent)

Attitude	Diocesan		Religious	
	Bishops	Active Priests	Major Superiors	Active Priests
I actively encourage boys to enter the seminary or novitiate, since I see the priesthood as a very rewarding vocation	89	64	71	56
I encourage boys but advise them about the uncertainties surrounding the role of the priest today	6	14	15	17
I neither discourage nor encourage boys, but allow them to make up their own minds	5	20	13	24
Abstracting from their personal qualities, I tend to discourage boys from entering now and advise them to wait until the future is more certain	0	0	0	1
Other	1	2	1	2
Total	101 [a]	100	100	100

[a] Not 100 per cent because of rounding.

which is the largest category) now take this "hands-off" approach. Clearly, then, there has been a dramatic change in the attitudes of priests on the appropriateness of actively encouraging young men to enter what the priests perceive as a rewarding vocation.

Furthermore, both Tables 14.3 and 14.4 show that compared to the other age groups, priests thirty-five and under — those most likely to be the most attractive role models for young men considering the priesthood — have been and still are the least likely to engage in active encouragement of a priestly vocation. Indeed, 41 per cent of this group say that they now neither encourage nor discourage young men from entering the priesthood. It should be noted, of course, that the young priests do not actively discourage entrance into the seminary (2 per cent), but the change in the levels of encouragement certainly can be assumed to play

TABLE 14.2

VOCATIONAL RECRUITING ATTITUDE TODAY, BY CLERICAL STATUS

(Per Cent)

Attitude	Diocesan		Religious	
	Bishops	Active Priests	Major Supe-riors	Active Priests
I actively encourage boys to enter the seminary or novitiate, since I see the priesthood as a very rewarding vocation	75	33	43	27
I encourage boys but advise them about the uncertainties surrounding the role of the priest today	18	27	38	31
I neither discourage nor encourage boys, but allow them to make up their own minds	6	36	18	36
Abstracting from their personal qualities, I tend to discourage boys from entering now and advise them to wait until the future is more certain	0	2	0	3
Other	1	2	1	4
Total	100	100	100	101 [a]

[a] Not 100 per cent because of rounding.

an important role in the sudden and sharp decline in vocations to the priesthood.

We need hardly observe that the situation recorded in the first four tables of this chapter represents an extremely serious problem for the Catholic priesthood in the United States. If priests are among the most effective recruiters of other priests and if their enthusiasm for recruitment has undergone a considerable decline, then it is not likely that the present vocation crisis will cease unless there is once again a return to some higher level of enthusiasm for vocational recruiting among the clergy.

In Table 14.5 we see that 59 per cent of the priests have not changed their recruiting attitudes in the last four or five years, but of those who have changed, 38 per cent have become less encouraging and only 4 per cent more encouraging. In other words, the net loss in vocation support is 34 per cent, a very high proportion indeed. Furthermore, 13 per cent

TABLE 14.3

VOCATIONAL RECRUITING ATTITUDE FOUR OR
FIVE YEARS AGO, BY AGE

(Per Cent of Active Diocesan and Religious Priests)

Attitude	Age			
	26-35	36-45	46-55	Over 55
I actively encourage boys to enter the seminary or novitiate, since I see the priesthood as a very rewarding vocation	52	61	62	64
I encourage boys but advise them about the uncertainties surrounding the role of the priest today	19	16	14	13
I neither discourage nor encourage boys, but allow them to make up their own minds	26	22	21	21
Abstracting from their personal qualities, I tend to discourage boys from entering now and advise them to wait until the future is more certain	1	1	1	0
Other	2	1	2	2
Total	100	101 [a]	100	100

[a] Not 100 per cent because of rounding.

of the priests in the country have moved from a position of actively encouraging boys to a position of either letting the boys make up their own minds or discouraging them. This sharp move away from the diagonal indicates how serious the recruiting crisis is becoming.

It is somewhat surprising that Table 14.6 shows no important correlation between recruiting attitude and age. We do know from previous tables in this chapter that the young are less likely than the old to enthusiastically recruit, but the correlation is below .2. Those who are most likely to recruit are those who have had religious experiences, who compare themselves favorably with other professionals, and who are satisfied with their work. Those who are least likely to recruit are those with "modern" religious values, those who see loneliness as a problem, those who would like to get married, and those who are thinking of leaving the priesthood.

We are only able to explain 16 per cent of the variance in recruiting attitudes by our causal model (Table 14.7). Thus, the same variables

TABLE 14.4

VOCATIONAL RECRUITING ATTITUDE TODAY, BY AGE

(Per Cent of Active Diocesan and Religious Priests)

Attitude	Age			
	26-35	36-45	46-55	Over 55
I actively encourage boys to enter the seminary or novitiate, since I see the priesthood as a very rewarding vocation	21	26	35	40
I encourage boys but advise them about the uncertainties surrounding the role of the priest today	32	30	26	26
I neither discourage nor encourage boys, but allow them to make up their own minds	41	39	33	30
Abstracting from their personal qualities, I tend to discourage boys from entering now and advise them to wait until the future is more certain	2	2	3	2
Other	4	3	3	2
Total	100	100	100	100

that were quite successful in explaining why men would leave the priesthood are considerably less successful in explaining why men are not vigorously encouraging vocations to the priesthood. This means that the present attitude operates in the priesthood rather independently of all the factors that we have considered in this study. The present spectrum of values on recruiting, in other words, tends to be found in most groups of priests — the young or the old. But if the decline in vocational enthusiasm is to be turned around, it will have to be through the influence of variables not under consideration in this study. Another, and more blunt, way of putting this is to say that on the basis of our evidence, we know very little about why vocational recruiting is less vigorously pursued today than it was four or five years ago.

To conclude with some questions:

1. *Has there been a decline in enthusiasm for encouraging vocations to the priesthood?* There has been a considerable decline over the last four or five years, though few priests actively discourage young men from seeking the priesthood. Instead, they encourage them less vigorously or let them make up their own minds.

TABLE 14.5

VOCATIONAL RECRUITING ATTITUDES FOUR OR
FIVE YEARS AGO AND TODAY

(Per Cent of Active Diocesan and Religious Priests)

Four or Five Years Ago	Today				
	A	B	C	D	Other
A. I actively encourage boys to enter the seminary or novitiate, since I see the priesthood as a very rewarding vocation	29	1	1	0	0
B. I encourage boys but advise them about the uncertainties surrounding the role of the priest today	18	9	2	0	0
C. I neither discourage nor encourage boys, but allow them to make up their own minds	12	5	19	0	0
D. Abstracting from their personal qualities, I tend to discourage boys from entering now and advise them to wait until the future is more certain	1	1	1	0	0
Other	0	0	0	0	2

Diagonal (no change)   =   59
Above (more encouragement) =   4
Below (less encouragement)   = 38
                     Total   = $\overline{101}$ [a]

[a] Not 100 per cent because of rounding.

TABLE 14.6

CORRELATES OF VOCATIONAL ENCOURAGEMENT

Variable	Pearson r
Age	.14
Family tension	—.14
Inner-directed	—.09
Religious experience	.19
"Modern" values	—.26
Professional comparison	.24
Work satisfaction	.19
Loneliness	—.25
Negative affect	—.18
Desire to marry	—.24
Inclination to stay in priesthood	.33

TABLE 14.7

EXPLANATION OF VARIANCE ON VOCATIONAL ENCOURAGEMENT

Variable	R^2	R^2 Change
Age	.02	.02
Family tension	.03	.01
Inner-directed	.04	.01
Religious experience	.06	.02
"Modern" values	.10	.04
Work satisfaction	.12	.02
Loneliness	.13	.01
Negative affect	.13	.00
Desire to marry	.14	.01
Inclination to stay in the priesthood	.16	.02

2. *Are there some particular groups of priests who are less likely to encourage priestly vocations?* The young and those with "modern" values are less likely to encourage young men to become priests, while those who have had religious experiences, like their work, and evaluate themselves highly in comparison with other professionals are more likely to do so. But the relationships are not strong and one must conclude that a lowering of enthusiasm for recruiting is widespread among all categories of the clergy.

CHAPTER 15

A LOOK AT THE RESIGNEES

There were two possible methods of presenting the data gathered by NORC in the separate questionnaire administered to resignees from the priesthood. The first method would have been to present a separate report, either as an appendix to the present report or as a separate report. The second strategy, and the one we elected to follow, was to present comparable data between the resignees and the active priests in the chapters that made up the main part of the report and then add a chapter toward the conclusion providing information on the questions that were specific to the resignees. (These questions are presented in Appendix G.) The disadvantage of such a strategy, of course, was that the various materials on the resignees would be scattered throughout the report. The advantage — and we believe the advantage outweighs the disadvantage — was that comparisons between the resignees' and the active priests' responses to the same questions could be easily made, though these would be comparisons and not attempts at causal analysis. The causal analysis took place in Chapter 13, where we attempted to determine not why those who have already resigned from the priesthood did in fact resign, but why those who presently consider resigning in fact made such a decision.

Material on the backgrounds, personality, religious experiences, attitudes, job satisfaction, and morale of those American priests who have resigned in the last four years can be found in the earlier chapters. In this chapter, we report on certain information pertaining more to their resignations: their experiences in the priesthood, their reasons for leaving, the resignation experience itself, and the events in their life since resignation — marriage career, relationship to the Church, and relationship to the priesthood. In preparing the data for this Chapter, a co-efficient of association was computed between each of the phenomena being discussed and the number of years since resignation from the priesthood. It turned out, however, that only on the matter of continued exercise of priestly liturgical functions was there any appreciable change in the pattern of responses across time. Therefore, only in that table will we present the associational statistics.

The principal findings reported in this chapter are as follows:

1. The reasons mentioned most frequently by resignees as "very important" to their decision to leave the priesthood are problems with the authority structure of the Church and the desire to marry.

2. The decision about resignation from the priesthood was a difficult and painful one, but apparently not one that the respondents regret.

3. Forty-three per cent of the wives (or fiancees) of resigned priests are former members of religious communities; 22 per cent of the wives (or fiancees) had been married before, of whom 13 per cent were divorcees.

4. A little less than one-third of the resignees make more than $12,000 a year, and a little more than one-third make less than $9,000.

5. More than three-quarters of the resigned priests consider themselves to be members of the Church but only two-fifths feel that they are actually within the structure of the Church itself. More than half still think of themselves as priests, though only two-fifths seem ready to return to the ministry and only a few of these would want to return to full-time ministry.

Resignation Rates

Since the definition of "resignation" differs from diocese to diocese as well as among religious communities, we established a common set of criteria to be applied uniformly across the nation. Thus, the term "resignee" refers to an ordained priest who was incardinated in a given diocese or was an official member of a given religious institute and who has resigned from his position in the diocese or institute and ceased to function as a Catholic priest in an official capacity. The resignation can have been voluntary or involuntary; it can be referred to as "a leave of absence," "leaving the priesthood," "suspension," "laicization," "dispensation from the obligations of Holy Orders," or simply as "walking off the job without notifying one's superior." To be included in the measures presented in this chapter, it must have occurred between January 1, 1966, and December 31, 1969. The term "resignee" does not include those priests who have left their dioceses or communities but are still actively pursuing some priestly ministry in another place (as, for example, graduate students).

We have computed the resignation rate for each of the calendar years

1966, 1967, 1968, and 1969. A rate is generally computed by dividing the number who experienced some event over a period of time by the total number who were exposed to the event over that period of time. Accordingly, the operational definition of "resignation rate" that we are using is the total number of resignees in a diocese or religious institute who resigned between January 1 and December 31 of a given year divided by the total number of priests who were potentially available for active service on January 1 of that same year. The number of priests potentially available for service is the sum of those priests who are defined by their diocese or religious institute as active in or outside of the diocese or community and those who are described as sick; it does not include those who are officially retired or those described as absent.

Table 15.1 presents the resignation rates (the number of resignations per 100 priests) for the years 1966 through 1969. The figures in the table can also be read as percentages. For example, in 1969, 2.0 priests per 100, or 2 per cent of the active priests in American dioceses, resigned between January 1 and December 31.

Table 15.2 shows the cumulative percentages that result from the resignation rates for the four years. The figures in this table represent the percentage of priests that would have been available for active service on January 1, 1970, if they had not resigned during the time from January 1, 1966, to December 31, 1969. The cumulative per cent of resignees was computed by dividing the number of resignees for the four years from 1966 through 1969 by the sum of the number of active priests

TABLE 15.1

AVERAGE RESIGNATION RATES IN AMERICAN DIOCESES AND
RELIGIOUS INSTITUTES, BY YEAR

(Number of Resignations per 100 Priests)

Year	Dioceses	Religious Institutes
1966	0.4	0.6
1967	0.9	0.9
1968	1.6	2.0
1969	2.0[a]	3.2
N	(85)	(87)

[a] Based on the statistical estimate of possible error due to sampling, the resignation rate for dioceses in 1969 would not go above 2.1 or below 1.9; see Appendix A for a discussion of the use of standard errors of estimate in probability samples.

TABLE 15.2

QUARTILE DISTRIBUTION OF CUMULATIVE PER CENT RESIGNEES
FROM AMERICAN DIOCESES AND RELIGIOUS INSTITUTES, 1966-69

Quartile	Dioceses	N	Religious Institutes	N
First	0.0- 2.7	20	0.0- 1.8	20
Second	2.8- 4.3	19	2.1- 4.9	21
Third	4.4- 5.8	20	5.1- 7.7	22
Fourth	6.1-10.9	20	7.9-24.6	19
Average	4.6		5.7	
Total N[a]		79		82

[a] Cases are omitted when information for any one year is missing.

available in the diocese or religious institute as of January 1, 1970, and the total number of resignees from 1966 through 1969. The number of priests available in a diocese or religious institute on January 1, 1970, was estimated by multiplying the number available in 1969 by the average per cent increase (or decrease) that had been experienced in the preceding four years; the increase or decrease was then added to or subtracted from, as the case may be, the 1969 figures.

Some dioceses have had no resignations within the last four years while others have experienced the resignation of 11 per cent of their active priests. Resignations among religious priests have been more frequent than among diocesan priests, resulting in the loss of one-fourth of the clergy in some religious institutes. We know from the responses to Question 75 in the actives' questionnaire that in the last weeks of December, 1969, and the first few months of 1970, another 3 per cent of the active priests in the United States were either probably or definitely planning to leave the priesthood. If all of these had left by the end of 1970 (and we have no way of knowing whether they did or not), approximately 8 per cent of the diocesan and 9 per cent of the religious priests would have resigned since the beginning of 1966. In those dioceses with exceptionally high resignation rates, the percentages would have been nearing 15 by the end of 1970, while some religious institutes would have gone beyond the 25 per cent mark.

Table 15.3 presents the resignation rates in terms of absolute numbers. The figures in this table as well as the preceding two are based on the official data supplied by the eighty-five dioceses and eighty-seven re-

TABLE 15.3

NUMBER OF RESIGNED PRIESTS FROM AMERICAN DIOCESES
AND RELIGIOUS INSTITUTES

Year	Dioceses	Religious Institutes	Total
1966	142	149	291
1967	306	267	573
1968	548	475	1,023
1969	753[a]	773	1,526
Total	1,749	1,664	3,413

[a] Based on the statistical estimate of possible error due to sampling, the total number of diocesan priests who resigned in 1969 would not go above 783 or below 723; see Appendix A for a discussion of the use of standard errors of estimate in probability samples.

ligious institutes in our sample and have been extrapolated by means of the sampling weights to produce an unbiased and highly accurate estimate of the national totals. Thus, 1,749 diocesan and 1,664 religious priests in the United States resigned between January 1, 1966, and December 31, 1969. If the 3 per cent who were probably or definitely planning to leave did in fact do so, the total number of priestly resignations for the past five-year period would be approximately 5,352.[1]

The Resignation Experience

It was argued in some of the preliminary discussions leading to the resignee study that the resignees might be especially likely to have come from very poor or black parishes and to have left the priesthood in disgust over the Church's inability to respond to the challenges of these communities. However, Table 15.4 indicates no confirmation for this assumption. While it is extremely difficult, of course, to rate the exact nature of a parish in the limited space available to one item in a questionnaire, nevertheless, it would appear from Table 15.4 that the majority of resignees come from parishes that are typical of American Catholicism — that is, middle- and working-class white parishes. Only 12 per cent of the resignees say that more than half of their parish was poor, and only 6 per cent report that more than half of their parish was black. Unquestionably, some men leave the priesthood because of frustration

TABLE 15.4

CHARACTERISTICS OF PARISHIONERS WITH
WHOM RESIGNED PRIESTS WORKED

Parishioners	Per Cent
More than half upper class	5
More than half middle class	42
More than half working class	25
More than half poor	12
More than half black	6

over the very difficult task of working with the poor or the black, but
men who were in this kind of parish make up only a rather small minority
of the resignee population.

Nor were the experiences in their relationships with their colleagues
in their last assignment completely intolerable. Thus, we see in Table
15.5 that 12 per cent describe their last pastor or superior as being very
much opposed to their work, but 19 per cent describe him as being very
supportive or helpful. Fourteen per cent think that the bishop or major
superior was very unhelpful, but 10 per cent think that he was very
helpful. Among resignees other than teachers or professionals, only very

TABLE 15.5

SUPPORT AND OPPOSITION FROM OTHER INDIVIDUALS IN
LAST ASSIGNMENT

(Per Cent of Resigned Priests)

Individual	Very Supportive (Helpful)	Very Much Opposed
Pastors, local Superiors you worked under	19	12
Lay leaders in the parish, institution	33	1
Priests your own age	30	1
Other priests in your diocese or community	10	5
Your family	34	2
Priests who worked in same parish or institution as you	25	6
Bishop and/or Major Superior	10	14
Other professional colleagues[a]	16	53

[a] Asked if teacher or other professional.

small percentages describe any of the other colleagues listed in Table 15.5 as very much opposed. The picture that emerges from Table 15.5 is one of a situation in which there was not intolerable opposition for the typical resignee, but neither was there extremely powerful support from one's colleagues.

Resignees also have mixed emotions about evaluating their experience in the ministry (Table 15.6). While 79 per cent say that it was psychosexually unhealthy and 54 per cent say that it was emotionally retarding, only minorities are willing to say it was generally self-negating (30 per cent), intellectually frustrating (41 per cent), spiritually impairing (37 per cent), and culturally narrowing (45 per cent).

When asked what crucial events may have been the turning point in their decision to leave (Table 15.7), 63 per cent of the resignees mentioned a relationship with a woman and 54 per cent mentioned falling in love. Whatever frustrations and difficulties may have preceded the decision to leave, for most resignees it was the experience of an emotional relationship with a woman that tipped the scales in the direction of resignation. Smaller minorities mentioned *Humanae Vitae* (28 per cent), the encyclical on celibacy (27 per cent), counseling experience (33 per cent), college or university experience (22 per cent), loss of faith (12 per cent), arbitrary reassignment by a superior (21 per cent), and injustice by a superior (28 per cent).

The most frequently mentioned "very important" reasons for leaving, as indicated by Table 15.8, are feeling that they could no longer live within the structure of the Church (53 per cent), a desire to marry (47 per cent), personal growth and development (46 per cent), and the irrelevancy of the Church (39 per cent). This order is in contrast

TABLE 15.6

EVALUATION OF EXPERIENCES IN THE MINISTRY

Statement	*Per Cent of Resigned Priests Agreeing*
Generally self-negating	30
Intellectually frustrating	41
Emotionally retarding	54
Spiritually impairing	37
Psychosexually unhealthy	79
Culturally narrowing	45

TABLE 15.7

CRUCIAL EVENTS INFLUENCING DECISION TO LEAVE

Event	Per Cent "Yes"
Humanae Vitae	28
Relationship with a woman	63
Encyclical on priestly celibacy	27
T-group experience or sensitivity training	14
Counseling or consultation experience	33
College or university experience	22
Realization of the loss of one's faith	12
Change from one national culture to another	7
Arbitrary reassignment by a superior	21
Resignation of prominent scholar from priesthood	15
Reading of a particular publication	15
Particular act of injustice by superior(s) to oneself or another	28
Falling in love	54
Told or advised to leave by bishop or superior	2

to that presented for resignees in Table 13.7, which shows that when they were asked to indicate the first and second most important reasons for leaving, the desire to marry was mentioned most frequently, with inability to live within the structure of the Church mentioned less frequently. However, as we can see in Table 15.8, the desire to marry is not the only reason given, nor, when compared with the combination of "structural dissatisfaction" factors, is it the single most important reason for leaving.

We see in Table 15.9 that the resignee was most likely to discuss his decision with other priests (86 per cent) and also extremely likely to receive support from other priests (66 per cent), but family support was not absent. Thus, 40 per cent report support from their mother, 45 per cent from their father, and 63 per cent from their brothers and sisters. While we have no information on how much support for resignation from the priesthood was available ten or fifteen years ago, presumably there would have been much more opposition from the family in years gone by. Thus, the data in Table 15.9 may actually represent a major change in attitude in the Catholic population, a change that one may speculate is both a cause and an effect of the increased resignation rate.

Forty-three per cent of the resignees sought some kind of professional counseling before resignation (Table 15.10), and most of those who went through the counseling experience found it a help in making their

TABLE 15.8

REASONS FOR LEAVING THE MINISTRY

Reason	Per Cent "Very Important for Me"
Bad relations with superiors	14
Desire to marry	47
Church was not facing the relevant problems of the day	39
Emotional problems made change necessary	17
Conflict with parishioners, or laity	1
No longer believed it was my vocation	26
Attracted to other work	8
Could no longer live within the structure of the institutional Church as a priest	53
Could no longer agree with some of the ethical and moral teaching of the Church	35
No longer got the satisfaction there used to be from being a priest	14
The work of a priest seemed irrelevant	21
Personal growth and development	46
Could no longer agree with some of the theological teaching of the Church	29
Talents were not being used sufficiently	23

TABLE 15.9

DISCUSSION AND SUPPORT FOR RESIGNATION FROM
OTHER INDIVIDUALS

(Per Cent of Resigned Priests)

Individual	Discussed With	Supportive and Accepting
Mother	43	40
Father	31	45
Siblings	55	63
Priests	86	66
Pastor or superior	40	24
Bishop or major superior	64	21
Lay friends	63	75
Member of local community	32	41
Spiritual director or confessor	50	49
Relatives	18	37
Professional colleagues	48	68

TABLE 15.10

COUNSELING BEFORE LEAVING THE MINISTRY

	Per Cent "Yes"
Sought counseling	43
Results of counseling:	
Confirmed a decision to leave I had in fact already made	59
Furnished an insight about myself or my situation which brought me to a decision to leave	60
Suggested that to leave would be an advisable step	7
Did not in fact enable me to feel settled with my decision to leave	11

decision to leave. On the other hand, more than half of those who sought the laicization process from the Roman Catholic Church experienced that process as very displeasing in three respects — length of time of the process, lack of information about the process, and conditions restricting the place or type of marriage (Table 15.11). On the other hand, only minorities found the attitudes of ecclesiastical officials toward themselves or their fiancees to be unsatisfactory, and only about a quarter objected to the secrecy surrounding the process. One must remark that in this table, as in many of the previous tables in this chapter, one does not get the impression that the resignees as a group are terribly angry at the Church, from whose active ministry they have withdrawn.

A majority of the resignees (53 per cent) report that their personal turmoil was severe before the decision to resign, and 60 per cent consider their turmoil to have been prolonged (Table 15.12). But almost half (48 per cent) found adjustment to the new life moderately easy. It might be remarked in passing that the data in Table 15.12 confirm from a completely different viewpoint the speculations about the relationships between psychological well-being and resignation that we discussed in Chapter 11. Finally, in response to a direct question on how they viewed their decision to leave the priesthood (table not shown), 86 per cent said that they were "very satisfied" with it.

Events since Resignation

Seventy per cent of the resigned clergy are married and 8 per cent more are engaged (Table 15.13). Forty-one per cent of those who resigned in 1970, 58 per cent of those who resigned in 1969, 77 per cent

TABLE 15.11

DISPLEASURE WITH ASPECTS OF THE LAICIZATION PROCEDURES

(Per Cent of Resigned Priests)

Aspect	Very Displeased	Somewhat Displeased	Total Displeased
Length of time to complete process	60	18	78
General attitudes of officials toward myself	12	6	18
General attitudes of officials toward my wife or fiancee	13	9	22
Secrecy surrounding the process	10	14	24
Information provided about progress of process	49	20	69
Conditions restricting place of work or residence	6	29	35
Conditions restricting place or type of marriage	50	10	60

TABLE 15.12

PERSONAL TURMOIL

(Per Cent of Resigned Priests)

Degree of Personal Turmoil	While Deciding To Leave	While Adjusting To New Life
Severe and prolonged	35	9
Severe but brief	18	7
Moderate but prolonged	25	19
Moderate but brief	14	29
Little or none	8	36
Total	100	100

of those who resigned in 1968, 81 per cent of those who resigned in 1967, and 87 per cent of those who resigned in 1966 are married (table not shown). Thus, about four-fifths of the resigned priests are either married or engaged, and the proportion married goes up as the number of years since resignation increases. On the other hand, 10 per cent of

TABLE 15.13

MARITAL STATUS OF RESIGNED PRIESTS

Marital Status	Per Cent
Single	21
Engaged	8
Married	70
Divorced, separated, or widowed	1
Total	100

the 1966 resignees are still neither married nor engaged. Of those resigned priests who are married, 40 per cent were married in a civil ceremony and 18 per cent in a non-Catholic religious service (Table 15.14). Only 13 per cent were married in an official Catholic service, though 22 per cent had some sort of "unofficial" Catholic service. Of those who were not married in an official Catholic service, 28 per cent later had their marriage "validated" by the Church. However, from the point of view of canon law, the majority of the marriages of resigned priests would at the present time still be considered "invalid."

We observe in Tables 15.15 and 15.16 that 22 per cent of the wives of resigned priests had been married before, and 43 per cent of the wives or fiancees had been members of a religious community. Eighty-four per cent of the wives or fiancees are Catholic, and 48 per cent attend Mass every week.

TABLE 15.14

KIND OF MARRIAGE CEREMONY

Kind of Ceremony	Per Cent of Married Resigned Priests
Catholic service	13
Unofficial Catholic service	22
Non-Catholic religious service	18
Civil ceremony	40
Other	7
Total	100

TABLE 15.15

MARITAL STATUS OF WIFE (OR FIANCEE) BEFORE
PRESENT MARRIAGE (ENGAGEMENT)

Wife's (or Fiancee's) *Marital Status*	*Per Cent of Married or Engaged Resigned Priests*
Never married	78
Separated	1
Previous marriage annulled by the Church	1
Divorced	13
Widowed	7
Total	100

TABLE 15.16

RELIGIOUS STATUS OF WIFE (OR FIANCEE)

Wife's (or Fiancee's) *Religious Status*	*Per Cent of Married or Engaged Resigned Priests*
Catholic	84
Was a member of a religious community	43
Attends Mass at least once a week	48

Resigned priests, then, tend to marry Catholics, particularly women who at one time were nuns. Even though they are unlikely to have been married with the Church's official blessing, many of their wives still seem to be devout Catholics.

The financial situation of most resigned priests is neither affluent nor impoverished (Table 15.17). The median income falls in the range of $9,000 to $12,000 a year, with 31 per cent of the respondents making more than $12,000 a year and 36 per cent making less than $9,000. The extremes of the income range are almost exactly the same, with 15 per cent making less than $6,000 a year and 16 per cent making more than $14,400 a year. There is a gamma coefficient of −.15 between annual income and recency of resignation, which means that the recent resignees make somewhat less money than resignees of several years ago. Thus, 24 per cent of the 1966 resignees make more than $14,400 and 14 per

TABLE 15.17

ANNUAL INCOME OF RESIGNED PRIESTS

Annual Income	Per Cent of Resigned Priests
Under $6,000	15
$6,000-$9,000	21
$9,000-$12,000	33
$12,001-$14,400	17
Over $14,400	14
Total	100

cent of the 1970 resignees earn that same amount. These figures possibly indicate that resigned priests are somewhat upwardly mobile in their new careers; but it is much more likely that it is too early to judge their progress in their secular careers and that any complete judgment about upward mobility will have to wait several more years.

Tables 15.18 and 15.19 show that in general they are more likely to see themselves as comparing favorably with other professionals now than they did when they were in the ministry and to feel that their talents are being used more now. Also, at the present time in their post-resignation careers, those who left the active ministry are more content with their jobs than they remember themselves as being when they worked as priests.[2]

TABLE 15.18

PROFESSIONAL STANDARDS IN MINISTRY AND IN PRESENT WORK

(Per Cent of Resigned Priests Reporting "More" or "About the Same"
As Professionals for Each Attribute)

Attribute	In Ministry	In Present Work
Depth of knowledge and skill	75	73
Autonomy to make decisions	24	79
Responsibility for an undertaking	40	86
Commitment to serving the needs of people	89	88

TABLE 15.19

USE OF TALENTS IN MINISTRY AND IN PRESENT WORK

(Per Cent of Resigned Priests)

Use of Talents	In Ministry	In Present Work
Feel talents used "a great deal"	29	53

Relationship to the Priesthood

We see in Table 15.20 that 53 per cent of the resignees are officially "laicized" and another 14 per cent are on approved leave; however, 25 per cent are either suspended or absent without leave. Table 15.21 shows that the most frequent reason given for not seeking laicization (among those who do not seek it) is that laicization is irrelevant to them (67 per cent). The next most frequent reasons are that the process is degrading (57 per cent) and that they hope to exercise some public ministry again (37 per cent).

How, then, do these resigned priests, some officially laicized, some deeming laicization to be irrelevant and degrading, view their present relationship to the Church? The largest single proportion (two-fifths) think of themselves as Roman Catholics within the structure of the Church (Table 15.22). Another two-fifths think of themselves as Catholics but outside of the Church, and only about one-tenth think of themselves as no longer Christian. Fifty-six per cent of them also still define themselves as priests (Table 15.23), though only 28 per cent of these seek any sort of official recognition for their priesthood from the Church.

TABLE 15.20

PRESENT "CANONICAL" STATUS OF RESIGNED PRIESTS

Present Status	Per Cent
Approved leave	14
Unapproved leave	11
Suspended	14
Laicized	53
Other	8
Total	100

TABLE 15.21

REASONS FOR NOT SEEKING LAICIZATION

(Resigned Priests Not Laicized Who Will Not Seek or
Are Uncertain about Seeking Laicization)

Reason	Per Cent
I am on an approved leave of absence and I plan to return to a diocese or religious community	2
Process is degrading	57
Church cannot withdraw sacramental character	34
I hope to again exercise some public ministry	37
I consider myself a priest independently of the Roman Catholic Church	20
"Laicization" is irrelevant to me	67
I want nothing further to do with the Roman Catholic Church	9
I would like to, but my marriage situation would make it impossible anyway	8

TABLE 15.22

PRESENT POSITION OF RESIGNED PRIESTS IN RELATION TO CHURCH

Position	Per Cent
Catholic within structure of the Church	40
Catholic outside structure of the Church	38
Orthodox	0
Denominational Protestant	1
Non-denominational Christian	8
Non-denominational religious humanist	7
Non-religious humanist	4
Agnostic or atheist	1
Total	99[a]

[a] Not 100 per cent because of rounding.

Concerning whether they intend to go back to the priesthood (Table 15.24), 40 per cent say they certainly would not return and another 18 per cent are uncertain about their return. Thus, only about 40 per cent would be definitely interested in acting as priests again, and only 10 per cent are interested in full-time ecclesiastical work. On the other hand, 58 per cent specify that they would return only under circum-

TABLE 15.23

PRESENT RELATIONSHIP TO THE PRIESTHOOD

	Per Cent of Resigned Priests
Consider self as a priest	56
Relationship to the Priesthood:[a]	
A priest and want to be recognized as such by the Roman Catholic Church	28
A priest recognized as such by the people I serve, though not in good standing with the hierarchy	8
A priest exercising new forms of ministry and wishing to be known as a priest	15
A priest exercising new forms of ministry but not caring to be known as a priest	24
A priest in transition to lay status where no longer wish to exercise the social role of the priesthood	15
A member of the universal priesthood in no way different from any other baptized Christian	10

[a] Of those who see themselves as priests.

stances where they had full-time secular jobs with part-time ecclesiastical work and 60 per cent say they would return only as a married priest.

It is appropriate for us to emphasize that we found no important association between number of years since resignation and a desire to return to the active ministry (gamma = .10) or one's perception of one's relationship to the Church (gamma = .07). Those who resigned five or six years ago are as likely to think of themselves as part of the "official" Church as are those who resigned recently. And those who have just resigned are as likely to define themselves as out of the Church as are those who resigned some years ago. This leads us to speculate that the perspective on the Church which shapes one's resignation persists in a relatively stable way for at least five years after resignation. If one still feels that one is a loyal member of the official Church as one leaves the priesthood, one will maintain that self-definition after resignation. If, on the other hand, one is going to "lose the faith," it will happen either before or during the time of resignation or not at all. As we noted earlier, 12 per cent describe a "loss of faith" as a turning point in their decision-making. Similarly, the same proportion now assert that they are no longer Christians.

TABLE 15.24

FUTURE PLANS IN PRIESTHOOD

Plans	Per Cent of Resigned Priests
Present situation or intentions:	
Presently working in a priestly ministry and celebrating Mass with "approval" of a bishop or pastor	1
Presently working in a priestly ministry and would like the approval of the hierarchy	4
Have definite plans to resume work in a diocese or community	0
Definitely would like to return to work as a priest under certain conditions	36
Am uncertain about going back	18
Definitely would *not* like to return to work as a priest in a diocese or community	40
Total	99[a]
Conditions for return:	
Under no condition	20
With adequate salary and living conditions	29
As a married priest	60
Full-time ecclesiastical work	10
Full-time secular job with part-time ecclesiastical work	58
Parochial work	16
Non-parochial work	17

[a] Not 100 per cent because of rounding.

One can rather easily categorize those who have definitely left the Church or even left Christianity and those who are still solidly in the Church. More puzzling is the situation of that two-fifths of our sample who see themselves as part of the "unofficial" Church. Their position seems to be "marginal" — neither "in" nor "out" — and the lot of marginal men is not easy. However, the fact that many are able to maintain this position for a number of years suggests that either of the two other alternatives is even less attractive: they do not want to be part of the official structure or to disaffiliate completely. Hence marginality is the only choice left.

Thirty-three per cent of the resigned priests have celebrated Mass in someone's home since their resignation and 15 per cent have said Mass in Church (Table 15.25). About one-tenth have administered the sacraments of penance or matrimony or baptism. The gamma coefficients in Table 15.25 indicate that these exercises of the priestly office decline

TABLE 15.25

EXERCISE OF THE PRIESTHOOD

(Resigned Priests Having Presided at
Sacramental Liturgy in Past Year)

Sacramental Liturgy	Per Cent	Gamma (with Years since Resignation)
Mass in homes or apartments	33	−.28
Mass in Church or chapels	15	−.34
Penance	12	−.36
Matrimony	12	−.26
Baptism	10	−.18

as the number of years since resignation increases. It is thus especially in the years immediately after resignation that a resigned priest is likely to exercise a priestly office.

Finally, two-fifths of the resigned priests say they attend Mass every week (table not shown). This is exactly the same proportion as those who consider themselves to be Catholics within the structure of the Church. Until further and more detailed analysis of the resignee data becomes possible, one can therefore summarize our impressions by saying that approximately two-fifths of the resigned priests are still very much a part of the Catholic Church, accept its regulations, and would be willing, under certain circumstances, to return to the exercise of the priestly ministry. Another two-fifths exist in a marginal area outside the official structure of the Church but are not yet ready to declare themselves as definitely out of the Church. Another group, about one-fifth, are pretty definitely no longer part of the Catholic Church. The proportions in each one of these three categories does not change greatly with time. One might have expected that there would be a drift through the years from being certainly in the Church to being certainly out of it; however, our data do not indicate that such a drift actually occurs (the gammas were .10 and .07).

Marriage Happiness among Resignees

In Chapter 11 we discussed the scores of the resigned priests on the measures of psychological well-being developed by Norman Bradburn. In addition to these "happiness" measures, Bradburn and his colleagues have also developed three measures, or indices, of "marriage adjustment"

(Bradburn, 1969; Orden and Bradburn, 1968, 1969). Two of the questions in the resignee questionnaire embodied these measures. The items for the "marital tension" index were contained in Question 41F, which asked the married resignees to indicate the sources of friction in their marriage.

   a. Time spent with friends
   b. Household expenses
   c. Being tired
   d. Being away from home too much
   e. Disciplining children
   f. In-laws
   g. Not showing love
   h. Your job
   i. How to spend leisure time
   j. Religion
   k. Irritating personal habits

The items for the "satisfactions" indices were contained in Question 41G, which asked for the sources of satisfaction in their marriage.

   a. Visited friends together
   b. Went out together to movie, etc.
   c. Entertained friends
   d. Ate out in restaurant
   e. Spent evening chatting
   f. Good laugh
   g. Drive or walk pleasure
   h. Did something other appreciated
   i. Affectionate

The first four items were used to measure marriage sociability and the last five to measure marriage companionship.

When the resignees as a whole are compared with a national sample of college-educated males (Table 15.26), they score higher on all three indices; that is, they report more marital tensions, but also more sociability and slightly more companionship. However, the amount of reported marital tension goes up with the number of years since resignation, while the amounts of sociability and companionship go down. Thus, the married resignees who left the priesthood in 1966 report twice as much marital tension as do college-educated males between twenty-six and thirty-five, a little less than twice as much as those between thirty-six and forty-five, and more than twice as much as those over forty-five.

TABLE 15.26

MARITAL ADJUSTMENT OF RESIGNED PRIESTS AND
COLLEGE-EDUCATED MALES

(Mean Scores)

Item	Marital Tension	Marital Sociability	Marital Companionship	N
Resigned priests (by year of resignation):				
1970	1.3	3.5	4.7	10
1969	1.6	3.5	4.7	177
1968	1.7	3.2	4.7	175
1967	1.8	3.2	4.5	100
1966	2.6	3.2	4.3	41
1964-65	2.3	3.1	4.3	15
Total	1.8	3.3	4.6	518
College-educated males (by age):[a]				
26-35	1.3	2.4	4.4	58
36-45	1.5	2.8	4.1	41
46-55	1.2	2.9	4.6	32
Over 55	.3	3.1	4.2	10

[a] Data from NORC Happiness Study, 1963.

On the other hand, those who resigned in 1966 report a bit more marriage sociability than any age group of the college-educated males and a little more marriage companionship than either those between thirty-six and forty-five or those over fifty-five, but less companionship than those under thirty-five or between forty-six and fifty-five. Further, the scores of the 1966 resignees on the sociability and companionship indices are lower than their colleagues who resigned in 1969 or 1970.

How is one to interpret the data in Table 15.26? First of all, there is some apparent confirmation for James Gill's prediction of serious marital tension among resigned clergy (*Medical Insight,* 1969). The tension levels are substantially higher than that of other married people and increase, as Gill's hypothesis would suggest, with the years since resignation. Furthermore, the compensations in sociability and companionship, once higher than that of the typical American marriage, also settle at average levels with the passage of time.

It may be, of course, that the pattern observed among the resignees is typical of recent marriages or of recent marriages of those who are older at marriage than most other Americans or, finally, of all marriages, recent or not, that are entered into at an older age. The national sample is not sufficiently large to enable us to examine any of these possibilities. If any of them could be confirmed, it would then follow that the pattern in Table 15.26 is not unique to the resigned clergy but is rather a function of either recency of marriage or age at marriage.

On the other hand, the pattern may be unique to resigned clergy; it may be that the seminary training, the years in the priesthood, and the emotional turmoil of resignation all combine to make the resignee somewhat less well equipped to deal with the strains of the marital relationship. However, there is little in our data to suggest that Catholic clergy are appreciably less mature than other American males. It may be that their apparent difficulty in coping with feelings of anger and aggression, as seen in Chapter 4, contributes to the tensions in their marriages.

We must also note that there is some conflict between the high level of psychological well-being reported by the resigned clergy (as described in Chapter 11) and the tensions in their marriages, especially since psychological well-being declines only moderately with years since resignation while marital tensions increase sharply.

In the conceptualization of Bradburn and his colleagues, marriage happiness is also a "balance of payments" between marital tensions and marital satisfactions. If one takes the difference between the marital tension score and a combination of the companionship and sociability scores, one sees that the score on the marriage adjustment balance scale (Table 15.27) for all resignees is higher than that of American college-educated males between twenty-six and forty-five (6.1 for the resignees and 5.5 and 5.4 for the two age cohorts of males, respectively). However, the marital balance score goes down from a very high 6.9 for those who have just left the priesthood (and presumably just married) to 5.0 for those who resigned in the mid-1960s.

There are two things to be noted about these marital adjustment balance scores. First of all, the resigned clergy reach their balances by a different route than most American males. Thus priests who resigned in 1967 have approximately the same score as males between twenty-six and thirty-five (5.8 and 5.5), but the balance is struck for the resigned priests by having both higher tension and higher satisfactions scores than do their male counterparts.

It would appear, then, that former priests score higher on both the positive and negative dimensions in the marriages than do typical American males. This is the third example we have of the strong feelings in the

TABLE 15.27

MARITAL ADJUSTMENT BALANCE SCALE SCORES OF RESIGNED
PRIESTS AND COLLEGE-EDUCATED MALES

Resigned priests (by year of resignation):	*Mean Scores*
1970	6.9
1969	6.6
1968	6.2
1967	5.8
1966	4.9
1964-65	5.0
Total	6.1
College-educated males (by age): [a]	
26-35	5.5
36-45	5.4
46-55	6.4

[a] Data from NORC Happiness Study, 1963.

lives of resigned clerics: their response to the POI test, their own psychological well-being, and their feelings about the adjustment of their marriages all display levels of emotionality not to be observed in comparable groups. Shostrom's phrase, "pathological freedom," may apply, as may Karen Horney's phrase, "a binge of health." But neither of these phrases is intended to be judgmental. They are merely a way of suggesting that if men keep their emotions pent up for a long period of time and then are able to release them through a process that is difficult and painful, one will certainly expect from them a period of strong emotionality.

The second observation is that priests who resigned in the mid-1960s score lower on the marital adjustment balance scale than the college-educated males. The sociability and companionship scores of these former priests have leveled out at scores roughly comparable with the college-educated males, but the tension scores have climbed to levels that are (for those who resigned in 1966) twice as high as those among the college-educated males. One is not able to say that these marriages are in "trouble," but one must say that their adjustment balance is lower than for comparable groups.

It would be unwise to attempt speculations at the present time beyond those contained in the previous paragraphs. The nature of our data for the general population makes further comparisons with the resignees quite tenuous. However, it is possible to report with some confidence that, whatever the explanation, former Roman Catholic priests do seem to experience greater tensions in marriage than the typical college-educated American male, and these tensions increase as the resignation date recedes into the past. On the other hand, only three of our respondents report that they are divorced.

Opinions of Resignees

Resignees were asked a series of open-ended questions that permitted them to express their own feelings and opinions about certain matters that it was thought might be of some particular concern to them. They were first asked, "In what capacity (kind of work) would you like to exercise the priesthood (if at all)?" Fifty-eight per cent of the resignees responded to this question. We observe in Table 15.28 that while 37 per cent of those who responded mentioned some form of traditional parochial ministry and 14 per cent mentioned education, almost half (42 per cent) mentioned some kind of activity — "free ministry," "counseling," "social service," "Christian presence," "campus ministry" — which would not be considered the kind of work in which most active priests presently engage.

TABLE 15.28

PREFERRED KIND OF WORK FOR EXERCISE OF THE PRIESTHOOD

Kind of Work	Per Cent of Resigned Priests
Traditional parochial	37
Free ministry	14
Education	14
Counseling	12
Social service and social change	8
Christian presence within professional, work, or community context	4
Campus ministry	4
Chaplaincy	2
Missionary work	1
Other	5
Total	101[a]
N	(435)

[a] Not 100 per cent because of rounding.

Under the category "free ministry," some of the expressions used were "liturgies where they are asked for," "floating parish," "a community in the process of living out the common humanity," "working with married couples in small communities," or "working with those currently dissatisfied with normal parish worship." Those who spoke of the ministry as Christian presence used terms such as "presence in the very secular world," "witness to the community of believers," "playing the role of a wise friend to my fellow men," or "a ministry concerned with each man you work with."

A second question asked the respondents whether they had themselves engaged in any new forms of priestly ministry. Of the approximately one-third of the respondents who said that they had, Table 15.29 shows that 67 per cent simply described their present occupation as their ministry and another 12 per cent thought of their life-style as Christian witness, while 9 per cent mentioned the so-called "free ministry," and 11 per cent more described a combination of "free ministry" and their present occupation.

In keeping with their own personal experiences, the respondents were also most likely to think of an occupational base when they were asked to speculate on "what kinds of activity can you imagine as possible new forms of meaningful ministry for priests." Table 15.30 shows that 44 per cent of those who responded to this question mentioned some form of priest-worker, 21 per cent mentioned liturgical innovative ministries, and 27 per cent more mentioned a combination of priest-worker and liturgical ministries. It is clear from the responses to this and the two previous open-ended questions that the majority of the resignees who answered

TABLE 15.29

FORMS OF PRIESTLY MINISTRY

Form of Ministry	Per Cent of Resigned Priests
Present occupation	67
Life-style as Christian witness	12
Free ministry	9
Present occupation plus free ministry	11
Other	1
Total	100
N	(271)

TABLE 15.30

POSSIBLE NEW FORMS OF MINISTRY FOR PRIESTS

Possible New Ministries	*Per Cent of Resigned Priests*
Principal categories:	
Priest-worker	44
Liturgical and related ministry	21
Priest-worker plus liturgical and related ministry	27
Life-style as Christian witness	7
Other	1
Total	100
N	(618)

these questions were not inclined to emphasize experimentation and innovation within the context of the parish ministry as it now stands.

Finally, the resignees were asked, "If you could make only *one* change in the Roman Catholic Church, what would it be?" Table 15.31 shows that almost half (47 per cent) suggested some modification of the structure of Church government — decentralization, election of church officials, co-responsibility, modifying uses of authority, etc. Celibacy was mentioned as the one principal change by 15 per cent of the respondents and various forms of becoming a "servant Church" by 16 per cent, while 12 per cent mentioned changes in selected doctrinal and moral teachings. There is in Table 15.31 more evidence for our impression that priests, both active and resigned, do not consider celibacy the principal problem facing the priesthood. Although 70 per cent of the resigned priests are married, when put in the artificial position of being forced to choose one change, celibacy is mentioned by less than one-sixth of them.

The Resignees Speak for Themselves

On the back cover of the questionnaire, the resignees were asked three final open-ended questions: "At the present time what would you most want to say to the following groups in the Roman Catholic Church? To Laymen? To Priests and Religious? To the Bishops?"

Of the responses directed to the laity (Table 15.32), 57 per cent stressed personal maturity or conversion, 29 per cent emphasized action within the Church, and 14 per cent mentioned action within the world.

TABLE 15.31

RECOMMENDED CHANGES IN THE ROMAN CATHOLIC CHURCH

Recommended Change	Per Cent of Resigned Priests
Restructuring Church government	47
Making celibacy optional	15
Changing clerical life-styles	5
Becoming servant Church	16
Changing selected doctrinal and moral teachings	12
Eliminating the Church	2
Other	3
Total	100
N	(809)[a]

[a] These data were computed using the final total case base for resignees of 873, of whom 64 did not respond to this question.

Some of the responses took a rather positive attitude toward religion and the Church, as we can see in the following six examples:[3]

Hold on to the best of the past and use it as productively as possible; be open to the present in both mind and emotion, be open to truth wherever it may be found, and respond to it authentically; have the audacity to become whatever you are capable of becoming, the drive to make your own little contribution to the future.

TABLE 15.32

ADVICE OF RESIGNEES TO LAYMEN

Recommendations to Laity	Per Cent of Responses[a]
Call to personal maturity and/or conversion	57
Call to action within the Church	29
Call to action within the world	14
Total	100
Number of recommendations	(1,209)

[a] Based on the multiple responses of those comprising the final total case base of 873.

There is still a God who guides. Faith means nothing if we forget this. The Church will grow, will change, will heal its defects. But we must not kill it with forced injections of whatever vitamins we think it needs.

Retain your faith in Christ, the Gospels and your own common sense.

Be of good cheer. Together we shall overcome the Roman bureaucracy. It will self-destruct under its own ponderousness and stupidity — Christ prevails (over Christiandom).

Hang in there. The authorities within the Church will eventually shed their antiquarian ways and the Catholic Church will be the most beautiful in the world.

For God's sake do not abandon the ship, even though it appears that a lot of the ship's officers are A.W.O.L.

On the other hand, many respondents urged the laity to act as independent agents within the Church.

From the days of struggling with Modernism the Church has become an overly-intellectual, rational institution. . . . We envision the Church as a true pilgrim — a people journeying toward a revealing God — a people becoming, in process — searching and finding, pursuing the light, believing and not believing. Each member free to be where he is in that pilgrimage.

Learn to make your own decisions. . . . Refuse to be shackled by facts without rational basis. Recognize that much of Roman Catholic teachings is without scriptural basis and is psychologically and religiously harmful — it produces moral infants.

Don't listen to all the junk Church authorities are laying on you. If you can't operate as a free human being and know you are loved by God, get yourselves a good therapist who can help you shake the hang-ups that the institutional Church has laid on you.

Quit asking "Father" what to do.

Think for yourselves and stop using the Church as a crutch.

And some respondents took a moderately or even strongly hostile attitude toward the Church, as seen in the following five examples:

Lay aside cultural Catholicism and folk-religion and accept or reject on a personal basis God as a vital and dynamic element.

Hang loose. Take the good things the Church has to offer, reject the rest. Sometimes you can be a good Christian only by being a "bad" Catholic.

Throw off the social and organizational increments that are choking
the real life you can receive from the Church.

The Catholic Church is America's invisible but all pervading pre-
server of social injustice. Supporting it is basically anti-Christian
and immoral.

The idea of Roman Catholicism being the one true church is a false
assumption based upon a misunderstanding of the nature of the
Church and the nature of God's election and promise. . . . The
present life-style of the Roman Church with its inherent legalism
and inordinate insistence upon authority as more important than
sensitivity to persons and service . . . was precisely what Christ
rejected in the Pharisees and Saducees. . . . In that sense, the R. C.
Church is perhaps the farthest denomination from the truth of
Christ. Real apostolic succession seems now to reside in those
denominations which follow Christ most closely.

The emphasis on maturity was maintained in their advice to priests and
religious (Table 15.33), with the most frequently mentioned suggestions
dealing with re-evaluation of the role of the priest (23 per cent) and a
call for closer identification with the people (27 per cent). Some respondents made vigorous and encouraging religious comments:

Be doers of the Gospel and imitators of the human Jesus. Lead by
example and not by some mystical sense of a superior call. Go
"everywhere" man goes and humanize him. Show that the power
of God in man is greater than the power of violence.

Live the Gospel. . . . Celibacy is valid and beautiful. If this is the
way you have to fulfill your commitment to Christ, be proud. A
priest or religious has no right to special privileges. . . . Only he who
loves God and man has a special privilege and that is to be called a
son of God.

On the other hand, many respondents attacked the position of those
who are still active clerics, urging them to break with their present role:

Many of you have been lulled by too much security. This has
caused some insensitivity to people. Don't be proud that you keep
the legal system perfectly — love more. If you don't feel in love
you won't act in love and then you are a negative sign of Christianity.
I warn you to question your role. . . . Most of you are still content
to see yourselves as "soul-savers" rather than catalysts, bringing
revolution to the world, making it more human, more conscious.

TABLE 15.33

ADVICE OF RESIGNEES TO PRIESTS AND RELIGIOUS

Recommendations to Priests and Religious	Per Cent of Responses[a]
Principal categories:	
Call to personal maturity and/or conversion ..	57
Call to effective ministry	43
Total	100
Number of recommendations	(1,308)
Principal categories with sub-categories:	
I. Call to maturity	
Re-evaluate present role	23
Be a Christian	17
Autonomy	13
Be a person	11
Authentic vs. unauthentic religion	9
Become informed	9
Positive attitude toward change	6
Persevere	5
New vision of Church	3
Follow conscience	2
Develop faith	2
Total	100
Number of recommendations	(743)
II. Call to effective ministry	
Identification with people	27
Effective teaching and preaching	14
Promote reform	14
Freer life-style	10
Work for co-responsibility	8
Positive attitude toward fellow clergy (active and inactive)	8
Involvement in social issues	7
Promote optional celibacy	4
Be a listener	4
Effective liturgy	3
Total	99[b]
Number of recommendations	(565)

[a] Based on the multiple responses of those comprising final total case base of 873.

[b] Not 100 per cent because of rounding.

You are wrong in trying to breathe life into a corpse — i.e., the institution as it stands; think Christ — get out — and do something if your Christianity is alive and honest.

Go read over again the parables about Pharisees. Your vows or contentions [sic] of poverty are so much self-confusion. Poverty as practiced by religious is security.

The principal advice to bishops, as seen in Table 15.34, was to urge them to strong pastoral leadership (42 per cent), followed by recommendations that the bishops engage more enthusiastically in the task of ecclesiastical reform (24 per cent). Many of the comments to the bishops showed some hostility and others were very hostile indeed. Among the printable comments (and some are certainly not printable) are the following three:

We see you as simply figureheads, administrators. You should be alive, concerned with all the issues, not just abortion and Catholic education. You, above all, should be crusading for human rights. You are too remote, selfish and lazy.

I am very happy to see the church involved in the negotiations of the United Farm Workers. I hope the church's involvement in social problems continues, especially the problems of the poor.

You have missed the opportunity to be real shepherds. Ten years ago people would have listened if you had said meaningful things about racial justice, community concern.

TABLE 15.34

ADVICE OF RESIGNEES TO BISHOPS

Recommendations to Bishops	*Per Cent of Responses*[a]
Call to pastoral leadership	42
Call to task of reform	24
Call to autonomy	14
Call to personal maturity and/or conversion	11
Call to evangelical life-style	6
Call to retire	2
Call to demise	1
Total	100
Number of recommendations	(1,669)

[a] Based on the multiple responses of those comprising the final total case base of 873.

Generally, the resignees advise against legalism and absolutism. The spirit of the law must triumph over the letter. Freedom of conscience is a Christian right. Thus, they made comments such as: "Allow for personal decisions and support them as unique and wholesome for Christian development." "Don't hold on so tight — then the horse knows you're afraid." "Let your priests define their ministry, their role in the world." "Free your Catholics of fear, repression, guilt and provincialism . . . freedom does not destroy but develops." "Your insensitive authoritarian approach is destroying the Church. It is not your keepsake. It belongs to everyone." "You are functioning in the security of the monarch who cut off the heads of messengers bringing bad news with the belief that that ended the bad news. Not so. You enjoy jurisdiction and orders but you have no right to claim omnipotence." "The 'Pharisees' of old were amateurs compared to you. . . . The tactics of the Mafia, though violent, are mild compared to yours."

Some of the responses were much more harsh: "Come off it, your excellency. Forget your chancery lackeys and your diocesan 'consenters.' If you really want to get the pulse of the 'People of God' . . . talk to the priests who are out where the action is." "Please communicate on a personal level with your priests insofar as it is possible. Learn to listen and accept them as persons, to love them and accept their love in return." "Your corporate treatment of and consequent loss of thousands of married priests is a *major scandal* to an ever increasing number of Christians." "Open yourself to your priests who have left the clergy to minister in new ways."

And some displayed considerable anger: "Climb off the throne, boys! You are so far out of contact, it is impossible to discuss with you what life is all about. Bishops have to join the human race." "For God's sake, wake up to what's happening today." "Read the signs of the times." "You are, perhaps, the most outdated group of men in contemporary America." "Get an education in the realities of the planet around you." "Make a sincere effort to evaluate Christian tradition apart from scholastic theology and philosophy with all their narrowing approach." "Take a year off to study the new theology, psychology and sociology, and get involved with people." "Take out the ear plugs, get a new set of glasses and go back to school."

Some offered ironic religious advice to their former leaders: "Brothers in Christ, lay aside your mitres, capes, croziers. Become humble and learn of Christ." "Be a model to the flock — or retire." "Bishops today are primarily committed to preserving the institution (which has little to do with following Jesus). They are a scandal to the poor." "Meditate on Matthew, Chapter 23." "Walk in the light of God's Word! Put away every other word." "To me most bishops are Pharisees and hypocrites. Money is their passion. . . . I see little of the poor Christ in them." "Make one final effort to be followers of Jesus or be even more reactionary so that the Church will die more quickly."

And a number of respondents accused the bishops of yielding to ambition: "Risk yourself. State your convictions, and don't be over-powered by the majority of the American hierarchy, many of whom have no guts and are motivated only by ambition." "All the bishops can't all think the same. I'm amazed some have not had the guts to sound off." "Don't become members of the Bishops' Club and have everything de-cided for you. You represent Christ (not the Club) in your diocese." "Learn to be true shepherds, courageous leaders . . . while the social fibre of the nation is torn apart, you have been content to sit tight and speak pious platitudes."

Finally a few seemed ready to despair about communicating with the bishops: "Cui bono?" "These men are too far gone by training and environment to be effective in any way. They serve a myth structure which is declining yet they act as if all were well." "Most of what you stand for is a bad dream of the past and I want very little to do with it."

Summary

To summarize this chapter we address ourselves to a number of questions:

1. *Are the resignees "angry" at the Church?* Some certainly are, as a reading of the responses to the open-ended questions would make clear. But many others are not. Rather they seem to have mixed emotions about the Church, their experiences in it, the treatment they received at resignation, and their present relationship to it.

2. *Why did they leave the priesthood?* They left because they found difficulties with the structure of the Church and the work they were doing as priests and because they wanted to get married.

3. *Does resignation indicate a problem of "faith"?* The "faith" issue is one that is clearly expressed by only a small minority — less than one-fifth. For another two-fifths, it does not seem to be a serious problem. The present state of our analysis does not enable us to make a judgment about the "faith" of the ambivalent two-fifths. However, there is nothing in their explicit testimony to indicate that they have "lost the faith."

4. *Are the resignees happy with their decision?* Eighty-six per cent say they are "very satisfied" with their decision to leave and this proportion remains roughly constant, no matter how many years intervene since resignation.

5. *What sort of work are the resignees doing?* Most seem to be engaged in some sort of teaching or social service occupations. About one-third make more than $12,000 a year.

6. *Do resignees still consider themselves as part of the Church?* About two-fifths think of themselves as part of the official Church and another two-fifths see themselves on the margin but still part of the Church. Around two-fifths attend Mass every week.

7. *Do many of them want to return to the active ministry?* Only about two-fifths seem interested in such a return, and many of these apparently do not want to return to any sort of "full-time" priestly work.

8. *Do they still exercise the ministry?* A minority do preside over liturgical functions, but this decreases as the resignation event recedes into the past.

9. *Are their marriages unhappy?* There seems to be a higher level of tension in their marriages than in most American marriages, and the tension increases with the passage of the years since resignation. But the marriage companionship and sociability scores are also high. There have been few divorces among the respondents.

10. *What sort of changes do the resigned priests want to see in the Church?* The most frequently mentioned change was some sort of reform of the ecclesiastical government structure. A change in the law of celibacy was mentioned only one-third as often as governmental change when the respondents were asked to choose only one reform.

1. Whether the resignation rate reported in the text is "high" or "low" depends on one's point of view. It is high by the standards of years before 1966 (at least insofar as impressions of very low resignation rates before then are valid). It is low compared to the situation during the French Revolution. It is high compared to the theoretical ideal of a "priest forever"; it is probably low according to the rates in other professions. Some of our colleagues at NORC who are not part of the team on this study expressed the opinion that a 2 per cent per year resignation rate from a profession was surprisingly low. On the other hand, it is very difficult to assess rates in other professions, since however poor the resignation records may be for priests, they are much worse for other professionals, mostly because professional associations take no official notice of someone who simply ceases to practice a given

profession. Our NORC colleagues have suggested that the resignation rate from the college professorate is very likely higher than 2 per cent per annum.

2. On the NORC occupational scale, almost one-half of the resignees fall into the category that included teachers and those engaged in a wide variety of social work activities.

3. It need hardly be said that the responses quoted in this chapter are cited for the information of the reader of this report and do *not* necessarily represent the opinions of anyone at NORC. They are presented here as illustrations of the answers to the open-ended questions and nothing more.

CHAPTER 16

SUMMARY AND CONCLUSION

We now turn to an evaluation of the "assets" and "liabilities" of the Catholic priesthood in the United States insofar as these can be determined by our research.[1] It must be emphasized that this assessment is made from a sociological and not a religious perspective.

Weighing the "Assets"

1. There is no evidence in our research that Catholic priests are any more or less deficient in emotional maturity than other groups in American society.

2. Priests maintain a high degree of personal morale, higher in fact than college-educated males in the same age categories.

3. No evidence could be found that either early entry into the seminary or dating experience affected either emotional maturity or personal morale among priests.

4. Most priests engage in some form of regular prayer, and a substantial proportion have had frequent religious experiences of union with God or Christ.

5. There is a fundamental acceptance by priests of the basic religious values to which the Church is officially committed, though there are some differences in the formulations according to which these values are expressed.

6. On certain social and racial matters, priests are more "liberal" than a sample of laity; and bishops are more "liberal" than priests. It therefore seems that one cannot assert that priests are lacking in social conscience.

7. There is support for ecumenism among the Catholic clergy and considerable involvement in ecumenical activity.

8. There is an acceptance among practically all priests of the bishop as the principal leader and decision-maker in the diocese.

9. Most priests feel that they have close friends, that the place where they live is "home," and that their relationships with their colleagues are adequate, although not always excellent.

311

10. Priests work moderately long hours, evaluate themselves quite favorably in comparison with other professionals, enjoy an adequate (though not spectacular) level of job satisfaction, are inclined to pursue a good deal of professional reading, and are committed to the need for more professional training.

11. A large majority of the clergy say that if they had the choice to make again, they would enter the priesthood.

12. While there is a moderate correlation between "inner-directedness" and inclination to leave and between having an M.A. and having already resigned, there is no evidence of a *massive* exodus of the most mature and best educated of the clergy. On the contrary, our data would indicate that such an exodus is not occurring.

And the "Liabilities"

On the other hand, there are serious problems facing the priesthood.

1. Large numbers of priests are dissatisfied with the way the ecclesiastical structure is shaped and the way decision-making power is distributed; but the leadership of the Church does not share this dissatisfaction. Furthermore, it would appear that differences between younger and older priests on the distribution of power and authority are rooted in ideological differences about the nature of the Church and religion.

2. There are systematic and substantial differences between bishops and priests on almost every matter we studied. In most cases, the bishops hold different points of view and positions than even the priests in their own age group. Given the disagreements over power and over appropriate reforms in the Church, these systematic differences of conviction indicate a serious and potentially dangerous "gap" between the priests and the hierarchy.

3. There are drastic differences between the priests and the bishops on the subject of sexual morality. The official position of the Church on birth control and divorce does not command majority support among the priests, and there has been a deterioration of support for the birth control position since the issuance of the encyclical *Humanae Vitae*.

4. The majority of the priests do not accept the present position on obligatory celibacy and expect that a change in the law is likely. Even though celibacy is still valued, and most priests (four-fifths of all, two-thirds of those under thirty-five) say that they would not be likely to marry if celibacy became optional, there is still strong support for a modification of this regulation, particularly among those under forty-five. The hierarchy, however, is strongly opposed to such a change.

5. About 5 per cent of the diocesan priests resigned in the four years from 1966 through 1969. Even though the annual rate may not be high in comparison with other professions, it is certainly high compared to impressions about what the rate was in the past. While only 3 per cent of our sample of active priests said that they either certainly or probably would leave the priesthood, many more were uncertain — particularly among the younger priests. The immediate reason for thinking about resignation is apparently the desire to marry, a desire which in its turn is partly based on the loneliness and discouragement of the priestly life.

6. There has been a considerable decline in enthusiasm for vocational recruiting, a phenomenon that may be far more serious than the resignation rate.

7. The condition of the associate pastor is poor. Job satisfaction in this group, for example, is generally lower than that of unskilled workers. Associate pastors also do not feel that they have very good relationships with their colleagues.

8. Finally, if one postulates for the clergy a high degree of self-actualization and psychological well-being, then they clearly fail to meet these standards.

The Resignees

A number of summary comments may also be made about the resignees.

1. The two reasons for resignation mentioned most frequently as "very important" are inability to live within the structure of the Church and the desire to marry. When forced to choose one recommendation for change in the Church, only 15 per cent of the resignees mentioned celibacy.

2. There is no evidence that the resignees regret their decision or are unhappy in their present state. On the contrary, there is considerable evidence that they are in a state of emotional euphoria, characterized by what Karen Horney has described as a "binge of health"— a binge that is understandable and probably inevitable in their circumstances.

3. Resignees are apparently moderately successful in their occupations, with about one-third making over $12,000 a year.

4. At the present time the resignees have attitudes and values that are sharply different from those of active priests, even those active priests under thirty-five. They also recollect much less satisfaction from priestly activities than do their opposite numbers among the active clergy. On the other hand, they find more satisfaction in their present career efforts than they did in their work as priests.

5. About two-fifths of the resignees still consider themselves to be Catholics and part of the official Church, another two-fifths are on the margins of the Church, and the remaining one-fifth are no longer affiliated with the Church. Apparently these proportions exist at the time of resignation and do not change much over time. Thus, one can tentatively conclude that the "faith" problem is overriding only in about one-fifth of the resignations — though there may be "faith confusion" among many of those on the margins of the official Church.

6. Only a minority of resigned priests (40 per cent) definitely wish to return to the priesthood. And only a minority of that minority seem interested in the exercise of full-time parochial or teaching ministries.

7. In the years immediately after marriage, the marital adjustment balance scores of married resignees are higher than those of the typical American marriage of college-educated males, but the scores become lower than those of the typical American marriage as the years pass. However, there were almost no divorces or separations recorded in our sample.

Analytic Postscript

One observation should also be made of more general social science interest. Two variables — recollection of family tension in one's childhood and experience of contact with God — make relatively small but consistent contributions to the explanation of priestly attitudes and behavior. In the explanation of the propensity to stay in the priesthood, they are almost as important as work satisfaction and values, though obviously less important than such powerful predictors as age and desire to marry. The family-tension variable was introduced into our research on the basis of theoretical considerations drawn from the increasing literature on religious apostasy. While the confirmation of the theory is not spectacular, confirmation is still to be found. One would not, after all, expect family tension to explain vast amounts of variance in values, morale, work satisfaction, and future plans. That it explains anything at all is, from a theoretical viewpoint, interesting and important.

That religious experience does contribute positively to work satisfaction, morale, and the desire to remain a priest may not be surprising to priests, but it is still a moderately important discovery for the rather undeveloped tradition of empirical research on mystical experiences.

Problem-Solving

As far as practical solutions are concerned, the two principal problems of priests that have emerged in this study — authority and resignation — are relatively independent. Thus even though loneliness is a strong predictor of the desire to marry, and the wish to marry is powerfully correlated with plans to leave, only 20 per cent of the priests in our sample think that they would be likely to marry even if they could. Loneliness is not such a problem for 80 per cent of the priests as to make them want to get married and to think of resigning as a result of that desire. On the other hand, problems with authority and work satisfaction are not nearly as strong predictors of the desire to marry as is loneliness.[2] Thus, if steps are taken to solve the work and authority problems in the priesthood but the problem of loneliness remains unresolved, the desire to marry and the resultant resignation rate will fall only somewhat. If, on the other hand, the loneliness problem can be solved, the desire to marry and the resignation rate will decline rather considerably, but the internal conflict problems will remain substantially unresolved.

Policy-makers will apparently have to face the fact that conflict over authority and feelings of loneliness may have to be approached as rather distinct problems. Reducing conflict within the authority structure may not reduce resignation rates very much; and reducing loneliness is not likely to have too much impact on internal conflict. We cannot make any absolute assertion about the relationship between authority as a problem and loneliness as a problem since the logic of our model does not permit us to postulate a causal relationship. However, we can say that an improvement in work satisfaction would not appreciably affect the loneliness problem. While there are obviously some priests for whom both authority and loneliness are problems, there are others who have one problem or the other but not both. One can conclude that no single solution will enable the priesthood to cope effectively with both problems.

One way to conceptualize this situation is to say that in a hypothetical model when all those who certainly or probably would marry if they could have left the priesthood (which would mean about one-fifth of all the priests and one-third of those under thirty-five), the amount of loneliness in the priesthood would be substantially diminished and resignation rates would become quite low once again, but there would be little change in the conflict over authority.

To attempt one final summary of our findings, we have discovered no evidence that the Catholic priesthood is in a state of collapse or even near collapse. There are many strong and positive forces at work in the priesthood, and it would be an unwise man who would conclude on the basis of our data that it will disappear. On the other hand, the priesthood has certain very serious problems, most of them centering around the highly volatile subjects of power and sex, which indicate trouble and conflict in the years ahead. Given the uneven nature of the social scientific study of professions, no certain answer can be given to the question of whether the Catholic priesthood has more problems or fewer problems than other professions; and given the nature of it as a profession *sui generis,* such a comparison would be of only marginal utility. And yet, by way of drawing all strands together, one might come away from a consideration of the NORC data with the conclusion that the priesthood has both more assets and more problems than most other professions.

1. The reader may now wish to reread the summary questions and responses in each of the preceding chapters.

2. The net regression weights with desire to marry when the prior variables in our model are included are $-.08$ for work satisfaction, $.12$ for authority as a problem, and $.33$ for loneliness as a problem.

APPENDIX A

SAMPLING METHODOLOGY

From the standpoint of sample design, the aim of this study was two-fold. A principal goal was the accurate description of the attitudes and characteristics of the population of diocesan and religious priests in the United States. Of equal importance, however, was the analysis of variation in reported attitudes in terms of other "explanatory" variables measured for each priest. Thus, we faced a problem that is common in survey research — that of striking an acceptable balance between a sample that is statistically efficient with respect to the estimation of population parameters and a sample that contains adequate representation of the full range of values of the independent variables that are expected in advance to have high explanatory potential.

It was believed that one of the most important explanatory variables in the analysis of a priest's attitudes and behavior would be the size (number of priests) of the diocese or religious order community with which he was affiliated, and that size would doubtless be highly correlated with other important variables such as the organizational characteristics of the diocese or religious institute. In order to ensure that priests from all size categories would be represented and, furthermore, to have sufficient numbers of priests from size groups of special interest (e.g., the very large urban dioceses), we decided to stratify dioceses and religious communities according to the number of priests contained in them and then to select them as first-stage sampling units or clusters. In addition to the size strata, in the case of religious institutes two special strata were formed for the Trappists and the United States Foundations in order to ensure representation from those groups.

The size categories for dioceses and religious institutes were defined as follows:

Dioceses:
  1. Small (1–100 priests)
  2. Medium (101–200)

3. Large (201–500)
4. Extra large (501 and above)

Religious institutes:

1. Extra small (1–20 priests)
2. Small (21–50)
3. Medium (51–135)
4. Large (136 and above)

After separation into size strata (or the two special strata for the Trappists and U.S. Foundations), the dioceses and religious communities were arranged in geographical order by the four major United States census regions (Northeast, North Central, South, and West) and then sampled within each stratum by systematic selection with probabilities proportional to size. In this manner, the benefits of finer stratification by size, as well as those of geographic stratification, were gained. In a second stage, subsamples of priests were selected from each of the dioceses or institutes chosen in the first stage. The method of sampling first-stage units with probabilities proportional to size made possible the selection of within-cluster subsamples of roughly equal size in the second stage while maintaining a constant overall probability of selection for each priest within a given stratum. After first-stage selection, we obtained by written request a complete list of priests within a selected unit from a contact person officially designated by the bishop or major superior. Subsampling was then performed at the desired rate by means of systematic selection.[1] At each sampling stage we used a replicated sample design in order to permit the computation of standard errors of estimate.

In summary, the main sample design may be described as *stratified two-stage cluster sampling with probabilities proportional to size*. The selection probabilities within the various strata were primarily determined by cell-size requirements in the eventual analysis and they should therefore be expected to vary considerably, requiring rather complicated weighting of individual responses in order to calculate the estimated characteristics for the total population of priests. The required weighting, however, presented no great problems in computer processing, and it was determined in advance that the variability in weights would have no appreciable impact on the efficiency of estimation. Thus, if an estimate of the proportion of priests in a particular subpopulation who express a particular response is desired, the appropriate combined ratio estimator is

$$r = \frac{\Sigma' w_j}{\Sigma'' w_j},$$

where w_j is the reciprocal of the selection probability for priest j, Σ' indicates summation over the set of all priests expressing the response, and Σ'' indicates summation over all priests in the relevant subpopulation. The w_j will be constant for all priests in a given diocese or community, and in many cases they will be constant within a given stratum. Adjustments for nonresponse may result in modification of the w_j in order to allow for representation of the assumed opinions of the nonresponse group. Appendix D contains a discussion of possible biases in our estimations due to nonresponse. Here we consider those that may be caused by sampling.

Since the sample for the American Catholic Priesthood Study was drawn in the form of two replicated subsamples, it is possible to compute a standard error for our estimates of the characteristics of both sampling units — the primary sampling units (dioceses and religious institutes) and the individual priests. In Chapter 15, data on resignations are presented for our sample of 85 dioceses and 87 religious institutes. With what degree of certitude can we say that the figures in Tables 15.1-15.3 are accurate for *all* dioceses and religious institutes in the United States rather than for just the 172 represented in the sample? To answer this question we computed the standard errors of estimate for the diocesan data in Tables 15.1 and 15.3; the results are given in Table A.1.[2] It is highly probable that in no year would the average resignation rate be off by more than .09 or the total number of resignees by more than 32 priests. Therefore, with a high degree of statistical certainty we can say that for 1968, the year for which the standard errors are the largest, the average resignation rate in *all* U.S. dioceses (given as 1.55) could be as low as 1.46 or as high as 1.64. Likewise, the total number of resignations for that year (given as 548) could be as low as 516 or as high as 580.

The standard errors of estimate were also computed for the percentages of individual priests in the United States holding certain opinions. The first column in Table A.2 presents the proportions giving certain responses on three issues as reported in the text.[3] (To simplify this discussion and to make the examples comparable with those included in the treatment of nonresponse bias in Appendix D, only the responses of active diocesan priests are considered here.) Fifty-six per cent of the active diocesan priests agree that celibacy should be a matter of personal choice (Table 12.1), 60 per cent in some fashion do not accept

TABLE A.1

STANDARD ERRORS OF ESTIMATE FOR AVERAGE DIOCESAN RESIGNATION
RATES AND TOTAL NUMBER OF RESIGNEES, BY YEAR

Year	Average Resignation Rate [a]	Standard Error	Coefficient of Variation [b]	Total Number of Resignees	Standard Error	Coefficient of Variation [b]	Weighted N
1966	.38	.03	.08	132.6 [c]	11.1	.09	139
1967	.87	.07	.08	302.1 [d]	22.5	.08	147
1968	1.55	.09	.06	548.2	32.3	.06	149
1969	1.98	.09	.04	753.2	30.0	.04	149

[a] Number of resignations per 100 priests.

[b] Coefficient of variation = $\dfrac{\text{standard error}}{\text{estimate}}$

[c] Supplying the mean for missing cases, the total number is 142.2.

[d] Supplying the mean for missing cases, the total number is 306.5.

the official teaching on birth control (Table 6.15), and 70 per cent support the election of bishops by the clergy of the diocese (Table 7.13). With what degree of certitude can we say that these figures are accurate for *all* diocesan priests in the country rather than for just those represented in our sample? The standard errors of estimate for the three percentages in Table A.2 provide an answer to the question. Once again with a confidence coefficient of .95 we can say that of all the diocesan priests in the United States, the percentage agreeing with optional celibacy lies between 55.2 and 55.9; the percentage not accepting the official teaching on birth control lies between 58.5 and 60.7; and the percentage advocating the election of bishops by the clergy of the diocese lies between 68.6 and 71.3.

We may conclude from these representative confidence statements that the sampling procedures used in this study have proved to be not only adequate but indeed highly satisfactory. (A tape containing all the basic data for the Priesthood Study prepared specifically for use in computing standard errors has been placed in the NORC data archives if a more complete set of standard errors of estimate is desired.) Therefore, the possible errors in the findings presented in this report that are due to sampling variability are relatively small.

TABLE A.2

STANDARD ERRORS OF ESTIMATE FOR PROPOSITION OF
ACTIVE DIOCESAN PRIESTS TAKING CERTAIN
POSITIONS ON THREE ISSUES

Item	Per Cent	Standard Error	Coefficient of Variation[a]	Weighted N
Celibacy should be a matter of personal choice for diocesan priests	55.5[b]	.18	.32	63,623
Personal convictions about artificial contraception	59.6[c]	.56	.94	60,675
Election of bishops by the priests of the diocese	69.9[d]	.67	.96	64,271

[a] Coefficient of variation $= \dfrac{\text{standard error}}{\text{estimate}}$.
[b] Per cent agreeing "strongly" or "somewhat."
[c] Per cent holding positions contrary to official teachings.
[d] Per cent who think such a change would help "very much" or "somewhat."

1. The following exceptions to this procedure must be mentioned:

a. *All* dioceses classified as *extra large* were included in the sample. Hence, a systematic subsample was selected from the total list of priests for this stratum, compiled from the separate lists obtained from the official contact person in each extra-large diocese.

b. Similarly, a subsample was selected directly from the list of priests in U.S. Foundations without intermediate first-stage selection of communities.

c. In the case of the stratum of *extra-small* religious communities, we decided after first-stage selection with probabilities proportional to size to include in the sample *all* priests within the selected units. Hence the overall selection probabilities within the stratum vary from unit to unit.

2. The resignation rates are given correct to two decimal places in Table A.1 because the standard errors are all below .10.

3. The figures in the original tables have been rounded to the nearest per cent; they are given correct to one decimal place in Table A.2 to facilitate interpretation of the standard errors.

APPENDIX B

FIELD WORK AND RESPONSE RATES

The NORC study of the American Catholic Priesthood began on March 1, 1969. On March 6, the study staff met with their consultants at Loyola University of Chicago to discuss the theoretical design of the research project.[1] From this meeting emerged the major theoretical perspectives and themes that have guided the study from its inception to its completion. Five thematic areas were chosen within which to study the priesthood:

1. *The personal life and development of the priest.* Within this area the study tried to determine whether, and to what extent, the spiritual, interpersonal, and cultural life-styles of the American priest contribute to his development as a human person.

2. *The priest's morale and role identity.* This theme was concerned with the priest's past, present, and future view of his role in the Church.

3. *The professional performance of the priest.* This theme aimed at determining the degree of professionalization of different sectors of the priesthood.

4. *The priest's attitude toward authority mechanisms in the Church.* The concern here was to see how authority is exercised in dioceses and religious orders, and to learn to what extent the priest disregards authoritative pronouncements. It sought to determine the actual and ideal distribution of power in religious organizations.

5. *The general cultural, demographic, and socialization background of priests.* Here the study focused on the priest's educational attainments and his job description (type of work, time spent on various activities, etc.), as well as early parental influences (parental affection, religiosity, marital adjustment, socio-economic status, type of work, and ethnicity).

In order to form a theoretical basis within each of these areas of investigation, an extensive review of the literature in related and parallel areas of research was undertaken, and a series of seminars was held to discuss the work of the reviewers.[2] These took place from the beginning

323

of April through July, 1969. On this theoretical basis, a number of hypotheses in each area were constructed as guides to the construction of a pretest questionnaire.

In September, 1969, a 75-page questionnaire was ready for pretesting. This included a Supplement for Religious, which contained questions pertaining only to religious priests.[3] The supplement was later incorporated into the main questionnaire. The pretest questionnaire was sent to 150 priests randomly selected from *The Official Catholic Directory, 1969.* The questionnaire was modified and refined in the light of the pretest results, and was sent to consultants and other interested persons for further criticism. After going through several further drafts, the questionnaire was presented to the Bishops' Committee on Pastoral Research and Practices for their criticism and approval.

The Bishops' Committee approved the questionnaire in late September, 1969, and after further revisions, the questionnaire was printed and prepared for fielding in November, 1969.[4]

The Samples

The study was divided into two phases: the first and major phase covered active priests, and the second phase covered those priests who had resigned from the ecclesiastical ministry in the last few years. Each phase will be described separately.

The Survey of Active Priests

It is estimated that as of the last quarter of 1969, the priest population of the United States (including American priests working abroad) was 64,496. This figure is based on the corrected data supplied to us by those dioceses and religious orders that fell into the sample, and the extrapolation of these figures to the total priest population. The ratio of diocesan to religious priests in the United States is approximately three to two — 36,900 diocesan and 27,600 religious priests.

The sample of active priests was drawn in two stages.[5] First, the 155 dioceses in the United States at the time the sample was drawn were stratified according to size and geographical region, and a sample of 85 dioceses was drawn. All 15 extra-large dioceses were chosen as a single stratum.[6] The sample of dioceses was chosen so as to represent the regional, cultural, ecological, and ethnic complexity of the American Catholic Church.

Similarly, a sample of religious institutes in the United States was drawn. Religious institutes vary widely in their size; Jesuits number approximately 6,000 priests in ten provinces, Camaldolese Hermits have only 7 men residing in a single monastery, and the Carthusians have only 5 priests in a single monastery. Hence, the institutes were reduced to their component self-governing subunits. Thus, a province is considered to be self-governing (as is, for example, a Benedictine monastery). At the time of the sample, the number of such subunits in the United States was 253. These were stratified according to size, region, canonical category (e.g., active or contemplative order), and country of foundation, and then a sample of 91 subunits was drawn.[7]

In the second stage of the sample, priests were randomly selected from the dioceses and religious subunits that were drawn in the first stage of the sample. The rate at which these priests were selected varied according to the size of the diocese or religious subunit. The overall design ensured that all priests in the United States, as well as American priests living abroad, had an equal chance of falling into the sample.

The research project was designed to produce approximately 6,000 cases for analysis and to allow analysis of the data at two levels. The unit of analysis on the first level would be the individual priest. The set of variables to be analyzed included measures of personal opinions, attitudes, and values. The focus on the second level of analysis would be the diocese or religious subunit. The effect of their organizational characteristics such as size or age on other attributes such as resignation rate, average morale, and average job satisfaction would be analyzed. At this level, also, the effects of ecological and demographic variables on attitudes, opinions, and values would enter into the investigation.

Before the sample of diocesan and religious priests could be drawn, of course, it was necessary to obtain the names of the priests in the dioceses and religious subunits that had fallen into the sample. The original intention of the study staff was to draw the sample of diocesan priests from lists supplied by *The Official Catholic Directory* and the sample of religious priests from lists that would be supplied by the religious subunits themselves. Unfortunately, several inadequacies in *The Official Catholic Directory* were discovered that would have caused errors as high as 20 per cent in some lists.[8] Hence, each diocese and religious subunit that fell into the sample was contacted and asked to supply an accurate listing of its men. One of the gratifying aspects of this part of the study was the friendly and extremely helpful cooperation that the vast majority of the dioceses and religious orders extended to the study staff. The listings they furnished formed the population from which the sample of active priests was drawn.

Research Instruments

The principal research instrument was a 46-page questionnaire. (This questionnaire is reproduced in Appendix F.) The questions were selected to test numerous hypotheses formulated in each of the areas of investigation already described. The length of the questionnaire was a cause of concern to the study staff, but its 110 questions were considered to be the absolute minimum necessary to realize the heuristic and theoretical goals of the research project. In addition to receiving the main questionnaire, a subsample of 1,500 priests received a Personal Orientation Inventory, which contains 150 dichotomous questions and is intended to measure personal maturity.[9]

In order to facilitate the flow of information from the dioceses and religious subunits in the sample, we requested that the bishop or major superior appoint a "contact person" and authorize him to supply statistical information on the men in the dioceses or religious subunits for the years 1965 through 1969, as well as up-to-date listings of men who had resigned from the ecclesiastical ministry. The information and cooperation that these key informants provided for the study staff were extremely helpful.

Survey of Resignees from the Ecclesiastical Ministry

The departure of men from the ecclesiastical ministry was an increasing phenomenon during the period from January 1, 1965, through the end of 1969. Therefore, we decided to include these men in the overall study of the American Catholic Priesthood. This aspect of the study, however, was much more difficult than the study of active priests because of the task of obtaining names and addresses of resignees. Many of these men are characterized by high geographical mobility and a desire for anonymity. Furthermore, "leaving the active ministry" is susceptible of various definitions. Hence, we decided to ask the contact man in the sample dioceses and religious subunits to supply listings of men in five categories: (1) leave of absence, (2) final canonical laicization, (3) suspension or faculties revoked, (4) a more general category of "those not engaged in priestly work of the diocese or religious institute but who have not applied for official separation from the diocese or institute," and (5) in the process of incardination (these men were considered to be "in transition" and their status had to be clarified so that they would not be included among those in the other four categories of resignees).

In addition to supplying names of men who fell into these five categories, the official contact men also supplied addresses when available, birth dates, and ordination dates, as well as dates of resignation or separation. Most of the dioceses and religious orders were helpful in supplying the information requested. However, a few were reluctant to do so for several reasons. In one case, the bishop was unwilling to release the information since he saw it as totally confidential. Others gave names but would not give addresses for fear that our contact with former members of the active clergy would damage the relationship of trust between the ordinary or superior and his former subject. Another reason was that a listing of names was not compiled and this would have involved too much time and effort for the chancery or order official. The majority of the names of men who had resigned from the sample dioceses and religious orders were obtained from the official contact men, but many priests had departed without leaving any forwarding address at all. To fill in the gaps of missing names and addresses, a number of organizations were asked to help in identifying and obtaining names and addresses for men whose whereabouts were not known by the chancery or religious order: these organizations included the Society of Priests for a Free Ministry, Bearings for Re-establishment, Next-Step, The National Association for Pastoral Review, and Transitional Resources of Los Angeles. The total number of names obtained from the official contact men and the organizations was 2,006.

These 2,006 names formed the population from which the sample of resignees was drawn. The sampling procedures and field work were designed to produce approximately 1,000 cases for analysis. Unfortunately, after all our efforts one-third of the addresses of the 2,006 names remained unknown, and therefore, special procedures had to be designed to try to contact those resignees with unknown addresses. The population was thus stratified on the basis of address-known and address-not-known, and 1,807 names were randomly selected. Of these 1,807, 1,435 names were with addresses and 372 without addresses. Different field-work strategies were required for the two separate groups and are discussed later.

Mailing Procedures and Response Rates

The Sample of Active Priests

The long and exacting work demanded by the gathering and verifying of the listings from the dioceses and religious orders caused a delay in the mailing of the main questionnaire. The study design envisaged a complete mailing of the main questionnaire before the end of December, 1969. But by then only about half the sample listings had been received and verified and address labels prepared for mailing. Consequently, it was decided to mail the main questionnaire in two waves. The first wave of 2,273 questionnaires was mailed in December, 1969. The second wave of 5,201 questionnaires was sent out in early February, 1970. Thus, a total of 7,474 questionnaires were mailed over a two-month period.

The first mailing of Waves I and II each resulted in a response rate of approximately 44 per cent (Table B.1). Two follow-up mailings took place for each wave, which resulted in a response rate of about 67 per cent for each wave. The final follow-up, in the form of a telegram, boosted the response rates for Waves I and II to 78.0 and 76.6 per cent, respectively. When the field work for the main questionnaire was completed on September 25, 1970, "late arrivals" and "converted incompletes" had raised the overall response rates for Waves I and II to 79.7 and 76.7 per cent. The total *overall* response rate for the main questionnaire stood at 78.8 per cent.

By *overall* response rate we mean the total number of "responses" actually received. However, these responses fall into several categories: (1) fully completed questionnaires, (2) deceased, (3) refusals, (4) incomplete questionnaires, (5) temporarily unavailable, and (6) nonlocatable. Some of the incomplete questionnaires were refielded and thus converted to completed questionnaires. The *usable* response rate comprises categories (1) and (4). We excluded 72 cases from the denominator in the calculation of the overall response rate when we discovered that these men were not priests but seminarians and brothers whose names were inadvertently given to us by some of the religious orders. We also excluded the deceased cases from the base in the calculation of the usable response rate. Table B.1 shows that the final total *usable* response rate for the main questionnaire was 71.0 per cent. We also mailed 1,500 Personal Orientation Inventories with the main questionnaire, and 917 of these were returned completed.

Questionnaires were also sent to all the 276 bishops and 208 major superiors in the American Church. The response rates were 59 per cent for the bishops and 76 per cent for the major superiors.

To obtain a picture of the chief characteristics of those priests who did not respond to the main questionnaire, telephone interviews were conducted with a randomly chosen sample of 150 nonrespondents. They proved to be very elusive indeed. We were unable to reach 66 on the list (after several calls), 18 refused outright to answer any questions whatsoever, and 7 said that they thought they had already answered the ques-

TABLE B.1

RESPONSE RATE BY WAVE AND MAILING FOR
SAMPLE OF ACTIVE PRIESTS

(Per Cent)

Mailing	Overall Response Rate	Usable Response Rate
Wave I		
After first mailing	45.0	43.5
After first follow-up	61.0	57.0
After second follow-up	67.2	62.5
After third follow-up (telegram)	78.0	71.5
Total (as of 9/25/70)	79.7	72.0
Wave II		
After first mailing	43.0	42.0
After first follow-up	58.0	54.5
After second follow-up	66.6	61.2
After third follow-up (telegram)	76.6	69.0
Total (as of 9/25/70)	76.8	70.0
Total overall response rate (Wave I and Wave II)	78.8	
Total usable response rate (Wave I and Wave II)		71.0

tionnaire and sent it in. Of those who gave excuses for not answering the questionnaire, two-fifths said that they were too busy and the questionnaire was too long; one-fifth reported that they were suspicious of surveys; one-sixth claimed bad health or old age; and the remainder excused themselves by saying they had forgotten, could not read English, had been away on vacation, or were in the midst of a transfer, and one even said that the rectory had been burglarized.

The average age of those who provided information by telephone was fifty-eight, and 50 per cent of them were pastors. This means that older American priests, especially those engaged in parish work and particularly those who are pastors, may be slightly underrepresented in the percentages presented in the main body of the report. The problem of underrepresentation is discussed in Appendix D, where the reader will also find excerpts from the telephone interview schedule with the percentage given for each question.

The Sample of Resignees

In order to maintain a basis of comparison between active and resigned priests, the 35-page questionnaire sent to the resignees was in many respects similar to that sent to active priests. (Excerpts from the resignee questionnaire are presented in Appendix G.) In addition to this questionnaire, 850 resigned priests were also sent a Personal Orientation Inventory.

Of the 1,807 names selected from the population of 2,006 men who had resigned from the ecclesiastical ministry, 1,435 had addresses and 372 had no addresses. In the case of the names with addresses, the mailing procedures were relatively straightforward. The first mailing of 1,435 questionnaires in July, 1970, produced 531 responses. The follow-up mailing of 904 questionnaires produced 178 more responses.

In order to protect the confidentiality of the resignees, some dioceses and religious institutes had refused to provide the study team with addresses of men who had resigned but instead requested that their questionnaires be sent to the designated contact person in the dioceses or religious institutes so that they could be forwarded from there. We followed this procedure for two mailings to resignees from six dioceses and five religious institutes.

The procedures used for the 372 names without addresses were even more complicated. Through the generous help of the various organizations mentioned earlier, we were able to obtain 69 of these missing addresses. We made two mailings to the new-found locations, spaced a month apart. Including this last batch, the total number of "up-to-date" addresses finally made available was 1,504. But of the 1,807 names initially selected, 303 names still remained without a known address. As a final effort, we decided to mail questionnaires to "the last known address," that is, to the last place where the priest had been assigned before his resignation, in the hope that it would be forwarded from there. We literally dug 260 addresses out of the last four editions of *The Official Catholic Directory* and fielded the questionnaires with a special label marked "Confidential-Urgent, Please Forward." Our efforts produced 24 additional responses.

The final follow-up procedure was a telegram sent in mid-November to all those in the original sample who had not yet responded and whose addresses we deemed "fresh" enough to warrant the expenditure. (No one on the list of 260 addresses of the last known assignment was sent a telegram.) The responses to the telegram, the results of the double mailings to the 69 recent addresses obtained from various organizations, the returns from the packets forwarded by the contact persons in the six dioceses and five religious communities, and the "late arrivals" from all previous mailings amounted to 140 more completed questionnaires. This number, added to the 531 responses to the original mailing, the 178 responses to the follow-up mailing, and the 24 responses from the mailing to the address of the last known assignment, brought the total number of usable completed questionnaires to 873 on December 16, 1970, the day when the field work for the sample of resignees was closed.[10] Four and one-half months had elapsed since we made the original mailing.

In summary, names and addresses of 1,504 resignees were obtained and the number of completed questionnaires totaled 873. Based on these figures, the usable response rate is 58.0, which is close to a projected rate of 60 per cent. However, based on the complete sample of 1,807, the usable response rate is only 48.3. The response rate for the resignees is considerably lower than that of the active priests, but given the many difficulties encountered in reaching the men who had resigned, their returns represent a rather respectable level of response. We may cite at least two factors for the difference in response rates. First, the names and addresses of the resignees were much more difficult to trace than those of active priests. Second, because of the difficulties inherent in obtaining the addresses and in executing some of the field work described above, less time, energy, and funds were available for a follow-up strategy as thorough as the one used for the active priests. However, it can be safely said that we obtained sufficient cases for analysis to make valid assertions about the resignees' general attitudes, values, and behavior.

1. The following were present at the Loyola meeting: Andrew M. Greeley (NORC), Richard A. Schoenherr (NORC), John Mulhearn (NORC), Eugene C. Kennedy (Loyola University), Victor Heckler (Loyola University), George Higgins (United States Catholic Conference), John Gorman (Loyola University), Donald Warwick (Harvard University), Charles Curran (Loyola University), Robert McNamara (Fordham University), Frank Kobler (Loyola University), James J. Vanecko (NORC), Sarah Charles (Notre Dame University), and Paul D'Arcy (Center for Applied Research in the Apostolate).

2. The following seminar members made major contributions to the development of the theoretical framework of the research project: Sister Esther Heffernan, O.P., Father John Dickson, M.M., and Father Charles Hegarty, S.J.

3. Father Dominic Maruca, S.J., contributed greatly to the development of the Supplement for Religious.

4. The following members of the Bishops' Committee on Pastoral Research and Practices were present at the meeting: His Eminence John Cardinal Krol, Arch-

bishop of Philadelphia, chairman; Most Rev. Leo C. Byrne, Archbishop of St. Paul-Minneapolis, chairman of the subcommittee on liturgy; Most Rev. James V. Casey, Archbishop of Denver, chairman of the subcommittee on spirituality; Most Rev. Ernest J. Primeau, Bishop of Manchester, chairman of the subcommittee on psychology and sociology; Most Rev. Alexander M. Zaleski, Bishop of Lansing, vice-chairman and chairman of the subcommittee on theology; and Rev. Edwin B. Neill, Associate General Secretary, National Conference of Catholic Bishops, general study coordinator.

On September 25, 1969, an *ad hoc* committee of the Conference of Major Superiors of Men met with the NORC study team at Loyola University in Chicago to discuss the questionnaire. They were unanimous in their endorsement of its content. The major superiors present were: Rt. Rev. Gerald Benkert, O.S.B., Very Rev. Dacian Bluma, O.F.M., Very Rev. Walter L. Farrell, S.J., Very Rev. Howard Kenna, C.S.C., Very Rev. Raymond J. Schmitt, C.Ss.R., and Very Rev. Malachy Smith, O.Carm. Also present at the meeting was the Most Rev. Joseph L. Bernardin, General Secretary, National Conference of Catholic Bishops.

5. Appendix A gives a theoretical description of the sampling methodology.

6. An extra-large diocese is defined as one with over 500 priests. The extra-large dioceses as of the last quarter of 1969 were the following: Boston (1,435), Brooklyn (1,094), Buffalo (654), Chicago (1,419), Cleveland (626), Detroit (840), Hartford (594), Los Angeles (718), Milwaukee (700), Newark (904), New York (1,250), Philadelphia (1,071), Pittsburgh (593), St. Louis (568), and St. Paul-Minneapolis (507).

7. Four religious subunits were later dropped from the sample. The members of two of these subunits, although working in the United States, were predominantly Canadians and had their headquarters in Canada. One religious subunit was predominantly Mexican and had its headquarters in Mexico. The fourth religious subunit consisted of two contemplative priests, who requested that they be dropped from the sample.

8. This is a statement of fact and not a criticism of this publication; it was not published with national surveys in mind. Thus, categories of priests such as seminary professors and retirees are omitted, while others are listed two or three times, such as, for example, chancery officials.

9. The Personal Orientation Inventory was developed by Everett L. Shostrom (1966), and is based on the concept of "self-actualization" proposed by Abraham Maslow (1962). See Chapter 4 of this report for a description of the inventory and a discussion of the findings based on the subsample.

10. Of these 873, only 750 are used throughout this report since the field work was completed too late to include the last 123 responses in the analysis. However, these additional 123 cases would not have significantly altered the percentages that we present.

APPENDIX C

DESCRIPTION OF INDICES

A number of indices were constructed to summarize different sets of highly interrelated items in the questionnaire. Some of the indices were used in exploratory analysis only, some have been incorporated into this report, while others were designed for use in further analyses of the data from the American Catholic Priesthood Study. The purpose of this appendix is to describe only those indices that are actually used in the present report. The others are described in the documentation on file in the data archives at NORC.

The indices appear in the order of causal precedence as outlined in Chapter 1. First each index is defined and then the source of the data in the main questionnaire is cited. Further details on the indices, including a complete set of correlation matrices showing the coefficients of association (Pearson r) between all the items in an index and tables presenting the results of pertinent factors analyses, are part of the documentation for the American Catholic Priesthood Study available at NORC.

1. Family Tension

Definition: Recollection of the quality of the relationship between one's parents and between oneself and each of one's parents scored on a continuous scale (1-5) with a high score indicating the recall of mostly tense and strained rather than close and intimate relationships. A similar measure of family tension was used by John Kotre (1971), whose study focused on religious apostasy as the dependent variable.

Source: The index was constructed from Question 92. The response categories were as follows: Very tense and strained, Somewhat tense and strained, Neutral, Somewhat close and intimate, Very close and intimate, and Does not apply.

92. Every family is not only a whole unit, but a number of twosomes. For each of the following twosomes in the family in which you grew up, circle the category which best describes the relationship.

A. Mother and father.
B. Mother and me.
C. Father and me.

2. Religious Experience

Definition: Frequency of having had a feeling of being close to God or Christ in the past two or three years scored on an integer scale (3-12), with a high score indicating many such experiences. Glock and Stark (1965) developed a taxonomy of personal religious experiences, two categories of which are the "confirming" and the "ecstatic" experiences. Our index attempts to measure the amount of what might be termed "normal mystical contact with God" that a religious person (but a non-saint) would claim for himself. The type of contact could be classified under the confirming and ecstatic labels discussed by Glock and Stark.

Source: The index was constructed from the following three items in Question 33. The response categories were as follows: Frequently, Occasionally, Once, and Never.

33. During the past two or three years how often have you experienced each of the following?
A. An overwhelming feeling of being at one with God or Christ.
B. A sense of being in the presence of God.
D. A deep feeling of being personally loved by Christ here and now.

3. Modern Priest

Definition: Beliefs and values regarding fifteen aspects of the priesthood scored on a continuous scale (1-5) with a high score indicating agreement with few "traditional" and many "modern" attitudes. The traditional statements were taken from standard manuals of Catholic dogmatic, spiritual, and pastoral theology reflecting formulations of beliefs and values prevalent before the mid-twentieth century. The modern statements reflect current formulations of ideas about the priesthood, some taken from the documents of the Second Vatican Council and others from contemporary Catholic and Protestant thinkers.

Source: The index was constructed from the following fifteen items in Question 12. The response categories were as follows: Agree strongly, Agree somewhat, Uncertain, Disagree somewhat, and Disagree strongly.

12. Here are some statements about the priesthood. For each of the statements below, circle the category of response that *best* fits your present thinking.

A. Since the priesthood is a lifelong commitment, there is almost never a good reason for leaving.

D. I think it would be a good idea if Christian communities such as parishes were to choose their own priest from among available ordained priests.

E. Ordination confers on the priest a new status or a permanent character which makes him essentially different from the laity within the church.

F. The idea that the priest is a "man set apart" is a barrier to the full realization of true Christian community.

H. Whatever else is said about the humanitarian preoccupations and interpersonal relationships of priests, we must remember that the priest is *the* man in society who proclaims God's Word and provides for sacramental encounter with God in Christ.

I. I feel that I am most a priest when I am saying Mass and hearing confessions.

J. In many cases a decision to resign from the priesthood is a wise and mature choice.

K. The priesthood as we know it is a transitory institutional role which will eventually be modified so that there will be much less difference between Christians who have Holy Orders and those who do not.

M. If being on the picket line alienates a priest from most Catholics in an area, a priest should not engage in social protest movements.

O. I think it would be a good idea if Christian communities such as parishes were to choose their own priest from among the parishioners. Such a man would acquire the proper training and then be ordained to act as the priest of the parish for some period of time.

Q. Priests who have resigned from the priesthood should be invited to re-apply for permission to function as priests again, whether they are married or single.

S. For some men being a priest could be a part-time job. Some ordained priests could earn their living at some other employment, and help out on weekends, while others would work full time in the parish and other ministries.

T. As a priest, I feel that I am a member of the bishop's team. When I am doing a job that has the local bishop's approval, I am doing priestly work.

U. Nowadays, you can hardly be an effective priest if you are assigned to a conventional parish.

V. There is no ontological difference between the priest and the laity, since all share in the common priesthood of Christ given at baptism; the difference is mainly one of assigned duties in the Church.

4. *"Modern" Values (Modern Church)*

Definition: Beliefs and values regarding twenty-one aspects of God, Jesus, and the Church scored on a continuous scale (1-5) with a high score indicating agreement with few "traditional" and many "modern" attitudes. The traditional statements were taken from standard manuals of Catholic dogmatic, spiritual, and pastoral theology reflecting formulations of beliefs and values prevalent before the mid-twentieth century. The modern statements reflect current formulations of ideas about God, Jesus, and the Church, some taken from the documents of the Second Vatican Council and others from contemporary Catholic and Protestant thinkers.

Source: The index was constructed from the following twenty-one items in Question 37. The response categories were as follows: Agree strongly, Agree somewhat, Uncertain, Disagree somewhat, and Disagree strongly.

37. Below are a number of statements which are frequently made today. Please indicate the extent of your agreement or disagreement with each of them.
    12) The mystery of the Trinity is so profound and so central that I feel I should humbly accept it as given and not seek to plumb its depths.
    14) I think of God primarily as the Supreme Being, immutable, all-powerful, and the Creator of the universe.
    15) The Catholic Church is the one true Church established by Christ with St. Peter and his successors as its head.
    16) For me, God is found principally in my relationships with people.
    17) God's Word comes to us through some of the great prophetic men of our times, such as Mahatma Gandhi and Martin Luther King.
    19) Today's Christian must emphasize more than ever openness to the Spirit rather than dependence on traditional ecclesiastical structures.
    21) The important thing to stress when teaching about Jesus is that He is truly God, and, therefore, adoration should be directed toward Him.
    23) The principal meaning of Christ's resurrection for me is that it proved His Divinity.
    24) I think of Jesus Christ as the God who humbled Himself by becoming man and dying for my sins.
    25) To doubt one article of faith that is *de fide* is to question the whole of revealed truth.
    26) I think of heaven as the state in which my soul will rest in blissful possession of the Beatific Vision.

27) I feel that the most important thing to recognize about the sacraments is that they are channels for receiving grace.

29) I think that priests who feel called to do so ought to be witnessing to Christ on the picket line or speaking out on controversial issues.

30) A Christian should look first to the salvation of his soul; then he should be concerned about helping others.

35) The Church should be a place of refuge and of quiet reflection away from the world.

36) The primary task of the Church is to encourage its members to live the Christian life rather than to try to reform the world.

37) For the most part, the Church has been inadequate in facing up to the civil rights issues.

38) Faith means essentially belief in the doctrines of the Catholic Church.

39) Faith is primarily an encounter with God in Christ Jesus, rather than an assent to a coherent set of defined truths.

43) There are times when a person has to put his personal conscience above the Church's teaching.

44) One's faith may be jeopardized by studying Protestant theologians.

5. *Anomie*

Definition: Attitudes regarding the confusion in seven aspects of priestly life scored on a continuous scale (1-5) with a high score indicating little tolerance for this confusion. The battery of questions for our scale includes five items adapted from the McClosky and Schaar (1965) anomie index; the changes in the wording of those items are meant to bring them more in line with the circumstances of the life of the priest. The remaining questions were designed to reflect other aspects of confusion and discontent likely to be voiced in clerical circles.

Source: The index was constructed from the following seven items in Question 37. The response categories were as follows: Agree strongly, Agree somewhat, Uncertain, Disagree somewhat, and Disagree strongly.

37. Below are a number of statements which are frequently made today. Please indicate the extent of your agreement or disagreement with each of them.

1) The important thing in the Church today is that people are really examining what has meaning for them.

4) The relationship between laity and priests was much better before Vatican II when everyone knew just how he was expected to act.

5) With the new roles for everyone in the Church that have developed since Vatican II, the relationships between priests and laity are much better.

6) Everything changes so quickly in the liturgy these days that I often have trouble deciding what rules to follow.

8) There is more opportunity now than before for real friendship for priests.

10) The diversity of liturgy provides a real choice which I enjoy.

40) The creative ferment in the Church today is bringing about a deepening of my Christian faith.

6. *Sexual Morality*

Definition: Moral convictions regarding masturbation, premarital intercourse, abortion, birth control, and divorce scored on a continuous scale (13-60) with a high score indicating few "conservative" and many "liberal" attitudes. The conservative statements were taken from standard manuals of Catholic moral theology reflecting formulations of the traditional teachings of the Catholic Church. The liberal statements reflect current formulations of sexual morality being propounded by certain humanistic psychologists and Christian moral theologians.

Source: The index was constructed from the following five questions:

48. There has been much discussion in recent years about questions of sexual morality regarding the individual and married couples. Within the Christian tradition moral theologians have undertaken new investigations in these areas. What is your *personal* opinion about the following statements? PLEASE DO NOT GIVE THE OPINIONS OF MORAL THEOLOGIANS, BUT WHAT YOU, YOURSELF, THINK.

A. Thinking about people in general, what is your opinion about masturbation?

1) Adolescent masturbation is a normal developmental phase in a person's maturing sexuality and among adults occasional masturbation is usually the result of stress or conflict, hence in most cases it is not sinful.

2) For both adolescents and adults, in most cases deliberate masturbation is sinful but no more than venially.

3) For both adolescents and adults, in most cases deliberate masturbation is a mortal sin.

4) Other.

B. What is your opinion about premarital sexual intercourse in the case of *mature* couples?

1) It is morally acceptable for couples who share affection.

2) It is morally acceptable for couples who are in love.

3) It is morally acceptable for couples who are engaged.

4) It is never morally acceptable: couples should wait until they are married.

5) Other.

C. The Church's teaching on direct abortion remains clear. Still, within society at large in the United States, there is great pressure for more permissive abortion laws. What is your opinion in this matter?

1) There is no need of theological development in the direction of change in the Church's teaching, since direct abortion is always wrong.

2) The Church has to allow open investigation of the issue, not only on moral, but also on medical and social grounds.

3) In certain well-defined circumstances, especially when the mother's life is endangered, direct abortion can be morally permissible.

4) Other.

49. Indicate which of the following statements comes closest to your personal convictions about artificial contraception. Please indicate your thinking for the current period after the issuance of Pope Paul's encyclical *Humanae Vitae*.

A. All artificial contraception is morally wrong because it is clearly forbidden by the natural law and by the Church's teaching.

B. It is not certain that all artificial contraception is morally wrong; still, the faithful are bound to follow the guidance of the teaching of the Church and avoid all methods of artificial contraception.

C. It is not certain that all artificial contraception is morally wrong; therefore, the faithful are morally justified in using *at least some methods* of artificial contraception when they have adequate reasons for avoiding more children.

D. There is no doubt that the responsible use of at least *some* methods of artificial contraception is morally acceptable, while the use of other methods may be morally wrong.

E. Judgment concerning the morality of artificial contraception should be left to the responsibly formed consciences of the individuals involved.

F. Given adequate reasons for avoiding children, all methods of artificial contraception are morally acceptable.

G. Other.

50. Since a priest's own personal convictions concerning a moral question and the action he would demand of others may differ, would you please indicate which one of the courses of action outlined below would be closer to your procedure in the confessional *after Humanae Vitae?*

A. Discourage the use of artificial contraception under pain of denial of absolution to a penitent who refused even to try to avoid the use of contraceptives.

B. Discourage the use of artificial contraception, but not deny absolution to a penitent who was convinced of his moral justification in using contraceptives.

C. Neither discourage nor encourage the use of artificial contraception, but accept the moral judgment of the responsibly formed conscience of the penitent who chooses to use contraceptives.
D. Encourage the penitent who has adequate reasons in a responsible use of artificial contraception.
E. Other.

51. There is some discussion within the Catholic Church as to the possibility of true divorce with freedom to remarry. Please indicate which one of the statements below comes closest to *your own* personal conviction (however formed) with regard to this question.
   A. Divorce with freedom to remarry in the case of a marriage *ratum et consummatum* is forbidden by divine law and can never be permitted by the Church.
   B. Divorce with the freedom to remarry in the case of *ratum et consummatum* marriages should continue to be forbidden by the Church *without exception,* but this is not clearly a matter of divine law.
   C. In some few extreme cases, divorce with freedom to remarry can and should be granted even though the marriage is *ratum et consummatum.*
   D. Divorce with freedom to remarry should be granted even in *ratum et consummatum* marriages if a divorce would alleviate a situation obviously damaging to the couple and their children (if any), and this even if such cases were to be fairly numerous.
   E. Other.

53. How would you rate your own attitudes toward sex as compared to those of most priests in your order or the diocese in which you work?
   Very liberal
   Somewhat liberal
   Moderate
   Somewhat conservative
   Very conservative

7. *Humanae Vitae*

Definition: An item, rather than an index, measuring acceptance or rejection of Pope Paul's encyclical *Humanae Vitae.*

Source: This item is based on Question 52.

52. Please indicate which one of the following statements most closely represents your view of the use of Papal teaching authority involved in the issuance of the encyclical *Humanae Vitae.*
   A. The issuance of *Humanae Vitae* was a competent and appropriate use of Papal teaching authority.
   B. In issuing *Humanae Vitae* the Pope acted within his authority to teach, but the encyclical was issued at an inappropriate time.

C. The Pope is competent to teach concrete directives of the natural law as he did in *Humanae Vitae,* but *Humanae Vitae* was a misuse of that authority because he failed to act with sufficient collegiality.

D. The Pope is incompetent to use his teaching authority in this way because he cannot *impose* concrete universal directives of the natural law.

E. Other.

8. Social Problems

Definition: Attitudes regarding the three social issues of guaranteed annual wage, authority on college campuses, and riots by urban Negroes scored on an integer scale (3-9) with low, medium, and high scores indicating "conservative," "liberal," and "radical" stances, respectively.

Source: The index was constructed from the following three sections of Question 82:

82. Many issues are currently being discussed by American citizens. Some are listed below. How do you judge them from your experience of them?

A. One solution that has been proposed for dealing with the problem of poverty in America is the "guaranteed annual wage" whereby all families whose annual income falls below an established level (say, $4,000 for a family of four) will automatically receive through the government the amount necessary to reach the established level. Which of the following most nearly represents your opinion on a guaranteed annual income?

a) It is a good way to make some progress in dealing with the problem of poverty.

b) It is not a good idea, for it would encourage people who would otherwise work for a living to do less work or none at all, and simply rely on other people's money to support them.

c) It is simply a surface reform, since poverty stems from the nature of the capitalistic system itself. The only way to wipe out poverty really is to get rid of capitalism and replace it with some other economic system.

B. If you had to choose only one, which of the following would you say should have the greatest power in determining the major policies of colleges and universities?

The students
The faculty
The administration

C. Which of the following most nearly describes your opinion of riots by urban Negroes?

a) They are understandable in the light of very slow progress of the movement to provide Negro Americans with equality.

b) They constitute a revolutionary response that is right, given the current condition of Negroes in American society.

c) They are wrong. Negroes who riot are going too far. Law and order must be preserved.

9. *Ecumenism*

Definition: Behavior and attitudes regarding interaction with Protestant ministers and Jewish rabbis scored on a continuous scale (1-5) with a high score indicating a favorable disposition and much activity in this area.

Source: The index was constructed from Question 46.

46. What kinds of relationships do you have with the Protestant clergy and Jewish rabbis? That is —

A. How often did you take part in ecumenical or interfaith gatherings or liturgies in the past year?
    About once a week
    About once a month
    Several times during the year
    Once during the year
    Never

B. In the past year how much contact on a social level did you have with Protestant clergy and Jewish rabbis in your house, in theirs, or going out together?
    About once a week
    About once a month
    Several times during the year
    Once during the year
    Never

C. How often did you work together with Protestant clergy and/or Jewish rabbis in the last year?
    About once a week
    About once a month
    Several times during the year
    Once during the year
    Never

D. How do you now see yourself in relation to the movement toward Christian unity?
    I am strongly committed to its goals.
    I am sympathetic with its aims.
    I am indifferent toward the movement.
    I don't see much point in the movement.
    I am strongly opposed to the type of unity it implies.

10. *Power Conflict*

Definition: Discrepancy between who a respondent thinks, in fact, has the authority or the most influence in a diocese to make decisions in eight areas and who he thinks ought to have the authority to make these decisions, scored on a continuous scale (-7 to $+7$) with a high score indicating a wide discrepancy between the actual and ideal distribution of authority.

Source: The index was constructed from the two sections of Question 40. The response categories were as follows: Bishop, Chancery and/or diocesan depts., Priests' senate, Deans or vicars, Elected board, Pastors, and Individual priests in any assignment.

40. *EVERYONE PLEASE ANSWER.*

    A. In your diocese, who, in fact, has the authority or the most influence in making the following decisions?
    1) Authorize Mass in homes or apartments.
    2) Determine where a priest is assigned.
    3) Determine where a priest has his living quarters.
    4) Authorize an expenditure of more than $500 from parish funds.
    5) Appoint pastors.
    6) Establish new parishes.
    7) Authorize construction.
    8) Retire pastors.

    B. Who do you think ought to have the authority to make these decisions?
    1) Authorize Mass in homes or apartments.
    2) Determine where a priest is assigned.
    3) Determine where a priest has his living quarters.
    4) Authorize an expenditure of more than $500 from parish funds.
    5) Appoint pastors.
    6) Establish new parishes.
    7) Authorize construction.
    8) Retire pastors.

11. *Initiative in Liturgical Matters*

Definition: The number of proscribed activities out of five involving sacramental ministry performed on one's own authority; the range is 0-5 (integer scale) with a high score indicating much initiative. These areas of initiative (described in vignettes) were used by Struzzo (1970) in his study of professional attributes of priests.

Source: The index was constructed from Question 41.

41. Have you ever done any of the following on your own authority?
    1) Said Mass in a home or apartment.
    2) Notably modify the rubrics to fit the occasion.

3) Said Mass without the proper vestments.
4) Given Communion to non-Catholics.
5) Given sacraments to those who are divorced and remarried.

12. *Church Reform*

Definition: Attitudes regarding twelve possible changes in ecclesiastical policy, practice, and organizational structure scored on an integer scale (-24 to $+24$) with a high score indicating a desire for many changes. The statements of possible changes in the Church were taken from different views on reform expressed by bishops, priests, and lay people in serious writings and in the popular press.

Source: The index was constructed from Question 47. The response categories were as follows: Would help very much, Would help somewhat, Would not help but would not hurt either, Would hurt somewhat, and Would hurt very much.

47. The phrase *ecclesia semper reformanda* was much used during the Second Vatican Council. What do you think of the effects of the following possible changes in the Church?
  A. Associate pastors choosing to live where they wish.
  B. All priests living in community when this is possible.
  C. A parish lay advisory board having some say in the transfer and selection of priests.
  D. Wider approval of household ministries, "small group parishes within a parish," and floating parishes.
  E. Elimination of Catholic school systems.
  F. Some priests holding secular jobs during the week.
  G. A court of appeals for all members of the Church distinct from the hierarchy, guaranteeing them due process of law.
  H. Some married priests working in a variety of ministries.
  I. Election of the Pope by the Synod of Bishops.
  J. Introduction of the married diaconate whenever and however the local church chooses.
  K. Election of bishops by the priests of the diocese.
  L. Election of bishops by the priests, religious, and laity of the diocese.

13. *Colleague Relationship*

Definition: Assessment of one's personal relationships between himself and those he lives with scored on a continuous scale (1-5) with a high score indicating much satisfaction with these relationships.

Source: The index was constructed from the following two parts of Question 69, in which the respondent was asked to answer whichever part applied better. The response categories were as follows: Excellent, Good, Fair, Poor, Very Poor, and Do not have.

69. [1] In general, how would you describe your personal relationships with your pastor, assistant(s), fellow assistant(s), resident priest(s), and housekeeper/cook?
   a) Pastor
   b) Assistant(s)
   c) Fellow assistant(s)
   d) Resident priest(s)
   e) Housekeeper/cook

   [2] If you live in a "non-parish" setting, e.g., in a religious house, how would you describe your personal relationships with the person in charge, other priest members of the community, brothers, student members of the community, and the lay help who live with you?
   a) Person in charge
   b) Priest members of the community
   c) Brothers
   d) Student members of the community
   e) Lay help

14. *Work Satisfaction*

Definition: Assessment of one's work based on seventeen short-phrase descriptions scored on an integer scale (1-52) with a high score indicating agreement with few unpleasant and many pleasant sounding descriptions. Patricia Smith and her colleagues developed the Job Description Index, one part of which is the work satisfaction scale. See Smith, Kendall, and Hulin (1969) for a full theoretical and empirical discussion of the work satisfaction measure.

Source: The index was constructed from Question 20.

20. Think of your present work. What is it like most of the time? In the blank beside each word given below, write . . .

   Y   for "Yes" if it describes your work
   N   for "No" if it does NOT describe it
   ?   if you cannot decide

Work on present assignment:

_____ Fascinating		_____ Tiresome
_____ Routine		_____ Healthful
_____ Satisfying		_____ Challenging
_____ Boring		_____ On your feet
_____ Good		_____ Frustrating
_____ Creative		_____ Simple
_____ Respected		_____ Endless
_____ Pleasant		_____ Gives sense of
_____ Useful		accomplishment

15. *Professional Comparison*

Definition: Assessment of one's standing regarding four major attributes of professionalism in comparison with other professionals, scored on an integer scale (4-16) with a high score indicating that the respondent judges himself to possess a comparatively high degree of professional qualities. A review of the current literature on professionalism revealed that the attributes of depth of knowledge and skill, autonomy, responsibility, and commitment to serving the needs of people are the four most frequently cited marks of a professional. See Vollmer and Mills (1966) for a well-chosen sampling of the literature.

Source: The index was constructed from Question 24. The response categories were as follows: I have more, I have about the same, I have less, I have much less, and Don't know.

24. Think of the professional men you know — for example, doctors, dentists, lawyers, scientists. How do you think you as a priest compare to them in regard to the following attributes?
    A. Depth of knowledge and skill.
    B. Autonomy to make decisions.
    C. Responsibility for an undertaking.
    D. Commitment to serving the needs of people.

16. *Positive Affect*

Definition: The number of pleasant emotional experiences out of five that one felt during the past few weeks; the range of scores is 0-5 with a high score indicating many pleasant experiences. See Bradburn (1969) for a full theoretical and empirical discussion of the three affect scales.

Source: The index was constructed from the following five items in Question 81. The response categories were "Yes" and "No."

81. During the past few weeks, did you ever feel—
    A. Particularly excited or interested in something?
    C. Proud because someone complimented you on something you had done?
    E. Pleased about having accomplished something?
    G. On top of the world?
    I. That things were going your way?

17. *Negative Affect*

Definition: The number of unpleasant emotional experiences out of five that one felt during the past few weeks; the range of scores is 0-5 with a high score indicating many unpleasant experiences.

Source: The index was constructed from the following five items in Question 81. The response categories were "Yes" and "No."

81. During the past few weeks, did you feel —
    B. So restless that you couldn't sit long in a chair?
    D. Very lonely or remote from other people?
    F. Bored?
    H. Depressed or very unhappy?
    J. Upset because someone criticized you?

18. *Affect Balance*

Definition: The difference between the number of pleasant emotional experiences out of five and the number of unpleasant ones out of five that one felt during the past few weeks; the range of scores is −5 to +5 with a high score indicating few unpleasant and many pleasant experiences.

Source: The index was constructed from all ten items in Question 81 as listed in 16 and 17 above.

APPENDIX D

NONRESPONSE

The purpose of this appendix is, first, to make available to the reader illustrations of the implications of various assumptions that might be made about the attitudes of those who did not respond to the mailed questionnaire. Secondly, we present the results of a brief telephone interview with a sample of the nonrespondents.

Estimating Bias Due To Nonresponse

Since 29 per cent of the active priests who were sampled either refused to complete the main questionnaire or for other reasons did not do so, what can be said about the accuracy of the percentages that are presented in this report? Do the findings of the Priesthood Study reflect the attitudes and opinions of *all* the active American clergy? Assessing the magnitude and direction of possible bias in estimates of population characteristics due to nonresponse is a tricky business at best, simply because nonrespondents, as it were, are the hardest of all nuts to crack. Without direct information, one is forced to rely on reasonable assumptions about the characteristics of the nonrespondent. (We were able to go one step better and gather some very limited data on fifty-nine nonrespondents by means of a telephone interview.) We shall discuss a number of assumptions about possible nonresponse bias; the reader can then weigh the relative merits of each and form his own opinion. Or he may wish to postulate assumptions of his own and form his judgment that way. The following information will enable him to proceed either way.

The first column in Table D.1 presents the percentages of active diocesan priests holding certain opinions on three issues as reported in the text. These percentages, strictly speaking, are applicable only to that part of the frame represented by the 71 per cent of the priests in the sample who returned usable questionnaires. Fifty-six per cent of the active diocesan priests who responded agree that celibacy should be a matter of personal choice (Table 12.1), 60 per cent in some fashion do not accept

TABLE D.1

ALTERNATIVE MODELS FOR VIEWING CERTAIN FINDINGS IN THE LIGHT OF NONRESPONSE

(Per Cent of Active Diocesan Priests)

Item	Model				
	Assuming nonrespondents would take:				
	(1) The same position as respondents	(2) Positions opposed to change	(3) "Liberal" positions half as often as respondents did	(4) The same positions as respondents over 55	(5) The same positions as nonrespondents who were interviewed by telephone
Celibacy should be a matter of personal choice for diocesan priests[a]	56	39	47	45	50
Personal convictions about artificial contraception[b]	60	41	50	50	—[c]
Election of bishops by the priests of the diocese[d]	70	49	60	64	—[c]

[a] Per cent agreeing "strongly" or "somewhat."
[b] Per cent holding positions contrary to official teachings.
[c] Not asked in the telephone interview.
[d] Per cent who think such a change would help "very much" or "somewhat."

the official teaching on birth control (Table 6.15), and 70 per cent support the election of bishops by the clergy of the diocese (Table 6.13). On the assumption that the nonrespondents would take the same positions as the respondents, these percentages would apply to all active diocesan priests in the United States. The second column in Table D.1 presents the results of a model that assumes that all the nonrespondents would take more "conservative" positions, that is, would oppose the possible changes. Under such circumstances, the proportions in the whole population supporting the three "liberal" stances would decline to 39 per cent, 41 per cent, and 49 per cent, respectively.

Such an assumption is, of course, rather drastic. A more moderate assumption would be that the nonrespondents would be half as likely as the respondents to take the "liberal" position. Column (3) shows that in this model 47 per cent would agree with a change in the celibacy ruling, 50 per cent would not accept the birth control teaching, and 60 per cent would concur on the election of bishops by priests. In Column (4) we assume that all the nonrespondents would answer in the same proportions as did priests over fifty-five. In such a model 45 per cent would agree with a celibacy change, 50 per cent would not accept the birth control teaching, and 64 per cent would support clerical election of bishops. Finally, in Column (5) the assumption is made that all the other nonrespondents would answer in the way that a sample of them did in a telephone interview. In this last model, 50 per cent would favor optional celibacy, the only item of the three included in the five-minute telephone interview.

In the last three models, it is clear that the descriptions made in the text would apply, though with somewhat less force. Even in the second model, approximately two-fifths of the population would be supporting the "liberal" positions on celibacy and birth control and one-half on the election of bishops.

The reader can, if he so desires, apply these models to all percentages reported in this study. Let us assume that X = the percentage presented in the tables in this report, Y = the percentage of those over fifty-five agreeing with a specific item, and Z = the percentage of those in the telephone interviews with nonrespondents who agree with the item. (The percentages for the responses to the items included in the telephone interview can be found in the excerpts from that interview presented at the end of this appendix.) Then the formula for determining the adjusted percentages based on the second model is $.7X$, where $.7$ stands for the usable response rate of $.71$ instead of the overall response rate of $.78$. The formula for the third model is .7X + (.3X/2); for the fourth model, .7X + .3Y; and for the fifth model .7X + .3Z.

By way of example, we shall compute the adjusted percentage using the formula from the fifth model. In the case of the celibacy ruling, 37 per cent of the nonrespondents who were interviewed by telephone were in favor of optional celibacy. Therefore, based on the assumptions underlying the fifth model, the percentage of the total population advocating a change would be:

$$(.7 \times 56) + (.3 \times 37) = 39.2 + 11.1 = 50.3 \text{ per cent.}$$

Telephone Interview with Nonrespondents

The procedures used in conducting the telephone interviews with nonrespondents are described in Appendix B, which is devoted to the various phases of the field work. Here we shall present excerpts from the interview schedule and next to each response give the percentage of those interviewed who took that position. These data will enable the reader to assess the characteristics of nonrespondents in order to judge the size and direction of the nonresponse bias in the percentages presented in the body of the report.

In the preceding section of this appendix, we described how the percentages given below enable one to adjust the figures presented in the chapter tables if one wishes to assume that all other nonrespondents would take the same positions as those who were contacted by telephone. Thus, to repeat the example, on the basis of such an assumption one would conclude that across the board 50 per cent of the American clergy rather than 56 per cent support optional celibacy. Likewise, using the same assumption and the formula based on it, the average age of the priests in the United States is 49.9 rather than 46.6, as reported in the text.

It should be stated, however, that this same kind of adjustment for nonresponse is not reasonable for the percentage breakdowns by age. The formulas for adjusting for nonresponse in each age category are more complicated. Furthermore, if the findings for each age category were adjusted for nonresponse, the changes in the percentages reported by age would be negligible. In other words, since the nonrespondents tend to be older than those who responded (the average age of the telephone respondents was fifty-eight), it is reasonable to assume that if there had been 100 per cent response to the questionnaire, the overall averages would change somewhat in the direction of those reported for the oldest age category. It is not reasonable to assume, however, that the percentages reported within each age category would change noticeably. Thus, continuing the example used above, although one would reasonably expect changes in Table 12.1 resulting from adjustments for nonresponse, the percentages reported by age in Table 12.2 would change little or not at all. Even with 100 per cent response, it is reasonable to assume the 84 per cent of active priests between the ages of twenty-six and thirty-five, 67 per cent between thirty-six and forty-five, 45 per cent between forty-six and fifty-five, and 21 per cent of those over 55 favor optional celibacy for diocesan priests.

The results of our efforts to contact 150 randomly selected nonrespondents may be summarized as follows. Fifty-nine completed the interview in some fashion, 48 entirely and 11 partially. We were unable to contact the others or some of them refused to cooperate for the reasons described in Appendix B. The results of the completed interviews are reported as percentages next to the questions in the excerpts presented below. The case base for the percentages ranges from 48 to 59; they are not recorded for each percentage.

Excerpts from Telephone Interview

Q. 83. First of all, in what year were you born—e.g., 1 9 2 6

Average age 58

Q. 5

	A. Before Ordination	B. Since Ordination
A. What is the highest educational level you had attained at the time of your ordination? B. And what is the highest level you have *completed since* ordination?		
1) Completed theology training but did not get a state or ecclesiastically accredited degree	37%	0%
2) Received a state accredited bachelor's degree	39	5
3) Received a state accredited master's degree	10	33
4) Received a state accredited doctor's or professional degree	4	6
5) Received an ecclesiastically accredited STB (Bachelor of Sacred Theology), or equivalent	2	6
6) Received an ecclesiastically accredited STL (Licentiate in Sacred Theology), or equivalent	4	11
7) Received an ecclesiastically accredited STD (Doctorate in Sacred Theology), JCD (Doctorate in Canon Law), DD (Doctor of Divinity), or equivalent	4	11
8) Other (SPECIFY) _____	0	0
9) No further degree	—	28
	100%	100%

Q. 16

A. What is your present status?
DIOCESAN PRIESTS AND RELIGIOUS PRIESTS WHERE
APPLICABLE:

	A. Current Position
Bishop	0%
Full-time chancery or tribunal official	2
Pastor with special work outside the parish	11
Pastor without special work outside the parish	34
Full-time associate pastor	13
Associate pastor with special work outside the parish	2
Special assignment	2
Retired	9
Other (SPECIFY) ———————————	4
RELIGIOUS PRIESTS ONLY:	
Major superior	0
Assistant to major superior	6
Local superior	2
Member	6
Other (DESCRIBE) ———————————	9
	100%

Q. 37

Below are a number of statements which are frequently made today. Please indicate the extent of your agreement or disagreement with each of them.

	Agree strongly	Agree some-what	Uncer-tain	Disagree some-what	Disagree strongly	Total
2) What is lacking today is that closeness among priests that used to be so evident	4%	17	10	33	35	99%
4) The relationship between laity and priests was much better before Vatican II when everyone knew just how he was expected to act	16%	37	12	12	22	99%
5) With the new roles for everyone in the Church that have developed since Vatican II, the relationships between priests and laity are much better	23%	38	11	11	17	100%

6) Everything changes so quickly in the liturgy these days that I often have trouble deciding what rules to follow	54%	8	6	19	13	100%
9) I often feel that many things the Church stood for are now disintegrating	40%	15	6	29	10	100%
C. Celibacy should be a matter of personal choice for diocesan priests	31%	6	2	16	45	100%
A. Since the priesthood is a lifelong commitment, there is almost never a good reason for leaving	42%	17	0	19	23	101%
R. I used to think I knew what a priest was supposed to do but I really don't know any more	11%	4	4	11	70	100%

Q. 65

Individual priests evaluate celibacy for themselves in different ways. Please tell me how you feel about the following aspects of the unmarried state for yourself. Celibacy is . . .

	Very much of an advantage	Somewhat of an advantage	Neither advantage nor disadvantage	Somewhat of a disadvantage	Very much of a disadvantage	Total
A. For doing my work better	78%	20	0	0	2	100%
B. For my personal growth and development	57%	22	8	6	6	99%
C. For the development of my love of God	71%	12	8	2	6	99%
D. For relating more fully to other people	63%	19	4	8	6	100%

Q. 66

	Certainly yes	Probably yes	Uncertain	Probably no	Certainly no	Total
If celibacy for priests became optional, do you think you would ever get married?	2%	5	10	11	72	100%

Q. 79

Taking things all together, how would you say things are these days—would you say you're very happy, pretty happy, or not too happy?

Very happy	49%
Pretty happy	41
Not too happy	10
	100%

Q. 80

Compared with your life today, how were things four or five years ago—were things happier for you then, not quite as happy, or what?

Happier	37%
Not quite as happy	18
About the same	45
Other (SPECIFY)	0
	100%

Q. 24

Think of the professional men you know—for example, doctors, dentists, lawyers, scientists. How do you think you as a priest compare to them in regard to the following attributes?

	I have more	I have about the same	I have less	I have much less	Don't know	Total
A. Depth of knowledge and skill	6%	58	25	4	6	99%
B. Autonomy to make decisions	8%	64	21	4	2	99%
C. Responsibility for an undertaking	13%	70	13	2	2	100%
D. Commitment to serving the needs of people	44%	46	6	4	0	100%

Q. 75

Have any of your friends left the priesthood in the last few years? Could you tell me which of the following statements best reflects your feelings about *your* future in the priesthood?

I definitely will not leave	77%
I probably will not leave	21
I am uncertain about my future	0
I will probably leave	2
I have definitely decided to leave	0
	100%

Q. 98
A. What is your national background on your father's side?
B. What is your national background on your mother's side?

	A. Father	B. Mother
English, Scotch, Welsh, English Canadian, Australian, New Zealand	6%	4%
African countries	2	4
Irish	38	42
German	10	12
Scandinavian	2	0
Italian	4	4
French, French Canadian, Belgian	6	6
Polish	6	4
Lithuanian	4	4
Russian or other Eastern European	6	6
Spanish, Portuguese, Latin American, including Puerto Rican	6	4
Other (SPECIFY) _____	8	8
Don't know	2	2
	100%	100%

Q. 94
What was the highest grade in school completed by your father and your mother?

	Father	Mother
No schooling	4%	8%
8th grade or less	65	65
Some high school	4	8
High school graduate	6	6
Some college	6	6
College degree	6	4
Master's degree or equivalent	0	0
Doctor's degree or equivalent	0	0
Don't know	8	2
	99%	99%

APPENDIX E

THE RELIGIOUS CLERGY

This appendix presents the data that pertain to religious priests. Much of this information has already been presented in the tables comparing the responses of diocesan and religious priests on the major items that comprise the body of this report. This procedure had the advantage of providing a composite profile of the two major groups that constitute the Roman Catholic clergy in the United States. There were some items in the NORC questionnaire, however, that pertained only to religious priests. Moreover, given the fact that the priesthood has traditionally been and continues to be a profession that admits of two generically different organizational styles of clerical life, there is some reason to focus, at least briefly, on diocesan and religious priests as two separate groups.

We first review the data scattered throughout the body of this report that pertain to differences between diocesan and religious priests. Secondly, we present the data relating only to religious clergy, specifically their attitudes toward the religious vows of chastity, poverty, and obedience and toward community life. Lastly, we analyze to what extent, if any, the specific values and attitudes of the religious clergy affect the causal model presented in Chapter 13.

One principal finding revealed by the data is that on almost all the major variables contained in this report, religious major superiors are much more like their subjects than the bishops are like diocesan priests. The similarity between religious priests and their superiors, on the one hand, and the difference between diocesan priests and their bishops, on the other, occur on such widely disparate items as family background, ethnicity, job satisfaction, clerical relationships, attitudes toward recruitment, and the adequacy of seminary training, as well as on other items such as theological values, attitudes toward celibacy, the ideal exercise of authority, spiritual practices, sources of priestly satisfaction, and perceptions of priestly problems.

359

A second principal finding is that taking the major variables as a whole, active diocesan and religious priests appear to be far more alike than different. Nevertheless, the data do reveal some important differences between the two groups, which can be summarized as follows:

1. Over twice as many diocesan as religious priests cite "parish work" as one of their current main jobs. More religious than diocesan priests cite one of the following as among their current main jobs: educational administration, counseling, university and college teaching, teaching in a major seminary, writing and research, or further studies.

2. Diocesan priests score consistently lower than religious priests on all measures of job satisfaction. Moreover, those jobs that correlate most highly with work satisfaction are jobs that are most likely to be performed by religious clergy.

3. Diocesan priests more often list "the joy of administering the sacraments," "satisfaction in organizing and administering work of the Church," and "the challenge of being the leader in the Christian community" as primary sources of priestly satisfaction. Religious priests, on the other hand, more often list community life and the opportunity to exercise intellectual and creative abilities as sources of their satisfaction.

4. Religious priests are slightly less likely than diocesan priests to say that loneliness is a major problem in their life and much less likely to agree that what is lacking today is that closeness among priests that used to be so evident.

5. Diocesan priests report more close friends among the laity than do religious priests; diocesan priests also appear to have much larger involvement in ecumenical activities.

6. Regarding reasons for leaving the priesthood, diocesan priests give a higher ranking to difficulties in living within the present structure of the Church, while religious priests place more emphasis on the need for personal development and growth.

In addition to these general and specific differences between diocesan and religious priests, one would also expect differences among religious groups themselves, especially between the more "monastic" and more "apostolic" orders. While the exploration of such differences will have to await a later and more detailed analysis, on the basis of the findings cited above it seems reasonable to hypothesize that there are fewer differences within religious institutes than one might expect from the history and varying traditions of each group.

In addition to the information gathered from both diocesan and religious clergy, the main questionnaire contained a number of items that pertained only to religious clergy. The principal findings from these data are the following:

1. Religious priests show a strong commitment to the religious life both for themselves personally and for the religious life itself as a "permanent" element in the Church. A large minority (44 per cent), however, feel that "religious life is so tied to institutions that its prophetic role is almost snuffed out."

2. About three-quarters of the religious priests agree that the vow of chastity is essential to the religious life, although about two-thirds agree that the traditional way of presenting chastity "has often allowed for the development of impersonalism and false spirituality."

3. There is little unanimity regarding the meaning and practice of religious poverty; well over half the religious priests think the name of the vow should be changed to "simplicity."

4. About three-quarters of the religious clergy do not think that "optional celibacy for diocesan priests would seriously hamper vocations to the religious life."

5. While most religious priests affirm the need for local superiors in all communities and oppose an authoritarian understanding of obedience, there is no strong leaning toward democratic government on the local level.

6. Three-tenths of the religious priests agree that community life demands uniformity in horarium, liturgical worship, residence, and dress, and about one-half agree that every member of the community should be allowed to involve himself in various movements and demonstrations without hindrance from the community.

7. Two-thirds of the religious priests are satisfied with the pace of updating in their communities, although opinion is considerably divided on whether this renewal has succeeded in recapturing the original spirit of the order's founder.

Description

As Table E.1 indicates, the attitude most commonly shared by religious priests is that religious life has been a major factor in their happiness and success in the priesthood (86 per cent). This strong affirmation takes on added meaning when it is compared with the responses to a question that dealt with the relationship between the priesthood and membership in a religious community (table not shown). Over half the group (55 per cent) indicated that the attraction of the priesthood was their primary reason for entering religious life; only 8 per cent said that they wanted primarily to be a religious and that the priesthood was a secondary motive; and 37 per cent reported that they regarded their membership in a religious community to be equally as important as their ordination to the priesthood. Within this context, then, it is not surprising that the majority of religious priests report little conflict between their dual membership in the priesthood and in a religious order or congregation (80 per cent).

While the data in Table E.1 show strong affirmation of the permanent value or religious life in the Church (67 per cent), there is also not very strong agreement with the attitude that the multiplicity of priestly orders and congregations presently existing in the Church should be abandoned (31 per cent). Moreover, only 24 per cent of the respondents feel that religious orders or congregations should give way to the secular institute as the most apt form of religious life today. The major difference between religious orders or congregations and secular institutes is that members of

TABLE E.1

ATTITUDES OF RELIGIOUS PRIESTS TOWARD THE RELIGIOUS LIFE

Attitude	*Per Cent Agreeing "Strongly" or "Somewhat"*
Religious life is a purely human phenomenon subject to radical reconsideration even to the point of allowing its disappearance	33
Religious life is a permanent element in the Church	67
Religious life is so tied to institutions that its prophetic role is almost snuffed out	44
For religious life to be relevant today, there should be a reemphasis of its contemplative dimension and a return to stricter discipline	37
The mode of religious life most apt for our day is that of the secular institute, not the religious order or congregation	24
Religious life is basically the same, so that the various orders with the same apostolates should be merged and united	31
Religious life has been a major factor of my happiness and success in the priesthood	86
For religious life to be relevant today it must adapt all of its structures to the secularized world	29
In my experience as a religious priest, there is seldom, if ever, any real conflict between being a member of an order and being an effective priest	80

the latter take no public vows and do not necessarily live in community. Thus, the data give strong indirect evidence that for most American religious clergy, community life and the vows are seen as essential to their total priestly life.

According to theologcian Edward Schillebeeckx, religious life is a vital expression of the charismatic and prophetic character of the Church. A religious order or congregation is, in fact, an institutionalized ecclesial charism. We can see clearly from Table E.1 that it is precisely this prophetic role that is most problematic for contemporary religious clergy. A large minority (37 per cent) feel that there should be an increased emphasis on the contemplative nature of religious life, and a smaller minority (29 per cent) feel that if religious life is to be relevant today, it must adapt more fully to the structures of the secularized world. Opinion is more evenly divided on how this prophetic element is to be embodied in the work of religious clergy; somewhat less than half (44 per cent) feel that religious life is so tied to institutions that its prophetic role is almost snuffed out. Evidently, the problem of recovering and maintaining their charismatic role in the Church is one of the most crucial issues facing religious clergy today.

Another problem is the practical meaning of the religious vows. As Table E.2 reveals, there is little variation in opinion among religious priests regarding the vow of chastity. Most agree it is essential to religious life (72 per cent) and also report that they were fully aware of its meaning when they pronounced this vow (80 per cent). Nor do most of the religious feel that if celibacy were optional for diocesan priests, this would seriously hamper vocations to the religious life (26 per cent). On the other hand, 68 per cent agree that the traditional way of presenting the vow of chastity during their religious training often allowed for the development of impersonalism and false spirituality.

Unlike opinions regarding chastity, attitudes toward the vow of poverty are much less clearly focused. Thus, 72 per cent of the group agree that poverty shields a person from the realistic cares of everyday living. However, it does not seem that the religious feel such a situation is undesirable, since only 38 per cent agree that the vow of poverty makes persons irresponsible and immature. It is clear, however, that there is little general agreement on the meaning of the vow of poverty. About half (54 per cent) of the religious clergy say that poverty means dependence on the community for all one's material needs. Again, 56 per cent agree that poverty is a charade and that religious live more comfortably and securely than the people with whom they work; 47 per cent feel that the spirit of

TABLE E.2

ATTITUDES OF RELIGIOUS PRIESTS TOWARD THE VOWS

Attitude	Per Cent Agreeing "Strongly" or "Somewhat"
Chastity:	
At the time of my perpetual vows, I was well aware of the implications of my vow of chastity	80
The vow of chastity is so essential to religious life that religious life would not survive without it	72
Optional celibacy for diocesan priests would seriously hamper vocations to the religious life	26
The traditional way of presenting the vow of chastity in religious formation has often allowed for the development of impersonalism and false spirituality	68
Poverty:	
Poverty means dependence on the community for all of one's material needs	54
Religious poverty is a charade; generally we live more comfortably and more securely than the persons with whom we are working	56
One cannot profess poverty and run expensive schools that cater to the rich	36
Poverty shields religious from the realistic cares of everyday human living	72
Poverty makes a person irresponsible, immature, and childish	38
The spirit of poverty is meaningless without poverty in fact	47
The term "poverty" should be changed to "simplicity" and its interpretation brought into line with modern economic realities	61
Obedience:	
The duty of the subject is to obey; it is the responsibility of the superior to discern God's will and declare it	30
The ideal decision-making process in a religious community is that of "dialogue obedience," i.e., the majority rules	40
All major superiors should be elected by the entire religious membership	69
There is no need for a local superior in a community of mature, religious men	18

poverty is meaningless without some poverty in fact. Yet, only 36 per cent say that religious cannot profess poverty and run expensive schools that cater to the rich. It is difficult to reconcile these contrary findings. What the data seem to point to is that while religious find their vow of poverty personally functional and individually demanding, there is no clear agreement about the meaning of corporate poverty or the practical implications of poverty in their apostolic work. Within this context, it is understandable that well over half (61 per cent) of the respondents agree that the term "poverty" is itself one of the major problems and that the vow should be changed to "simplicity."

As for the vow of obedience, there seems to be a large-scale rejection of any authoritarian understanding of the roles of superior and subject. Less than one-third agree that it is the duty of the subject to obey and the responsibility of the superior to command. Although the data indicate support of democratic procedures in selecting all major religious superiors, there is no indication of a trend toward "democratic" government on the local level. While 69 per cent of the religious feel that all major superiors should be elected by the entire religious membership, only 40 per cent agree that the ideal decision-making process is one of "majority rule." At the same time, only 18 per cent of the religious priests feel that there is no longer a need for local superiors, a finding that seems to support the position that somehow the superior provides a source of unity for the community and that religious life would not be "quite right" without superiors.

The remaining questions directed specifically to the religious clergy dealt with their attitudes toward community life. The data presented in Table E.3 indicate a rather strong acceptance of pluralism in community life and a rejection of sheer uniformity. Only 30 per cent of the religious agree that life in community demands uniformity in horarium, liturgical worship, residence, and dress. Almost half (48 per cent) agree that each member of the community should be allowed to involve himself in various movements and demonstrations without hindrance from his community. At the same time, there is also confirmation that religious priests do not generally support a principle of natural selection in the formation of their communities; only one-third of them agree that local communities should have the right to choose their own members. The recent updating and renewal undertaken by religious orders and congregations in response to the urging of the Second Vatican Council does not seem to have

TABLE E.3

ATTITUDES OF RELIGIOUS PRIESTS TOWARD COMMUNITY LIFE

Attitude	Per Cent Agreeing "Strongly" or "Somewhat"
A religious community demands uniformity in horarium, liturgical worship, residence, and dress	30
Each member of the community should be allowed to involve himself in various movements and demonstrations without hindrance from his community	48
In its efforts toward renewal, our community or order has not recaptured the original spirit of our Founder	45
Updating has created disorder and confusion which is harmful to our community	33
Our pace of change has lacked a sense of realism and urgency. Adaptation has been only marginal	34
Each local community should have the right to choose its own members	33

occasioned much disorder and confusion; only one-third of the respondents think that there has been resulting harm. This finding should be a source of comfort not only to religious institutes themselves but also to the Church as a whole. Religious renewal has demanded some severe and sudden changes in attitudes and ideology as well as in the lifestyle of many religious. The fact that only one-third feel that this change has been harmful attests to a rather large measure of flexibility in men who for long years have been accustomed to total institutionalism.

Analysis

As a first step in a more detailed analysis of the data on religious priests, the various attitude items discussed above were grouped into a religious-life index parallel to the "modern"-values index used in the analysis of theological beliefs and attitudes toward the priestly life (cf. Chapter 6). The first interesting finding that emerges from an inspection of the scores on the items in the index is that there is no clean division between "traditional" and "modern" attitudes toward religious life and the vows. In other words, most religious priests tend to agree with a certain number of both sets of attitudes. Thus, while most of the religious agree with the more modern position that the vow of poverty shields them from life and is more a fiction than fact, that poverty should be renamed "simplicity," that the traditional presentation of chastity has been dysfunctional, and that priests should not be hindered by the community in their involvement in social movements, most would also affirm the need for local superiors, reject the demand for more adaptation to the secularized world, and not agree that religious should cease to run schools for the wealthy or that poverty breeds irresponsibility. Likewise, most of the religious affirm the traditional values of the permanency of religious life, the meaning of poverty as total dependence on the community, and the essential role of chastity in religious life, and yet most would also reject the traditional values of uniformity within religious communities, an authoritarian understanding of obedience, and the need for more contemplation in religious life.

A closer inspection of these items of agreement and disagreement, however, reveals a subtle logic. In their attitudes toward the nature of religious life as such (its permanency, evangelical character, etc.), religious priests still hold "traditional" attitudes. Their acceptance of "modern" values seem to relate to the way in which these "traditional" values are worked out in practice and to the pluralism required in contemporary religious life.

We also carried out a more extensive analysis of the difference between diocesan and religious priests using multiple regression. As we commented in Chapter 9, one of the variables in our correlation matrix was whether a priest was a member of a religious community. Since no correlation in excess of .2 was found between being a religious and any of the other variables in our analytic model, we concluded that as far as the variables in our model are concerned, there is little difference between diocesan and religious priests. However, this preliminary test of the hypothesis was based only on an inspection of the simple correlations. A simple correlation sometimes hides more complicated indirect relationships and even at times appears to be very small because the strong effect of another variable is cancelling out the equally strong but opposite effect of the variable whose correlation coefficient is being examined. Therefore, to discover whether being a religious priest makes any appreciable difference in explaining future plans to remain in the priesthood, we decided to execute a more efficient (and much more complex) test of the hypothesis. This investigation allowed us to inspect all the variables at one time, taking into consideration not just the simple relationships with future plans to stay in the priesthood, but all the direct and indirect effects of the variables on one another as well as on future plans.

Because of space limitations, we cannot present a full discussion of the differences discovered when the causal model that was applied to all active priests in the sample (see the "Analysis" sections of Chapter 5-13) was applied separately to the diocesan and to the religious priests. However, Table E.4 contains a summary of those differences. Though presentation of merely the R^2 and R^2 changes omits many of the technical details, it highlights the important findings rather clearly.

The table shows that the combination of variables in the analytic model enables us to explain a higher per cent of the variance of future plans when the sample has been divided into separate groups of diocesan and religious than when the two types of priests are taken together. In Table 13.9 we saw that the model accounts for 52 per cent of the variance on future plans of all American priests, but taken separately the explanatory power is increased to 59 per cent for diocesan priests and 56 per cent for religious priests.

Aside from the increase in the amount of variance explained, the effects exerted by the prior variables characterizing diocesan priests change only somewhat, but those exerted by the attributes of religious are altered rather markedly. The five characteristics that are most predictive of the plans of all priests to stay in the ministry in order of importance are age, desire to marry, loneliness, work satisfaction, and "modern" values (Table 13.9). However, if one tries to explain the future plans of religious priests only, the five most powerful predictors in order of importance (accounting for 53 per cent of the variance) are desire to

TABLE E.4

EXPLANATION OF VARIANCE ON FUTURE PLANS OF DIOCESAN
AND RELIGIOUS PRIESTS TO STAY IN THE PRIESTHOOD

Variable	R^2		R^2 Change	
	Diocesan	Religious	Diocesan	Religious
Age	.18	.16	.18	.16
Family tension	.21	.21	.03	.05
Inner-directed	.25	.23	.04	.02
Religious experience	.29	.23	.04	.00
"Modern" values	.33	.26	.04	.03
Work satisfaction	.44	.27	.11	.01
Loneliness	.50	.37	.06	.10
Negative affect	.50	.37	.00	.00
Desire to marry	.59	.56	.09	.19

marry, age, loneliness, the recollection of family tensions, and "modern" values. Inner-directedness contributes 2 per cent to the overall explanatory power of the model when it is limited to religious priests. Work satisfaction explains only 1 per cent, and quasi-mystical experiences and negative affect have no influence at all on religious priests' future plans when prior variables are controlled. When we consider the path coefficients, we find that only two variables in the model have a direct effect on future plans to stay in the priesthood that is above .90: the direct path of desire to marry is −.53 and that of loneliness is −.16.

For diocesan priests, age still has the highest explanatory power of all the variables in the model, adding 18 per cent to the total explanation. Age is followed by work satisfaction (11 per cent), desire to marry (9 per cent), and loneliness (6 per cent). Inner-directedness, religious experiences, and "modern" values each contribute 4 per cent, while family tension accounts for 3 per cent of the variance in diocesan priests' plans to remain in the priesthood. Again, negative affect has no influence on the dependent variable. In contrast to the path coefficients for religious priests, six prior variables have direct paths leading to diocesan priests' future plans to stay in the priesthood: desire to marry (−.39), work satisfaction (.24), loneliness (−.16), "modern" values (−.12), inner-directedness (−.10), and religious experiences (.09).

If one asks why some religious priests are inclined to resign from their ecclesiastical ministries, we would say on the basis of our analytic model that the chief explanation is the desire to marry combined with a serious problem of loneliness. Answers to the questions of why they are lonely and why they want to get married are bound up in their age, recollection of family tensions, and "modern" values.

If, on the other hand, one asks why some diocesan priests are planning to leave the priesthood, we would say that the chief explanation is also the desire to marry, but this is combined with low work satisfaction, being lonely, having "modern" values, having an inner-directed personality, and not experiencing contracts with God or Christ.

The model for explaining the future plans of religious priests turns out to be less complicated than the one for diocesan priests. In comparison with their counterparts in dioceses, much more importance must be given to the desire to marry among those contemplating leaving religious communities, while only one other factor, loneliness, has a direct impact on their future plans. Work satisfaction has only a slight influence. The desire to marry is likewise the chief explanatory variable in the diocesan priests' model but its predictive power is lessened somewhat. Work satisfaction, on the other hand, greatly influences diocesan priests' plans for the future, and to a lesser extent so does the problem of loneliness. However, three other variables — "modern" values, inner-directedness, and religious experience — also have a direct impact for diocesan but not for religious priests' plans.

Table 12.3 shows that in comparison with diocesan priests, fewer religious priests actually desire to marry, and Table 9.6 provides evidence that religious priests on the average have higher work satisfaction than diocesan priests. Why, then, is the desire to marry more important and work satisfaction less important in explaining the future plans of religious than they are in explaining those of diocesan priests? The explanation seems to be that precisely because work satisfaction is so high among religious clergy, it does not cause them to want to resign from their jobs. That leaves the desire to marry and loneliness as the two single predictors of whether a religious priest will remain in his community. Although comparatively few religious would probably or certainly want to marry if celibacy became optional and an equally small proportion report loneliness as a great problem, nevertheless, when these factors are present they greatly influence a religious priest's decision to stay or leave. These same two factors are not as important in the decision of a diocesan priest because he is also influenced by low work satisfaction and (though to a lesser extent) by his "modern" values, inner-directed personality, and lack of religious experiences.

Finally, the index constructed from the items dealing with attitudes and values regarding the vows and community life was inserted into the model, first in place of and then along with the "modern"-values index, to analyze whether the special values of religious priests affect their plans to stay in the priesthood. The religious-life index behaved exactly like the "modern"-values index. This result provides further evidence that the traditional-modern dimension consistently underlies all the various values indices that were constructed and tested in this analysis.

The findings presented in this appendix indicate that while religious and diocesan priests appear to be fundamentally alike, nevertheless several important and interesting differences between them emerge that should be subjected to a more thorough investigation.

APPENDIX F

MAIN QUESTIONNAIRE

December, 1969

Dear Colleague,

The American bishops have commissioned the National Opinion Research Center, a professional research organization affiliated with the University of Chicago, to conduct a comprehensive study of the Catholic priesthood in the United States and of American priests living abroad.

You are one of 6,000 diocesan and religious priests who have been selected by scientific probability sampling methods to participate in this study. To enable us to determine with a high degree of accuracy the opinions and attitudes of priests regarding the vital issues confronting them, we chose an exceptionally large sample for this research. A slightly amended version of the questionnaire will be sent to a separate sample of those priests who have recently resigned from the active ministry.

This booklet is the outcome of many months of discussion and consultation with research scholars in the fields of theology, scripture, Church history, ascetics, sociology, and psychology; with bishops and major superiors; with representatives of priests' associations; and with many priests active in various ministries.

The questionnaire has been studied and approved by the Bishops' Committee on Pastoral Research and Practices and also has been endorsed by an *ad hoc* committee of major superiors appointed by the president of the Conference of Major Superiors of Men. Nevertheless, it goes without saying that it is entirely up to you whether you want to complete the questionnaire.

None of the questions should be interpreted as calling for a manifestation of conscience. Some of the items concern controversial issues, but no question is worded to impute or imply any judgment on our part. Your freedom to omit a response is always respected.

The anonymity of your answers is professionally guaranteed. NORC cannot release respondents' names to anyone, including sponsoring clients. The purpose of the code number on this page is to permit us to send follow-up letters to persons who do not return the questionnaire so that we can get a high completion rate. Ultimately your responses will be linked only to the first part of the identification number, which refers to your diocese or religious community, thereby allowing us to make a variety of statistical comparisons. No researcher will examine the questionnaire until after personal identification has been removed.

When you have filled out the entire questionnaire as completely and candidly as possible, please send it to us in the prepaid return envelope at your earliest convenience.

We would like to thank you for the time and thoughtful consideration we hope you will give to this questionnaire. It is long, but it covers a lot of ground: good ground we hope, which will yield much for the Church in the United States and particularly for you and all our fellow priests.

Fraternally,

(Signed) RICHARD A. SCHOENHERR

(Rev.) Richard A. Schoenherr
Senior Study Director

(Signed) JOHN MULHEARN, S.J.

(Rev.) John Mulhearn, S.J.
Research Associate

(Signed) NEAL W. MCDERMOTT, O.P.

(Rev.) Neal W. McDermott, O.P.
Research Associate

CONFIDENTIAL
Survey 5029

BEGIN DECK 01

PLEASE NOTE:

Almost all of the questions can be answered by drawing a circle around one or more numbers to the right of the categories. Thus:

Are you a U.S. citizen?	Yes, U.S. born......... 1	No, and I do not expect
CIRCLE ONE CODE.	Yes, naturalized....... 2	to stay in the U.S..... 4
	No, but expect to stay in	
	the U.S.............. 3	

After each question there are instructions. Please follow these instructions closely as they are very important for data processing.

A. If it says "CIRCLE ONE CODE," draw a circle around only the one number which *best describes* your answer, even though one or more other alternatives might be relevant.

B. If it says "CIRCLE ONE CODE IN EACH COLUMN," or "CIRCLE ONE CODE IN EACH ROW," please look to see that you have circled one and only one number in each of the appropriate columns or rows.

C. If it says "CIRCLE AS MANY CODES AS APPLY," circle as many or as few numbers in the columns or rows as you think are relevant.

- -

1. What was the highest grade in school you completed *before* entering the seminary or novitiate? CIRCLE ONE CODE.

8th grade or less..... 1	College degree (ANSWER A) ..5 10/0
Some high school.... 2	Master's degree (ANSWER A).. 6
High school graduate 3	Doctorate (ANSWER A).. 7
Some college........ 4	Professional degree (ANSWER A).. 8
	Other (SPECIFY). 9
	_____

A. *IF "DEGREE":* In what field?

Medicine.............. 01	Social work................ 11 11–12/00
Law.................. 02	Agriculture and related subjects 12
Biological sciences....... 03	Business and administration.. 13
Physical sciences........ 04	Art....................... 14
Social sciences (including history)............. 05	Counselling................ 15
Humanities (including philosophy)........... 06	Theology and related subjects (catechetics, church history, liturgy, etc.).............. 16
Mathematics........... 07	Other (SPECIFY)........... 17
Engineering.............08	_____
Education............. 09	_____
Other health professions.. 10	

2. What type of educational institutions have you attended for a year or more? CIRCLE APPROPRIATE CODES IN

EACH COLUMN. IN-CLUDE ANY YOU ARE CURRENTLY ATTENDING.	Catholic	Public or private non-religious	DECK 01 Other religious (*Not* Catholic)
A. Grade school	1 13/0	2 14/0	3 15/0
B. High school	4 16/0	5 17/0	6 18/0
C. College	7 19/0	8 20/0	9 21/0
D. University (beyond A.B.)	2 22/0	3 23/0	4 24/0
E. Other (SPECIFY)	5 25/0	6 26/0	7 27/0

3. How old were you when you first entered the seminary or novitiate?

years old   28–29/00

4. What seminaries did you attend?

	Name of Seminary	City and State (or City and Country, if not U.S.)
High school:		
College:		
Philosophy:		
Theology:		
Other:		

5. A. What is the highest educational level you had attained at the time of your ordination? CIRCLE APPROPRIATE CODE IN COLUMN A BELOW.

B. And what is the highest level you have *completed since* ordination? CIRCLE APPROPRIATE CODE IN COLUMN B.

	A. Before Ordination	B. Since Ordination
1) Completed theology training but did not get a state or ecclesiastically accredited degree..........................	1 30/0	1 31/0
2) Received a state accredited bachelor's degree..........................	2	2
3) Received a state accredited master's degree..........................	3 (ANSWER C)	3 (ANSWER C)
4) Received a state accredited doctor's or professional degree.................	4 (ANSWER C)	4 (ANSWER C)
5) Received an ecclesiastically accredited STB (Bachelor of Sacred Theology), or equivalent........................	5	5
6) Received an ecclesiastically accredited STL (Licentiate in Sacred Theology), or equivalent........................	6	6
7) Received an ecclesiastically accredited STD (Doctorate in Sacred Theology), JCD (Doctorate in Canon Law), DD (Doctor of Divinity), or equivalent....	7	7

8) Other (SPECIFY)	8	8
9) No additional degree *since* ordination..	–	9

C. *IF MASTER'S OR DOCTOR'S DEGREE IN A FIELD OTHER THAN THOSE ABOVE:*

Please indicate the field in which you received this degree. LIST THE CODE NUMBER USED IN Q. 1A (PAGE 1) WHICH INDICATES THIS FIELD.

Field in which I received this degree before ordination............................ 32–33/00

Field in which I received this degree since ordination.. 34–35/00

6. A. Are you currently engaged in full-time or part-time study at any college or university? CIRCLE ONE CODE.

Yes, full time (ANSWER B, C, & D)........... 1 36/0

Yes, part time (ANSWER B, C, & D).......... 2

No, not currently studying (ANSWER B)....... 3

IF "YES" TO A, ANSWER B, C & D:

B. Do you have fairly definite plans to begin (another course of) full-time or part-time study at any college or university in the near future? CIRCLE ONE CODE.

Yes, plan to study full-time (ANSWER E & F). 1 37/0

Yes, plan to study part-time (ANSWER E & F). 2

No, have no definite plans (GO TO Q. 7, PAGE 4). 3

	C. *CURRENT:* What type of program? CIRCLE ONE CODE.	E. *IF "YES" TO B—FUTURE:* What type of program? CIRCLE ONE CODE.
Ph.D. or equivalent at a Catholic university or Catholic professional school...................	01 38–39/0	01 40–41/00
Ph.D. or equivalent at a secular university.........	02	02
M.A. or equivalent at a Catholic university........	03	03
M.A. or equivalent at a secular university.........	04	04
A.B. at a Catholic college.......................	05	05
A.B. at a secular college........................	06	06
Other degree at a Catholic college................	07	07
Other degree at a secular college.................	08	08
Yes, but not for a degree.......................	09	09
Other (SPECIFY)	10	10

	D. *CURRENT:* In what field? CIRCLE ONE CODE.		F. *IF "YES" TO B—* *FUTURE:* In what field? CIRCLE ONE CODE.	
Medicine....................................	01	42–43/00	01	44–45/00
Law..	02		02	
Biological sciences...........................	03		03	
Physical sciences............................	04		04	
Social sciences (including history)...............	05		05	
Humanities (including philosophy)...............	06		06	
Mathematics.................................	07		07	
Engineering.................................	08		08	
Education...................................	09		09	
Other health professions......................	10		10	
Social work.................................	11		11	
Agriculture and related subjects.................	12		12	
Business and administration....................	13		13	
Art...	14		14	
Counselling.................................	15		15	
Theology and related subjects (catechetics, church history, liturgy, etc.)........................	16		16	
Other (SPECIFY)	17		17	

7. How well would you say your seminary training has prepared you to do the major duties of your priestly work? CIRCLE ONE CODE.

Very well............ 1   46/0
Moderately well...... 2
So-so............... 3
Not very well........ 4
Very badly.......... 5

8. A number of criticisms have been made about seminary training. Please indicate whether you agree or disagree with each of the following statements by circling one code on each line.

		Agree	Disagree	
A.	Most of the courses were too theoretically oriented	1	2	47/0
B.	Too many courses too superficially presented.....	3	4	48/0
C.	Many of the courses were irrelevant to modern pastoral needs.............................	5	6	49/0
D.	Few attempts made to help the seminarian learn how to deal with people......................	7	8	50/0
E.	The seminary was too sheltered from the main stream of life, intellectual and social...........	1	2	51/0
F.	Other (PLEASE SPECIFY)	3	5	52/0

9. Do you approve of sending boys to the seminary for their high school training? CIRCLE ONE CODE.

Yes.................. 1   53/0
No.................. 2
No opinion.......... 3

10. How frequently did you date girls before entering the seminary and during your seminary training? CIRCLE ONE CODE ON EACH LINE.

	Never	Several times a year	Two or three times a month	One or more times a week	
A. Before entering the seminary........	1	2	3	4	54/0
B. During the seminary........	5	6	7	8	55/0

11. To what extent do you feel you are utilizing your important skills and abilities in your present assignment? CIRCLE ONE CODE.

Not at all............ 1   56/0
Comparatively little... 2
To some degree...... 3
Fairly much......... 4
A great deal........ 5

12. Here are some statements about the priesthood. For each of the statements below, circle the category of response that *best* fits your present thinking. CIRCLE ONE CODE ON EACH LINE.

	Agree strongly	Agree some-what	Un-certain	Dis-agree some-what	Dis-agree strongly	
A. Since the priesthood is a lifelong commitment, there is almost never a good reason for leaving.	1	2	3	4	5	57/0
B. Being a priest-psychologist, priest-sociologist, or a priest-social worker is as priestly as working in parishes and missions.	6	7	8	9	0	58/5
C. My own ideas about the priesthood are pretty much the same as those of most priests I know.	1	2	3	4	5	59/0
D. I think it would be a good idea if Christian communities such as parishes were to choose their own priest from among available ordained priests	6	7	8	9	0	60/5

		Agree strongly	Agree some-what	Un-certain	Dis-agree some-what	Dis-agree strongly	
E.	Ordination confers on the priest a new status or a permanent character which makes him essentially different from the laity within the church.	1	2	3	4	5	61/0
F.	The idea that the priest is a "man set apart" is a barrier to the full realization of true Christian community.	6	7	8	9	0	62/5
G.	Being a chancery official, an administrator in the Province, or the administrator of a Catholic institution is as priestly as working in parishes and missions.	1	2	3	4	5	63/0
H.	Whatever else is said about the humanitarian preoccupations and interpersonal relationships of priests, we must remember that the priest is *the* man in society who proclaims God's Word and provides for sacramental encounter with God in Christ.	6	7	8	9	0	64/5
I.	I feel that I am most a priest when I am saying Mass and hearing confessions.	1	2	3	4	5	65/0
J.	In many cases a decision to resign from the priesthood is a wise and mature choice.	6	7	8	9	0	66/5
K.	The priesthood as we know it is a transitory institutional role which will eventually be modified so that there will be much less difference between Christians who have Holy Orders and those who do not.	1	2	3	4	5	67/0
L.	Being a priest really means being the liturgical leader of the Christian community. Anything else that is said about the priest could really be said about every Christian.	6	7	8	9	0	68/5
M.	If being on the picket line alienates a priest from most Catholics in an area, a priest should not engage in social protest movements.	1	2	3	4	5	69/0
					BEGIN DECK 02		
N.	Most of the laity with whom I work have ideas about what a priest is and what he should do that are very different from my own.	6	7	8	9	0	10/5

		Agree some-what	Un-certain	Dis-agree some-what	Dis-agree strongly	
	Agree strongly					

O. I think it would be a good idea if Christian communities such as parishes were to choose their own priest from among the parishioners. Such a man would acquire the proper training and then be ordained to act as the priest of the parish for some period of time.   1   2   3   4   5   11/0

P. It is the job of the priest to call into question the values of his parishioners.   6   7   8   9   0   12/5

Q. Priests who have resigned from the priesthood should be invited to re-apply for permission to function as priests again, whether they are married or single.   1   2   3   4   5   13/0

R. I used to think I knew what a priest was supposed to do but I really don't know any more.   6   7   8   9   0   14/5

S. For some men being a priest could be a part-time job. Some ordained priests could earn their living at some other employment, and help out on weekends, while others would work full time in the parish and other ministries.   1   2   3   4   5   15/0

T. As a priest, I feel that I am a member of the bishop's team. When I am doing a job that has the local bishop's approval, I am doing priestly work.   6   7   8   9   0   16/5

U. Nowadays, you can hardly be an effective priest if you are assigned to a conventional parish.   1   2   3   4   5   17/0

V. There is no ontological difference between the priest and the laity, since all share in the common priesthood of Christ given at baptism; the difference is mainly one of assigned duties in the church.   6   7   8   9   0   18/5

13. A. Circle the code in Column A following the statement which most accurately reflects your attitude toward recruiting for the priesthood and religious life *today*.

B. In Column B, circle the code that comes closest to your attitude *four or five years ago*.

DECK 02

	A.	B.
		4–5
	Today	years ago

a) I actively encourage boys to enter the seminary or
novitiate, since I see the priesthood as a very
rewarding vocation 1   19/0   1   20/0

b) I encourage boys but advise them about the uncertainties surrounding the role of the priest
today   2   2

c) I neither discourage nor encourage boys, but
allow them to make up their own minds 3   3

d) Abstracting from their personal qualities, I tend
to discourage boys from entering now and advise
them to wait until the future is more certain 4   4

e) Other (SPECIFY)   5   5

14. In what diocese did you grow up?   Diocese (City):   21–24/
                                       State (or Country if
                                       outside U.S.):

15. In what diocese are you now working?
                                       Diocese (City):   25–28/
                                       State (or Country if outside U.S.):

                                       IF OUTSIDE U.S.:
                                       ANSWER A

A. *IF OUTSIDE U.S.:* Are you engaged in
missionary work?

                                       Yes (ANSWER [1]) . . . 1   29/0
                                       No 2

[1] *IF YES TO A:* How long have you
been in the missions?   ———— years   30–31/99

16. A.   What is your present status? CIRCLE ONE CODE UNDER A.
    B.   How many of these positions have you held for at least one year since ordina-
         toin? CIRCLE AS MANY AS APPLY UNDER B.

	A.	B.
DIOCESAN PRIESTS AND RELIGIOUS	Current	Previous
PRIESTS WHERE APPLICABLE:	position	positions
Bishop	01 32–33/00	1 34/0
Full-time chancery or tribunal official	02	2 35/0
Pastor with special work outside the parish .	03	3 36/0
Pastor without special work outside the		
parish	04	4 37/0
Full-time associate pastor	05	5 38/0
Associate pastor with special work		
outside the parish	06	6 39/0
Special assignment	07	7 40/0
Retired . . . . (ANSWER C)	08	8 41/0
Other (PLEASE DESCRIBE)	09	9 42/0

	A. Current position		B. Previous positions
RELIGIOUS PRIESTS ONLY:			
Major superior........................	10	1	43/0
Assistant to major superior..............	20	2	44/0
Local superior.......................	30	3	45/0
Member............................	40	4	46/0
Other (PLEASE DESCRIBE)	50	5	47/0

C. *IF RETIRED*:
   1) What was your last position before retirement? LIST THE CODE NUM-
      BER USED IN A. WHICH INDICATES THIS POSITION.

   LAST POSITION:_____ 48–49/00

   2) At what age did you retire? _____ Age   50–51/00

17. How many years have you been in your current position?

   _____years   52–53/99

BEGIN DECK 03

18. [1] Both diocesan and religious priests may have either one full-time job or divide
       their time among a number of jobs. For example, a parish priest may work
       part time at the chancery and a man with a special assignment may do weekend
       work. Please indicate the type of work(s) in which you are *mainly* engaged.
       Do not indicate anything as one of your *main* jobs unless you spend approxi-
       mately one working day at it over a period of a week. CIRCLE AS MANY
       AS APPLY UNDER [1].

   [2] How many of the following jobs have you *ever* been engaged in for at least one
       year since your ordination? Again, do not consider the work as one of your
       former jobs unless you regularly spent at least one working day at it almost
       every week for a year's time. CIRCLE AS MANY AS APPLY UNDER [2].

		[1] Current main jobs		[2] Former main jobs	
A.	Diocesan administration	1	10/0	1	36/0
B.	Administrative work in a religious institute	2	11/0	2	37/0
C.	Administrative work in an educational or other institution	3	12/0	3	38/0
D.	Parish work	4	13/0	4	39/0
E.	Counselling work	5	14/0	5	40/0
F.	Chancery or tribunal work	6	15/0	6	41/0
G.	Retreat work, mission band	7	16/0	7	42/0
H.	Pilgrimages and shrines, pious societies (e.g., Apostleship of Prayer)	8	17/0	8	43/0
I.	Home missions in U.S.	9	18/0	9	44/0
J.	Religious instruction (e.g., catechetics, information center)	1	19/0	1	45/0
K.	Campus ministry	2	20/0	2	46/0
L.	Institutional chaplaincies (e.g., hospital, school, convent, prison)	3	21/0	3	47/0

		[1] Current main jobs	[2] Former main jobs
M.	Military chaplaincies (including ship chaplain)	4 22/0	4 48/0
N.	Social work (e.g., welfare agencies, poverty program, youth organizations)	5 23/0	5 49/0
O.	Publications, press	6 24/0	6 50/0
P.	Monastic observances	7 25/0	7 51/0
Q.	Teaching (other than in seminary): university and college levels	8 26/0	8 52/0
R.	Teaching (other than in seminary): high school and grade school levels	9 27/0	9 53/0
S.	Major seminary work (college level and above)	1 28/0	1 54/0
T.	Minor seminary work (high school)	2 29/0	2 55/0
U.	Writing/research	3 30/0	3 56/0
V.	Further studies	4 31/0	4 57/0
W.	Mass media (e.g., TV, films)	5 32/0	5 58/0
X.	Arts (e.g., music, painting)	6 33/0	6 59/0
Y.	Experimental ministry (PLEASE DESCRIBE)	7 34/0	7 60/0
Z.	Other (PLEASE DESCRIBE)	8 35/0	8 61/0

BEGIN DECK 04

[3] Now please write down the code letter(s) of your current job(s) and the percentage of your working week you devote to each; write in the code letter of the job (given in 18 [1]) and then the percentage next to it. E.g.:

Current job	% of time spent on job
D	50%
Q	25%
E	25%
Total	100%

Code letter of current job	Percentage of working week spent on job	
10/0		11–13/000
14/0		15–17/000
18/0		19–21/000
22/0		23–25/000
26/0		27–29/000
30/0		31–33/000
Total	100%	34–39/R

19. One of the activities that all priests share in common is pastoral work of one form or another, full time or part time. Likewise, all priests spend varying amounts of time on personal development and leisure. This question tries to find out how much time priests spend on these three types of activity. Please indicate the approximate number of hours you devote to each of the following activities in an average week. (If you devote no time, or hardly any, to a particular activity, write "0.")

	Activity	Hours spent on activity during average week
1)	Mass in church, homes, convents, etc.	40–41 /99
2)	Confessions	42–43 /99
3)	Marriages, baptisms, visiting sick, funerals and wakes	44–45 /99
4)	Preparation for sermons	46–47 /99
5)	Preparations for liturgy: choir, servers, lectors, etc.	48–49 /99
6)	Counselling: marriage, individuals	50–51 /99
7)	Adult and CCD instruction	52–53 /99
8)	Youth work: physical and religious development	54–55 /99
9)	Parish administration: finances, maintenance, correspondence, etc.	56–57 /99
10)	Meetings: deanery, senate, priests, laity	58–59 /99
11)	Parish school administration	60–61 /99
12)	Own spiritual development: prayer, breviary (alone or in choir), etc.	62–63 /99
13)	Own intellectual development (as opposed to further study): study, reading, conferences, etc.	64–65 /99
14)	Leisure: reading, TV, films, concerts, sports, etc.	66–67 /99
15)	Social involvement: civil rights, anti-poverty program, community affairs	68–69 /99
16)	Other (PLEASE DESCRIBE)	70–71 /99

BEGIN DECK 05

NOTE: CONCERNING QUESTIONS 20–26:

Some of the following questions about the work you do may not apply exactly to your situation; for example, if you are a member of a monastic community that is devoted mainly to contemplation. But in each case, try to answer all parts of the questions as best you can.

20. Think of your present work. What is it like most of the time? In the blank beside each word given below, write. . . .

   Y for "Yes" if it describes your work
   N for "No" if it does NOT describe it
   ? if you cannot decide

Work on present assignment:

———Fascinating 10/	———Tiresome 19/
———Routine 11/	———Healthful 20/
———Satisfying 12/	———Challenging 21/
———Boring 13/	———On your feet 22/
———Good 14/	———Frustrating 23/
———Creative 15/	———Simple 24/
———Respected 16/	———Endless 25/

Work on present assignment:

Pleasant   Gives sense of accomplishment

17 /   26 /

Useful

18 /

21. Do you have a supervisor—that is, do you get some sort of supervision in your work?

Yes (ANSWER A & B)... 1   27 /0

No (GO TO Q. 22)........2

IF "YES":

A. Who is the supervisor? IDENTIFY HIM BY POSITION, NOT NAME.

28–29 /

B. Think of the kind of supervision that you get in your work. How well does each of the following words describe this supervision? In the blank beside *each* word, below, put....

Y   if it describes the supervision you get on your job

N   if it does NOT describe it

?   if you cannot decide

Supervision on present assignment:

Asks my advice

30 /

Hard to please

31 /

Impolite

32 /

Praises good work

33 /

Tactful

34 /

Influential

35 /

Up-to-date

36 /

Doesn't supervise enough

37 /

Quick-tempered

38 /

Tells me where I stand

39 /

Annoying

40 /

Stubborn

41 /

Knows job well

42 /

Bad

43 /

Supervision on present assignment:

Intelligent

44/

Leaves me on my own

45/

Around when needed

46/

Lazy

47/

22. A. Considering all your duties together, how long do you consider your average work day to be? (Think of your work day as that amount of time that you are *actually engaged* in various duties; do not include leisure time or time spent in personal matters.) CIRCLE ONE CODE.

4 hours or less	1	48/0
5 hours	2	
6 hours	3	
7 hours	4	
8 hours	5	
9 hours	6	
10 hours	7	
11 hours	8	
12 or more hours	9	

B. How many days a week do you usually work for that number of hours? CIRCLE ONE CODE.

3 days a week or less	1	49/0
4 days a week	2	
5 days a week	3	
6 days a week	4	
7 days a week	5	

23. Do you belong to any priests' associations? CIRCLE ONE CODE.

Yes (ANSWER A)	1	50/0
No (GO TO Q. 24)	2	

A. Which priests' associations do you belong to? CIRCLE AS MANY CODES AS APPLY.

Diocesan Senate (currently or formerly)	1	51/0
Diocesan Association of Priests	2	52/0
National Association for Pastoral Renewal	3	53/0
Society of Priests for a Free Ministry	4	54/0
Local Ministerial Association	5	55/0
Other (SPECIFY)	6	56/0

24. Think of the professional men you know—for example, doctors, dentists, lawyers, scientists. How do you think you as a priest compare to them in regard to the following attributes? CIRCLE ONE CODE ON EACH LINE.

	I have more	I have about the same	I have less	I have much less	Don't know	
A. Depth of knowledge and skill.	1	2	3	4	5	57/0
B. Autonomy to make decisions.	1	2	3	4	5	58/0
C. Responsibility for an undertaking.	1	2	3	4	5	59/0
D. Commitment to serving the needs of people.	1	2	3	4	5	60/0

25. Think of the pay you get now, or, if you have a vow of poverty, think of the arrangements made for your living expenses. How well does each of the following words describe your present pay arrangement? In the blank beside *each* word, put....

Y   if it describes your pay
N   if it does NOT describe it
?   if you cannot decide

Present pay:
61/   Income adequate for normal expenses
62/   Barely live on income
63/   Bad
64/   Income provides luxuries
65/   Less than I deserve
66/   Highly paid
67/   Underpaid

BEGIN DECK 06

26. Think of the opportunities for promotion that you have now. How well does each of the following words describe these? In the blank beside each word, put....

Y   for "Yes" if it describes your opportunities for promotion
N   for "No" if it does NOT describe them.
?   if you cannot decide.

Opportunities for promotion

10/   Good opportunity for advancement
11/   Opportunity somewhat limited
12/   Promotion on ability
13/   Dead-end assignment
14/   Good chance for promotion
15/   Unfair promotion policy
16/   Infrequent promotions
17/   Regular promotions
18/   Fairly good chance for promotion

27. How often do you *usually* celebrate Mass each week? CIRCLE ONE CODE.

Every day................................... 1 19/0
5–6 times................................... 2
2–4 times................................... 3
Once a week............................... 4
Less than once a week....................... 5

28. In what kind of situation do you *usually* celebrate Mass? CIRCLE ONE CODE.

For parish, religious community, or institution..... 1 20/0
Generally in private........................ 2
Concelebrated Mass......................... 3
For small informal groups.................... 4
Other (SPECIFY)........................... 5

29. How frequently do you say the Breviary? CIRCLE ONE CODE.

Daily for all of the Hours.................... 1 21/0
Daily for some of the Hours.................. 2
All or some of the Hours several times a week..... 3
All or some of the Hours several times a month.... 4
Not at all.................................. 5

30. How often do you read the Bible outside of the context of the Liturgy and the Divine Office? CIRCLE ONE CODE.

Never, or so rarely that it probably shouldn't count.. 1 22/0
Only on very special occasions................. 2
About once a month......................... 3
About once a week.......................... 4
Several times a week........................ 5
Every day.................................. 6

31. How often do you pray or meditate privately? CIRCLE ONE CODE.

Seldom or never............................ 1 23/0
On very special occasions.................... 2
About once a week.......................... 3
Several times a week........................ 4
Daily..................................... 5
Other (SPECIFY).......................... 6

32. Which of the following statements best describes your feelings? CIRCLE ONE CODE.

A. I find that celebrating Mass has become a matter of routine or duty, and I pray better at other times............................. 1 24/0

OR

B. I find that celebrating Mass is usually a very important form of prayer and worship for me personally............................... 2

33. During the past two or three years how often have you experienced each of the following? CIRCLE ONE CODE ON EACH LINE.

	Frequently	Occasionally	Once	Never	
A. An overwhelming feeling of being at one with God or Christ.	1	2	3	4	25/0
B. A sense of being in the presence of God.	5	6	7	8	26/0
C. A feeling of being afraid of God.	1	2	3	4	27/0
D. A deep feeling of being personally loved by Christ here and now.	5	6	7	8	28/0
E. A feeling of being tempted by the devil.	1	2	3	4	29/0
F. A feeling of being abandoned by God.	5	6	7	8	30/0
G. Other (SPECIFY)	1	2	3	4	31/0

34. How do you evaluate the following as contributing to your spiritual and personal fulfillment? If you don't engage in a particular activity, CIRCLE THE "I do not do this" CODE.

	I do not do this	No value	Doubtful value	Somewhat valuable	Very valuable	
A. Visiting the sick.	5	6	7	8	9	32/0
B. Helping people who are poor.	1	2	3	4	5	33/0
C. Participating in some significant social action such as a rally or demonstration.	5	6	7	8	9	34/0
D. Private devotion to Mary, e.g., rosary.	1	2	3	4	5	35/0
E. Small group discussions of spiritual concerns.	5	6	7	8	9	36/0
F. Supporting the causes of minority peoples.	1	2	3	4	5	37/0
G. Preparing sermons.	5	6	7	8	9	38/0
H. Active concern for mentally ill or retarded.	1	2	3	4	5	39/0
I. Regular confession (at least monthly).	5	6	7	8	9	40/0
J. Working for better political leadership.	1	2	3	4	5	41/0
K. Spiritual reading.	5	6	7	8	9	42/0
L. Providing recreational facilities for the young or the deprived.	1	2	3	4	5	43/0
M. Having a good time at a social gathering.	5	6	7	8	9	44/0
N. Personal donations of money to worthy causes.	1	2	3	4	5	45/0
O. Literature, drama, film, art.	5	6	7	8	9	46/0

35. There are many sources of satisfaction in the life and work of the priest. Would you indicate how important each of the following is *as a source of satisfaction* to you? CIRCLE ONE CODE ON EACH LINE.

As a source of satisfaction, this is of. . . .

	Great importance	Some importance	Little importance	No importance	
A. Joy of administering the sacraments and presiding over the liturgy.	1	2	3	4	47/0
B. Respect that comes to the priestly office.	5	6	7	8	48/0
C. Satisfaction in organizing and administering work of the Church.	1	2	3	4	49/0
D. Opportunity to exercise intellectual and creative abilities.	5	6	7	8	50/0
E. Spiritual security that results from responding to the divine call.	1	2	3	4	51/0
F. Challenge of being the leader of the Christian community.	5	6	7	8	52/0
G. Engaging in efforts at social reform.	1	2	3	4	53/0
H. Being part of a community of Christians who are working together to share the good news of the gospel.	5	6	7	8	54/0
I. Opportunity to work with many people and be a part of their lives.	1	2	3	4	55/0
J. The well-being that comes from living the common life with like-minded confreres.	5	6	7	8	56/0
K. Other (SPECIFY) _____	1	2	3	4	57/0

36. There are many problems which face priests today. A. Would you indicate (in Column A) how important the following problems are *to you* on a day-to-day basis? B. Then, in Column B, indicate how important they seem to be to most of the priests you know. CIRCLE TWO CODES ON EACH LINE.

Importance of problem to:

	A. Myself					B. Most priests I know				
	A great problem to me personally	Somewhat of a problem	Very little problem	No problem at all		A great problem to them personally	Somewhat of a problem	Very little problem	No problem at all	
a) Lack of clear idea of what a priest is.	1	2	3	4	58/0	5	6	7	8	59/0
b) Theological change in the concept of the priesthood.	1	2	3	4	60/0	5	6	7	8	61/0
c) Absence of challenge in priestly work.	1	2	3	4	62/0	5	6	7	8	63/0
d) The way authority is exercised in the Church.	1	2	3	4	64/0	5	6	7	8	65/0
e) Relationships with superiors or pastor.	1	2	3	4	66/0	5	6	7	8	67/0

BEGIN DECK 07

36. Continued.

Importance of problem to:

PLEASE CIRCLE TWO CODES ON EACH LINE.

	A. Myself					B. Most priests I know				
	A great problem to me personally	Somewhat of a problem	Very little problem	No problem at all		A great problem to them personally	Somewhat of a problem	Very little problem	No problem at all	
f) Celibacy.	1	2	3	4	10/0	5	6	7	8	11/0
g) Relevance of the work that priests do.	1	2	3	4	12/0	5	6	7	8	13/0
h) Uncertainty about the future of the Church.	1	2	3	4	14/0	5	6	7	8	15/0
i) Unrealistic demands and expectations of lay people.	1	2	3	4	16/0	5	6	7	8	17/0
j) Loneliness of priestly life.	1	2	3	4	18/0	5	6	7	8	19/0
k) Too little work.	1	2	3	4	20/0	5	6	7	8	21/0
l) Too much work.	1	2	3	4	22/0	5	6	7	8	23/0
m) Conflict with parishioners or laity about issues of the day.	1	2	3	4	24/0	5	6	7	8	25/0
n) Lack of opportunity for personal fulfillment.	1	2	3	4	26/0	5	6	7	8	27/0
o) Difficulty of really reaching people today.	1	2	3	4	28/0	5	6	7	8	29/0
p) Other (SPECIFY) _____	1	2	3	4	30/0	5	6	7	8	31/0

37. Below are a number of statements which are frequently made today. Please indicate the extent of your agreement or disagreement with each of them by CIRCLING ONE CODE ON EACH LINE.

	Agree strongly	Agree somewhat	Uncertain	Disagree somewhat	Disagree strongly	
	1	2	3	4	5	
1) The important thing in the Church today is that people are really examining what has meaning for them.	1	2	3	4	5	32/0

Item		1	2	3	4	5	6	7	8	9	Code
2)	What is lacking today is that closeness among priests that used to be so evident.					5	6	7	8	9	33/0
3)	The basic values of the Church remain the same, but their expression is changing.	1	2	3	4	5					34/0
4)	The relationship between laity and priests was much better before Vatican II when everyone knew just how he was expected to act.					5	6	7	8	9	35/0
5)	With the new roles for everyone in the Church that have developed since Vatican II, the relationships between priests and laity are much better.	1	2	3	4	5					36/0
6)	Everything changes so quickly in the liturgy these days that I often have trouble deciding what rules to follow.					5	6	7	8	9	37/0
7)	The trouble with the Church today is that most people really don't believe in anything.	1	2	3	4	5					38/0
8)	There is more opportunity now than before for real friendship for priests.					5	6	7	8	9	39/0
9)	I often feel that many things the Church stood for are now disintegrating.	1	2	3	4	5					40/0
10)	The diversity of liturgy provides a real choice which I enjoy.					5	6	7	8	9	41/0
11)	I feel that everything that has value in human life will somehow be retained in heaven.	1	2	3	4	5					42/0
12)	The mystery of the Trinity is so profound and so central that I feel I should humbly accept it as given and not seek to plumb its depths.					5	6	7	8	9	43/0
13)	The experience of dialogue among persons who are open and trusting provides the human analogy for understanding the Trinity as a life of communication and communion.	1	2	3	4	5					44/0
14)	I think of God primarily as the Supreme Being, immutable, all-powerful, and the Creator of the universe.					5	6	7	8	9	45/0
15)	The Catholic Church is the one true Church established by Christ with St. Peter and his successors as its head.	1	2	3	4	5					46/0
16)	For me, God is found principally in my relationships with people.					5	6	7	8	9	47/0

37. Continued.
PLEASE CIRCLE ONE CODE ON EACH LINE.

	Agree strongly 1	Agree somewhat 2	Uncertain 3	Disagree somewhat 4	Disagree strongly 5	
17) God's Word comes to us through some of the great prophetic men of our times, such as Mahatma Gandhi and Martin Luther King.	5	6	7	8	9	48/0
18) I think of Jesus principally as the man who has given me my ideals for truly human living.	1	2	3	4	5	49/0
19) Today's Christian must emphasize more than ever openness to the Spirit rather than dependence on traditional ecclesiastical structures.	5	6	7	8	9	50/0
20) If God has meaning, I can recognize Him only in Jesus the Christ who makes God plausible and credible.	1	2	3	4	5	51/0
21) The important thing to stress when teaching about Jesus is that He is truly God, and, therefore, adoration should be directed toward Him.	5	6	7	8	9	52/0
22) I feel that diversity in individual men, among peoples, and in many cultures helps me appreciate the meaning of the Incarnation.	1	2	3	4	5	53/0
23) The principal meaning of Christ's resurrection for me is that it proved His Divinity.	5	6	7	8	9	54/0
24) I think of Jesus Christ as the God who humbled Himself by becoming man and dying for my sins.	1	2	3	4	5	55/0
25) To doubt one article of faith that is *de fide* is to question the whole of revealed truth.	5	6	7	8	9	56/0
26) I think of heaven as the state in which my soul will rest in blissful possession of the Beatific Vision.	1	2	3	4	5	57/0
27) I feel that the most important thing to recognize about the sacraments is that they are channels for receiving grace.	5	6	7	8	9	58/0
28) I think of the Mass as a sacramental event which anticipates heaven as the joyous union of humanity: risen, redeemed, and glorified in Christ.	1	2	3	4	5	59/0

	1	2	3	4	5	
29) I think that priests who feel called to do so ought to be witnessing to Christ on the picket line or speaking out on controversial issues.	1	2	3	4	5	60/0
30) A Christian should look first to the salvation of his soul; then he should be concerned about helping others.	5	6	7	8	9	61/0
31) When I experience moments of deep communication and union with other persons, these sometimes strike me as a taste of what heaven will be like.	1	2	3	4	5	62/0
32) The contemplative and mystical life is absolutely essential for Christianity.	5	6	7	8	9	63/0
33) People can be good Christians without spending much time in solitary reflection and prayer.	1	2	3	4	5	64/0
34) In a secular age like our own, the Church must abandon much of its past emphasis on the sacred.	5	6	7	8	9	65/0
35) The Church should be a place of refuge and of quiet reflection away from the world.	1	2	3	4	5	66/0
36) The primary task of the Church is to encourage its members to live the Christian life rather than to try to reform the world.	5	6	7	8	9	67/0
37) For the most part, the Church has been inadequate in facing up to the civil rights issues.	1	2	3	4	5	68/0
38) Faith means essentially belief in the doctrines of the Catholic Church.	5	6	7	8	9	69/0
39) Faith is primarily an encounter with God in Christ Jesus, rather than an assent to a coherent set of defined truths.	1	2	3	4	5	70/0
40) The creative ferment in the Church today is bringing about a deepening of my Christian faith.	5	6	7	8	9	10/0
41) The problem with the Church after Vatican II is that many of the certainties we used to have have been taken away.	1	2	3	4	5	11/0

BEGIN DECK 08

37. Continued.
PLEASE CIRCLE ONE CODE ON EACH LINE.

	Agree strongly	Agree somewhat	Uncertain	Disagree somewhat	Disagree strongly	
42) The turmoil following Vatican II is resulting in a gradual weakening of my own religious beliefs.	5	6	7	8	9	12/0
43) There are times when a person has to put his personal conscience above the Church's teaching.	1	2	3	4	5	13/0
44) One's faith may be jeopardized by studying Protestant theologians.	5	6	7	8	9	14/0

38. Sometimes some rather sharp criticisms have been made of a local situation. Do you think any of the following describe the situation in your diocese? CIRCLE ONE CODE ON EACH LINE.

	Agree strongly	Agree somewhat	Uncertain	Disagree somewhat	Disagree strongly	
A. Religious priests usually get the best parishes and use the money to support their order.	1	2	3	4	5	15/0
B. Diocesan priests, especially pastors, live too extravagantly.	5	6	7	8	9	16/0
C. Religious orders are too aggressive in vocational recruitment in the diocese.	1	2	3	4	5	17/0
D. It is actually unjust that religious priests helping on weekends get a higher monthly stipend than the regular assistant's monthly salary.	5	6	7	8	9	18/0

39. The evangelical counsels of poverty and obedience still remain a challenge to priests. What is your opinion about the following statements? CIRCLE ONE CODE ON EACH LINE.

	Agree strongly	Agree somewhat	Uncertain	Disagree somewhat	Disagree strongly	
A. The essence of priestly poverty is to have an effective solidarity with the poor and under-privileged by a style of life similar to theirs.	1	2	3	4	5	19/0
B. The gift of one's time and talents for the service of neighbor is a better manifestation of priestly poverty than material privation.	5	6	7	8	9	20/0
C. Values that come from the corporate strength of the vow or promise of obedience can more than compensate for individual frustrations.	1	2	3	4	5	21/0

39. Continued.

PLEASE CIRCLE ONE CODE ON EACH LINE.

	Agree strongly	Agree somewhat	Uncertain	Disagree somewhat	Disagree strongly	
D. The promise or vow of obedience has kept me from fulfilling my priestly role as a leader of God's people.	5	6	7	8	9	22/0
E. When an individual judges that apostolic effectiveness demands it, he may disregard the directive of his superior or bishop.	1	2	3	4	5	23/0
F. *DIOCESAN PRIESTS ONLY*: As a diocesan priest, I do not see any particular value in my promise of obedience to the bishop.	5	6	7	8	9	24/0
G. With regard to the promise or vow of obedience, a person violates his human integrity by submitting his autonomy to the will of another.	1	2	3	4	5	25/0

40. *EVERYONE PLEASE ANSWER.*

A. In your diocese, who, in fact, has the authority or the most influence in making the following decisions? CIRCLE ONE CODE ON EACH LINE.

	Bishop	Chancery and/or diocesan depts.	Priests' senate	Deans or vicars	Elected board	Pastors	Individual priests in any assignment	
1) Authorize Mass in homes or apartments.	1	2	3	4	5	6	7	26/0
2) Determine where a priest is assigned.	1	2	3	4	5	6	7	27/0
3) Determine where a priest has his living quarters.	1	2	3	4	5	6	7	28/0
4) Authorize an expenditure of more than $500 from parish funds.	1	2	3	4	5	6	7	29/0
5) Appoint pastors.	1	2	3	4	5	6	7	30/0
6) Establish new parishes.	1	2	3	4	5	6	7	31/0
7) Authorize construction.	1	2	3	4	5	6	7	32/0
8) Retire pastors.	1	2	3	4	5	6	6	33/0

B. Who do you think *ought* to have the authority to make these decisions? CIRCLE ONE CODE ON EACH LINE.

	Bishop	Chancery and/or diocesan depts.	Priests' senate	Deans or vicars	Elected board	Pastors	Individual priests in any assignment	
1) Authorize Mass in homes or apartments.	1	2	3	4	5	6	7	34/0
2) Determine where a priest is assigned.	1	2	3	4	5	6	7	35/0
3) Determine where a priest has his living quarters.	1	2	3	4	5	6	7	36/0
4) Authorize an expenditure of more than $500 from parish funds.	1	2	3	4	5	6	7	37/0
5) Appoint pastors.	1	2	3	4	5	6	7	38/0
6) Establish new parishes.	1	2	3	4	5	6	7	39/0
7) Authorize construction.	1	2	3	4	5	6	7	40/0
8) Retire pastors.	1	2	3	4	5	6	7	41/0

41. Have you ever done any of the following on your own authority? CIRCLE ONE CODE ON EACH LINE.

	Yes	No	
1) Said Mass in a home or apartment.	1	2	42/0
2) Notably modified the rubrics to fit the occasion.	3	4	43/0
3) Said Mass without the proper vestments.	5	6	44/0
4) Given Communion to non-Catholics.	7	8	45/0
5) Given sacraments to those who are divorced and remarried.	1	2	46/0

42. Do you think you *ought* to have the authority to do these things? CIRCLE ONE CODE ON EACH LINE.

	Yes	No	
1) Say Mass in a home or apartment.	3	4	47/0
2) Notably modify the rubrics to fit the occasion.	5	6	48/0
3) Say Mass without the proper vestments.	7	8	49/0
4) Give Communion to non-Catholics.	1	2	50/0
5) Give sacraments to those who are divorced and remarried.	3	4	51/0

43. A. In general, how much influence do you think the following groups *in fact* have in determining policies and actions in your diocese? IF THERE IS NO SUCH PERSON OR GROUP IN YOUR DIOCESE, CIRCLE "DO NOT HAVE" CODE. CIRCLE ONE CODE ON EACH LINE.

	Do not have	A very great deal	A great deal	Some	A little	None	
1) The ordinary.	1	2	3	4	5	6	52/0
2) Auxiliary bishops.	1	2	3	4	5	6	53/0
3) Chancery officials and heads of diocesan departments.	1	2	3	4	5	6	54/0
4) Deans or vicars.	1	2	3	4	5	6	55/0
5) Priests' senate.	1	2	3	4	5	6	56/0
6) Pastors.	1	2	3	4	5	6	57/0
7) Other priests.	1	2	3	4	5	6	58/0
8) Laity.	1	2	3	4	5	6	59/0

B. How much influence do you think the following groups *should* have in determining policies and actions in your diocese? CIRCLE ONE CODE ON EACH LINE.

	Do not have	A very great deal	A great deal	Some	A little	None	
1) The ordinary.	1	2	3	4	5	6	60/0
2) Auxiliary bishops.	1	2	3	4	5	6	61/0
3) Chancery officials and heads of diocesan departments.	1	2	3	4	5	6	62/0
4) Deans or vicars.	1	2	3	4	5	6	63/0
5) Priests' senate.	1	2	3	4	5	6	64/0
6) Pastors.	1	2	3	4	5	6	65/0
7) Other priests.	1	2	3	4	5	6	66/0
8) Laity.	1	2	3	4	5	6	67/0

BEGIN DECK 09

DIOCESAN PRIESTS NOW SKIP TO Q. 46. RELIGIOUS PRIESTS ONLY.

44. A. In your province, abbey, or institute, who has the authority or the most influence in making the following decisions? CIRCLE ONE CODE ON EACH LINE.

DECK 09

RELIGIOUS PRIESTS ONLY.

44. Continued.

	General chapter	Major superior	Local superior	House council (elected)	House chapter or meeting of whole community	Individual alone	
Decisions regarding:							
1) Place of residence.	1	2	3	4	5	6	10/0
2) Choice of ministry.	1	2	3	4	5	6	11/0
3) Use of money.	1	2	3	4	5	6	12/0
4) Daily meditation.	1	2	3	4	5	6	13/0
5) Celebration of, or attendance at, Mass.	1	2	3	4	5	6	14/0
6) Annual retreat.	1	2	3	4	5	6	15/0

B. In your province, abbey, or institute, who do you think *ought* to have the authority to make these decisions? CIRCLE ONE CODE ON EACH LINE.

	General chapter	Major superior	Local superior	House council (elected)	House chapter or meeting of whole community	Individual alone	
Decisions regarding:							
1) Place of residence.	1	2	3	4	5	6	16/0
2) Choice of ministry.	1	2	3	4	5	6	17/0
3) Use of money.	1	2	3	4	5	6	18/0
4) Daily meditation.	1	2	3	4	5	6	19/0
5) Celebration of, or attendance at, Mass.	1	2	3	4	5	6	20/0
6) Annual retreat.	1	2	3	4	5	6	21/0

RELIGIOUS PRIESTS ONLY.

45. A. In general, how much do you think the following individuals or groups have in determining policies and actions in your province, abbey, or institute? IF THERE IS NO SUCH PERSON OR GROUP IN YOUR PROVINCE, ABBEY, OR INSTITUTE, CIRCLE "DO NOT HAVE" CODE. CIRCLE ONE CODE ON EACH LINE.

	A very great deal	A great deal	Some	A little	None	Do not have	
1) General chapter.	1	2	3	4	5	6	22/0
2) Major superior.	1	2	3	4	5	6	23/0

	A very great deal	A great deal	Some	A little	None	Do not have	
3) Assistants to major superior.	1	2	3	4	5	6	24/0
4) Local superior.	1	2	3	4	5	6	25/0
5) House council or chapter.	1	2	3	4	5	6	26/0
6) Individual priests.	1	2	3	4	5	6	27/0

B. In general, how much influence do you think the following groups *should have* in determining policies and actions in your province, abbey, or institute? IF THERE IS NO SUCH PERSON OR GROUP IN YOUR PROVINCE, ABBEY, OR INSTITUTE, CIRCLE "DO NOT HAVE" CODE. CIRCLE ONE CODE ON EACH LINE.

	A very great deal	A great deal	Some	A little	None	Do not have	
1) General chapter.	1	2	3	4	5	6	28/0
2) Major superior.	1	2	3	4	5	6	29/0
3) Assistants to the major superior.	1	2	3	4	5	6	30/0
4) Local superior.	1	2	3	4	5	6	31/0
5) House council or chapter.	1	2	3	4	5	6	32/0
6) Individual priests.	1	2	3	4	5	6	33/0

EVERYONE PLEASE ANSWER.

46. What kinds of relationships do you have with the Protestant clergy and Jewish rabbis? That is—

A. How often did you take part in ecumenical or interfaith gatherings or liturgies in the past year? CIRCLE ONE CODE.

About once a week.	1 34/0
About once a month.	2
Several times during the year.	3
Once during the year.	4
Never.	5

B. In the past year how much contact on a social level did you have with Protestant clergy and Jewish rabbis in your house, in theirs, or going out together? CIRCLE ONE CODE IN EACH COLUMN.

	Clergy	Rabbis
About once a week.	1 35/0	1 36/0
About once a month.	2	2
Several times during the year.	3	3
Once during the year.	4	4
Never.	5	5

DECK 09

C. How often did you work together with Protestant clergy and/or Jewish rabbis in the last year? CIRCLE ONE CODE IN EACH COLUMN.

About once a week.............	1	37/0	1	38/0
About once a month...........	2		2
Several times during the year........	3		3
Once during the year........	4		4
Never...........	5		5

D. How do you now see yourself in relation to the movement toward Christian unity? CIRCLE ONE CODE.

I am strongly committed to its goals........	1	39/0
I am sympathetic with its aims............	2	
I am indifferent toward the movement...........	3	
I don't see much point in the movement............	4	
I am strongly opposed to the type of unity it implies....	5	

47. The phrase *ecclesia semper reformanda* was much used during the Second Vatican Council. What do you think of the effects of the following possible changes in the Church? CIRCLE ONE CODE AFTER EACH STATEMENT.

	Would help very much	Would help somewhat	Would not help but would not hurt either	Would hurt somewhat	Would hurt very much	
A. Associate pastors choosing to live where they wish.	1	2	3	4	5	40/0
B. All priests living in community when this is possible.	5	6	7	8	9	41/0
C. A parish lay advisory board having some say in the transfer and selection of priests.	1	2	3	4	5	42/0
D. Wider approval of household ministries, "small group parishes within a parish," and floating parishes.	5	6	7	8	9	43/0
E. Elimination of Catholic school systems.	1	2	3	4	5	44/0
F. Some priests holding secular jobs during the week.	5	6	7	8	9	45/0
G. A court of appeals for all members of the Church distinct from the hierarchy guaranteeing them due process of law.	1	2	3	4	5	46/0

H. Some married priests working in a variety of ministries.   5   6   7   8   9   47/0

I. Election of the Pope by the Synod of Bishops.   1   2   3   4   5   48/0

J. Introduction of the married diaconate whenever and however the local church chooses.   5   6   7   8   9   49/0

K. Election of bishops by the priests of the diocese.   1   2   3   4   5   50/0

L. Election of bishops by the priests, religious, and laity of the diocese.   5   6   7   8   9   51/0

48. There has been much discussion in recent years about questions of sexual morality regarding the individual and married couples. Within the Christian tradition moral theologians have undertaken new investigations in these areas. What is your *personal* opinion about the following statements? PLEASE DO NOT GIVE THE OPINIONS OF MORAL THEOLOGIANS, BUT WHAT YOU, YOURSELF, THINK.

A. Thinking about people in general, what is your opinion about masturbation? CIRCLE THE CODE OF THE *ONE* STATEMENT YOU AGREE WITH MOST.

  1) Adolescent masturbation is a normal developmental phase in a person's maturing sexuality and among adults occasional masturbation is usually the result of stress or conflict, hence in most cases it is not sinful. 1   52/0

  2) For both adolescents and adults, in most cases deliberate masturbation is sinful but no more than venially 2

  3) For both adolescents and adults, in most cases deliberate masturbation is a mortal sin. 3

  4) Other (SPECIFY)   4

B. What is your opinion about premarital sexual intercourse in the case of *mature* couples? CIRCLE ONE CODE.

  1) It is morally acceptable for couples who share affection. . 1

  2) It is morally acceptable for couples who are in love. 2

  3) It is morally acceptable for couples who are engaged. . . . 3

  4) It is never morally acceptable: couples should wait until they are married. 4   53/0

  5) Other (SPECIFY). 5

C. The Church's teaching on direct abortion remains clear. Still, within society at large in the United States, there is great pressure for more permissive abortion laws. What is your opinion in this matter? CIRCLE ONE CODE. [NOTE: Direct abortion in this context means the *deliberate* termination of a pregnancy.]

  1) There is no need of theological development in the direction of change in the Church's teaching, since direct abortion is always wrong. 1

  2) The Church has to allow open investigation of the issue, not only on moral, but also on medical and social grounds. . . 2

  3) In certain well-defined circumstances, especially when the mother's life is endangered, direct abortion can be morally permissible. 3   54/0

  4) Other (SPECIFY). 4

49. Indicate which of the following statements comes closest to your personal convictions about *artificial* contraception. First, please indicate your thinking in the period a few months *prior* to the issuance of Pope Paul's encyclical *Humanae Vitae*, and then your thinking for the current period after promulgation.

[NOTE: Artificial contraception is understood in this and the following question as referring to all methods of contraception except abortion, complete abstinence, and the use of "rhythm." Moreover, it is presumed that the discussion here concerns the use of contraception by married couples and that the several statements refer to the "objective" morality of contraception, not the "subjective" state of a person's soul.]

	CIRCLE ONE CODE IN EACH COLUMN	
	Before *Humanae Vitae*	After *Humanae Vitae*
A. All artificial contraception is morally wrong because it is clearly forbidden by the natural law and by the Church's teaching..............	1 55/0	1 56/0
B. It is not certain that all artificial contraception is morally wrong; still, the faithful are bound to follow the guidance of the Church and avoid all methods of artificial contraception....	2	2
C. It is not certain that all artificial contraception is morally wrong; therefore, the faithful are morally justified in using *at least some methods* of artificial contraception when they have adequate reasons for avoiding more children.............	3	3
D. There is no doubt that the responsible use of at least *some* methods of artificial contraception is morally acceptable, while the use of other methods may be morally wrong..........	4	4
E. Judgment concerning the morality of artificial contraception should be left to the responsibly formed consciences of the individuals involved...........	5	5
F. Given adequate reasons for avoiding children, all methods of artificial contraception are morally acceptable.........	6	6
G. Other (SPECIFY)	7	7

50. Since a priest's own personal convictions concerning a moral question and the action he would demand of others may differ, would you please indicate which one of the courses of action outlined below would be closest to your procedure in the confessional? CIRCLE ONE CODE FOR THE PROCEDURE USED BEFORE AND ONE FOR AFTER *HUMANAE VITAE*.

[NOTE: The point of this question is the moral stance, not the medical or psychological difficulties, which may be involved in the use of one or another type of contraceptive. Therefore, let it be presumed that medical and psychological considerations are taken into account in each of the courses of action outlined below.]

	CIRCLE ONE CODE IN EACH COLUMN	
	Before *Humanae Vitae*	After *Humanae Vitae*
A. Discourage the use of artificial contraception under pain of denial of absolution to a penitent who refused even to try to avoid the use of contraceptives.	1 57/0	1 58/0
B. Discourage the use of artificial contraception, but not deny absolution to a penitent who was convinced of his moral justification in using contraceptives.	2	2
C. Neither discourage nor encourage the use of artificial contraception, but accept the moral judgment of the responsibly formed conscience of the penitent who chooses to use contraceptives.	3	3
D. Encourage the penitent who has adequate reasons in a responsible use of artificial contraception.	4	4
E. Other (SPECIFY)	5	5

51. There is some discussion within the Catholic Church as to the possibility of true divorce with freedom to remarry. Please indicate which one of the statements below comes closest to *your own* personal conviction (however formed) with regard to this question. CIRCLE ONE CODE.

[NOTE: The question concerns the possibility of true divorce, not the problem of determining if a marriage is truly *ratum et consummatum*. Therefore, let it be presumed that all requisites exist for a truly valid and consummated sacramental marriage.]

A. Divorce with freedom to remarry in the case of a marriage *ratum et consummatum* is forbidden by divine law and can never be permitted by the Church. 1   59/0

B.   Divorce with the freedom to remarry in the case of *ratum et consummatum* marriages should continue to be forbidden by the Church *without exception*, but this is not clearly a matter of divine law.......... 2

C.   In some few extreme cases, divorce with freedom to remarry can and should be granted even though the marriage is *ratum et consummatum*. 3

D.   Divorce with freedom to remarry should be granted even in *ratum et consummatum* marriages if a divorce would alleviate a situation obviously damaging to the couple and their children (if any), and this even if such cases were to be fairly numerous 4

E.   Other (SPECIFY) 5

BEGIN DECK 10

52. Please indicate which one of the following statements most closely represents your view of the use of Papal teaching authority involved in the issuance of the encyclical *Humanae Vitae*. CIRCLE ONE CODE.

A.   The issuance of *Humanae Vitae* was a competent and appropriate use of Papal teaching authority. 1

B.   In issuing *Humanae Vitae* the Pope acted within his authority to teach, but the encyclical was issued at an inappropriate time. 2

C.   The Pope is competent to teach concrete directives of the natural law as he did in *Humanae Vitae*, but *Humanae Vitae* was a misuse of that authority because he failed to act with sufficient collegiality. 3

D.   The Pope is incompetent to use his teaching authority in this way because he cannot *impose* concrete universal directives of the natural law.......... 4

E.   Other (SPECIFY) 5

10/0

53. How would you rate your own attitudes toward sex as compared to those of most priests in your order or the diocese in which you work? CIRCLE ONE CODE.

Very liberal.......... 1   11/0
Somewhat liberal.......... 2
Moderate.......... 3
Somewhat conservative.......... 4
Very conservative.......... 5

54. A. Other than during leisure time or liturgical functions, how do you think a priest should dress today? CIRCLE ONE CODE UNDER A.

B. Which of the statements below best describes how you usually dress outside of leisure time or liturgical functions. CIRCLE ONE CODE UNDER B.

	A. Way priest should dress today (other than during leisure time or liturgical functions)	B. My usual dress today (other than during leisure time or liturgical functions)
1) A priest should almost always wear the Roman collar and black suit	1 12/0	1 13/0
2) He need not wear the Roman collar but he should wear a black suit	2	2
3) He should sometimes wear the Roman collar and black suit and sometimes ordinary clothes	3	3
4) What a priest wears should not be much different from that of the people with whom he is working, whatever occupation or social standing they may have	4	4
5) Other (SPECIFY)	5	5

55. *FOR RELIGIOUS PRIESTS ONLY; DIOCESAN PRIESTS SKIP TO QUESTION 57, PAGE 32.*
Choose *one* of the following statements which best describes your opinion. CIRCLE ONE CODE.

1) I regard my membership in this religious order or congregation as important as my ordination to the priesthood 6   14/0
2) The priesthood was my primary reason for entering religious life 7
3) I wanted to be a religious primarily; the priesthood was a secondary motive 8

FOR RELIGIOUS PRIESTS ONLY:

56. Below are some statements about the nature and relevance of religious life. For each, circle the code under the category which best fits your *present* thinking.

	Agree strongly	Agree somewhat	Uncertain	Disagree somewhat	Disagree strongly	
	1	2	3	4	5	
1) Religious life is a purely human phenomenon subject to radical reconsideration even to the point of allowing its disappearance.	1	2	3	4	5	15/0
2) Religious life is a permanent element in the Church.	5	6	7	8	9	16/0
3) Religious life is so tied to institutions that its prophetic role is almost snuffed out.	1	2	3	4	5	17/0
4) For religious life to be relevant today, there should be a re-emphasis of its contemplative dimension and a return to stricter discipline.	5	6	7	8	9	18/0
5) The mode of religious life most apt for our day is that of the secular institute, not the religious order or congregation.	1	2	3	4	5	19/0
6) Religious life is basically the same, so that the various orders with the same apostolates should be merged and united.	5	6	7	8	9	20/0
7) Religious life has been a major factor of my happiness and success in the priesthood.	1	2	3	4	5	21/0
8) For religious life to be relevant today it must adapt all of its structures to the secularized world.	5	6	7	8	9	22/0
9) In my experience as a religious priest, there is seldom, if ever, any real conflict between being a member of an order and being an effective priest.	1	2	3	4	5	23/0
10) A religious community demands uniformity in horarium, liturgical worship, residence, and dress.	5	6	7	8	9	24/0
11) Each member of the community should be allowed to involve himself in various movements and demonstrations without hindrance from his community.	1	2	3	4	5	25/0
12) In its efforts toward renewal, our community or order has not recaptured the original spirit of our Founder.	5	6	7	8	9	26/0

Item	Statement	Scale					Code
13)	Updating has created disorder and confusion which is harmful to our community.	1	2	3	4	5	27/0
14)	Our pace of change has lacked a sense of realism and urgency. Adaptation has been only marginal.	5	6	7	8	9	28/0
15)	Each local community should have the right to choose its own members.	1	2	3	4	5	29/0
16)	At the time of my perpetual vows, I was well aware of the implications of my vow of chastity.	5	6	7	8	9	30/0
17)	The vow of chastity is so essential to religious life that religious life would not survive without it.	1	2	3	4	5	31/0
18)	Optional celibacy for diocesan priests would seriously hamper vocations to the religious life.	5	6	7	8	9	32/0
19)	The traditional way of presenting the vow of chastity in religious formation has often allowed for the development of impersonalism and false spirituality.	1	2	3	4	5	33/0
20)	Poverty means dependence on the community for all of one's material needs.	5	6	7	8	9	34/0
21)	Religious poverty is a charade; generally we live more comfortably and more securely than the persons with whom we are working.	1	2	3	4	5	35/0
22)	One cannot profess poverty and run expensive schools that cater to the rich.	5	6	7	8	9	36/0
23)	Poverty shields religious from the realistic cares of everyday human living.	1	2	3	4	5	37/0
24)	Poverty makes a person irresponsible, immature, and childish.	5	6	7	8	9	38/0
25)	The spirit of poverty is meaningless without poverty in fact.	1	2	3	4	5	39/0
26)	The term "poverty" should be changed to "simplicity" and its interpretation brought into line with modern economic realities.	5	6	7	8	9	40/0
27)	The duty of the subject is to obey; it is the responsibility of the superior to discern God's will and declare it.	1	2	3	4	5	41/0

56. Continued.

	Agree strongly	Agree somewhat	Uncertain	Disagree somewhat	Disagree strongly	
28) The ideal decision-making process in a religious community is that of "dialogue obedience," i.e., the majority rules.	5	6	7	8	9	42/0
29) All major superiors should be elected by the entire religious membership.	1	2	3	4	5	43/0
30) There is no need for a local superior in a community of mature, religious men.	5	6	7	8	9	44/0

57. *EVERYONE PLEASE ANSWER.*

Thinking of all the people (including relatives) whom you consider really close friends—people you feel free to talk with about personal things—would you say you have many, a few, or no such friends? CIRCLE ONE CODE.

Many (ANSWER A & B)......	1	45/0
A few (ANSWER A & B)......	2	
None....................	3	

IF "MANY" OR "A FEW":

A. Who are these good friends? CIRCLE ALL CODES THAT APPLY IN COLUMN A.

B. Of these close friends, with whom do you associate most often? CIRCLE ALL CODES THAT APPLY IN COLUMN B.

	A. Close friends		B. Associate most often	
1) Members of my immediate family or other relatives.	1	46/0	1	57/0
2) Fellow priests with whom I was in the seminary.	2	47/0	2	58/0
3) Fellow priests from my religious order or congregation.	3	48/0	3	59/0
4) Fellow priests whom I met after leaving the seminary.	4	49/0	4	60/0
5) Laymen from the parish where I am now, or connected with my present work.	5	50/0	5	61/0
6) Laywomen from the parish where I am now, or connected with my present work.	6	51/0	6	62/0
7) Laymen from outside my present parish, or whom I met while involved in other work.	7	52/0	7	63/0
8) Laywomen from outside my present parish, or whom I met while involved in other work.	8	53/0	8	64/0
9) Women religious.	1	54/0	9	65/0
10) Ministers from a Protestant church.	2	55/0	2	66/0
11) Other (PLEASE DESCRIBE)	3	56/0	3	67/0

BEGIN DECK 11

58. Of your good friends, how many are priests? CIRCLE ONE CODE.

None	1	10/0
1–2	2	
3–5	3	
6–9	4	
10 or more	5	

59. How many priests live in the same residence with you?

Number of priests   11–13/999

60. How many of the priests with whom you live do you consider to be close friends? CIRCLE ONE CODE.

Don't live with any priests	1	14/0
None	2	
1–2	3	
3–5	4	
6–9	5	
10 or more	6	

61. How often do you take time off? Think of time off as a day or part of a day in which you do not have to be concerned with ordinary duties but spend your time however you wish. CIRCLE ONE CODE.

Never or almost never have a day off	1	15/0
One day or less a month	2	
Half a day or less a week	3	
One day almost every week	4	
Two days almost every week (e.g., an "overnight")	5	
Other (SPECIFY)	6	

DECK 11

62. When was your last vacation—that is, a week or longer? CIRCLE ONE CODE.

Within a year..................... 1   16/0
2 years ago....................... 2
3 years ago....................... 3
4 years ago....................... 4
Other (SPECIFY)   5

63. With whom did you spend your last vacation? CIRCLE AS MANY AS APPLY

With one or more fellow priests.... 1   17/0
With some member(s) of my family.. 2
With one or more lay friends....... 3
Alone............................ 4
Other (SPECIFY)   5

64. How would you rate your general health at present? CIRCLE ONE CODE.

Excellent......................... 1   18/0
Quite good........................ 2
Fair.............................. 3
Poor.............................. 4
Very bad.......................... 5

65. Individual priests evaluate celibacy for themselves in different ways. Please indicate how you feel about the following aspects of the unmarried state for yourself. CIRCLE ONE CODE ON EACH LINE.

Celibacy is.....

	Very much of an advantage	Somewhat of an advantage	Neither advantage nor disadvantage	Somewhat of a disadvantage	Very much of a disadvantage	
A. For doing my work better.	1	2	3	4	5	19/0
B. For my personal growth and development.	1	2	3	4	5	20/0
C. For the development of my love of God.	1	2	3	4	5	21/0
D. For relating more fully to other people.	1	2	3	4	5	22/0

66. If celibacy for priests became optional, do you think you would ever get married? CIRCLE ONE CODE.

Certainly yes	Probably yes	Uncertain	Probably no	Certainly no	
1	2	3	4	5	23/0

67. *RELIGIOUS PRIESTS ONLY*: CIRCLE ONE CODE. If celibacy became optional for diocesan priests, would you transfer to a diocese to get married?

1 2 3 4 5   24/0

68. Some people think that the present law of celibacy will be changed allowing priests to be married if they wish. Do you agree? CIRCLE ONE CODE.

Yes (ANSWER A)... 6   25/0
No........................ 7

A. *IF "YES"*: How long do you think it will take before the law is changed? CIRCLE ONE CODE.

Within:
5 years........... 1   26/0
10 years.......... 2
20 years.......... 3
50 years.......... 4

69. Where are you living now, i.e., have your private quarters? CIRCLE ONE CODE.

A. In a rectory, religious house, or suite of rooms near Catholic institution (ANSWER [1] OR [2], WHICHEVER APPLIES BETTER)... 5   27/0

B. With my parents or relatives in their home (GO TO Q. 73)......... 6

69. Continued.
  C. In my own private home or apartment which is not part of any church related complex (GO TO Q. 73) 7
  D. Other arrangements (SPECIFY) (ANSWER [1] OR [2], IF APPROPRIATE) 8

[1] In general, how would you describe your personal relationships with your pastor, assistant(s), fellow assistant(s), resident priest(s), and housekeeper/cook? CIRCLE ONE CODE ON EACH LINE.

	Excellent	Good	Fair	Poor	Very poor	Do not have	
a) Pastor	1	2	3	4	5	6	28/0
b) Assistant(s)	1	2	3	4	5	6	29/0
c) Fellow assistant(s)	1	2	3	4	5	6	30/0
d) Resident priest(s)	1	2	3	4	5	6	31/0
e) Housekeeper/cook	1	2	3	4	5	6	32/0

[2] If you live in a "non-parish" setting, e.g., in a religious house, how would you describe your personal relationships with the person in charge, other priest members of the community, brothers, student members of the community, and the lay help who live with you? CIRCLE ONE CODE ON EACH LINE.

	Excellent	Good	Fair	Poor	Very poor	Do not have	
a) Person in charge.	1	2	3	4	5	6	33/0
b) Priest members of the community.	1	2	3	4	5	6	34/0
c) Brothers.	1	2	3	4	5	6	35/0
d) Student members of the community.	1	2	3	4	5	6	36/0
e) Lay help.	1	2	3	4	5	6	37/0

70. Do you consider the place where you live to be your own home, for example, a place where you can be yourself, relax, or entertain if you wish? CIRCLE ONE CODE.   Yes...... 1   No 2   38/0

71. A. How often do you, or any of your close priest friends, go out with women socially—other than for necessary professional reasons? CIRCLE ONE CODE IN EACH COLUMN.

	Myself	My priest friends
	39/0	40/0
Several times a year..............	1	5
Several times a month..........	2	6
One or more times a week.......	3	7
Never.......................	4	8

B. When you or your friends do go out with women socially, is it usually with a group or as a couple? CIRCLE ONE CODE IN EACH COLUMN.

	Myself	My priest friends
	41/0	42/0
With a group.....................	1	4
As a couple......................	2	5
Do not go out with women socially.	3	6

C. How do you feel about these social relations with women? (EXPLAIN BRIEFLY.)

43/
44/
45/
46/

D. How do you think most of the priests you know feel about these social relations? (EXPLAIN BRIEFLY.)

47/
48/
49/
50/

72. You have probably heard many of the statements listed below. Please indicate the extent of your agreement or disagreement. CIRCLE THE CODE THAT COMES CLOSEST TO THE WAY YOU FEEL.

	Agree strongly	Agree somewhat	Uncertain	Disagree somewhat	Disagree strongly	
A. Usually, it is unwise for priests to have women as close friends.	1	2	3	4	5	51/0
B. Celibacy is essential in order to realize the full potential of the priesthood.	1	2	3	4	5	52/0
C. Celibacy should be a matter of personal choice for diocesan priests.	1	2	3	4	5	53/0
D. When a priest has a warm friendship with a woman, it usually helps him become more fully human.	1	2	3	4	5	54/0
E. Priestly companionship with God means an experiential union so close and so strong as to exclude companionship with another in marriage.	1	2	3	4	5	55/0
F. The present requirement of celibacy keeps many men from entering the priesthood who would actually make excellent priests.	1	2	3	4	5	56/0
G. A married clergy would better understand the problems of the laity.	1	2	3	4	5	57/0
H. Today's deeper understanding of the person is helping us to realize that celibacy is in fact harmful for some priests.	1	2	3	4	5	58/0
I. The celibate life allows more time for the priest to be available to the people.	1	2	3	4	5	59/0
J. There are quite a few women who like to chase after priests.	1	2	3	4	5	60/0
K. Marriage contributes to the fullness of human life and therefore can contribute to the fullness of priestly life.	1	2	3	4	5	61/0
L. The *primary* reason for celibacy is that it witnesses to the future life with God.	1	2	3	4	5	62/0
M. Temptations to impurity are the most serious temptations in the lives of most priests.	1	2	3	4	5	63/0

73. In a period of rapid change and self-study one must consider the reasons for his choices. Which of the following reasons come closest to the explanation of why you remain a priest today? PLEASE MARK TWO OF THE REASONS IN ORDER OF IMPORTANCE; PLACE "1" NEXT TO THE MOST IMPORTANT AND "2" NEXT TO THE SECOND MOST IMPORTANT REASON.

1) Happiness in priestly work.
2) To save my soul.
3) I am convinced this is my personal vocation.
4) Self-fulfillment.
5) To try to renew the structures of the Church.
6) To give witness to Christ in the modern world.
7) I feel comfortable in this way of life.
8) I consider myself too old to leave.
9) Loyalty to the community.

10) Fear of adjusting to secular life.   64–65 /
11) I'd like to leave, but would be afraid of going   66–67 /
    against God's will.
12) I would not like to hurt my parent(s) by leaving.
13) Other (PLEASE DESCRIBE)

_____

BEGIN DECK 12

74. A number of priests today are facing the decision of whether they should remain priests or leave the active ministry. Have any of your friends left the priesthood since the beginning of 1966? CIRCLE ONE CODE.

Yes (ANSWER A & B)......... 1   10/0
No (GO TO Q. 75)........... 2

IF "YES":

A. How many? _____ priest-friends have left

B. Did a friend's leaving cause you to re-think your status as a priest?   11–12/00
    CIRCLE ONE CODE.

Yes, a great deal.......... 6   13/0
Yes, somewhat.............. 7
No, not much............... 8
No, not at all............. 9

75. Which of the following statements most clearly reflects your feelings about your future in the priesthood?
CIRCLE ONE CODE.

I definitely will not leave (ANSWER Q. 76A)............. 1   14/0
I probably will not leave (ANSWER Q. 76A)............. 2
I am uncertain about my future (ANSWER Q. 76A & B).... 3
I will probably leave (ANSWER Q. 76A & B)............. 4
I have definitely decided to leave (ANSWER Q. 76A & B)... 5

76. There are many reasons given for leaving the priesthood.

A. Which of the following do you think applies to priests in general who leave, and which to your friends who have left? IN COLUMN A, PLEASE MARK TWO OF THE REASONS IN ORDER OF IMPORTANCE: PLACE "1" NEXT TO THE MOST IMPORTANT AND "2" NEXT TO THE SECOND MOST IMPORTANT REASON.

B. IF UNCERTAIN, PROBABLE, OR DEFINITE: Which two of the following do you think would apply to yourself? IN COLUMN B, PLEASE MARK TWO OF THE REASONS IN ORDER OF IMPORTANCE: PLACE "1" NEXT TO THE MOST IMPORTANT AND "2" NEXT TO THE SECOND MOST IMPORTANT REASON.

	A. Priests in general who leave	My friend(s) who left	B. Myself, if I were to leave
1) Bad relations with superiors	15–16/	19–20/	23–24/
2) Desire to marry	17–18/	21–22/	25–26/
3) Personal development and growth			
4) No longer believe it is one's vocation			
5) Attracted to other work			
6) Can no longer live within the structure of the Church as a priest			
7) Emotional problems make a change necessary			
8) Conflict with parishioners or laity			
9) No longer get the satisfaction there used to be from being a priest			
10) No longer agree with some of the ethical and moral teachings of the Church			
11) Talents are not being used sufficiently			
12) The work of a churchman seems irrelevant			
13) No longer agree with some of the theological teachings of the Church			
14) The Church is not facing the relevant questions of the day			
15) Other (SPECIFY)			

77. If you had your choice again, would you enter the priesthood? CIRCLE ONE CODE.   27/0

Definitely yes.............. 1   Probably not.............. 4

Probably yes................. 2   Definitely not................. 5

Uncertain.................. 3

78. During the normal (non-vacation) week, about how many times do you take a drink (beer, whiskey, or any other alcoholic drink)?
CIRCLE ONE CODE.   28/0

Less than once a week......... 1   Twice a day............ 5

Once a week............ 2   Three or more times a day...... 6

Three or four times a week...... 3   Do not drink....... 7

Once a day........ 4

79. Taking things all together, how would you say things are these days—would you say   Very happy............ 1   29/0
you're very happy, pretty happy, or not too happy? CIRCLE ONE CODE.   Pretty happy......... 2

Not too happy........ 3

80. Compared with your life today, how were things four or five years ago—were things   Happier.......... 1   30/0
happier for you then, not quite as happy, or what? CIRCLE ONE CODE.   Not quite as happy..... 2

About the same........ 3

Other (SPECIFY)......... 4

81. During the past few weeks, did you ever feel—   CIRCLE ONE CODE ON EACH LINE.

	Yes	No
A. Particularly excited or interested in something?	1	2	31/0
B. So restless that you couldn't sit long in a chair?	3	4	32/0
C. Proud because someone complimented you on something you had done?	5	6	33/0
D. Very lonely or remote from other people?	7	8	34/0
E. Pleased about having accomplished something?	1	2	35/0
F. Bored?	3	4	36/0
G. On top of the world?	5	6	37/0
H. Depressed or very unhappy?	7	8	38/0
I. That things were going your way?	1	2	39/0
J. Upset because someone criticized you?	3	4	40/0

82. Many issues are currently being discussed by American citizens. Some are listed below. How do you judge them from your experience of them?

A. One solution that has been proposed for dealing with the problem of poverty in America is the "guaranteed annual wage" whereby all families whose annual income falls below an established level (say, $4,000 for a family of four) will automatically receive through

82. Continued.

the government the amount necessary to reach the established level. Which of the following most nearly represents your opinion on a guaranteed annual income? CIRCLE ONE CODE.

a) It is a good way to make some progress in dealing with the problem of poverty. 1   41/0

b) It is not a good idea, for it would encourage people who would otherwise work for a living to do less work or none at all, and simply rely on other people's money to support them. 2

c) It is simply a surface reform, since poverty stems from the nature of the capitalistic system itself. The only way to wipe out poverty really is to get rid of capitalism and replace it with some other economic system. 3

B. If you had to choose only one, which of the following would you say *should* have the greatest

    The students. 4   42/0

power in determining the major policies of colleges and universities? CIRCLE ONE CODE.

    The faculty. 5

    The administration. 6

C. Which of the following most nearly describes your opinion of riots by urban Negroes? CIRCLE ONE CODE.

a) They are understandable in the light of very slow progress of the movement to provide Negro Americans with equality. . 7   43/0

b) They constitute a revolutionary response that is right given the current condition of Negroes in American society. 8

c) They are wrong. Negroes who riot are going too far. Law and order must be preserved. 9

D. When you think of Vietnam today, how do you think of the following factors in the war? MARK EACH FACTOR WITH NUMBERS 1 TO 5 ACCORDING TO THE EXTENT OF YOUR CONCERN. CIRCLE 5's BESIDE THOSE THAT ARE MOST IMPORTANT TO YOU, 4's NEXT TO THOSE THAT ARE NEXT MOST IMPORTANT, ETC.

	Least important				Most important	
a) The destruction of life and property due to use of weapons.	1	2	3	4	5	44/0
b) The Communist danger.	1	2	3	4	5	45/0
c) The rights of the native population to an opportunity for self-development.	1	2	3	4	5	46/0
d) The use of our military forces in an unnecessary war.	1	2	3	4	5	47/0
e) The deflection of American tax money to armament rather than health, education, and welfare at home.	1	2	3	4	5	48/0
f) The urgency of fighting the war to a successful finish as soon as possible.	1	2	3	4	5	49/0
g) The value of a settlement in conference that will be respected by all as a substitute for victory in the field.	1	2	3	4	5	50/0

83. In what year were you born—e.g.,   1   9   2   6 | 51–52/70
84. And what year were you ordained? | 53–54/70
85. Are you a United States citizen? CIRCLE ONE CODE. | 55/0
     Yes, U.S. born (ANSWER A)............ 1
     Yes, naturalized (ANSWER B & C)........ 2
     No, but I expect to stay in the United States (ANSWER B & C)........ 3
     No, and I do not expect to stay in the United States (ANSWER B & C)............ 4

   A. *IF U.S. BORN:* Where were you born?   State: | 56–57/00
      City:
   IF BORN OUTSIDE U.S.:
   B. Where were you born?   Country: | 58–59/99
      City:
   C. How old were you when you came to the U.S.? ___ years old | 60/0

86. Are you a born Catholic? CIRCLE ONE CODE.
     Yes................ 1
     No (ANSWER A).... 2

   A. *IF "NO":* How old were you when you became a Catholic? ___ years old | 61–62/99

87. For the most part, by whom were you brought up—up to the age of 14? CIRCLE ONE CODE. | 63/0
     Both parents........ 1   Foster parents........ 5
     Mother alone........ 2   Grandparents........ 6
     Father alone........ 3   Other relatives........ 7
     Stepparent(s)........ 4   Other arrangement (SPECIFY)........ 8

ANSWER QUESTIONS 88–96 FOR YOUR NATURAL PARENTS, STEPPARENT(S), OR PARENT SUBSTITUTES—OR CODE "DOES NOT APPLY"—AS IS MOST APPROPRIATE FOR YOUR SITUATION WHEN GROWING UP. | 64/R

88. Are both your mother and father still living? CIRCLE ONE CODE. | 65/0
     Yes, both living................ 1   Father only, living (ANSWER B)........ 3
     Mother only, living (ANSWER A)........ 2   No, neither living (ANSWER A & B)........ 4

   A. How old were you when your father died? ___ years old | 66–67/99
   B. How old were you when your mother died? ___ years old | 68–69/99

89. Were your parents ever divorced or separated from each other? CIRCLE ONE CODE. IF PARENT HAD DIED, CIRCLE "DOES NOT APPLY."

    No 1   Yes, divorced (ANSWER A) 3   70/0

    Yes, separated but not divorced (ANSWER A) . 2   Does not apply 4

A. IF "YES": How old were you when your parents first lived separately? CIRCLE ONE CODE.

    5 years or younger 1   16–20 years old 4   71/0

    6–10 years old 2   21 or older 5

    11–15 years old 3

BEGIN DECK 13

90. A. What was the usual occupation of the head of your household when you were growing up? CIRCLE CODE IF "DON'T KNOW" OR IF HOUSEHOLD HEAD WAS A WOMAN.

    Main Occupation:

    Don't know 1   10–14/0

    If head of household was a woman, also circle code here   2   15/R

B. What is/was this person's *most recent* occupation?

    Occupation: 16–20/0

91. For the most part, was your mother employed when you were growing up? CIRCLE ONE CODE.

    Yes, full time 1   No, not employed 3   21/0

    Yes, part time 2   Does not apply 4

92. Every family is not only a whole unit, but a number of twosomes. For each of the following twosomes in the family in which you grew up, circle the category which best describes the relationship. CIRCLE ONE CODE IN EACH ROW. IF NO SUCH TWOSOME, CIRCLE "DOES NOT APPLY."

	Very tense and strained	Somewhat tense and strained	Neutral	Somewhat close and intimate	Very close and intimate	Does not apply	
A. Mother and father.	1	2	3	4	5	6	22/0
B. Mother and me.	1	2	3	4	5	6	23/0
C. Father and me.	1	2	3	4	5	6	24/0

93. With regard to drinking habits, in which category would you place your father and mother when you were growing up? CIRCLE ONE CODE IN EACH COLUMN. IF PARENT WAS NOT PRESENT WHEN YOU WERE GROWING UP, CIRCLE "DOES NOT APPLY."

	Father 25/0	Mother 26/0
Total abstainer	1	1
Light drinker	2	2
Moderate drinker	3	3
Heavy drinker	4	4
Alcoholic	5	5
Does not apply	6	6

94. What was the highest grade in school completed by your father and your mother? CIRCLE ONE CODE IN EACH COLUMN.

	Father 27–28/00	Mother 29–30/00
No schooling	01	01
8th grade or less	02	02
Some high school	03	03
High school graduate	04	04
Some college	05	05
College degree	06	06
Master's degree or equivalent	07	07
Doctor's degree or equivalent	08	08
Don't know	09	09

95. What was your father's and your mother's religion when you were growing up? CIRCLE ONE CODE IN EACH COLUMN.

	Father 31/0	Mother 32/0
Catholic (born)	1	1
Catholic (convert)	2	2
Protestant	3	3
Other (DESCRIBE)	4	4

96. How devout would you say your father and mother were when you were growing up? CIRCLE ONE CODE IN EACH COLUMN. IF PARENT NOT PRESENT WHEN GROWING UP, CIRCLE "DOES NOT APPLY."

	Father 33/0	Mother 34/0
Very devout	1	1
Fairly devout	2	2
Indifferent to religion	3	3
Agnostic	4	4
Anti-religion	5	5
Does not apply	6	6

97. Were your natural father and natural mother born in the United States? CIRCLE ONE CODE IN EACH COLUMN.

	Father 35/0	Mother 36/0
Yes	1	1
No	2	2
Don't know	3	3

98. A. What is your national background on your natural father's side?

B. What is your national background on your natural mother's side?

CIRCLE ONE CODE IN EACH COLUMN UNDER A & B. IF YOU HAVE MIXED ANCESTRY ON EITHER SIDE, INDICATE THE BACKGROUND YOU CONSIDER MOST DOMINANT.

99. When you were growing up, did your family belong to a "national" parish, i.e., one that was noticeably influenced by a particular nationality group? If a parish had one or more Masses at which the scriptural readings and the sermon were in a foreign language, or in other ways had a distinct "national" flavor, e.g., mostly Irish clergy and parishioners, consider it a national parish. (The use of the term "national" parish for the purposes of this question goes beyond the well-known distinction between territorial and national parishes in the strict sense.) CIRCLE ONE CODE.

Yes (ANSWER A) . . . . 1　37/0

No 2

	Q. 98		Q. 99 A. What nationality group attended the parish?
	A. Father	B. Mother	
	38–39/00	40–41/00	42–43/00
English, Scotch, Welsh, English Canadian, Australian, New Zealand	01	01	01
African countries	02	02	02
Irish	03	03	03
German	04	04	04
Scandinavian	05	05	05
Italian	06	06	06
French, French Canadian, Belgian	07	07	07
Polish	08	08	08
Lithuanian	09	09	09
Russian or other Eastern European	10	10	10
Spanish, Portuguese, Latin American, including Puerto Rican	11	11	11
Other (SPECIFY)	12	12	12
Don't know	13	13	13

100. When you were growing up, did your family identify with any nationality group? CIRCLE ONE CODE.

    Yes, strongly (ANSWER A)............ 1   44/0

    Yes, somewhat (ANSWER A)............ 2

    No, hardly at all............ 3

  A. IF "YES": With which nationality group did they identify themselves?

                           45–46/00

    PLEASE LIST THE CODE NUMBER USED IN Q. 99A WHICH INDICATES NATIONALITY GROUP:

101. Do *you* now identify with any particular nationality group? CIRCLE ONE CODE.

    Yes, strongly (ANSWER A)............ 1   47/0

    Yes, somewhat (ANSWER A)............ 2

    No, hardly at all............ 3

  A. IF "YES": With which nationality group do you identify?

                           48–49/00

    PLEASE LIST THE CODE NUMBER USED IN Q. 99A WHICH INDICATES NATIONALITY GROUP:

102. How many brothers and sisters (do/did) you have? PLEASE GIVE THE NUMBER OF EACH, OR CIRCLE THE CODE FOR "NONE":

Brothers	50–51/99
Sisters	52–53/99
0 None	

103. *UNLESS "0" CIRCLED IN QUESTION 102:* What was the rank order of your birth—were you firstborn, second born, or what?

	Rank:	born	54–55/00

104. *ANSWER IF ANY BROTHERS AND/OR SISTERS:* How many of your brothers and sisters ever entered the priesthood, brotherhood, or sisterhood? PLEASE GIVE THE NUMBER OF EACH, OR CIRCLE THE CODE FOR "NONE."

were professed sisters	56–57/99
were professed brothers	58–59/99
were ordained priests	60–61/99
were in training but left before profession or ordination	62–63/99
0 None	

—— (ANSWER A)——

A. How many of your brothers and sisters ever left the priesthood, brotherhood, or sisterhood? PLEASE GIVE THE NUMBER OF EACH, OR CIRCLE THE CODE FOR "NONE."

have left the priesthood	64–65/99
have left the sisterhood	66–67/99
have left the brotherhood	68–69/99
0 None	

105. What is your race? CIRCLE ONE CODE.

White	1	Oriental	3 70/0
Negro	2	Other	4

106. A. What was the size of the town or city in which you grew up (or think of most as home)?
    B. And what is the size of the town or city in which you now work? CIRCLE ONE CODE IN EACH COLUMN.

	A. Where I grew up 71–72/00	B. Where I now work 73–74/00
Farm or open country	01	01
Non-suburban town of:		
Less than 10,000	02	02
10,000 to 49,999	03	03

Suburb in a metropolitan area with an *area* population of:

More than 2 million. ... 04
500,000 to 2 million. ... 05
100,000 to 499,999 ... 06
60,000 to 99,999 ... 07

Central city in a metropolitan area with an *area* population of:

More than 2 million. ... 08
500,000 to 2 million. ... 09
100,000 to 499,999 ... 10
50,000 to 99,999 ... 11

BEGIN DECK 14

10–11/00

107. In what region of the country did you live most of the time when you were growing up? CIRCLE ONE CODE.

New England (Maine, New Hampshire, Massachusetts, Connecticut, Rhode Island, Vermont). ... 01
Middle Atlantic (New York, New Jersey, Pennsylvania). ... 02
East North Central (Ohio, Indiana, Illinois, Michigan, Wisconsin). ... 03
West North Central (Minnesota, Iowa, Missouri, N. Dakota, S. Dakota, Nebraska, Kansas). ... 04
Mountain (Montana, Idaho, Wyoming, Colorado, N. Mexico, Arizona, Utah, Nevada). ... 05
Pacific (Washington, Oregon, California, Alaska, Hawaii). ... 06
South Atlantic (Delaware, Maryland, D.C., Virginia, W. Virginia, S. Carolina, N. Carolina, Georgia, Florida). ... 07
East South Central (Kentucky, Tennessee, Alabama, Mississippi). ... 08
West South Central (Arkansas, Louisiana, Oklahoma, Texas). ... 09
Didn't grow up in United States. ... 10

108. How much encouragement did you receive from each of the following individuals in becoming a priest? IF THE PERSON HAD NO INFLUENCE OR IF THERE WAS NO SUCH PERSON, CIRCLE CODE 3. IF MORE THAN ONE PERSON IN A CATEGORY, CODE THE MOST INFLUENTIAL.

	Encouraged strongly	Encouraged somewhat	No influence or No such person	Discouraged somewhat	Discouraged strongly	
A. Mother.	1	2	3	4	5	12/0
B. Father.	1	2	3	4	5	13/0
C. Other member of my family.	1	2	3	4	5	14/0
D. Priest.	1	2	3	4	5	15/0
E. Nun.	1	2	3	4	5	16/0
F. Brother.	1	2	3	4	5	17/0
G. Other person (SPECIFY)	1	2	3	4	5	18/0

109. Please indicate the extent to which you read the following publications. CIRCLE ONE CODE ON EACH LINE.

	Most issues	An occasional issue	Never read this	
A. Cross Currents	1	2	3	19/0
B. Homiletic and Pastoral Review	4	5	6	20/0
C. National Catholic Reporter	7	8	9	21/0
D. American Ecclesiastical Review	1	2	3	22/0
E. The Priest	4	5	6	23/0
F. Commonweal	7	8	9	24/0
G. America	1	2	3	25/0
H. The Critic	4	5	6	26/0
I. Concilium	7	8	9	27/0
J. The Wanderer	1	2	3	28/0
K. The Catholic Mind	4	5	6	29/0
L. Worship	7	8	9	30/0
M. Theology Digest	1	2	3	31/0
N. Theological Studies	4	5	6	32/0
O. Your diocesan newspaper	7	8	9	33/0
P. The Way	1	2	3	34/0
Q. Catholic Biblical Quarterly	4	5	6	35/0

110. What about your more "solid" reading?

  A. Have you read at least one of the books of the following authors in the last few years? CIRCLE ONE CODE ON EACH LINE UNDER A, BELOW.

  B. *FOR EACH "YES":* INDICATE HOW MUCH EACH AUTHOR HAS INFLUENCED YOUR PRESENT THINKING. B. FOR EACH "YES," CIRCLE ONE CODE.

	A. Yes (1)	A. No	B. Has influenced my present thinking greatly	B. Has influenced my present thinking somewhat	B. Has not influenced my present thinking	
1) Gregory Baum	(1)	2	3	4	5	36/0
2) Cardinal Bea	(1)	2	3	4	5	37/0
3) Dietrich Bonhoeffer	(1)	2	3	4	5	38/0
4) Robert McAfee Brown	(1)	2	3	4	5	39/0
5) Daniel Callahan	(1)	2	3	4	5	40/0
6) Yves Congar	(1)	2	3	4	5	41/0
7) Harvey Cox	(1)	2	3	4	5	42/0
8) Teilhard de Chardin	(1)	2	3	4	5	43/0
9) Henri de Lubac	(1)	2	3	4	5	44/0
10) Avery Dulles	(1)	2	3	4	5	45/0
11) Louis Evely	(1)	2	3	4	5	46/0
12) Bernard Häring	(1)	2	3	4	5	47/0
13) Eugene Kennedy	(1)	2	3	4	5	48/0
14) Hans Küng	(1)	2	3	4	5	49/0
15) Jacques Maritain	(1)	2	3	4	5	50/0
16) Martin Marty	(1)	2	3	4	5	51/0
17) John L. McKenzie	(1)	2	3	4	5	52/0
18) Gabriel Moran	(1)	2	3	4	5	53/0
19) John Courtney Murray	(1)	2	3	4	5	54/0
20) Marc Oraison	(1)	2	3	4	5	55/0
21) Pope Paul VI	(1)	2	3	4	5	56/0
22) Karl Rahner	(1)	2	3	4	5	57/0
23) Rosemary Reuther	(1)	2	3	4	5	58/0
24) Edward Schillebeeckx	(1)	2	3	4	5	59/0
25) Cardinal Suenens	(1)	2	3	4	5	60/0
26) Documents of Vatican II	(1)	2	3	4	5	61/0

DECK 14

111. How much do you feel a need for the following during 1970? CIRCLE ONE CODE IN EACH ROW CORRESPONDING TO THE DEGREE OF NEED YOU FEEL.

	Do not need					Need very much	
A. Training in how to plan and evaluate the Church's work.	1	2	3	4	5	6	62/0
B. Preparation for another occupation.	1	2	3	4	5	6	63/0
C. Time to reflect on and evaluate the direction of my ministry.	1	2	3	4	5	6	64/0
D. Training in ministerial skills (preaching, counseling, etc.).	1	2	3	4	5	6	65/0
E. Learning how to be a change agent in Church and community.	1	2	3	4	5	6	66/0
F. Updating in Biblical, theological, and related fields.	1	2	3	4	5	6	67/0
G. Study to relate Christian faith to our rapidly changing society.	1	2	3	4	5	6	68/0
H. Other (SPECIFY)			4		5	6	69/0

112. This questionnaire has touched upon many aspects of the priesthood. It has covered a number of the crucial issues, but surely not all of them. You may have an observation or insight concerning an area that was omitted or insufficiently highlighted. If so, please use as much of the remaining space as you need to describe it.

THANK YOU.

APPENDIX G

RESIGNEE QUESTIONNAIRE

The questionnaire that was sent to resigned priests was a modified version of the main questionnaire sent to active priests. The resignee questionnaire was shorter and contained not only some of the same questions as in the main questionnaire but also questions that pertained only to resignees. On the following pages are presented the latter questions.

Dear Sir,

As you may know, the National Opinion Research Center at the University of Chicago, under contract to the United States Catholic Conference, is conducting a comprehensive in-depth study of the American Catholic priesthood to determine "what priests see as the past, present, and future role of the priesthood and the Catholic Church in the United States." Questionnaires have been completed by over 5,000 priests, 1,000 of whom also completed the "Personal Orientation Inventory" mentioned below.

As you will readily understand, the circumstances surrounding the priesthood today demand that we include in the study the opinions of those men who have resigned or taken a leave of absence from the ecclesiastical ministry in the past few years. You are one of a scientifically selected sample of over 1,000 individuals who have worked as priests in the dioceses and religious communities of the United States and who have resigned from their positions or have taken a leave of absence.

This booklet is the outcome of discussion and consultation with research scholars in the fields of theology, sociology, and psychology; with representatives of various formal and informal priests' associations and other interested organizations; and with many men formerly active in the ecclesiastical ministry.

May we ask you to fill out the questionnaires as completely and candidly as possible and send it to us in the prepaid return envelope at your earliest convenience. A number are also being invited to complete a "Personal Orientation Inventory." If one is enclosed in your booklet, please follow the instructions on the front page. It is easy and quick to fill out.

The anonymity of your answers is professionally guaranteed. NORC cannot release respondents' names to anyone, including sponsoring clients. The purpose of the code number on this page is to permit us to send followup letters to persons who do not return the questionnaire so that we can get a high completion rate. All reports will be based only on statistical tabulations.

We would like to thank you for the time and thoughtful consideration we hope you will give to this questionnaire.

Sincerely yours,

(Rev.) Richard A. Schoenherr
Senior Study Director

Survey 5029-R
Confidential

8. C. During the last two years of your ecclesiastical ministry, what percentage of the people with whom you worked (most of the time) fell into each of the four social groups below? CIRCLE YOUR ESTIMATE TO THE NEAREST 10 PER CENT FOR EACH.

Per Cent

Upper class............	00	10	20	30	40	50	60	70	80	90	100
Middle class............	00	10	20	30	40	50	60	70	80	90	100
Working class............	00	10	20	30	40	50	60	70	80	90	100
Poor or lower class............	00	10	20	30	40	50	60	70	80	90	100

D. In the last two years of your ecclesiastical ministry, what percentage of the following groups made up your parish (the people with whom you worked)? CIRCLE YOUR ESTIMATE TO THE NEAREST 10 PER CENT FOR EACH GROUP.

Per Cent

White—no predominant ethnic composition..........	00	10	20	30	40	50	60	70	80	90	100
White—some predominant ethnic composition (SPECIFY)_____											
Black..........	00	10	20	30	40	50	60	70	80	90	100
Other (SPECIFY)_____	00	10	20	30	40	50	60	70	80	90	100

E. Were you ever engaged in missionary work?   Yes (ANSWER [1] & [2])...... 1
   No...... 2

IF YES:
[1] How long were you in the missions? _____ years
[2] In what country?

9. Do you presently belong to or participate in the activities of any formal or informal association(s) of priests or ministers? CIRCLE ONE CODE.

Yes (ANSWER A & B)........... 1
No (GO TO Q. 10)............. 2

IF YES:

A. Which formal or informal associations are these? CIRCLE AS MANY CODES AS APPLY.

Diocesan association of priests..... 1
National Association for Pastoral Renewal..... 2
Society of Priests for a Free Ministry..... 3
Local ministerial association..... 4
Bearings..... 5
Next Step..... 6
Informal group affiliated with former diocese or community..... 7
Other (PLEASE DESCRIBE)_____ 8

B. How often do you participate in meetings or informal get-togethers of this (these) group(s)? CIRCLE ONE CODE.

About once a week........ 1
Several times a month........ 2
Several times a year........ 3
About once a year........ 4
Never........ 5

11. At the present time, what kind of work are you engaged in?

If not employed, circle the code........ 1

13. What is your current "canonical" status in the Roman Catholic Church? CIRCLE ONE CODE.

a. On approved leave of absence (ANSWER A)........ 1
b. On unapproved leave of absence (ANSWER A)........ 2
c. Suspended (ANSWER A)........ 3
d. "Laicized" ("dispensed from the obligations arising from sacred order") or in process of "laicization" (ANSWER B). 4
e. I applied only for dispensation from celibacy but was laicized (or put in process) automatically (ANSWER B)........ 5
f. Other (PLEASE DESCRIBE)........ 6

A. IF ON LEAVE OF ABSENCE OR SUSPENDED: Do you intend to seek "laicization"?

Yes (GO TO Q. 14)........ 7
No (ANSWER [1])........ 8
Uncertain (ANSWER [1])........ 9

[1] IF "NO" OR "UNCERTAIN" ABOUT "LAICIZATION": Is this for any of the following reasons? CIRCLE AS MANY CODES AS APPLY.

a. I am on an approved leave of absence and I plan to return to a diocese or religious community........ 1
b. Process is degrading........ 2
c. Church cannot withdraw sacramental character........ 3
d. I hope to again exercise some public ministry........ 4
e. I consider myself a priest independently of the Roman Catholic Church........ 5
f. "Laicization" is irrelevant to me........ 6
g. I want nothing further to do with the Roman Catholic Church........ 7
h. I would like to, but my marriage situation would make it impossible anyway........ 8
i. Other (SPECIFY)........ 9

13. Continued.

B. *IF "LAICIZED" OR IN THE PROCESS OF "LAICIZATION"*: Please give the following information:

	Month	Year
A. Date of request....		
B. Date when finalized....		
C. Diocese that finally handled the papers....		
D. Circle code if "laicization" is still pending............1		

C. Many people have commented on the process of "laicization." Please indicate to what extent you were pleased or displeased with the following aspects of the laicization procedures. CIRCLE ONE CODE ON EACH LINE. (IF THE ITEM DOES NOT APPLY IN YOUR CASE, CIRCLE THE MIDDLE CATEGORY.)

	Very pleased	Somewhat pleased	Neither pleased nor displeased or does not apply	Somewhat displeased	Very displeased
a. Length of time to complete process	1	2	3	4	5
b. General attitudes of officials toward myself	6	7	8	9	0
c. General attitudes of officials toward my wife or fiancee	1	2	3	4	5
d. Secrecy surrounding the process	6	7	8	9	0
e. Information provided about progress of process	1	2	3	4	5
f. Conditions restricting place of work or residence	6	7	8	9	0
g. Conditions restricting place or type of marriage	1	2	3	4	5
h. Other (PLEASE DESCRIBE)	6	7	8	9	0

14. Do you at the present time see yourself as a priest? CIRCLE ONE CODE.

Yes (ANSWER A & B)..............1
No (ANSWER B)..............2
Uncertain (ANSWER A & B).......3

IF YES:

A. Which of the following statements best describes *how* you see yourself as a priest? CIRCLE ONE CODE.

I am . . . a priest and I want to be recognized as such by the Roman Catholic Church. 4
a priest recognized as such by the people I serve, though not in good standing with the hierarchy. 5
a priest exercising new forms of ministry and wishing to be known as a priest. 6
a priest exercising new forms of ministry but not caring to be known as a priest. 7
a priest in transition to lay status where I no longer wish to exercise the social role of the priesthood. 8
a member of the universal priesthood in no way different from any other baptized Christian. 9
Other (PLEASE DESCRIBE) 0

B. *IF YES, NO, OR UNCERTAIN:* Which of the following statements best describes your present situation or intentions? CIRCLE ONE CODE.

I am presently working in a priestly ministry (full or part time) and celebrating Mass with "approval" of a bishop or pastor. 1
I am presently working in a priestly ministry and would like the approval of the hierarchy (ANSWER C). 2
I have definite plans to resume work in a diocese or community (ANSWER C). 3
I definitely would like to return to work as a priest under certain conditions (ANSWER C). 4
I am uncertain about going back (ANSWER C). 5
I definitely would *not* like to return to work as a priest in a diocese or community (ANSWER C). 6

C. Under which of the following work conditions or lifestyles would you be willing to resume some exercise of the priesthood? CIRCLE AS MANY CODES AS APPLY.

a. Under no condition. 1
b. With adequate salary and living conditions. 2
c. As a married priest. 3
d. Full-time ecclesiastical work. 4
e. Full-time secular job with part-time ecclesiastical work. 5
f. Parochial work. 6
g. Nonparochial work. 7
h. Other (SPECIFY) 8

D. In what capacity (kind of work) would you like to exercise the priesthood (if at all)? (DESCRIBE BRIEFLY). If uncertain, write "uncertain."

15. A number of priests have pointed to a *crucial* event or experience influencing their decision to leave. Were any of the following events or experiences *crucial* in your case? CIRCLE ONE CODE ON EACH LINE.

	Yes	No
1) *Humanae Vitae*	1	2
2) Relationship with a woman	3	4
3) Encyclical on priestly celibacy	5	6
4) T-group experience or sensitivity training	7	8
5) Counseling or consultation experience	1	2
6) College or university experience	3	4
7) Realization of the loss of one's faith	5	6
8) Change from one national culture to another	7	8
9) *Arbitrary* reassignment by a superior	1	2
10) Resignation of prominent scholar from priesthood	3	4
11) Reading of a particular publication	5	6
12) Particular act of injustice by superior(s) to oneself or another	7	8
13) Falling in love	1	2
14) Told or advised to leave by bishop or superior	3	4
15) Other (PLEASE DESCRIBE)	5	6

20. At the present time there is a great deal of interest shown in new forms of priestly ministry. Some people, however, have said that there is no element of priestly ministry in some of the new careers ordained men have chosen for themselves. Have you yourself entered upon some activity which you consider to be a new form of priestly ministry? CIRCLE ONE CODE.

Yes (ANSWER A & B) 1
No (ANSWER B) 2

IF YES:

A. Please describe.

B. (*IF YES OR NO*): Aside from your own practice or nonpractice of any new form of ministry, what kinds of activity can you imagine as possible new forms of meaningful ministry for priests?

21. Think of the following circle as representing degrees of closeness to or distance from Roman Catholicism. CIRCLE THE ONE CODE that best represents your position.

   1) Catholic within the structure of the Roman Church... 1
   2) Catholic outside the structure of the Roman Church... 2
   3) Orthodox... 3
   4) Denominational Protestant (ANSWER A)... 4
   5) Non-denominational Christian... 5
   6) Non-denominational religious humanist... 6
   7) Non-religious humanist (SKIP TO Q. 23)... 7
   8) Agnostic or atheist (SKIP TO Q. 23)... 8

   A. *IF MEMBER OF ANOTHER DENOMINATION:* State the denomination.

   B. Are you active as a clergyman in any other religious denomination?

   Yes (ANSWER [1])... 1
   No... 2

   [1] *IF YES:* State the denomination.

23. In the past year (or since the time you left the ecclesiastical ministry, if within the past year), about how often did you preside at or participate in the following sacramental liturgies? **CIRCLE TWO CODES ON EACH LINE.**

	Presided at or concelebrated as priest				Participated in as layman			
	Never	Several times a year	At least once a month	At least once a week	Never	Several times a year	At least once a month	At least once a week
A. Mass in homes or apartments	1	2	3	4	5	6	7	8
B. Mass in Church or chapels	5	6	7	8	1	2	3	4
C. Penance	1	2	3	4	5	6	7	8
D. Matrimony	5	6	7	8	1	2	3	4
E. Baptism	1	2	3	4	5	6	7	8

25. If you could make only *one* change in the Roman Catholic Church, what would it be? DESCRIBE BRIEFLY:

29. Overall, during the last two years of your ecclesiastical ministry, how supportive (helpful) were the following people, and how much were they opposed or indifferent to your work? CIRCLE ONE CODE ON EACH LINE.

	Very supportive (helpful)	Somewhat supportive (helpful)	Indifferent	Somewhat opposed	Very much opposed
A. Pastors, local Superiors you worked under	1	2	3	4	5
B. Lay leaders in the parish, institution	6	7	8	9	0
C. Priests your own age	1	2	3	4	5
D. Other priests in your diocese or community	6	7	8	9	0
E. Your family	1	2	3	4	5
F. Priests who worked in same parish or institution as you	6	7	8	9	0
G. Bishop and/or Major Superior [If teacher or other professional]	1	2	3	4	5
H. Other professional colleagues	6	7	8	9	0

33. Here are some of the possible reasons for leaving the ecclesiastical ministry. How important were these for you? CIRCLE CODE 1 TO 5 FOR THE DEGREE OF IMPORTANCE FOR EACH OF THE REASONS BELOW.

Ratings of degree of importance

	Not important for me				Very important for me
1) Bad relations with superiors	1	2	3	4	5
2) Desire to marry	6	7	8	9	0
3) Church was not facing the relevant problems of the day	1	2	3	4	5
4) Emotional problems made change necessary	6	7	8	9	0
5) Conflict with parishioners, or laity	1	2	3	4	5
6) No longer believed it was my vocation	6	7	8	9	0
7) Attracted to other work	1	2	3	4	5
8) Could no longer live within the structure of the institutional Church as a priest	6	7	8	9	0
9) Could no longer agree with some of the ethical and moral teaching of the Church	1	2	3	4	5
10) No longer got the satisfaction there used to be from being a priest	6	7	8	9	0
11) The work of a priest seemed irrelevant	1	2	3	4	5
12) Personal growth and development	6	7	8	9	0

13) Could no longer agree with some of the theological teaching of the Church 1 2 3 4 5

14) Talents were not being used sufficiently 6 7 8 9 0

15) Other (SPECIFY) 1 2 3 4 5

A. Among the 15 items above, which two had the most importance for you?
(WRITE IN THE NUMBER OF EACH.)

First in importance: #
Second in importance: #

34. Please state the month and year (e.g., 7, 1969) of each of the following:

Month *Year*

Birth...
When first entered seminary or novitiate.........
Ordination....................................
First seriously considered leaving..............
Effective withdrawal..........................
First secular job.............................
Engagement (if applicable)....................
Marriage (if applicable)......................

36. A. In arriving at your decision to withdraw from the ecclesiastical ministry, did you discuss it with any of the following people? CIRCLE ONE CODE UNDER A.

B. What has been the overall reaction of the following people to your decision to leave? CIRCLE ONE CODE UNDER B.

IF NO SUCH PERSON, CIRCLE "NOT APPLICABLE" CODE.

	A.			B.			
	Yes	No	Not applicable	Supportive and accepting	Tolerant	Opposed	Hostile and rejecting
1) Mother..........................	1	2	3	1	2	3	4
2) Father..........................	4	5	6	5	6	7	8
3) Brothers and sisters............	7	8	9	1	2	3	4
4) Priest-friends..................	1	2	3	5	6	7	8
5) Local pastor or local superior..	4	5	6	1	2	3	4
6) Bishop/major superior..........	7	8	9	5	6	7	8
7) Lay friends.....................	1	2	3	1	2	3	4
8) Members of your local community.	4	5	6	5	6	7	8
9) Spiritual director, confessor...	7	8	9	1	2	3	4
10) Relatives.....................	1	2	3	5	6	7	8
11) Professional colleagues.......	4	5	6	1	2	3	4

37. Did you seek psychiatric or psychological consultation from the time you first seriously considered leaving the ecclesiastical ministry through the time when you felt settled with your decision? CIRCLE ONE CODE.

Yes (ANSWER A & B)......... 1
No (GO TO Q. 38).............. 2

IF YES:

A. Did you seek consultation for any of the following reasons? CIRCLE ONE CODE ON EACH LINE

	Yes	No
1) I was advised to do so	1	2
2) I wanted to clarify a confused state of mind and feeling brought about by the consideration of leaving	3	4
3) I wanted to discuss a long-term problem	5	6
4) Other (PLEASE DESCRIBE)	7	8

B Did consultation have any of the following results? CIRCLE ONE CODE ON EACH LINE.

	Yes	No
1) Confirmed a decision to leave I had in fact already made	1	2
2) Furnished an insight about myself or my situation which brought me to a decision to leave	3	4
3) Suggested that to leave would be an inadvisable step	5	6
4) Did not in fact enable me to feel settled with my decision to leave	7	8
5) Other (PLEASE DESCRIBE)	1	2

38. Did your diocese or community make available financial support for A, B, C, below? CIRCLE ONE CODE ON EACH LINE.

	Fully adequate	Partial	Token	None at all	Did not inquire
A. Psychiatric or psychological consultation services	1	2	3	4	5
B. Professional job counseling	6	7	8	9	0
C. Any other financial help to get a start	1	2	3	4	5

39. Through the period of A) deciding to leave up until the time you left, and B) adjusting to a new life style, to what extent did you experience personal turmoil? CIRCLE ONE CODE ON EACH LINE.

	Severe and prolonged	Severe but brief	Moderate but prolonged	Moderate but brief	Little or none
A. While deciding to leave	1	2	3	4	5
B. While adjusting to new life style	6	7	8	9	0

40. Taking all things together, how satisfied would you say you are now with your decision to leave the ecclesiastical ministry? CIRCLE ONE CODE.

Very satisfied......... 1
Pretty satisfied......... 2
Not too satisfied......... 3

41. What is your marital status? CIRCLE ONE CODE.

Single......... 1
Engaged (ANSWER C, D, & H)......... 2
Married (ANSWER A, B, C, D, E, F, G, H)......... 3
Divorced (ANSWER A & B)......... 4
Separated (ANSWER A & B)......... 5
Widowed (ANSWER A & B)......... 6

IF EVER MARRIED:

A. In what kind of ceremony was your marriage performed? CIRCLE ONE CODE.

Roman Catholic service......... 1
Unofficial Roman Catholic service (ANSWER [1])......... 2
Non-Catholic religious service (ANSWER [1])......... 3
Civil ceremony (ANSWER [1])......... 4
Other (SPECIFY) (ANSWER [1])......... 5

[1] Has your marriage since been "validated" by the Roman Catholic Church?

Yes......... 1
No......... 2

B. How many dependent children do you have from this or a previous marriage?

C. *IF PRESENTLY MARRIED OR ENGAGED:*

(1) What is your wife's or fiancee's present age?

(2) What was your wife's or fiancee's marital status before present marriage/engagement? CIRCLE ONE CODE.

Never married......... 1
Separated (ANSWER a)......... 2
Previous marriage annulled by Roman Catholic Church (ANSWER a)......... 3
Divorced (ANSWER a)......... 4
Widowed (ANSWER a)......... 5

a) *IF SEPARATED, "ANNULLED," DIVORCED, WIDOWED:* How many dependent children does she bring to your present or contemplated marriage?

(3) What is your wife's or fiancee's religion?

Catholic (ANSWER [1])......... 1
Protestant (state denomination)......... 2
Jewish......... 3
Basically religious but not associated with any organized religion......... 4
Other (SPECIFY)......... 5

41. Continued.

[1] *IF CATHOLIC:* Was your wife or fiancee ever a member of a religious community?

Yes (ANSWER [2])........ 1
No........ 2

[2] *IF YES TO* [1]: For how long was she a member of a religious community?

_____ years

D. *IF PRESENTLY MARRIED OR ENGAGED:* During the past year, about how often has your wife or fiancee attended Mass in church or homes? CIRCLE ONE CODE.

At least once a week........ 1
At least once a month........ 2
Several times a year........ 3
Never........ 4

IF NOT PRESENTLY MARRIED, GO TO Q. 42.

IF MARRIED:

E. Taking all things together, would you say that your marriage is very happy, pretty happy, or not too happy? CIRCLE ONE CODE.

Very happy........ 1
Pretty happy........ 2
Not too happy........ 3

F. Below are some issues about which husbands and wives sometimes disagree. Please indicate which ones were sources of friction in your marriage *during the past few weeks.* CIRCLE ONE CODE IN EACH ROW.

	Yes	No
a. Time spent with friends	1	2
b. Household expenses	3	4
c. Being tired	5	6
d. Being away from home too much	7	8
e. Disciplining children	1	2
f. In-laws	3	4
g. Not showing love	5	6
h. Your job	7	8
i. How to spend leisure time	1	2
j. Religion	3	4
k. Irritating personal habits	5	6
l. Other (SPECIFY)	7	8

G. Please indicate which of the items below were sources of satisfaction in your marriage *during the past few weeks.* CIRCLE ONE CODE ON EACH LINE.

	Yes	No
a. Visited friends together	1	2
b. Went out together to movie, etc.	3	4
c. Entertained friends	5	6
d. Ate out in restaurant	7	8
e. Spent evening chatting	1	2
f. Good laugh	3	4
g. Drive or walk pleasure	5	6
h. Did something other appreciated	7	8
i. Affectionate	1	2
. Other (SPECIFY)	3	4

H. *IF MARRIED:* How long did you go with your wife before marrying her? _____ months

42. A. What is your gross average *monthly* income from your own job (or income you may have from scholarships, assistantships or other stipends awarded to students)? CIRCLE ONE CODE UNDER A.
B. What do you regard as an adequate monthly income for a person in your circumstances? CIRCLE ONE CODE UNDER B.
C. *IF MARRIED:* What is your wife's gross monthly income? CIRCLE ONE CODE UNDER C.

	A. My gross monthly income	B. Monthly income I regard as adequate	C. Wife's gross monthly income
Under $200	1	1	1
$201–500	2	2	2
$501–750	3	3	3
$751–1,000	4	4	4
$1,001–1,200	5	5	5
$1,201–1,400	6	6	6
$1,401–1,600	7	7	7
$1,601 and over	8	8	8
Not currently employed or studying	9	9	9

46. Looking back on the time spent in the ecclesiastical ministry, how would you evaluate that part of your life? Below is a set of descriptive opposites. First, *decide which side you agree with* and then circle the point which reflects the strength of your agreement on each line. *CIRCLE ONLY ONE CODE ON EACH LINE.* CIRCLE: 0—when you agree strongly this way

    o—when you agree somewhat this way

    .—when you agree only slightly this way

	Strongly agree	Somewhat agree	Slightly agree	Slightly agree	Somewhat agree	Strongly agree	
Generally self-fulfilling	0	o	.	.	·o	0	Generally self-negating
Intellectually frustrating	0	o	.	.	o	0	Intellectually satisfying
Emotionally satisfying	0	o	.	.	o	0	Emotionally retarding
Spiritually impairing	0	o	.	.	o	0	Spiritually enriching
Psychosexually healthy	0	o	.	.	o	0	Psychosexually unhealthy
Culturally narrowing	0	o	.	.	o	0	Culturally expanding

68. At the present time what would you most want to say to the following groups in the Roman Catholic Church?

To Laymen:

To Priests and Religious:

To the Bishops:

REFERENCES

Bradburn, Norman M. *The structure of psychological well-being.* NORC Monographs in Social Research, no. 15. Chicago: Aldine, 1969.

Duncan, Otis Dudley. "Path analysis: Sociological examples." *American Journal of Sociology,* 1966, *72* (July), 1-16.

Glock, Charles Y., and Stark, Rodney. *Religion and society in tension.* Chicago: Rand McNally, 1965.

Greeley, Andrew M., and Rossi, Peter H. *The education of Catholic Americans.* NORC Monographs in Social Research, no. 6. Chicago: Aldine, 1966.

Greeley, Andrew M., and Spaeth, Joe L. "Stratification, poverty, and social conflict in American white ethnic groups." In S. M. Lipset and S. M. Miller (eds.), *Stratification and poverty.* New York: Basic Books, forthcoming.

Kotre, John. *The view from the border: A social psychological study of current Catholicism.* Chicago: Aldine, 1971.

Krump, J. A., "Personality in Catholic college freshmen." Unpublished M.A. thesis, St. Xavier College, 1970.

McClosky, Herbert, and Schaar, John H. "Psychological dimensions of anomy." *American Sociological Review,* 1965, *30* (February), 14-40.

Maslow, Abraham. *Toward a psychology of being.* New York: Van Nostrand, 1962.

Medical Insight. "Why we see it in priests." An interview with James J. Gill, S.J., M.D. 1969 (December), 21-32.

Moynihan, Daniel P. *Maximum feasible misunderstanding: Community action in the war on poverty.* New York: Free Press, 1969.

The Official Catholic Directory. New York: P. J. Kenedy & Sons, 1965, 1966, 1967, 1968, 1969, 1970.

Orden, Susan R., and Bradburn, Norman M. "Dimensions of marriage happiness." *American Journal of Sociology,* 1968, *73* (May), 715-31.

Orden, Susan R., and Bradburn, Norman M. "Working wives and marriage happiness." *American Journal of Sociology,* 1969, *74* (January), 392-407.

Riesman, David. *The lonely crowd: A study of the changing American character.* New Haven, Conn.: Yale University Press, 1950.

Shostrom, Everett L. *EITS manual for the Personality Orientation Inventory (POI): An inventory for the measurement of self-actualization.* San Diego: Educational and Industrial Testing Service, 1966.

Smith, Patricia C.; Kendall, Lorne M.; and Hulin, Charles L. *The measurement of satisfaction in work and retirement: A strategy for the study of attitudes.* Chicago: Rand McNally, 1969.

Spaeth, Joe L., and Greeley, Andrew M. *Recent alumni and higher education: A survey of college graduates.* New York: McGraw-Hill, 1970.

Struzzo, John A. "Professionalism and the resolution of authority conflicts among the Catholic clergy." *Sociological Analysis,* 1970, *31* (Summer), 92-106.

Vollmer, Howard M., and Mills, Donald L., eds. *Professionalism.* Englewood Cliffs, N. J.: Prentice-Hall, 1966.

Webster, Allan C., and Stewart, Robert A. C. "Psychological attitudes and beliefs of ministers." *Anvil Quarterly,* 1969, 1 (March), 11-16.

INDEX

The categories which appear in most tables (age; bishops; active diocesan priests; resigned diocesan priests; major superiors; active religious priests; resigned religious priests, etc.) are generally to be found by reference to the specific topic with which the table is concerned: celibacy, education, friendship, etc. No separate entry is made each time these categories appear in the tables.

Page reference is usually to the page on which the table appears; the text around the tables comments on or interprets the findings, and it is assumed in this index that the commentary can be found easily enough once the table is located.

abortion: attitude re, 83, 119-120
  opinion on, 339
  questionnaire, 403
absolutism, 306
acculturation, 28, 30
active diocesan priests
  (see note at beginning of index)
active religious priests
  (see note at beginning of index)
Ad Hoc Committee for the Study of the
    Life and Ministry of the Priest, 7
advanced education. *See* education.
affect balance: definition, 347
  see also negative affect; positive affect
affect scale:
  active priests and resignees, 220
  items in question, 215-216
  the married compared in, 216(1)
  priests and college-educated males,
    219
  priests compared with married males,
    216(3)
  scores by age, 217
  scores by clerical status, 217
age: negative influence, 226
  status of American Catholic clergy;
    table, 24
  (see also note at beginning of index)
American Catholic males
  (see note at beginning of index)
American priests: assets, 311
  general background, 23, 323(5)
  liabilities, 312
  serious problems, 315-316

anger: personality and, 59
anomie, 89-91
  definition, 337
  index source, 337-338
apostasy: family background, 31
associate pastor: poor conditions, 313(7)
assumptions: in models, 10
  summary, 11, 13
attitudes: age as cause of differences,
    128(2)
  anomic, 90-91
  anomic; by age, 91
  correlation of indices, 127
  correlation with age, 87
  description of, as goal, 317
  flexible and orthodox, 83(1)
  intercorrelations of indices; table, 130
  modern; by age, 98
  modern; by clerical status, 97
  survey, 81
  traditional; by clerical status, 93
  see also social attitudes
authority: actual centralization of, 138-
    139
  attitude towards, 323(4)
  dissatisfaction with, 312(1)
  ideal centralization of, 140-142
  loneliness and, 214(4)
  major problem, 207, 315
  most serious problem, 199(2)
  power conflict, 343
  as problem, 209
  see also decision making; power
authors, influential, 187, 190, 429

autonomy: in decision-making, 182
  inner-directedness, 63
  of priests, 70
behavior: factors in shaping, 23
bias: nonresponse and, 349
  in research, 9

Bible: reading, 71, 389
bibliography: preparation of, 7
birth, place of. *See* place of birth.
birth control: attitude re, 83, 101, 104-
  105
  attitudes before and after *Humanae
    Vitae,* 105-108
  confession and, 109-113, 339-340
  nonresponse affecting, 350
  opinion on, 339
  questionnaire, 404
  standard errors of estimate, 321
bishops: election of, 321, 350
  leadership, 311(8)
  major superiors and, 139
  need for strong, 133(3)
  power, 134
  resignees' advice to, 305
  response rate, 328
  strong; attitude of priests, 147(1)
  (see also note at beginning of index)
bishops and priests:
  age comparison, 23
  conservatism, 84
  interpretation of tables, 20
  potential conflict, 148(5)
  substantial differences in views,
    312(2)
Bishops' Committee on Pastoral Research and Practices, 331(4)
books and reading:
  influential authors read; tables, 187-
    190
  professional study, 191(4)
  see also periodicals
Bradburn, Norman M., 6, 215, 218, 294
Breviary: daily recitation, 71(2)
  obligation disregarded, 74
  questionnaire, 389
  recitation, 79(2)
  recitation; by age, 74
  recitation; by clerical status, 74

capitalism, 121
Catholic Church: attitude re, 93
  changes recommended by resignees,
    301

  see also Church
celibacy: attitudes toward sexuality,
    240-242
  attitudes toward value of, 238
  change in law supported, 239, 312(4)
  controversy on obligation, 233
  nonresponse affecting, 350
  opinions on future of, 236-237
  optional; by age, 235
  optional; by clerical status, 234
  optional; religious priests, 361(4), 363
  personal choice, 233
  as problem, 207, 209
  questionnaire, 355
  reason for supporting change, 247(4)
  resignation related to, 13
  standard errors of estimate, 321
  strong support for change, 246(2)
  value, 233, 238, 247(3)
  vow, 237
  see also marriage
chancery officials: power, 134
change: with age, 82
  questionnaire on possible, 402
chastity: vow, 361(2), 363
  vow; attitude of religious priests, 364
Christian unity. *See* ecumenism.
Church: attitude re, 94
  world and, iii
church reform. *See* reform in the
  church.
church structure. *See* structure.
civil rights, 97
clergy: background on American Catholic, 23
  socio-economic background, 26
  see also bishops; life in the ministry;
  priests
colleague relationship: questionnaire,
  344
colleges and universities, 341
Committee on Pastoral Research and
  Practices, iv
Communion to non-Catholics, 142
community life: attitudes of religious
  priests, 366
  uniformity in, 361(6), 365
Conference of Major Superiors of Men,
  332(4)
confession: birth control in, 109-113
confusion, 124(2)
conservatism: bishops and priests,
  126(5)
contraception. *See* birth control.

correlation coefficients: in causal
  models, 19
counseling: before leaving the ministry;
  table, 284
  popular field of study, 43
court of appeals, 145
courtship, 243, 247(5)
culture: clerical, 155, 165(1)

dark night of the soul, 75
data collection: problems; response, 7
data processing, 8
dating: experience with women, 52(1)
  maturity and, 311(3)
  questionnaire, 379
  subsequent behavior and, 52(4)
  in youth; by age, 49
  in youth; analysis, 50
  in youth; by clerical status, 48
day off, 222
decision-making: attitudes on, 138
  change in processes, 140
  decentralization of, 147(2)
  power conflict, 343
  primary, 139
  questionnaire, 343, 397-401
dependency: excessive, 69(5)
depression, 220
desire to marry: assumption re, 13(7)
  explanation of, 266
  explanation of variance on, 250
  future plans and, 265
  leaving the priesthood, 265, 313(5)
  loneliness and, 14, 212, 214, 248,
    265, 315
  loneliness and other factors, 250
  major problem, 315
  not strong, 246(1)
  path diagram, 249
  principal explanations for, 250
  reason for leaving ministry, 282
  resignations and, 265, 313(5)
  simple correlations; independent ef-
    fects of added variables, 251
  social interaction with women and,
    248
devotion: dropped from model, 14
  family tension and, 35
  religious backgrounds, 32
diaconate, married, 145
dioceses: extra-large, 332(6)
  size categories, 317-318
divorce: attitude re, 83(2), 116-117
  family background, 31

opinion on freedom to remarry, 340
  questionnaire, 405
doctrine: "new" vocabulary, 82
  traditional vs. modern, 81
dress of clergy, 407
drinking, 419, 423

ecumenism: attitudes towards, 118, 120-
  121
  opinion on, 342
  questionnaire, 342, 402
  support for, 311(7)
education: backgrounds, 28
  pre-seminary; table, 39, 40
  questionnaire on level of, 375
  of resignees, 52(2)
education since ordination:
  by age; table, 43
  by clerical status; table, 42
  further training needed; tables, 183-
    184
election of bishops:
  nonresponse affecting, 350
  standard errors of estimate, 321
emotions, 419
  pent up, 297
  problems in the priesthood, 68(3)
encouragement of vocation. *See* vocation.
ethnicity: of the father; table, 29
euphoria, 221
  resigned priests, 221-222, 313(2)
experience, religious. *See* religious experience.

faith: attitude re, 93
  modern attitude, 97
family experiences: by age, table, 32
  by clerical status; table, 31
  religious experience and, 75
family problems: by age, table, 35
  broken family, 31
  by clerical status; table, 34
family-tension index, 35, 333
family-tension variable, 314
family twosomes, 422
fathers: ethnicity, table, 29
feeling, 419
  see also emotions
Fichter, Joseph, 7
field of study. *See* study.
firstborn: resignations and, 26
free ministry, 299
friends and friendship:

by age; table, 156
assets, 311(9)
classification of close friends; tables, 157-158
by clerical status; table, 155
frequent associates; table, 159-160
future plans, and friends who have left, 255
intimate, 69(9)
leaving the priesthood, 255-256, 417
loneliness, 166(2)
with priests; tables, 160-161
questionnaire, 410
religious and diocesan priests, 360(5)
fulfillment: spiritual and personal, 200, 390
future plans: by age, 254
by clerical status, 254
corrrelates of plans to stay, 260
desire to marry, 265
explanation of variance; diocesan and religious priests, 368
explanation of variance on staying, 262
four direct paths, 260
important reasons for staying, 256
likely to leave, 255
path diagram, 261
principal findings, 253
questionnaire, 356, 417
reasons for leaving, 258
religious priests; predictors, 368
of resignees, 292
simple correlations; independent effects of added variables, 263
status rethought because of friends leaving, 255

generation gap, 128(1), 152
generational change, 82
Gill, James J., 219, 295
God: attitude towards, 93
modern attitude re, 97
Graduate Record Examination:
age and education; path diagram, 17
correlation with age and education, 18
graduate work. *See* education since ordination.
Greeley, Andrew M., vii
guaranteed annual wage, 124, 341, 419

Hadden, Jeffrey, 7
happiness: Bradburn index, 6
incidence of, 224

measures of, 215
measure (Bradburn), 223
priests and resignees, 223(3)
questionnaire, 356, 419
reasons for, 226(1)
as reason for staying in priesthood, 257
work satisfaction, 225
young and older priests, 226(2)
health, 412
heaven, 93
Higgins, George, 7, 124
high school seminaries, 45
Holy Spirit, iv
home Masses, 140
Horney, Karen, 64
hours of work. *See* work.
housekeepers, 163
human condition: description as problem, 21
human relations. *See* interpersonal relations.
Humanae Vitae, 83, 105, 109
attitude towards; by age, 115
attitude towards; by clerical status, 114
consent to, 126(4)
opinion on, 340-341
questionnaire, 405
humanistic psychology, 70(3)

image of God, 75
income: questionnaire, 388
wives of resignees, 445
indices: construction of, 8
description, 333
initiative: actual exercise of personal, 143
ideal exercise of, 144-145
inner-directedness: idiosyncratic, 70
meaning, 63
insight: in scientific activity, 22(5)
intentions. *See* future plans.
interpersonal relations:
change in clerical culture, 166(4)
clerical culture, 166(3)
colleagues in nonparish setting; tables, 164-165
colleagues in parish setting; tables, 163-164
correlates of colleague-relationship index, 167
explanation of variance, 167
with ministers and rabbis, 401

path diagram relating colleague support to prior variables, 168
questionnaire, 344-345
satisfaction with, 155
unsatisfactory, 169
interviews: nonrespondents, by telephone, 352
Irish: acculturation, 28, 30

Jesus Christ: attitude re, 93
job satisfaction. *See* work satisfaction.
jobs. *See* work.
journals. *See* periodicals.

Kotre, John, 333
Krol, John Cardinal, vi

laicization:
 displeasure with procedures; table, 285
 process displeasing, 284
 questionnaire, 435
 reason for not seeking, 289, 290
laity: recommendations by resignees, 301
 relations with priests, 89
 Vatican Council, and, 91
leadership: proportion of clergy, 69(6)
leaving the priesthood. *See* future plans; resignation.
legalism, 306
Leo XIII, Pope, iv
liberal attitudes, 311(6)
liberal (the word), 131(1)
literature review, 323-324
liturgy: ignoring rules, 149(7)
 initiative in, 343
life in the ministry:
 preliminary research, 6
 rewarding activities, 199
 spiritual and personal fulfillment, 200-201
living quarters, 162, 413
loneliness: added to model, 14
 correlates on, as problem, 212
 desire to marry and, 14, 212, 214, 248, 250, 265, 315
 explanation for, 262
 explanation of variance on, 214
 morale, 229
 negative affect, 225, 264
 path diagram relating to prior variables, 213
 personal relationships, 165

as problem, 212
religious and diocesan priests, 360(4)
summary questions on, 214
love: capacity to show, 59
 resignees, 281
Loyola University, Chicago, 53, 323

McDermott, Neal W., O.P., vii, 374
McNamara, Robert, 7
major superiors: bishops and, 139
 (see also note at beginning of index)
marriage: adjustment balance scale, 297
 adjustment in; measures, 294
 desired. *See* desire to marry.
 friction in, 294
 happiness in, 296
 invalid; sacraments, 142
 optional celibacy; table, 237
 satisfactions in, 294
 tensions in, 296, 298
 see also celibacy; divorce
married priests: attitude towards, 146
Maslow, Abraham, 53
Mass: importance, 71
 questionnaire, 388
 rubrics; modification, 142
masturbation: attitude re, 83, 100
 questions, 338
maturity: age and education as factors, 70
 emotional, 53
 of priests, 311(1)
meditation: daily, 73
mental health: happiness, 215
 see also psychological well being
metropolitan areas: resignees from, 26
Mills, Edgar, 7
models: building, 13
 causal relationships, 10
modern priest: definition, 334
 index; response items, 334-335
morale: assumption re, 11(6)
 crisis in, 215
 higher, 226
 interpretations of problem of, 20
 loneliness, 229
 now and a decade ago, 4
 of priests, 311(2)
 as theme, 323(2)
mothers: employment, 31
 vocational encouragement, 47
motivation: in priesthood, 171
Mulhearn, John, vii, 374
Murray, John Courtney, 189

mystical experiences, 77, 314
  frequency of prayer and, 79(4)

National Opinion Research Center, v
national parish, 424
nativity. *See* place of birth.
Neal, Sr. Marie Augusta, 7, 121
negative affect: analysis, 223
  causes, 224
  explanation of variance, 225
  path diagram, 231
  questionnaire, 346
  simple correlations; independent effects of selected variables, 228
non-Catholics, Communion to, 142
normal (the word), 55
normlessness, 89

obedience: questionnaire, 396
  vow; attitude of religious priests, 364
occupational prestige index, 26
Official Catholic Directory, 325
orthodoxy, 83(1), 124(1)

parents: devotion, 424
  unsatisfactory relations with, 75
parochial schools, 147
  attitude towards closing, 149(9)
pastoral implementation, vi
pastoral work:
  activities; questionnaire, 384-385
path diagrams: in causal models, 19
Paul VI, Pope, v, 189
  see also Humanae Vitae
periodicals, 183
  questionnaire, 428
  titles read; tables, 185-186
perseverance. *See* future plans.
personal initiative. *See* initiative.
Personal Orientation Inventory, 53, 58, 60-61, 66-67
personal relations. *See* interpersonal relations.
personality: causes, 11(2)
  inner-direction, 54
  mean scores; by age; table, 62
  mean scores; table, 57
  measurement of, 53
  measurement; sub-scales, 54-55
  self-actualizing, 53
  strengths of priests, 68(4)
piety, 71
  see also devotion
place of birth; tables, 25, 26

plans. *See* future plans.
policy decisions: researcher's role and, 5
positions. *See* work.
positive affect: euphoria after resignation, 221
  explanation of variance, 225
  path diagram; prior variables, 230
  principal explanations of, 223
  questionnaire, 346
  scale. *See* affect scale.
  simple correlations and independent effects of added variables, 227
poverty: problem of, 122
  questionnaire, 396
  vow, 361(3), 363
  vow; attitude of religious priests, 364
power: actual distribution in diocese, 134
  actual distribution in diocese; tables, 135
  attitudes on, 133
  bishops on centralization of, 147(4)
  conflict, 342-343
  correlations and total independent effects; table, 153
  correlates with structure indices, 150
  decentralization of, 147(2)
  distribution of, 312(1)
  explanation of variances, 152
  ideal distribution in diocese, 136-137
  intercorrelations with power indices, 150
  major problem, 316
  path diagram; power conflict and prior variables, 151
  redistribution of, 135
  trouble re dissatisfaction with distribution of, 154(3)
prayer: daily, 73
  mystical experiences, 79(4)
  by priests, 79
  questionnaire, 389
  regular, 311(4)
  role; analysis, 75
premarital sex, 83, 101-103, 338, 403
presence of God, 75
priesthood: attitudes towards, 84-92
  attitude; by age, 88
  attitude; by clerical status, 85
  five thematic areas of study, 323
  leaving. *See* future plans.
  profession, as, 171

response to statements on (text), 379-381

satisfactions and frustrations in, 199

priests: American. *See* American priests.

choice again. 312(11)

life and ministry; purpose of research, 3

model for causal analysis of, 12

number in U.S., 324

personal life and development, 323(1)

ratio of diocesan to religious, 324

resigned. *See* resignees.

see also associate pastor; clergy; married priests; modern priest; religious priests; seminarians.

priests and bishops. *See* bishops and priests.

priests' associations: questionnaire, 387

priests' senate: controversial, 149(6)

increasing power of, 136

power, 134-135, 147(3)

subject of controversy, 138

problems in the priesthood, 312

for others; tables, 210-211

principal problems, 211(2)

questionnaire, 391

for self, tables, 206-208

summary, 315

professional comparison, 346, 356

path diagram, 194

professionalization of priesthood, 323(3)

professions: attributes of, 171

priests' self-evaluation, 191(1)

questionnaire, 387-388

research on, 82

resignation rate in, 308(n 1)

promotion: opportunities for, 388

Protestant theologians: study of, 92

psychological well being, 215

correlates of, 224

correlates of affect, 224

priests compared with other males, 218

at resignation, 221

questionnaire: approved, 324

cover letter, 373

drafts, 6

nonresponse, 349

pretest, 324

research instrument, 326

response rate, 328

Rahner, Karl, 189

reading. *See* books and reading.

recommendations, 4-5

recreation, 222-223

recruiting, vocational. *See* vocational recruiting.

reforms in the church:

attitudes on, 145

popular ideas, 149(8)

questionnaire, 344

regions of the U.S., 425-427

religious attitudes. *See* attitudes.

religious background: by age; table, 34

by clerical status; table, 33

religious experience: assumption re, 11(3)

family tension and, 75

frequency tables, 76-77

importance, 314

index, 334

path diagram; relation to prior variables, 78

questionnaire, 390

summary, 79(3)

vocational recruiting and, 270

religious institutions: differences, 360(6)

renewal in, 361(7)

size categories, 318

religious life:

attitudes of religious priests, 362

charismatic role, 363

commitment to, 361(1)

democratic government in, 361(5)

index, 366

prophetic role, 363

religious priests:

comparison with diocesan priests, 360

differences from diocesan priests, 369-370

findings on, 359

future plans; factors in, 368

questionnaire, 361, 407-410

as resignees, 278

religious superiors, 359, 365

religious values. *See* values.

research: causal explanation in, 10

six phases of the project, 6

resignation(s):

annual rate, 313(5)

decision, influences on, 282

inclination; causes, 4

lowering rate of, 266(4)

by the mature and the educated, 312(12)

rate of, 259, 266(4), 313(5)

rate; definition, 277
rate: 1966-1969, 277
rate; standard errors of estimate, 320
reason for, 259(4)
reasons for; questionnaire, 418
speculation on causes, 4
values and, 259
young priests, 266(3)
resignees: advice to bishops, 305
advice to priests and religious, 304
age; table, 23-24
anger at the Church, 307(1)
annual income, 288
attitudes and values, 84, 313(4)
careers; upward mobility, 288
changes in the Church, 301
Christian witness, 299
Christianity and, 292
the Church and, 291
as church members, 276(5), 314(5)
colleague support, 281
counseling, 282
crucial influence on decision, 438
decision painful, 276(2)
decision to leave; reasons, 276
decision; turning point, 281
discussion and support, 283
emphasis on social role, 205
euphoria on deciding to resign, 216(4), 221-222, 313(2)
evaluation of experiences in ministry, 281
evaluation of life as priest, 446
exercise of priestly office, 292-293
explanation for plans to leave, 368
faith, 307(3)
family opposition, 282
family support, 282
financial situation, 287
forms of priestly ministry, 299
as friends, 259
fulfillment, 202
future plans in priesthood, 292
happiness, 222-223
income, 313(3)
a look at the, 275
loss of faith, 291
marginality, 292
marital adjustment, 314(7)
marital adjustment; table, 295
marital happiness, 293-294
marital status, 443
marital status; table, 286
marriage ceremony; table, 286

marriages, 308(9)
Mass attendance, 293
number: 1966-1969, 279
occupations, 309(2)
parishioners of, 280
percent married, 285
personal turmoil, 285
poor or black parishes, 279
possible new ministries, 300
preferred kind of work in priesthood, 298
present canonical status, 289
present position re the Church, 289, 290
present relationship to priesthood, 291
principal reason for resignation, 253, 257
professional standards, 288
psychiatric consultation, 442
questionnaire; cover letter, 433
questionnaire (text), 431
reasons for leaving, 283, 307(2), 313(1), 440-441
recommendations to laity, 301
religious and diocesan priests, 360(6)
religious priests, 278
response rate, 331
return to priesthood, 314(6)
salary, 276(4)
the sample of, 330
sampling population, 327
satisfaction with decision, 284, 308(4), 443
self-image as priest, 436-437
sources of satisfaction, 204
summary, 307-308, 313-314
support and opposition from others, 280, 440
survey, 326
talents, use of, 289
the term, 21(n3), 276
view of present church relationship, 289
wives of, 276(3), 287
see also laicization
respondents. *See* sample.
response rate, 328
Riesman, David, 54
riots, 124, 341
role identity, 323(2)
Ryan, John, 124

sacraments: attitude re, 94
salaries. *See* income.

salvation: attitude re, 94
sample and sampling:
  active priests, 324-325
  age distribution, 15
  analysis of 6,000 cases, 325
  distribution by clerical status, 15
  geographic stratification, 318
  methodology, 317
  preparation of, 7
  random selection, 325
  of religious institutes, 325
  selection, 6
satisfaction: sources, 391
  sources; table, 203, 205
Schillebeeckx, Edward, 363
Schoenherr, Richard A., vii, 374
secular institutes, 362
secularism, iii
self-actualization:
  active priests and others; table, 65
  American Catholic clergy, 55-56
  declining with age, 62
  factors in background and training, 69(8)
  high degree of, 313(8)
  hyper and hypo, 64
  priesthood and emotional development, 68
  resignees, 68(2), 69(7)
  youthfulness and, 59
seminarians:
  age at entry, 52(4)
  age at entry; by age; table, 41
  age at entry; by clerical status, 40
  early entry into seminaries, 311(3)
  slump in number of, 267
  time of entry; analysis, 50
seminaries: drop in enrollment, 267
  educational system, 37
seminary training: critics of; analysis, 51
  opinion of, 52(3)
  opinion; by age; table, 47
  opinion; by clerical status, 46
  questionnaire, 378
senate of priests. *See* priests' senate.
sex: attitude towards, 240-242, 340
  major problem, 316
  premarital. *See* premarital sex.
sexual morality:
  attitudes towards, 99
  differing views on, 312(3)
  index, 338
  questionnaire, 403
  support for Church's position, 125(3)

Sheatsley, Paul B., 9
Shostrom, Everett L., 53, 55, 332(9)
simplicity, 361(3), 365
size of community, 317
  dropped from model, 197
Smith, Patricia C., 6, 197(n3)
social attitudes: by age, table, 125
social change, iii
social conscience, 311(6)
social problems: attitudes towards, 122-125
  questionnaire, 341
social research: policy decisions and, 5
socio-economic background, 26
  by age; table, 28
  by clerical status; table, 27
Spaeth, Joe L., 9
spiritual life: activities; by age, 73
  activities; by clerical status, 72
  prayer and work, 199
  of priests, 71
standard errors of estimate, 319
staying in the priesthood. *See* future plans.
structure: attitudes on, 133
  correlates with power indices, 150
  dissatisfaction with, 154(1), 312(1)
  intercorrelations with power indices, 150
  the young and, 154(2)
study: fields of, table, 44
  full-time, 43
  maintaining professional skills, 191(4)
  need for higher training; continuing education, 182
superiors, religious, 359, 365
supervisors, 386

tables: general description of, 14
talents: of resignees, 289
  use of, 196
telephone interviews, 352-355
theology: field of study, 43
tradition: majority support for, 87
  younger clergy and, 87
training. *See* education; study.
Trappists, 317
Trinity, 93
truth, ix

uncertainty, 124(2)
United States: Catholic population, ix
United States Catholic Conference, 124

vacation, 222, 411, 412

values:
  acceptance of religious, 311(5)
  assumption re, 11(4)
  gap, 152
  modern, 128
  modern; explanation of variance on, 128
  modern expression of, 96
  modern; index, 336
  modern related to age, 128
  path diagram: modern related to prior values, 129
  plans related to, 10
  in religious life, 367
  resignation and, 259
  survey of, 81

Vanecko, James J., 7

variables: specification of, 6

Vatican Council II, iii
  documents of, 186, 189
  morale crisis, 215

Vietnamese war, 420

vocation: encouragement; by age; table, 50
  encouragement; by clerical status, 49
  mothers' encouragement of, 47
  sense of, 257

vocational recruiting, 45
  attitude, by age, 270-271
  attitude 4 or 5 years ago, 268, 270
  attitude 4-5 years ago, and today, 272
  attitude today, 269, 271
  as cause of decline in vocations, 268-269
  correlates of, 272
  decline in, 267, 313(6)
  decline in enthusiasm for, 271
  enthusiasm, 269, 271
  explanation of variance on, 273
  groups less likely to recruit, 273
  questionnaire, 381-382
  religious experiences and, 270

vows: essential, 363
  religious; practical meaning of, 363

Warwick, Donald, 7

wives: of resigned priests, 276(3)
  of resignees; previous marital status, 287
  of resignees; religious status, 287

women: as close friends, 239
  correlates of social interaction with, and desire to marry, 248
  going out with, socially, 244-245, 414-415
  opinions on social relations with, 246-247
  patterns of social interaction with, 245
  resignees; decision to leave, 281
  see also dating

work: assets, 312(10)
  current main positions; table, 173
  current main positions by age, 175
  current positions; table, 172
  hard, 191(2)
  hours of work; questionnaire, 387
  long hours, 174
  questionnaire, 383-384
  spiritual life and, 199

work satisfaction: assumption re, 11(5)
  correlates of, and professional-comparison indices, 192
  current main job; table, 180
  by current position; table, 178
  explanation of variance; tables, 193
  happiness and, 225
  highest level of, 177
  importance of, 193
  job reactions by age; table, 182
  job reactions by clerical status, 181
  loneliness and, 214(1)
  long hours, 197(2)
  major problem, 315
  mean scores; tables, 176-177
  measurement, 174
  negative influence, 226
  path diagram, 195
  principal satisfactions, 211
  questionnaire, 345, 385
  religious and diocesan priests, 197(3)
  religious community members, 196
  religious priests, 360
  serious problem, 191(3)
  size of community, 197(4)
  Smith index, 6, 176
  those most likely to be satisfied, 197(1)

world and the Church, iii
  priestly vocation in, iii

youth: and age, 82(2)
  ideas of one generation, 83(4)
  wave of the future, 82